D1322196

Novell NetWare 6.5 CNA Cram Sheet

INTRODUCTION TO NETWORKING. NETWORK ADMINISTRATION, AND NETWARE 6.5

1. NDS was introduced with NetWare 4.

2. eDirectory was introduced with NetWare 6.

3. NCS 1.7 supports, out of the box, a 2-server cluster and can be upgraded to support a maximum of 32 nodes in a cluster.

4. iFolder lets users have access to their files from home, the office, or while on the road without copying files back and forth to a floppy disk.

5. eGuide is a Web-based address book.

6. The five major Open Source Services or applications that Novell ships with NetWare 6.5 are Apache, MySQL, Perl, PHP, and Tomcat.

7. The kernel is launched from SERVER.EXE, which is found in C:\NWSERVER.

INSTALLING AND CONFIGURING NETWARE 6.5

8. NetWare 6.5 requires a minimum of a PII CPU, 512 MB of RAM, a 500-MB DOS partition, 2 GB of space for SYS, a PS/2 or USB mouse, an SGVA video adapter, and one or more network adapters.

9. If you are using a multiprocessor server, the minimum CPU requirement is two PIII 700-MHz CPUs.

10. You must have Supervisor rights to the Tree object, Supervisor rights to the container object where the server will be installed, and Read rights to the Security container.

11. To prepare an existing NetWare environment for a NetWare 6.5 server, you run Deployment Manager from root of the operating system CD. The Deployment Manager executable is NWDEPLOY.EXE.

12. You cannot introduce a NetWare 6.5 server into an environment that contains a NetWare 4.10 server.

13. When introducing a NetWare 6.5 server into an existing environment, NetWare 4.11 and 4.2 servers must have SP6a, NetWare 5.0 servers must have SP4, and NetWare 5.1 servers must have SP3 installed.

14. You need a DOS partition on a NetWare 6.5 server to boot the server.

15. The executable that launches the install routine is Install.bat, found at the root of the operating system CD.

16. NET.CFG configures the DOS-based Novell client for an across-the-wire installation and configures the Preferred tree, Preferred server, First network drive, and Name context. It is most often found in the C:\NWCLIENT or C:\Novell\Client32 directory.

17. There are two types of NetWare 6.5 installations: default and manual. If you choose the Default option, the SYS volume will be 4 GB.

18. The extension for storage adapters is .ham, for storage devices is .cdm, for network adapters is .lan, for namespace modules is .nam, and for NetWare Loadable Modules is .nlm.

19. The default frame type for IPX is Ethernet_802.2.

20. The three NetWare 6.5 architectural layers are Applications/Services, Kernel (where the operating system is found), and Drivers.

21. Know the four keystroke combinations Alt+Esc, Ctrl+Esc, Alt+Ctrl+Esc, and Left-Shift+Right-Shift+Alt+Esc.

22. Startup.NCF configures storage adapters and devices, and Autoexec.NCF configures LAN adapters, time synchronization, Server ID, and file server name. Autoexec.NCF also establishes search paths and launches NLMs.

23. The load order for server configuration files is CONFIG.SYS, AUTOEXEC.BAT, SERVER.EXE, STARTUP.NCF, and AUTOEXEC.NCF.

24. Notable SERVER.EXE switches include -nl, -na, and -ns.

25. You can locate iManager by using the following URL:
https://ip_address/nps/iManager.html.

26. You can locate Remote Manager by using the following URL: https://ip_address:8009 or http://ip_address:8008. You can substitute a DNS name for the IP address if you have DNS configured. You can also locate Remote Manager through Web Manager by using the following URL: https://ip_address:2200.

27. You can locate OpenSSH in Web Manager, Open Source, OpenSSH. OpenSSH provides ssh, sftp, and scp. The generic path to open an ssh session is ssh user@remote_ip_address.

INSTALLING AND CONFIGURING THE NOVELL CLIENT

28. Four protocol options are available with the Novell client: IP Only, IPX Only, IP and IPX, and IP and IPX Compatibility Mode.

29. Four main methods are available for accessing the Novell Client Login screen.

 a. Choose Start, Novell (common), Novell Login.

 b. Go to My Network Places.

 c. Right-click the red N in the System Tray.

 d. Reboot the workstation.

30. `Winsetup.exe` launches the Novell Client installation routine when the Client CD does not autorun.

31. /508 is the option that you should append to the installation executable if you have users with special accessibility needs.

32. Typical and Custom are the two installation methods.

33. Typical installation automatically installs four Client components.

34. NDS and Bindery are two Login Authenticator options.

35. NDS, Script, Windows, Dial-up, and NMAS are the five tabs available when you select the Advanced button on the opening Novell Client screen.

36. You can set the Novell Client Properties for numerous users with ZENworks for Desktops 3 or higher. You can set the Client IP properties for multiple users using a DHCP server.

37. eDirectory is made up of the schema, objects, properties, and values.

38. Objects are one of three types: Tree objects, Container objects, and Leaf objects.

39. Three main types of Container objects exist: Country objects, Organization objects, and Organizational Unit objects. Other container objects include Role Based Service container, License container, Domain container, and Security container.

40. An eDirectory tree is required to have a Tree object (some utilities call it the [Root]) and an Organization object. The Country object and Organizational Unit object are optional.

41. The Tree object can contain the Country object, an Organization object, an Alias of the Country, an Organization, or a Security container. An Organization object can contain an Organizational Unit or Leaf objects. It cannot contain an Organization object.

42. The schema defines the rules of object creation and where in the tree an object can be created.

43. An object's properties can be single valued or multivalued. Some properties are required, whereas others are optional. The same class of objects has the same properties but different values for the required properties.

44. Leaf objects are resources, such as Server, Volume, User, Group, Organizational Role, LDAP group, and LDAP server.

45. The Organizational Role is a task-oriented Group object.

46. Distinguished names are identified by a leading period. Relative distinguished names have no leading period.

47. Contextual elements in an eDirectory name are separated by periods.

48. eDirectory names can be typeful or typeless.

49. An object's context is where the object exists in the tree.

50. Current context, name context defines where the computer you are sitting at is currently looking in the tree.

51. Inheritance controls the flow of rights down the tree from object to object.

52. You can use NetWare Administrator, ConsoleOne, iMonitor, and iManager to administer the tree.

53. You can find NetWare Administrator at `SYS:\Public\Win32\Nwadmn32.exe`.

54. You can find ConsoleOne at `SYS:\Public\Mgmt\ConsoleOne\1.2\Bin\ConsoleOne.exe`.

55. The URL of iMonitor is `http://ip_address_or_dns_name:8008/nds`.

56. The traditional file system is made up of volumes (the most fundamental unit of NetWare data storage), directories, subdirectories, files, and attributes.

57. When compared to a traditional paper-based file system, the file server is like a file cabinet, a volume like a drawer, a directory like a hanging folder, a subdirectory like a manilla folder, and paper files in the manilla folder like the files.

58. Volume storage has two types: Traditional and NSS.

59. Traditional volumes can span drives, be stored on a single drive, or be stored with other volumes on a single drive.

60. NSS volumes are made up of partitions, pools, and logical volumes. Volumes are created from the free space that is available on your server's hard drives.

61. The process of creating an NSS volume is Partition, Pool, and then Volume.

62. NSS attributes include overbooking, in which you have multiple volumes in a pool competing for the available space.

63. Volume SYS is the first created when a server is installed and should be kept for the operating system and nonvolatile system-related files.

64. Create additional volumes for applications and data.

65. The `Public` directory contains publicly accessible NetWare utilities.

66. The `System` directory contains files and NLMs for the admin and system's use.

67. Novell recommends that you create Shared, Users, and Applications parent directories. You should also create the storage locations for configuration files, such as INI files and ZENworks profile directories.

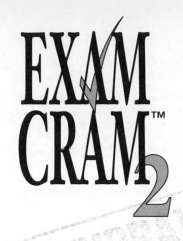

EXAM CRAM™2

WITHDRAWN

Novell®
NetWare® 6.5
CNA

LEARNING RESOURCES
CENTRE

Havering College
of Further and Higher education

Warren E. Wyrostek

CERTIFICATION

Novell NetWare 6.5 CNA Exam Cram 2

International Standard Book Number: 0-7897-2787-0

Library of Congress Catalog Card Number: 2002091628

Printed in the United States of America

First Printing: April 2005

07   06   05   4   3   2   1

Trademarks

All terms mentioned in this book that are known to be trademarks or service marks have been appropriately capitalized. Que Publishing cannot attest to the accuracy of this information. Use of a term in this book should not be regarded as affecting the validity of any trademark or service mark.

Warning and Disclaimer

Every effort has been made to make this book as complete and as accurate as possible, but no warranty or fitness is implied. The information provided is on an "as is" basis. The author and the publisher shall have neither liability nor responsibility to any person or entity with respect to any loss or damages arising from the information contained in this book or from the use of the CD or programs accompanying it.

Bulk Sales

Que Publishing offers excellent discounts on this book when ordered in quantity for bulk purchases or special sales. For more information, please contact

U.S. Corporate and Government Sales

1-800-382-3419

corpsales@pearsontechgroup.com

For sales outside the U.S., please contact

International Sales

international@pearsoned.com

Publisher
Paul Boger

Executive Editor
Jeff Riley

Acquisitions Editor
Jenny Watson

Development Editor
Susan Brown-Zahn

Managing Editor
Charlotte Clapp

Project Editor
Andy Beaster

Copy Editor
Karen A. Gill

Indexer
John Sleeva

Proofreader
Cindy Long

Technical Editors
Mark Hall
Ted Simpson

Publishing Coordinator
Pamalee Nelson

Multimedia Developer
Dan Scherf

Cover Designer
Anne Jones

Interior Designer
Gary Adair

CERTIFICATION

Que Certification • 800 East 96th Street • Indianapolis, Indiana 46240

A Note from Series Editor Ed Tittel

You know better than to trust your certification preparation to just anybody. That's why you, and more than 2 million others, have purchased an Exam Cram book. As Series Editor for the new and improved Exam Cram 2 Series, I have worked with the staff at Que Certification to ensure you won't be disappointed. That's why we've taken the world's best-selling certification product—a two-time finalist for "Best Study Guide" in CertCities' reader polls—and made it even better.

As a two-time finalist for the "Favorite Study Guide Author" award as selected by CertCities readers, I know the value of good books. You'll be impressed with Que Certification's stringent review process, which ensures the books are high quality, relevant, and technically accurate. Rest assured that several industry experts have reviewed this material, helping us deliver an excellent solution to your exam preparation needs.

This Exam Cram 2 book also features a special edition of ExamForce's powerful, full-featured test engine, which is trusted by certification students throughout the world.

As a 20-year-plus veteran of the computing industry and the original creator and editor of the Exam Cram Series, I've brought my IT experience to bear on these books. During my tenure at Novell from 1989 to 1994, I worked with and around its excellent education and certification department. At Novell, I witnessed the growth and development of the first really big, successful IT certification program—one that was to shape the industry forever afterward. This experience helped push my writing and teaching activities heavily in the certification direction. Since then, I've worked on nearly 100 certification related books, and I write about certification topics for numerous Web sites and for *Certification* magazine.

In 1996, while studying for various MCP exams, I became frustrated with the huge, unwieldy study guides that were the only preparation tools available. As an experienced IT professional and former instructor, I wanted "nothing but the facts" necessary to prepare for the exams. From this impetus, Exam Cram emerged: short, focused books that explain exam topics, detail exam skills and activities, and get IT professionals ready to take and pass their exams.

In 1997 when Exam Cram debuted, it quickly became the best-selling computer book series since "...*For Dummies*," and the best-selling certification book series ever. By maintaining an intense focus on subject matter, tracking errata and updates quickly, and following the certification market closely, Exam Cram established the dominant position in cert prep books.

You will not be disappointed in your decision to purchase this book. If you are, please contact me at etittel@jump.net. All suggestions, ideas, input, or constructive criticism are welcome!

Ed Tittel

This is for my mom and dad. Dad, I know you are with the Saints, but your presence is surely felt. You both gave me the source of my faith, a deep respect for family, a desire to excel in education, the belief that hard work is a good thing, and above all a sense of humor. I love you both.

In nomine Patris, et Filii, et Spiritus Sancti. Amen!

About the Author

Warren E. Wyrostek is the owner of Warren E. Wyrostek, M.Ed. (a Novell Authorized Partner), and 3WsCertification.com (a portal dedicated to Novell Training and Support). He holds a master's degree in Vocational-Technical Education from Valdosta State College, a Master of Divinity from New York's Union Theological Seminary, and is devoted to technical education as reflected by his list certifications. He currently holds 25 Novell certifications including the CNI, MCNE, and CDE. Warren has been teaching over 20 years and has taught on the college and secondary school levels. He has taught Novell authorized courses since 1996. Professionally, his main joy comes as a freelance writer, course developer, and contract trainer for various technologies that revolve around integrated networking. He has been the Technical Editor for over 20 certification titles in the last few years. At heart, he is a teacher who loves what technical education offers. Many of Warren's certification articles can be found on Informit.com, including "Now What? A Career Changer's Odyssey." You can reach Warren at wyrostekw@msn.com.

Acknowledgments

Right after I signed up to write this book, Murphy showed up with his whole family and decided to check in for the year and even wanted to know what time meals were being served. On top of that he brought along 4 hurricanes. Amidst all of that this book came to fruition. A miracle in and of itself, but the direct result of the understanding and patience of the folks at Pearson Education. It is the product of many people, not just the guy who wrote it. I am only one small cog in this team effort. First and foremost to everyone who let me spout off when things went nuts this year but still kept me laughing at life and myself, I am forever in your debt.

Jenny Watson for giving me the opportunity to do something I dreamed of and pitched for so long. You never gave up on me, and for that you have my deepest respect and thanks. Emmett Dulaney, there are no words to express my gratitude to you for your advice when I was considering this project. As we have worked together on many projects over the last few years, my respect for you has continually grown. Thanks for your friendship and all of the advice. This book would not be here if not for you.

Mark Taber, Jeff Riley, and Steve Rowe and all of the folks at Pearson that I had the pleasure of meeting and talking with in September, my thanks for allowing me to contribute to your library. Your patience with me and my schedule will never be forgotten.

Susan and Karen, for all of your patience and professionalism making this book something I am very proud of, *thanks* does not come close to expressing my gratitude for cleaning up my lousy typing and grammar and doing everything you did. A major thanks to Mark and Ted for a fantastic TE job. I have been in your shoes many times and fully appreciate what it takes to TE a book. Your suggestions and corrections are invaluable. Andy, what can I say? It was a pleasure meeting you, and thanks for pulling all of the strings together; your availability for my questions and concerns have meant so much and got me over some high hurdles. Many many thanks especially for keeping me laughing.

To all of my students over the years who freely shared their knowledge and experience with me, your inspiration is the foundation for my love of Technical Education. And to my teachers, mentors, and clerics who shared with me their love of teaching and inspired me. Thanks just does not seem to be enough. You all openly and honestly shared your sense of vocational call and divine direction. This book is a result of all those conversations and debates.

For all who read this, I thank you for letting me share what I know of NetWare administration, for allowing me to be your teacher for a few hours. I hope that this book will motivate you as my teachers and authors before me motivated me. And more than anything I thank you for letting me be your tour guide to the CNA.

Dominus Vobiscum!

Contents at a Glance

Introduction   xix

Self-Assessment   xxxiii

Chapter 1   The Novell Certifications   1

Chapter 2   Introduction to Networking, Network Administration, and NetWare 6.5   9

Chapter 3   Installing and Configuring NetWare 6.5   25

Chapter 4   Installing and Configuring the Novell Client   69

Chapter 5   Introduction to eDirectory   89

Chapter 6   Introduction to the NetWare 6.5 File System   113

Chapter 7   Basic Management Tasks—eDirectory and File System   133

Chapter 8   File System Security   167

Chapter 9   eDirectory Security   203

Chapter 10   NetWare 6.5 Network Security   231

Chapter 11   NetWare 6.5 Printing   253

Chapter 12   iFolder and Virtual Office   279

Chapter 13   Practice Exam 1   307

Chapter 14   Answer Key for Practice Exam 1   323

Chapter 15   Practice Exam 2   343

Chapter 16   Answer Key for Practice Exam 2   357

Glossary   377

Appendix A   NetWare 6.5 Port Reference   397

Appendix B   NetWare 6.5 File System: Effective Rights
              Practice Scenarios   403

Appendix C   Workstation Utilities   409

Appendix D   Sample Response File   413

Appendix E   NetWare 6.5: New Server Installation Planning
              Table   421

Appendix F   References (Web and Print)   427

Appendix G   Commonly Used NetWare 6.5 Management
              URLs   437

Appendix H   CD Contents and Installation Instructions   439

              Index   443

Table of Contents

Introduction ....**xix**

Self-Assessment ....**xxxiii**

Chapter 1
The Novell Certifications **1**

    Novell Certifications   2
        Certified Novell Administrator (CNA)   2
        Certified Novell Engineer (CNE)   3
        Master Certified Novell Engineer (MCNE)   4
        Certified Directory Engineer (CDE)   5
        Certified Novell Instructor (CNI)   6
        Novell Authorized Instructor (NAI)   7
        Certified Linux Engineer (CLE)   7
        Certified Linux Professional (CLP)   7
    Conclusion   7

Chapter 2
Introduction to Networking, Network Administration, and
NetWare 6.5 ....**9**

    A Brief History of the NetWare Operating System   10
    Identify NetWare 6.5 Features   13
        Business Continuity Services   14
        Productivity-Enhancing Services   14
        Open Source Services   15
        Web Application Services   16
    Describe How NetWare Works with Other Operating Systems   16
        How NetWare Interacts with DOS   17
        Operating System Platforms That Can Function as a NetWare
        6.5 Client   18
        Platforms That Can Function as a Server if eDirectory Is
        Installed   18
    Exam Prep Questions   20

Chapter 3

Installing and Configuring NetWare 6.5 ....**25**

Identify Prerequisite Requirements 26
    System Requirements 28
    Software Requirements 29
    Configuration Requirements 30
    New Server Installation Requirements 30
Prepare the Existing Network 32
Prepare the Designated Computer 33
    Preparing the DOS Partition 34
Install NetWare 6.5 40
Identify the Operating System Components of NetWare 6.5 46
Use Server Console Commands to Manage NetWare 6.5 47
    Console Commands 48
    NLMs 51
Use Configuration Files 53
    Five-Step Load Order 53
    Server.exe Switches 56
Identify the Utilities to Remotely Manage NetWare 6.5 57
    iManager 57
    Remote Manager 58
    OpenSSH 61
Exam Prep Questions 64

Chapter 4

Installing and Configuring the Novell Client **69**

Describe the Novell Client 70
    Novell Client Features 70
    Protocols and Login Scripts 71
    Client Login Methods 73
Install the Novell Client 75
Log In to eDirectory and the Workstations 78
    NDS 78
    Script 79
    Windows 80
    Dial-up 81
    NMAS 81
Set Client Properties 83
    Client Properties That Can Be Set 83
    Setting Client Properties for Individuals and for Multiple
    Users 84
Exam Prep Questions 85

Chapter 5

Introduction to eDirectory **89**

    Identify the Role and Benefits of eDirectory   90

    Identify How eDirectory Works   92

    Identify and Describe eDirectory Components   93

    Identify and Describe eDirectory Object Classes   95

    Identify the Flow and Design of the eDirectory Tree   99

    Identify eDirectory Tools and When to Use Them   105

    Exam Prep Questions   109

Chapter 6

Introduction to the NetWare 6.5 File System **113**

    Identify Network File Service Components   114

    Identify Types of NetWare Volume Storage   116

        Traditional Volumes   117

        NSS Volumes   117

    Identify the Guidelines for Planning Network Volumes   119

    Identify the Content and Purpose of NetWare SYS Directories   121

    Identify the Types of Directories Used for Organizing a File
System   125

    Evaluate Directory Structures   127

    Exam Prep Questions   129

Chapter 7

Basic Management Tasks—eDirectory and File System **133**

    Describe the Admin Object   134

    Create User Objects   135

    Modify User Objects   139

    Move Objects   141

    Delete User Objects   142

    Create Traditional and NSS Volumes   144

        Create Traditional Volumes   147

        Create NSS Volumes   149

    Access Volumes Through Mapped Network Drives   153

        Types of Drive Mappings   153

        Map Syntax   156

        Map Options   157

        NetWare 6.5 Login Scripts   158

    Exam Prep Questions   162

Chapter 8
File System Security **167**

Identify the Types of Network Security Provided by NetWare   168
Identify How NetWare File System Security Works   170
    What Are Rights, and What Are the NetWare File System
    Rights?   171
    What Are the Default Assignments Granted in
    NetWare 6.5?   173
    What Are Trustees, ACLs, and Inheritance?   173
    What Are the Two Ways to Change a Trustee
    Assignment?   181
    What Are Effective Rights?   182
    What Are the Rules of NetWare 6.5 File System
    Security?   187
    Effective Rights Practice   188
Plan File System Rights   192
Identify Directory and File Attributes   193
Exam Prep Questions   199

Chapter 9
eDirectory Security **203**

Describe eDirectory Security   204
    eDirectory Rights and the eDirectory ACL   206
    Granting eDirectory Rights: The Utilities   210
    Default Rights   214
    The Rules and Guidelines for eDirectory Rights   215
Determine How Rights Flow   217
Block Inherited Rights   218
Determine eDirectory Effective Rights   220
    Scenario 1   221
    Scenario 2   224
Troubleshoot eDirectory Security   226
Exam Prep Questions   227

Chapter 10
NetWare 6.5 Network Security...**231**

Internally Secure a Network   232
    Guidelines for Physically Securing the Server   234
    File System Security Guidelines   234
    Login Security and Intruder Lockout Guidelines   235
    Password Guidelines   239
    eDirectory Rights Guidelines   241

Administrative Access Guidelines   242
Virus Protection Guidelines   243
Troubleshoot Common Internal Security Problems   244
Identify How to Provide External Network Security with a
Firewall   245
Exam Prep Questions   248

Chapter 11
NetWare 6.5 Printing **253**

Identify the Features of NDPS   256
Identify the Types of Printers   257
Describe NDPS Components   258
   Printer Agent   259
   NDPS Manager   259
   Printer Broker   259
   Printer Gateway   259
Set Up NDPS   260
   Set Up the Broker   261
   Set Up the NDPS Manager   263
   Set Up the Printer Agents   264
   Set Up RPM (Remote Print Management)   266
Manage NDPS   267
Implement iPrint   270
Exam Prep Questions   275

Chapter 12
iFolder and Virtual Office **279**

Implement iFolder   280
   iFolder: Its Benefits and Features   280
   Installing iFolder and the iFolder Client   281
   Configuring iFolder   284
   Global Settings   286
   User Management   290
   System Monitoring   291
   Reporting   291
Describe Virtual Office   292
Install Virtual Office   293
Configure Virtual Office   294
   Virtual Office Configuration Using iManager   294
   Virtual Office Configuration Using the Virtual Office
   Interface   300
Conclusion   302
Exam Prep Questions   303

Chapter 13
Practice Exam 1 307

Chapter 14
Answer Key for Practice Exam 1 323

Chapter 15
Practice Exam 2 343

Chapter 16
Answer Key for Practice Exam 2 357

Glossary 377

Appendix A
NetWare 6.5 Port Reference 397

Appendix B
NetWare 6.5 File System: Effective Rights Practice Scenarios 403

    File System Inheritance Scenarios   403
        Simple File System Inheritance   404
        Complex File System Inheritance   405
    File System Inheritance Scenarios—Answer Keys   406
        Simple File System Inheritance   406
        Complex File System Inheritance   407

Appendix C
Workstation Utilities 409

    Workstation Utilities Native to NetWare 6.5   409
    Legacy Workstation Utilities That Are Compatible with
    NetWare 6.5   411

Appendix D
Sample Response File 413

Appendix E
NetWare 6.5: New Server Installation Planning Table 421

Appendix F
References (Web and Print) 427

    Introduction   428
    Chapter 1   429
    Chapter 2   429

Chapter 3   430
Chapter 4   431
Chapter 5   431
Chapter 6   432
Chapter 7   432
Chapter 8   433
Chapter 9   433
Chapter 10   434
Chapter 11   434
Chapter 12   435
Appendixes   435

Appendix G
Commonly Used NetWare 6.5 Management URLs **437**

Appendix H
CD Contents and Installation Instructions **439**
The CramMaster Engine   439
Multiple Test Modes   439
Pretest Mode   440
Adaptive Drill Mode   440
Simulated Exam Mode   440
Installing CramMaster for the Novell NetWare 6.5 Exam   440
Using CramMaster for the Novell NetWare 6.5 Exam   441
Customer Support   442

Index **443**

We Want to Hear from You!

As the reader of this book, *you* are our most important critic and commentator. We value your opinion and want to know what we're doing right, what we could do better, what areas you'd like to see us publish in, and any other words of wisdom you're willing to pass our way.

As an executive editor for Que Publishing, I welcome your comments. You can email or write me directly to let me know what you did or didn't like about this book—as well as what we can do to make our books better.

Please note that I cannot help you with technical problems related to the topic of this book. We do have a User Services group, however, where I will forward specific technical questions related to the book.

When you write, please be sure to include this book's title and author as well as your name, email address, and phone number. I will carefully review your comments and share them with the author and editors who worked on the book.

Email: feedback@quepublishing.com

Mail: Jeff Riley
Executive Editor
Que Publishing
800 East 96th Street
Indianapolis, IN 46240 USA

For more information about this book or another Que Certification title, visit our Web site at www.examcram2.com. Type the ISBN (excluding hyphens) or the title of a book in the Search field to find the page you're looking for.

Introduction

Terms You'll Need to Understand

✓ Form test

✓ Adaptive test

✓ Practicum test

✓ Hot-spot question

✓ Drag-and-drop question

✓ Mutiple-choice question

✓ Fill-in-the-blank question

Techniques You'll Need to Master

✓ Test-taking strategies

✓ Identify the differences among a form test, an adapative test, and a practicum

✓ Identify the differences among the various question types

I would like to welcome you to *Novell NetWare 6.5 CNA Exam Cram 2*. The sole purpose of this book is to help you earn the CNA by passing the Novell Foundations of Novell Networking: NetWare 6.5 exam (050-686). Sometimes I simply call this the Foundations exam. At those occasions, I am abbreviating the title of the exam simply to conserve on space. Realize when I say the Foundations exam that I am referring to the Foundations of Novell Networking: NetWare 6.5 exam (050-686).

The NetWare CNA is an introductory certification that requires you to pass a single test, the 050-686. This is not a difficult exam if you have some background in networking and a bit of hands-on experience with NetWare 6.5. Even a complete network novice can pass this exam if he is willing to work and study diligently. The test is not a cakewalk, but a true test of your ability to perform basic workstation-based administrative tasks. You will also be tested on a few server-based tasks and the steps and requirements for installing a fresh NetWare 6.5 server.

Quite honestly, because I've taught the CNA courses as a Novell contract instructor for the past eight years, my students are my main motivation for writing this text. Students come into the Foundations class seeking knowledge and leave enthusiastic about what they can do based on the knowledge they have learned. The real success stories are the students who contact me after earning their CNA. Their pride is amazing. For my future students and those of you whom I will never meet in a classroom, I hope you leave this Exam Cram 2 with the enthusiasm that my in-class students have, and more importantly, with the CNA in NetWare 6.5.

At the beginning of every class, I ask my students what their objectives are for the class. Some come to learn a skillset, some come because their employer forced them, some come because they want to take a week off from work, and some come because they want to earn the CNA and realize its value. This book is not the *War and Peace* of NetWare 6.5 administration. Its sole purpose is to help you pass the Foundations exam.

If you are looking for more detailed information on administrative skills, I encourage you to take the instructor-led Novell authorized course, 3016, "Foundations of Novell Networking: NetWare 6.5"; purchase the authorized self-study kit from Novell; or seek out one of the great titles from Novell Press on NetWare 6.5 (`http://www.novell.com/training/books/`). You can find further information on Novell training options at `http://www.novell.com/training/`.

As we begin this journey together, I hope you have as much fun preparing for this exam as I have presenting the information to you. I wish you all good things as you prepare to earn the CNA.

About This Book

Each chapter in this Exam Cram 2 follows a regular pattern and offers graphical cues about important or useful information. Following is the structure of a typical chapter:

➤ **Opening hotlists**—This is a list of the terms, tools, and techniques that you must learn to fully understand the chapter's subject matter.

➤ **Topical coverage**—Each chapter covers the main content that is related to the chapter's subject title. Each chapter has sections that relate to one of the published test objectives.

➤ **Exam alert**—Throughout each chapter, topics or concepts that are likely to appear on a test or specific pieces of exam advice are highlighted using a special Exam Alert layout, like this:

 An Exam Alert stresses concepts, terms, software, or activities that are likely to relate to one or more certification test questions. They reflect the information you need to know as defined in the exam objectives laid out by Novell.

➤ **Tips**—In addition to Exam Alerts, Tips are included to give you an alternative method of accomplishing a NetWare 6.5 administrative task. This is more practical real-world information that might or might not be on the test.

 This is an example of a tip. Although Novell is moving away from NetWare Administrator in NetWare 6.5, NetWare Administrator can still perform many administrative functions more efficiently than some of the newer utilities.

➤ **Notes**—The Note icon flags information that is related to the material within the chapter body but is not meant to be part of the content flow. A note is also known as an aside.

 This is what a note looks like. A note details or clarifies information in the chapter body.

➤ **Exam Prep questions**—These practice questions appear at the end of every chapter. These exam-like questions are similar to what you will find on the Foundations of Novell Networking: NetWare 6.5 (050-686) exam.

➤ **Further details and resources**—On the CD you will find a document that provides direct pointers to Novell and third-party resources offering more details on the chapter's subject.

In addition, Chapters 13, "Practice Exam 1," and 15, "Practice Exam 2," include two sample tests that review the material presented throughout this book to ensure that you're ready for the exam. Chapters 14, "Answer Key for Practice Exam 1," and 16, "Answer Key for Practice Exam 2," offer the answer keys to the sample tests that appear in Chapters 13 and 15. Take the sample tests when you think you're ready for the live exam.

This book also offers appendixes that provide technical resources, additional practice questions for file system rights, commonly used management URLs and ports, the low-down on what's on the CD-ROM that accompanies this book, and instructions for using the ExamForce software (again, see the CD-ROM). Concluding this book are a Glossary, which explains terms, and an index, which you can use to track down terms as they appear in the text.

Finally, the tear-out Cram Sheet that is attached to the inside front cover of this *Exam Cram 2* book represents a condensed and compiled collection of facts, exam alerts, and tips that you should memorize before taking the test. It is a summary of key testable points that you might encounter on the Foundations exam.

Exam Experience

The Foundations of Novell Networking: NetWare 6.5 exam is a straightforward computer-based assessment of your knowledge. Authorized exam providers administer this test.

Arrive at the test center, after registering with your provider, at least 15 minutes before your scheduled appointment. This gives you time to sign in with the test proctor; provide two forms of identification, one of which must be a photo ID; deposit any books, bags, cell phones, or study aids with the proctor; and take a deep breath. Remember that all Novell tests, including the Foundations exam, are closed book exams.

The proctor then escorts you into a test room that has a window or closed-circuit camera system enabling him to monitor the test. Each test room has one or more computers, generally separated from each other by a partition. You are given a sheet of scrap paper and a pen or pencil (some provide erasable boards and an erasable pen) to write down any notes before or during the exam. After you compose yourself and before you start the exam, write down on the notepad any facts or mnemonics you want to remember during the exam. This includes any lists that you memorized during your study time. You must surrender all notes when you leave the test room.

When the proctor leaves the room, you can click Start for the Foundations exam. The proctor has the exam preloaded for you.

The computer has a clock in the upper-right corner of the screen. This tells you how much time you have left in the exam.

As you proceed through the exam, answer every question. You cannot mark a question and return to it at the end of the exam. You have only one chance at each question. Take your time, look at the possible answer choices, and provide the best possible answer. If you leave a question blank, it is scored as incorrect. For this reason, it's better to guess than to skip a question entirely.

After you answer the final question, the test is scored automatically. You are notified immediately on your computer screen if you earned a passing score. A score report is routed to a printer that the proctor monitors and given to you when you leave the test center. The score report provides your score, the passing or cut-off score, and the objectives that correspond to questions that you answered incorrectly. This gives you an immediate reference to this *Exam Cram 2* and any authorized courseware you might have used to study from. When you leave the test center, you are asked to sign out and return any notepads that were given to you at the beginning of the exam. Your personal possessions are then returned to you.

Test-Taking Strategies

The exam experience is an exhilarating one. Depending on whether this is your first Novell exam or the hundredth, you will take the exam with a certain amount of nervous anticipation. Here are a couple of hints for doing the best you can:

➤ Take your time and read each question and answer carefully. Don't read too quickly, or you might miss a key component that is there to trick you.

➤ Most of the questions are short and straightforward, but some contain a short scenario. Read through the scenario and make sure you know the key element that the scenario is addressing. Many of these questions have extraneous information that is there strictly to confuse you.

➤ If you have no idea what the correct answer is for a question, try to narrow the choices down to two or three and then guess. Don't leave a question blank.

➤ Don't spend too much time on any one question because that could mean running out of time at the end of the exam. Answer all questions. If you have to, use every minute to do so.

➤ Refer to any notes that you made before starting the exam to see if any might help you on a particularly difficult question.

➤ If you encounter a question that you have no idea how to answer, provide an answer and move on with a positive attitude. Remember that it is only one question. Be patient with yourself and the test. You might know more than you think you know.

➤ Make sure you answer the questions the way that Novell wants you to. If you have a boatload of certifications from other vendors but have never taken a Novell exam, you might have problems if you answer the questions the way you are accustomed. For example, if you answer a Novell question the way that Microsoft, CompTIA, or Cisco would have you answer it, you might get it wrong. Remember that this is a Novell CNA exam, not a Microsoft MCP, CompTIA Network+, or Cisco CCNA exam.

➤ The worst thing that will happen is that you might fail the exam. That is financially costly but not life threatening. You can take the exam again, and it's likely you will pass it if you take what you learn from the experience, study the objectives you got wrong, and patiently work through the material again. The only students I have had who have failed are those who did not study the material I pointed them to, those who were overly nervous, or those who did not answer the questions the Novell way.

Exam Providers

Most Novell computer-based tests, including the Foundations of Novell Networking: NetWare 6.5 (050-686), cost $125 each. Each time you take the exam, you are assessed an additional $125 fee. Several of Novell's newer practicum exams, which are discussed in the "Exam Types" section, have a higher price associated with them. In the United States and Canada, most Novell tests are administered by Pearson VUE and by Thomson Prometric. The newer practicum exams are being administered by Novell through their authorized training partners. You can contact Pearson VUE and Thomson Prometric at the following addresses and phone numbers, respectively:

➤ **Pearson VUE**—Sign up for a test or get the phone numbers for local testing centers through the Web page at www.vue.com/novell. You can also register by phone at 800-TEST-CNE (in North America) or 800-837-8263.

➤ **Thomson Prometric**—Sign up for a test through the company's Web site at www.2test.com. You can also call 800-RED-EXAM (in North America) to register.

You can find information about Novell's practicum exams at the Novell Practicum Portal (http://practicum.novell.com/).

Exam Scoring

Each Novell exam has a defined passing score. Based on the number of people who have taken an exam and where a test is in its life cycle, the passing score might change. When you are preparing to take a Novell exam, check Novell's Test Data Web site (http://www.novell.com/training/testinfo/testdata.html) for the current passing score.

At the time that I am writing this *Exam Cram 2*, the passing score for the Foundations of Novell Networking: NetWare 6.5 (050-686) exam is 650 out of a possible 800 points. Currently, the exam has 66 questions, and you have 75 minutes to complete it.

When you look at Novell's Test Data Web site (see Figure I.1), notice that there are two Foundations of Novell Networking: NetWare 6.5 exams. The 050-686 exam is for CNAs and CNEs. The 050-886 is for Novell instructors, or CNIs. There is no difference in content between the 050-686 and 050-886 exams. The only difference is that the passing score is higher for Novell instructors who want to be authorized by Novell to teach the class for

Novell training partners using the authorized courseware. If a Novell instructor takes the 050-686 exam and passes it with a score higher than the 050-886 passing score, he will be authorized by Novell to present the class. Novell encourages instructors to take the 050-886 exam, but it accepts the 050-686 exam as long as the score for instructional authorization is above the passing score for the 050-886 exam.

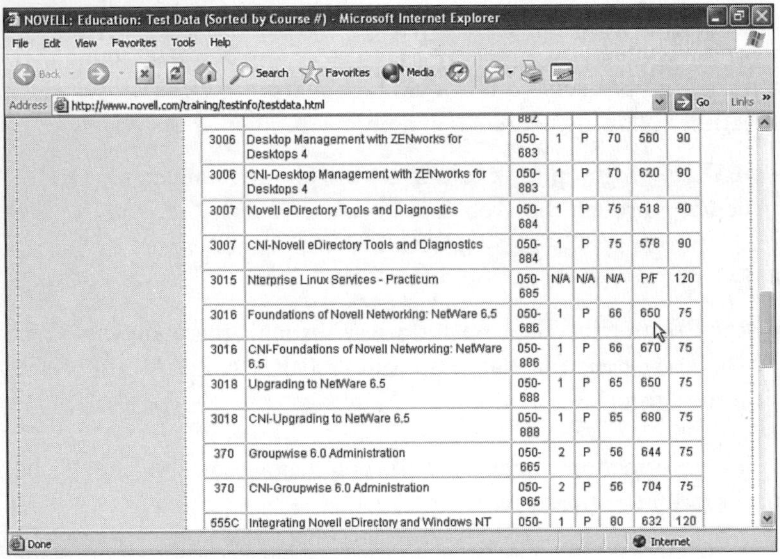

Figure I.1 Test 050-686 test data.

Retake Policy

Novell's current retake policy permits you, should you fail this exam on your first attempt, to take the exam again as soon you want. However, should you fail an exam twice, you must wait a minimum of 30 days before attempting to pass the exam on a third or fourth attempt. This is to prevent folks from stealing Novell's test content and publishing it to a braindump site.

After passing an exam, you can retake the same exam no sooner than 12 months later, unless Novell has changed the published objectives or modified the content.

If you violate these policies, Novell denies or revokes your Novell certification(s).

Exam Readiness

Before tackling the Foundations of Novell Networking: NetWare 6.5 exam, read through the Self-Assessment, which follows this Introduction. This document gives you a good sense of whether you're ready for the exam or if you need to brush up on a topic or two.

The best way to prepare for a Novell exam, after working through this *Exam Cram 2*, its practice tests, its end-of-chapter review questions, and other third-party sources, is to set up a NetWare 6.5 test lab. The lab should consist of a Windows 2000/XP workstation with the Novell Client, networked with a NetWare 6.5 server.

This type of lab environment can get expensive. To work around purchasing additional computers for your practice lab, you can set up a virtual network on a computer using VMWare workstation, which you can find at http://www.vmware.com/products/desktop/ws_features.html. You can download VMWare for a 30-day trial period before purchasing it. If you are seriously interested in pursuing Novell certifications, VMWare is a great product to invest in for study and research. To establish your network, your computer should have at least 1 GB of RAM installed, be running a Linux or Windows platform, and have enough hard disk space to install NetWare 6.5 and Windows XP Professional.

After you have your network up and running, get familiar with the utilities, the interfaces, the paths to those utilities discussed in this text, the server console commands, and the steps needed to accomplish basic administrative tasks. Practice, practice, practice. That is the best teacher.

After all that practice, return to the review questions at the end of each chapter and the practice tests at the end of this text. These questions alert you to what you know and what you don't know. You should score a minimum of 80 percent without help to feel comfortable with the material. If you fail to score 80 percent or higher, make a list of what you don't know and perform additional study. Do some additional practice. Look at the help screens that each interface offers. You might want to visit Novell's NetWare 6.5 Documentation Web site (http://www.novell.com/documentation/nw65/index.html) to fully research any sticking point.

Exam Types

Novell currently offers computer-based exams using three formats: form-based, adaptive, and practical (commonly called practicums). Adaptive and form-based exams are scored on a 200–800 scale. Practicums are scored on a pass-fail basis.

A form exam is a standard or traditional exam in which you are presented with 60–70 questions in a defined period of time. Your final score is based on the number of questions you answer correctly. All Novell exams start out as form-based exams. The Foundations exam (050-686) is currently a form-based exam.

After a form-based exam has been live for an extensive period of time, and after the test has been taken at least 1,000 times, Novell might convert it to the adaptive exam format. An adaptive exam is a condensed, efficient testing format in which you are presented with 15–25 questions. You are initially presented with a question of moderate difficulty. If you get that question correct, the testing algorithm presents you with a second question that meets or exceeds your ability level, gauged from your response to the first exam question. If you get a difficult question wrong, the next question you are presented with is easier. If you get a question correct, the next one is generally more difficult. A question of moderate difficulty is normally the first question. You are presented with questions until the algorithm concludes that it knows your ability level. You might see only 15 questions, or you might see 25.

Novell's adaptive algorithm is a mystery to most test takers. The important thing to remember is that although the test is relatively short in scope and duration, it is still testing your knowledge and ability as accurately as a form-based exam. Your final score on an adaptive exam is based on the difficulty level of the questions you answered correctly and incorrectly. The score is not simply based on the number or percentage of questions you answered correctly. It is based on a weighted average, with the weights corresponding to the question difficulty level. You might answer almost all of the questions correctly, but if you only do well on easy and moderately difficult questions, you might not receive a perfect score of 800. The Foundations exam is not currently an adaptive exam.

The third and newest type of exam format is the practicum. Practicums were released a few years ago as the definitive exam format for those pursuing the CDE (Certified Directory Engineer). The practicum was offered through the Pearson VUE testing provider. That certification path is no longer available. Novell is now using the practicum for the CLE (Certified Linux Engineer) and CLP (Certified Linux Professional) certifications. Practicums are now offered only through authorized Novell training partners. See the earlier section titled "Exam Providers" for the practicum Web site.

In a practicum exam, you are presented not with a knowledge-based exam format, but with a task-oriented exam format. You are connected, across the

Internet, to a bank of servers at Novell headquarters where you must perform a series of tasks, including installing and troubleshooting products. The exam format tests your ability to perform these tasks in a defined period of time. If you perform a task incorrectly, you fail the exam. Either you perform all tasks to perfection, or you fail. The exam is scored on a pass-fail basis. Novell is currently trying to work out some bugs for the CLE practicum. The CLP practicum is currently in beta and has not gone live. The current pricing for the CLE and CLP practicums is $195 each. The CDE practicum was in excess of $300. Novell has hinted that its long-range goal for certification testing, including testing for the CNA and CNE, is to go with all practicum tests. Only time will tell.

Question Types

The Foundations of Novell Networking: NetWare 6.5 exam (050-686) is a form-based one. You can expect to see several types of questions on this exam. These question types have been used for years in paper-based exams and have been adapted for computer-based exams. The question types are multiple-choice, fill-in-the-blank, matching (which is now graphically accomplished through a drag-and-drop interface), and hot-spot or identification.

Multiple-choice questions come in two formats. Either the question has one correct response, which is represented by a radio button, or it has several correct responses, which are represented by square check boxes. Multiple-choice questions have a short question or scenario and four or more response options. Those questions that have several correct responses have more than four options available. Generally, on Novell exams, if a multiple-choice question has several correct responses, you are told at the end of the question to "Choose 2" or "Choose 3." Rarely have I seen "Choose all that apply" on a Novell exam. On those questions that have several correct responses, you must select all the correct options. For example, if the question says to "Choose 3" and you choose two of the correct options but get the third one wrong, that question is marked as incorrect. Many multiple-choice questions have associated exhibits that you must examine so that you can respond correctly. Take time to carefully look at the exhibits so that on multiple-choice questions that have several correct responses, you select all of the correct responses.

Fill-in-the-blank questions are simply statements in which you have to provide a missing term, command, word, phrase, or path that completes the statement. It is best on these to use all lowercase when entering your response, although Novell says that these responses are not case sensitive. I have seen instances in which student answers were marked incorrect if all uppercase was used, and the students had to dispute this with Novell. To avoid aggravation and a later dispute with the testing provider, I encourage you to use all lowercase. Many consider the fill-in-the-blank the toughest type of question. This is a matter of opinion based on how well you have studied. If you know your commands, glossary terms, and paths to management utilities, fill-in-the-blanks are the easiest of all of the questions.

Matching or drag-and-drop questions are graphical questions in which you click and drag a term to its associated definition. Sometimes these questions involve reordering a series of steps to accomplish a task. For example, on a DOS-based computer, you might drag the boxes containing the terms Command.com, Config.sys, and Autoexec.bat to a part of the screen where you would show their correct order of execution. Some drag-and-drop questions have choices in which you do not have to match to a term, whereas other questions require you to match multiple terms to the same definition. You must match all items or order all items correctly to receive credit for the question. If you match any element incorrectly or put one thing out of order, this question is marked as wrong.

Hot-spot or identification questions ask you to click on an interface option where you would perform a task. For example, you might be asked to click on the menu option in ConsoleOne where you would begin the process of creating a user. If you click on the wrong part of the interface, this question is marked as incorrect.

Each chapter's Exam Prep Questions and the practice exams at the end of this book provide you with all but the matching type of question. Because we are dealing with a paper medium with this text, I cannot provide you with drag-and-drop type questions, but I can offer you some practice on hot-spot, fill-in-the-blank, and multiple-choice questions.

Practice Test Providers

The best way to prepare for the Foundations exam is to take a few practice tests. This book has more than 200 practice questions. If you are looking for additional practice questions, I would also encourage you to look toward ExamForce (http://www.examforce.com) for practice tests that will help you toward passing the Foundations exam. This book features a trial version of their popular CramMaster product.

Test Objectives

Without hesitation, I encourage you to research one other Novell Web site before taking the Foundations exam. Tests change, and so do their objectives. I have already pointed you toward the Novell Test Data Web site to verify the current passing score for the Foundations exam. The other critical site is the Novell Test Objectives site for the Foundations of Novell Networking: NetWare 6.5 exam (`http://www.novell.com/training/testinfo/objectives/3016tobj.html`).

All of the questions on the live exam are based on the objectives that are published on this site. In addition, this *Exam Cram 2* is structured around the published test objectives. This book presents the material based on published objectives to maximize your ability to pass the Foundations exam in the shortest period of time. As time moves along, the objectives might change, and you need to be aware of this.

Onto the CNA

Now that you have an idea of what the exam is like and what this book is all about, look at the Self-Assessment that follows. Chapter 1, "The Novell Certifications," then takes you through all of Novell's current certification offerings. These documents should help you become enthused about why you bought this book and where you can go after earning the CNA. After you know your goal and have assessed your ability to attain the CNA goal, dive into Chapters 2, "Introduction to Networking, Network Administration, and Netware 6.5," through 12, "iFolder and Virtual Office." Together, we will take a phenomenol journey toward your becoming a Novell CNA in NetWare 6.5. Enjoy the ride!

If you have any questions during your study, don't hesitate to contact me at `wyrostekw@msn.com`. You can also visit my Web site (`www.3WsCertification.com`), where you can see a virtual installation of NetWare 6.5, a Novell Links page, and a host of classroom notes. Best wishes on your journey, and thanks for letting me help you toward your goal.

Self-Assessment

Based on recent statistics, thousands of individuals are at some stage in the Novell certification process. And with the release of NetWare 6 and more recently NetWare 6.5, many more are considering whether to obtain a Novell certification of some kind. That's a huge audience!

This book includes a self-assessment to help you evaluate your readiness to tackle the CNA. It should also help you understand what you need to master Novell's 050-686 exam, "Foundations of Novell Networking: NetWare 6.5," which is unofficially known as the NetWare 6.5 CNA exam. However, before you tackle this self-assessment, it's important to talk about concerns you might face when pursuing the CNA and what an ideal CNA candidate might look like.

CNAs in the Real World

The following section describes an ideal CNA candidate, even though only a few real candidates will meet this ideal. In fact, the description of that ideal candidate might seem downright scary. But take heart: Although the requirements to obtain a CNA might seem pretty formidable, they are by no means impossible to meet. However, you should be keenly aware that certification does take time, requires some expense, and consumes substantial effort to get through the process.

Thousands of folks have already earned Novell's CNA, so it's obviously an attainable goal. You can get all the real-world motivation you need from knowing that many others have gone before, so you'll be able to follow in their footsteps. If you're willing to tackle the process seriously and do what it takes to obtain the necessary experience and knowledge, you can take and pass the one certification test involved in obtaining a CNA. In fact, *Exam Cram 2s* are designed to make it as easy on you as possible to prepare for exams. But prepare you must!

The Ideal CNA Candidate

Just to give you some idea of what an ideal CNA candidate is like, here are some relevant statistics about the background and experience such an individual might have. Don't worry if you don't meet these qualifications because this is far from an ideal world, and where you fall short is simply where you'll have more work to do. An ideal CNA candidate should have the following:

➤ Academic or professional training in network theory, concepts, and operations. This includes everything from networking media and transmission techniques through network operating systems, services, protocols, routing algorithms, and applications.

➤ Four-plus years of professional networking experience, including experience with Ethernet, Token Ring, modems, and other networking media. This must include installation, configuration, upgrading, and troubleshooting experience, in addition to some experience working with and supporting users in a networked environment.

➤ Two-plus years in a networked environment that includes hands-on experience with NetWare 6.x or NetWare 5.x. Some knowledge of NetWare 4.x is helpful, especially on networks where this product remains in use. Individuals must also acquire a solid understanding of each system's architecture, installation, configuration, maintenance, and troubleshooting techniques. An ability to run down and research information about software, hardware components, systems, and technologies on the Internet and elsewhere is also becoming an essential job skill.

➤ A thorough understanding of key networking protocols, addressing, and name resolution, including Transmission Control Protocol/Internet Protocol (TCP/IP), Internetwork Packet Exchange/Sequenced Packet Exchange (IPX/SPX), Lightweight Directory Access Protocol (LDAP), and Service Location Protocol (SLP) version 2.

➤ A thorough understanding of Novell's naming conventions, directory services, and file and print services. This is absolutely essential.

➤ Familiarity with key NetWare-based TCP/IP-based services, including Hypertext Transfer Protocol (HTTP) Web servers, Dynamic Host Configuration Protocol (DHCP), Domain Name System (DNS), plus familiarity with one or more of the following: ZENWorks, BorderManager, GroupWise, ManageWise, and other supporting Novell products and partner offerings.

➤ Working knowledge of Windows NT, Windows 2000 (the server and workstation versions), and Windows XP Professional. This is an excellent accessory to this collection of facts and skills, as is knowledge of Microsoft implementation of key technologies, such as Internet Information Server (IIS), Internet Explorer, and Windows Internet Naming Service (WINS).

Fundamentally, this boils down to a bachelor's degree in computer science, plus three or more years of work experience in a technical position involving network design, installation, configuration, and maintenance. In reality, though, less than half of all CNA candidates meet these requirements, and most meet less than half of these requirements when they begin the certification process. But because hundreds of thousands who already have been certified have survived this ordeal, you can survive it, too, especially if you heed what the self-assessment can tell you about what you already know and what you need to learn.

Don't worry if you do not meet all the previously mentioned criteria. Motivation has a great deal to do with success on Novell's CNA exam. If you want the certification badly enough and are willing to study and work toward your goal, you can be successful. When you look back on it, you will realize how much you have learned in the process. By all means, you should enjoy the certification process.

Many of my students wonder how they will get through the exam process and earn the CNA. When students leave the exam room, having successfully passed the CNA exam, the air of accomplishment that surrounds them is quite noticeable. It is a thrill. Those who have to take the exam a second time do so for one of two reasons. Either they did not focus on the material covered and spend a reasonable amount of time studying, or they had a bad case of nerves during the test. For those taking their first IT certification exam, being nervous is normal. Knowledge goes a long way to overcoming a case of nerves. The focus of this book is to provide you with the information you need to not only get over being nervous, but also to successfully pass exam 050-686, "Foundations of Novell Networking: NetWare 6.5."

Putting Yourself to the Test

The following series of questions and observations is designed to help you figure out how much work you must do to pursue Novell certification and what types of resources you can consult on your quest. Be absolutely honest in your answers, or you'll end up wasting money on exams you're not yet ready to take. There are no right or wrong answers, only steps along the path to certification. Only you can decide where you really belong in the broad spectrum of aspiring candidates.

Two things should be clear from the outset, however:

➤ Even a modest background in computer science is helpful.

➤ Hands-on experience with Novell products and technologies is an essential ingredient to certification success. If you don't already have this experience, you'll need to get some along the way; if you do already have some, you still need to get more!

Educational Background

1. Have you ever taken computer-related classes? [Yes or No]

If Yes, proceed to question 2; if No, proceed to question 4.

2. Have you taken any classes on computer operating systems? [Yes or No]

If Yes, you'll probably be able to handle Novell's architecture and system component discussions. If you're rusty, brush up on basic operating system concepts, especially virtual memory, multitasking regimes, program load and unload behaviors, and general computer security topics.

If No, consider some basic reading in this area. You should probably read a good general operating systems book, such as *Operating System Concepts, 6th Edition* by Abraham Silberschatz, Peter Baer Galvin, and Greg Gagne (Wiley Publishing, 2001, ISBN: 0-471-41743-2). If this title doesn't appeal to you, check out reviews for other, similar titles at your favorite online bookstore.

3. Have you taken any networking concepts or technologies classes? [Yes or No]

If Yes, you'll probably be able to handle Novell's networking terminology, concepts, and technologies. (Brace yourself for occasional departures from normal usage.) If you're rusty, brush up on basic networking concepts and terminology, especially networking media, transmission types, the OSI reference model, networking protocols and services, and networking technologies, such as Ethernet, Token Ring, Fiber Distributed Data Interface (FDDI), and wide area network (WAN) links.

If No, you might want to read several books in this topic area. Two good ones are *Network+ Study Guide 3rd Edition*, by David Groth (Sybex, 2002, ISBN: 0-7821-4014-9) and *Networking Complete* (Sybex, 2000, ISBN: 0-7821-2610-3). Another good one is the Laura Chappell book, *Novell's Guide to LAN/WAN Analysis* (Hungry Minds/Novell Press, 1998, ISBN:

0-7645-4508-6), for its outstanding coverage of NetWare-related proto-cols and network behavior. (Even though it is a bit out of date, it's still a worthwhile reference.) Or try *Understanding Directory Services* by Sheresh and Sheresh (Sams, 2002, ISBN: 0-672-32305-2). One of the best texts on the market, and one that should be in every CNA's toolkit, is the Novell Press title, *Novell's NetWare 6.5 Administrator's Handbook*, by Jeff L. Harris (Que/Novell Press, 2004, ISBN: 0-7897-2984-9). Yet another comprehensive reference for NetWare 6.x is *Guide to Novell NetWare 6.0 Administration*, by Ted L. Simpson and Michael T. Simpson (Course Technology, 2003, ISBN: 0-619-12037-1). For a list of self-study references that revolve around networking, see the following arti-cle on InformiT.com titled "Now What? A Certification Resource List for Self-Study Career Changers," by Warren E. Wyrostek (http:// www.informit.com/content/index.asp?product_id={393BE5F3-4249-415C-856A-204148F4048A}).

Skip to the next section, "Hands-On Experience."

4. Have you done reading on operating systems or networks? [Yes or No]

If Yes, review the requirements stated in the first paragraphs after ques-tions 2 and 3. If you meet those requirements, move on to the next sec-tion. If No, consult the recommended reading for both topics. A strong background will help you prepare for the Novell exams better than just about anything else.

Hands-On Experience

The most important key to success on all the Novell tests is hands-on expe-rience, especially with NetWare 6.5, plus the many system services and other software components that cluster around NetWare, such as GroupWise and ZENworks, which appear on many of the Novell certification tests. If you're left with only one realization after taking this self-assessment, it should be that there's no substitute for time spent installing, configuring, and using the various Novell and ancillary products upon which you'll be tested repeated-ly and in depth. For in-depth coverage of installing NetWare 6.5 compo-nents that will be covered on the CNA 6.5 exam, see Chapters 3, "Installing and Configuring NetWare 6.5" and 4, "Installing and Configuring the Novell Client," and Appendix E, "NetWare 6.5: New Server Installation Planning Table."

5. Have you installed, configured, and worked with the following:

➤ NetWare 6.5? [Yes or No]

The more times you answer Yes, the better off you are. Please make sure you understand basic concepts as covered in Test 050-686.

You can download objectives, practice exams, and other information about Novell exams from the company's education pages on the Web at **http://www.novell.com/ training**.

If you haven't worked with NetWare and eDirectory, you must obtain one or two machines and a copy of NetWare 6.5. Then you must learn the operating system and TCP/IP, IPX, and be familiar with ZENworks.

In fact, it is recommended that you obtain two computers, each with a network board, and set up a two-node network on which to practice. With decent NetWare-capable computers selling for less than $600, this shouldn't be too much of a financial hardship. Evaluation copies of many Novell products are available, but you'll have to browse each product offering at http://www.novell.com/products.

One Web site that now offers an online presentation of a NetWare 6.5 installation is http://www.3wscertification.com/.

For any and all Novell exams, check to see if Novell Press (an imprint of Pearson Education) offers related titles.

6. For any specific Novell product that is not itself an operating system (such as ZENworks, GroupWise, BorderManager, and so forth), have you installed, configured, used, and upgraded this software? [Yes or No]

If the answer is Yes, skip to the next section. If it's No, you must get some experience. Read on for suggestions on how to do this.

Experience is a must with any Novell product test, be it something as simple as Web Server Management or as challenging as eDirectory installation and configuration. Here again, explore Novell's product Web site for available evaluation copies at http://www.novell.com/ products.

If you have the funds, or if your employer will pay your way, consider checking out one or more of the many training options that Novell offers. This could be something as expensive as taking a class at a Novell Training Service Partner (NTSP) to as inexpensive as Novell's Self-Study Training programs. Be sure to check out the training options that Novell offers and that it authorizes third parties to deliver at **http://www.novell.com/training/train_product**.

Before you even think about taking a Novell test, make sure you've spent enough time with the related software to understand how it can be installed and configured, how to maintain such an installation, and how to troubleshoot that software when things go wrong. This will help you both on the exam and in real life!

Testing Your Exam Readiness

Whether you attend a formal class on a specific topic to get ready for an exam or use written materials to study on your own, some preparation for the Novell certification exams is essential. At $125 per try, pass or fail, you want to do everything you can to pass on your first try. That's where studying comes in.

This book includes two sample tests, and there's a third on the CD-ROM. Take all of them. If you still don't hit a score of at least 76 percent after two or more tests, keep at it until you get there. For any given subject, consider taking a class if you've tackled self-study materials, taken the test, and failed anyway. The opportunity to interact with an instructor and fellow students can make all the difference, if you can afford that privilege. For information about Novell courses, visit Novell Training at `http://www.novell.com/training` and follow the Training by Product link.

If you can't afford to take a class, you should still invest in some low-cost practice exams from commercial vendors because they can help you assess your readiness to pass a test better than any other tool. The following Web sites offer practice exams online for less than $100 apiece (and some are significantly cheaper than that):

➤ `www.boson.com`—Boson

➤ `www.certify.com`—CyberPass

➤ `www.stsware.com`—Self-Test Software

➤ `www.real-questions.com`—realQuestions.com

7. Have you taken a practice exam on your chosen test subject? [Yes or No]

If Yes, and your score meets or beats the cut score for the related Novell test, you're probably ready to tackle the real thing. If your score isn't above that crucial threshold, keep at it until you break that barrier.

If No, obtain all the free and low-budget practice tests you can find (see the previous list) and get to work. Keep at it until you can break the passing threshold comfortably.

Taking a good-quality practice exam and beating Novell's minimum passing grade, known as the *cut score*, is the best way to assess your test readiness. When I am preparing for a Novell exam, I shoot for 10 percent over the cut score—just to leave room for the "weirdness factor" that sometimes shows up. Murphy and weird seem to walk hand in hand.

Assessing Readiness for Exam 050-686

Novell exam mavens recommend checking the *Novell Application Notes*, the *Novell Support Resource Library*, and the Novell Product Documentation Web site found at `http://www.novell.com/documentation/`. The *Novell Support Resource Library* provides "meaningful technical support" information that relates to your test's topics. I have noticed some overlap between technical support questions on particular products and troubleshooting questions on the tests for those products. For more information on the *Novell Support Resource Library*, go to `http://support.novell.com/subscriptions/subscription_products/nsrl19.html`.

Let the Journey Begin!

After you've assessed your readiness, undertaken the right background studies, obtained the hands-on experience that will help you understand the products and technologies at work, and reviewed the many sources of information to help you prepare for a test, you'll be ready to take a round of practice tests. When your scores come back positive enough to get you through the exam, you're ready to go after the real thing. If you follow this book's assessment regimen, you'll not only know what you need to study, but also when you're ready to make a test date at Pearson VUE or THOMSON Prometric. Good luck!

The Novell Certifications

. . . .

Terms you'll need to understand:

✓ CNA
✓ CNE
✓ MCNE
✓ CDE
✓ CNI
✓ CLE
✓ CLP

Techniques you'll need to master:

✓ Assessing which certification(s) is right for you professionally

Novell Certifications

In late 1994, when my employer told me that she wanted me to install, administer, configure, and manage a new Novell network, I had no idea what a Novell network was, nor did I know how to install, administer, configure, or manage one. I asked for training and was told no. I spent my own money for training and took the first of many authorized Novell courses: a CNA 3 course. Within two weeks of completing the class, I was a Novell CNA; within a few months, I was a CNE. I have since earned four of Novell's Master CNE titles as well as the Novell CNI, Master CNI, and CDE. I am currently preparing for Novell's CLE. It all started with the Novell CNA.

The CNA is the doorway to many of Novell's other certifications. It never ceases to amaze me when I am teaching this class how many students want to know what the other Novell certifications are and what tests they have to pass to reach a particular certification level.

The purpose of this chapter is to briefly describe Novell's current line of certifications and their requirements, as of June 2004, so that you will have an informed idea of what you are getting yourself into.

One caveat is in order. Novell certifications are continually changing as the technology is changing. What you will be learning in this chapter and in this book as a whole is the state of Novell certifications in the early summer of 2004. Keep a keen eye on Novell's Certification Web site (`http://www.novell.com/training/certinfo/`) so that you can monitor changes to Novell's current line of certifications and their associated requirements. Now onto the wonderful world of Novell certifications!

Certified Novell Administrator (CNA)

The *CNA*, or *Certified Novell Administrator*, is the entry-level Novell certification. The CNA is designed for those who are setting up workstations, managing users and groups, administering a printing environment, and automating network access. It is a one-test, one-course certification. Depending on the operating system that you support, you can earn the CNA in NetWare 5.1, NetWare 6, and NetWare 6.5. Novell's offerings for the CNA in NetWare 4.11, NetWare 5.0, and GroupWise 5 are no longer available.

If you want to earn the NetWare 5.1 CNA, you must pass the 050-653 exam, "NetWare 5.1 Administration." If you want to earn the NetWare 6 CNA, you must pass the 050-677 exam, "Foundations of Novell Networking: NetWare 6." The NetWare 6 exam is currently a 68-question form exam.

You can earn the NetWare 6.5 CNA by passing exam 050-686, "Foundations of Novell Networking: NetWare 6.5." The Introduction discusses the differences among form exams, adaptive exams, and performance-based exams.

If you want to pursue authorized, instructor-led training for these certifications, you can take Novell's course 560, "NetWare 5.1 Administration," for the NetWare 5.1 CNA, course 3001, "Foundations of Novell Networking: NetWare 6," for the NetWare 6 CNA, or course 3016, "Foundations of Novell Networking: NetWare 6.5," for the NetWare 6.5 CNA. You can also obtain self-study kits from Novell and Novell's training partners.

Novell's   self-study   portal   for   training   products   is
```
http://shop.novell.com/dr/v2/ec_MAIN.Entry16?SP=10024&PN=29&xid=27477&V1=300
10406&V2=30010406&V3=1&V5=11000021&V4=10&S1=&S2=&S3=&S4=&S5=&DSP=0&CUR=840&P
GRP=0&CACHE_ID=0.
```

Certified Novell Engineer (CNE)

The *CNE*, or *Certified Novell Engineer*, is one of Novell's premier certifications. Depending on the CNE track that you pursue, you will take either five or seven exams. The CNE is designed for networking professionals who are responsible for keeping their networks up and running. These are the folks who are charged with designing a TCP/IP internetwork and designing a directory services implementation. Two tracks are currently offered: the CNE 5 and the CNE 6.

To earn the NetWare 5 CNE, you must pass seven exams:

➤ NetWare 5.1 Administration (exam 050-653)

➤ NetWare 5.1 Advanced Administration (exam 050-654)

➤ NetWare 5.1 Design and Implementation (exam 050-664)

➤ Networking Technologies (exam 050-632, or pass CompTIA's Network+ or earn Microsoft's MCSE)

➤ Service and Support (exam 050-658)

➤ Upgrading to NetWare 6 (exam 050-676. All NetWare 5 CNEs must complete this exam. Upon completion, a CNE 5 will also be a CNE 6.)

➤ One elective

Following are the electives:

➤ Desktop Management with ZENworks 4 (exam 050-683)

➤ Internet Security Management with BorderManager Enterprise Edition (exam 050-650)

➤ Network Management Using ManageWise 2.7 (exam 050-660)

➤ TCP/IP for Networking Professionals (exam 050-649)

➤ Integrating Novell eDirectory and Windows NT (exam 050-669)

➤ Integrating Novell eDirectory and Active Directory (exam 050-663)

➤ GroupWise 6 Administration (exam 050-665)

To earn the NetWare 6 CNE, you must pass five exams:

➤ Foundations of Novell Networking (the NetWare 6 CNA exam—exam 050-677) or the NetWare 6.5 CNA exam (exam 050-686)

➤ Novell Network Management (exam 050-681)

➤ Advanced Novell Network Management (exam 050-682)

➤ Novell eDirectory Design and Implementation (exam 050-664)

➤ Desktop Management with ZENworks for Desktops 4 (exam 050-683)

The current list of authorized courses that lead to the NetWare 6 CNE are Foundations-3001 or 3016, Network Management-3004, Advanced Network Management–3005, Design and Implementation-575, and ZENworks 4-3006. These are also available as self-study guides.

If you currently hold the CNE 5 and want to upgrade to a CNE 6, you can choose one of two tests to accomplish this: "Upgrading to NetWare 6" (exam 050-676), or "Upgrading to NetWare 6.5" (exam 050-688). Novell offers authorized courses and self-study guides for both of these courses. You do not have to take both exams to upgrade to a CNE 6. If you are currently working on a NetWare 6 platform, upgrade your CNE to NetWare 6 with exam 050-676. If you are currently working on a NetWare 6.5 platform, upgrade your CNE to NetWare 6 with exam 050-688.

Master Certified Novell Engineer (MCNE)

The *MCNE*, or *Master Certified Novell Engineer*, is designed for those individuals who are responsible for integrating eDirectory and Novell Directory Services (NDS) with the platforms of other vendors. The MCNE is first and foremost an integration specialist. MCNEs are one of the most respected certified professionals involved in network management, infrastructure, and design.

The MCNE track has recently undergone a major overhaul. Until July 31, 2001, Novell had six tracks that led to the MCNE. These tracks included Management, Connectivity, Messaging, Internet/Intranet Solutions, NetWare and Unix Integration, and NetWare and Windows NT Integration. Now one track leads to the MCNE. After achieving the NetWare 6 CNE, a candidate can earn the MCNE by passing four additional exams. Those exams include the following:

➤ TCP/IP for Networking Professionals (exam 050-649)

➤ CompTIA's IT Project+ (exam PK0-001)

➤ Two electives

Following are the electives:

➤ Desktop Management with ZENworks for Desktops 4 (exam 050-683)

➤ Internet Security Management with BorderManager Enterprise Edition (exam 050-650)

➤ Integrating Novell eDirectory and Active Directory (exam 050-663)

➤ GroupWise 6 Administration (exam 050-665)

➤ eDirectory Tools and Diagnostics (exam number is currently in beta release)

Check Novell's Test data Web site (`http://www.novell.com/training/testinfo/testdata.html`) for the latest exam numbers.

Certified Directory Engineer (CDE)

The *CDE*, or Novell's *Certified Directory Engineer*, is one of Novell's newest certifications. It is designed for advanced support persons who need to know how to integrate and troubleshoot directory service issues. The focus of this certification is the power of directory services, regardless of the parent platform: NetWare, Unix, or Windows 2000 Server.

To earn the Novell CDE, you must pass three exams, two of which are traditional cognitive, computer-based exams. The third exam is a performance-based practicum. The two cognitive exams include Advanced NDS Tools and Diagnostics (exam 050-648) and Directory Server Technologies (exam 050-661). The practicum is a 2-hour exam where you connect remotely to 5 live servers at Novell headquarters from your test site. Those servers include both NetWare 4.11 and 5.0 servers in a single tree. Each test taker is asked to repair up to 10 directory service errors and then to perform 5–10 simple administrative tasks in less than 2 hours. If you leave any task undone or any error remains in the tree at the end of the exam, you fail. This is a fantastic test of one's understanding of practical concepts and techniques involved in working with directory services.

As of June 2004, Novell is still recognizing the CDE but no longer offering admission to new candidates. The CDE is still listed on Novell's certification Web pages. As powerful as this certification is, it might well make a comeback. For that reason, I have continued to list it here, for both historical and information purposes.

Certified Novell Instructor (CNI)

The Novell *CNI*, or *Certified Novell Instructor*, certification is one of the elite technical instructor certifications that is recognized worldwide. You can find the current CNI requirements on Novell's CNI Program Requirements Web site at http://www.novell.com/training/certinfo/cni/requirements.html.

There is no formal CNI exam, but CNIs are required to hold a current Novell CNE, such as a CNE 6, and pass all exams at a higher level than is required of CNEs, CNAs, or MCNEs. The exams that CNIs take are the same as for the other certifications, but the candidate must have a higher passing score than is required of the other certification candidates. For example, at the time of this writing, a person seeking the CNA 6 must pass exam 050-677 with a score of 608 out of 800. The CNI candidate, who wants to teach the Foundations of Novell Networking: NetWare 6 course, must pass the same exam (although the CNI exams have a different Novell number—in this case, 050-877) with a score of 668 out of 800. The passing score for NetWare 6.5 CNAs (exam 050-686) and CNIs who want to teach Foundations of Novell Networking: NetWare 6.5 (exam 050-886) is 650 and 710 respectively.

New CNI candidates must also hold CompTIA's CTT+ certification. You can find information on the CTT+ at http://www.comptia.org/certification/ctt/default.asp.

The CNI must also go through a formal registration process with Novell, meet all yearly continuing certification requirements, and pay any required yearly dues if full benefits are desired.

Novell Authorized Instructor (NAI)

The *NAI*, or *Novell Authorized Instructor*, certification is one of Novell's newer trainer certifications. The NAI is the instructor certification that is designed for those who want to teach authorized Novell courses for a Novell Academic Training Partner or Novell Technical Institute (NATP/NTI).

NAIs must pass all exams for courses that they want to teach on the CNI level, be employed by an Academic Training Partner, and submit an NAI application.

Certified Linux Engineer (CLE)

This is the one of Novell's newest certification offerings. At the time this is being written, the *Certified Linux Engineer* (*CLE*) program is in its early beginnings. The CLE is an advanced certification geared to Linux administrators who incorporate Novell Nterprise Linux Services and eDirectory in their network environment. There is no written (cognitive) exam for the CLE. The only exam that a candidate must pass is a practicum (050-685), similar in nature to the practicum offered for the CDE.

Monitor Novell's CLE Web site (`http://www.novell.com/training/certinfo/cle/`) if this is a certification that you are interested in.

Certified Linux Professional (CLP)

Geared toward Linux administrators, this is the latest Novell certification offering. Skills that are targeted include creating and managing users and groups and installing, managing, administering, and troubleshooting a SuSE Linux server, Linux kernel, and associated network processes and services. The only test that a candidate must pass to earn the CLP is practicum (050-689), which at the time of this writing is in beta. Monitor Novell's CLP Web site (`http://www.novell.com/training/certinfo/clp/`) for up-to-date information.

Conclusion

Are the Novell certifications right for you? That is where you come in and hopefully where I come in as your Novell CNA 6.5 instructor. If I do my job, you will have the information you need to successfully tackle Novell's entry-level certification—the CNA.

What will drive your decision to pursue Novell certification is your present circumstance. You have to decide whether your employer, your region of the country, your region of the world, or you have adopted NetWare as a viable networking standard. It makes no sense to pursue a certification that has no value to you personally or to your employer because of predetermined decisions.

When I faced the decision in the early 1990s, my initial answer was driven by the outstanding instruction and guidance I received from a Novell instructor. Because I was working in a Novell environment, my instructor motivated me to aggressively reach for the stars. I did, and I have never regretted it. It all started with Novell's CNA. The CNE, CNI, MCNE, and CDE followed. Those certifications have allowed me to enjoy my time in the world of IT.

Will it be the same for you? There is no way to know until you try. What I have tried to do here is provide you with the same information I provide to my students on the first day of a certification track. The answer generally does not come on the first day of class, as it did with me, but on the journey that follows. And it all begins with the CNA. Let us begin the journey.

2

Introduction to Networking, Network Administration, and NetWare 6.5

. . . .

Terms you'll need to understand:

✓ Bindery
✓ NDS
✓ eDirectory
✓ SAN
✓ NCS
✓ iSCSI
✓ iFolder
✓ eGuide
✓ Virtual Teams

✓ File Versioning
✓ iPrint
✓ Open Source Services
✓ NSS
✓ Native File Access Protocol
✓ DOS
✓ NWSERVER
✓ SERVER.EXE

Techniques you'll need to master:

✓ Identify major occurrences in the evolution of NetWare
✓ Identify NetWare 6.5 features

✓ Describe how NetWare 6.5 works with other operating systems

The first thing you need to do as you begin your NetWare 6.5 journey is to briefly look at the historical roots of NetWare 6.5. You will look at some of the new features of NetWare 6.5 and how Novell has classified some of these features and services. Then you will see how NetWare works with other operating systems. For example, you will learn which systems can function as a NetWare client and which can function as a server in a NetWare 6.5 network environment. Let the journey begin!

> The first objective in this chapter is the only one that is not on the list of official test objectives. The content for this section is covered in the Novell authorized courseware under the objective "Identify NetWare 6.5 Features." The material covered in this section is on the exam, so don't overlook it.

A Brief History of the NetWare Operating System

Novell NetWare has a long and winding history. From the early 1980s on, NetWare has gone through many version upgrades. It is beyond the scope of this book to go all the way back to the early days of NetWare, when it was called ShareNet or S-Net. The versions that are of interest to you, as you prepare for the exam, start with NetWare 3. The versions, their major features and services, and their importance are covered in Table 2.1.

Table 2.1 A Brief History of NetWare	
NetWare Version	**Features and Services**
NetWare 3.x, including the following versions: NetWare 3.0 NetWare 3.11 NetWare 3.12 NetWare 3.2	NetWare 3.0 shipped in the fall of 1989. With the release of 3.11, NetWare became a full 32-bit operating system that supported NetWare Loadable Modules (NLMs). NetWare 3.x primarily provided file and print services. NetWare 3.x stored user accounts in the *bindery*, which is a *flat-file database* that is stored on each server. The bindery was made up of three files: ➤ NET$OBJ.DAT ➤ NET$PROP.DAT ➤ NET$VAL.DAT

(continued)

Table 2.1 A Brief History of NetWare *(continued)*	
NetWare Version	**Features and Services**
	The only objects you would see in the bindery, when working in the SYSCON management utility, would be users, groups, printers, print servers, and print queues.
	Users had to log in to each server that they wanted to access. The process was to *log in* to the first server and *attach* to the second and subsequent servers.
	Rights assignments, also known as Trustee assignments, were made to users and groups. A group *EVERYONE* existed when you wanted to grant rights to all users in the bindery.
NetWare 4.x, including the following versions: NetWare 4.0 NetWare 4.10 NetWare 4.11 IntraNetWare NetWare 4.2	NetWare 4.0 was introduced in early 1993. NetWare 4.x offered the same file and print services that were the mainstay of NetWare 3.x. NetWare 4.x supported up to 1,000 users, with licenses becoming additive with the release of NetWare 4.10.
	Novell Directory Services (NDS) was introduced with NetWare 4. NDS is a directory naming service. It keeps track of all network resources through a hierarchical, relational database that is distributed and loosely consistent. Many consider it the main network service provided by NetWare 4.x. It is the precursor to the current directory service called *eDirectory*.
	With NDS, users no longer logged in to a server, but to a tree. After they were authenticated, based on the rights assigned, users could access all network resources available to them in the tree. It no longer mattered which server an application, service, or resource was on. If a tree had 10 servers installed, a user could potentially access all 10 servers if the appropriate rights were assigned.
	The three major components of NDS were objects, properties, and values.

(continued)

Table 2.1 A Brief History of NetWare *(continued)*	
NetWare Version	**Features and Services**
	With NetWare 4.x and NDS, the directory was not housed on a single server. The directory, through the processes of partitioning and replication, was distributed to strategically placed servers throughout the tree. This provided a degree of fault tolerance.
	NetWare 4.x also provided enhanced TCP/IP and Macintosh support.
	In 1996, IntraNetWare was released, enhancing the network capabilities available with NetWare 4.11. The primary enhancements were the capability to function as a Web server, FTP server, router, Internetwork Packet Exchange/Sequenced Packet Exchange (IPX/IP) gateway, and application launcher. NAL (NetWare Application Launcher) was the precursor to the modern-day ZENworks for Desktops.
NetWare 5.x, including the following versions: NetWare 5.0 NetWare 5.1	In the late 1990s, NetWare 5.0 was released. Up until NetWare 5.0, NetWare was primarily a network operating system that used IPX/SPX. The main reason behind this was that NetWare before NetWare 5 was considered a LAN operating system. With the release of NetWare 5.0, a *native TCP/IP protocol stack* was made available with the core operating system. This enabled NetWare to shed its LAN chains and move into the world of WANs. IPX/SPX was still available, but Novell encouraged its customers to migrate to TCP/IP. For those who could not, two strategies were made available:
	➤ Both IP and IPX stacks could be used simultaneously.
	➤ A Compatibility Mode Driver, with a Migration Agent, was made available for those who were transitioning from IPX to IP.
	NetWare 5.x, using the native TCP/IP stack, enhanced its capabilities by including a Web server, FTP server, NNTP server, and the capability to function as a DNS/DHCP server.

(continued)

Table 2.1 A Brief History of NetWare *(continued)*	
NetWare Version	**Features and Services**
NetWare 6.x, including the following versions: NetWare 6.0 NetWare 6.5	With the release of NetWare 6.0, Novell has begun its move toward OneNet, anytime, anywhere access to networked resources, regardless of the operating system platform. With NetWare 6, Novell also began its entrance into the world of open source services and applications. One of the main features and services introduced with NetWare 6 is eDirectory and the multitude of platforms that it can work on. eDirectory is the successor to NDS, introduced with NetWare 4. eDirectory is more mature and robust than its predecessors, and it still provides centralized administration of network resources through a distributed, replicated directory.

 Table 2.1 includes a great deal of information. All of it is relevant to your understanding, but of particular interest to you should be three facts: when NDS was introduced; what existed before NDS; and when TCP/IP was introduced as a native protocol.

Now that this chapter has explored some of NetWare's history, it will examine the new features and services introduced with NetWare 6.5.

Identify NetWare 6.5 Features

Novell, with the release of NetWare 6.5, has introduced a host of new features and services. For the sake of organization, Novell has divided these features and services into four categories:

➤ Business Continuity Services

➤ Productivity-Enhancing Services

➤ Open Source Services

➤ Web Application Services

Business Continuity Services

To provide customers with high availability, support for the branch office, consolidation of servers, and backup, Novell has included several features with NetWare 6.5. The following are Business Continuity services:

➤ Internet Small Computer Systems Interface (iSCSI) support is included. With iSCSI, you can create an economically affordable Storage Area Network (SAN) using an existing Ethernet infrastructure. A fibre-channel SAN is also possible with iSCSI, although it is much more expensive.

➤ Novell Cluster Services (NCS) has been enhanced from its origin in NetWare 6.0. NCS 1.7 is a server clustering system that provides fail-back, failover, and load balancing for mission-critical environments. Some of the major features of NCS 1.7 are as follows:

➤ NCS supports SANs that are based on SCSI, iSCSI, or fibre-channel technology.

➤ NetWare 6.5 supports, out of the box, a 2-server cluster.

➤ You can upgrade NCS 1.7 to support a maximum of 32 nodes in a cluster.

➤ You can manage NCS by using ConsoleOne or Remote Manager, a browser-based management utility.

Productivity-Enhancing Services

Novell labels services that help users securely access their data in a timely manner as productivity-enhancing services. These include the following:

➤ eDirectory is the latest generation of NDS. It can run on a multitude of platforms including Linux and Windows 2003 Server, and it is LDAP-enabled. One of the major benefits of eDirectory is that it is scalable and has an extensible schema. This book discusses the role of the schema in Chapter 5, "Introduction to eDirectory."

➤ iPrint is Novell's anytime, anywhere printing solution based on Novell Distributed Print Services (NDPS) and Internet Printing Protocol (IPP). Users can print from their home to their office printer by using a Web browser interface.

➤ iFolder lets users have access to their files from home, the office, or while on the road. Without copying files back and forth to a floppy disk, users can access the latest version of their data when and where they need it with an Internet connection and a browser that is Java enabled.

➤ Virtual Teams lets users create a team for real-time collaboration purposes.

➤ eGuide is a Web-based address book, enabling users to find the names, addresses, and phone numbers that are stored in eDirectory.

➤ File Versioning lets users restore earlier versions of their files without having to call you or one of your help desk technicians.

➤ Novell Storage Services (NSS) provides NetWare 6.5 users quick file access to large data stores, such as large databases that are common today.

➤ Native File Access Protocol in NetWare 6.5 supports numerous file protocols that are native to Macs, Unix, Linux, and Windows. Clients no longer need to have the Novell Client installed to access data that is stored on a NetWare 6.5 server.

 You might see the information that follows on Open Source Services in Novell Authorized courseware under two different objectives. For the sake of brevity, I am addressing it under the "NetWare 6.5 Features" objective.

Open Source Services

Novell is rapidly becoming a major player in the open source environment. One of the indications of this is the inclusion of five major Open Source Services/applications with NetWare 6.5. These let you take advantage of the flexibility of open source solutions while remaining with a historically stable networking operating system.

The phrase *open source* means that the source code for operating systems and associated applications is freely distributable. It is not proprietary. Those who make changes are asked to freely distribute those changes to all interested parties. If you develop an open source application, you can license it and distribute it yourself. However, you are asked to make all code available.

Following are the five major Open Source Services/applications that Novell ships with NetWare 6.5:

➤ Apache Web Server version 2.0.45 is the most popular Web server available today.

➤ Tomcat Servlet Engine version 4.0.18 is an open source engine for running Java applications.

➤ MySQL Database version 4.0.12 is a popular open source database solution.

➤ Perl 5.8 for NetWare is an open source language for creating dynamic Web sites.

➤ PHP 4.2.3 for NetWare is a cross-platform, server-side scripting language that is capable of quickly hosting Web applications.

 You must know the five Open Source Services/applications for the exam. Do not worry about the version numbers. Just know that Apache, Tomcat, Perl, PHP, and MySQL make up the Open Source Services feature set.

 One piece of trivia that you might come across in your NetWare 6.5 research is that the acronym AMP is a shortcut for Apache, MySQL, Perl/PHP. The only open source solution missing in the AMP acronym is Tomcat, which is the application engine.

Web Application Services

The Novell exteNd application server version 5.0 that comes with NetWare 6.5 gives administrators and developers a method of deploying standards-based applications that are cross-platform and high performance. It is a high-performance J2EE Web application server.

Describe How NetWare Works with Other Operating Systems

No major network environment can be solely dependent on a single network operating system. Most environments today are made up of two or more platforms. It is imperative that you know how NetWare 6.5 interoperates with each platform. Three relationships are of particular importance:

➤ How NetWare interacts with DOS

➤ Which operating system platforms can function as a NetWare 6.5 client

➤ Which platforms can function as a server if eDirectory is installed

How NetWare Interacts with DOS

NetWare 6.5 has an interesting relationship with DOS. NetWare 6.5 cannot by itself boot a computer. It relies on DOS to boot the computer. Therefore, a DOS partition is required on a NetWare 6.5 server. DOS partition requirements are discussed in Chapter 3, "Installing and Configuring NetWare 6.5."

During the boot process, depending on whether you are running MS-DOS or DR-DOS, three system files are required.

If you are using MS-DOS, these are the three files:

➤ Io.sys

➤ Msdos.sys

➤ Command.com

If you are using DR-DOS, which comes with the NetWare 6.5 operating system, these are the three files:

➤ Ibmbio.com

➤ Ibmdos.com

➤ Command.com

After you boot the computer, you are at a C: prompt. You can then load the NetWare 6.5 operating system by entering two commands:

➤ cd\NWSERVER

➤ SERVER.EXE

 The preceding description assumes that you are not autoloading the server operating system by placing the two commands in your **AUTOEXEC.BAT** file. Chapter 3 discusses the **CONFIG.SYS** and **AUTOEXEC.BAT** files and their role in a NetWare 6.5 installation.

The NWSERVER directory is the DOS folder that holds the executable that launches the server operating system. The server operating system is launched when SERVER.EXE is run.

After the server is up and running, NetWare no longer needs DOS to function. You can run the following server console command to remove DOS from server RAM:

➤ SECURE CONSOLE

In earlier versions of NetWare, you could also use the REMOVE DOS command to remove DOS from server memory. However, REMOVE DOS is not supported in NetWare 6.5.

Now that you have your NetWare 6.5 server booted, using DOS, the following question arises: Which operating system platforms can function as a NetWare 6.5 client?

Operating System Platforms That Can Function as a NetWare 6.5 Client

To answer the question of which operating system platforms can function as a NetWare 6.5 client, you must fully understand what a server is and what a client is. A *server* is a computer that provides resources and services. A *client* is a computer that requests resources and services from a server. NetWare 6.5 is a client/server operating system. Part of the operating system resides on the server, whereas the requesting part resides on a client.

A host of operating system platforms can serve as NetWare 6.5 clients. Some use the Novell Client, whereas others access a server either with a browser or through the Native File Access Protocol (NFAP). Those that are of interest for this test involve the platforms that use the Novell Client. They include the following:

➤ DOS

➤ Linux/Unix

➤ Windows 9x/Me

➤ Windows NT Workstation and Server

➤ Windows 2000 Professional and Server

➤ Windows XP Home and Professional

➤ Windows 2003 Server

Platforms That Can Function as a Server if eDirectory Is Installed

Now that you know the platforms that can function as a NetWare 6.5 client, you need to be able to identify those that can function as an eDirectory server. The following server platforms can interoperate with NetWare 6.5:

➤ Linux/UNIX

➤ Windows NT Server

➤ Windows 2000 Server

➤ Windows Server 2003

It is important to note here that we are not talking about NetWare servers, but server platforms that can interoperate with NetWare 6.5 when eDirectory is installed on them. In other words, we are referring to the platforms that eDirectory can be installed on.

Although this is Novell's official list of platforms that eDirectory can be installed on, and you must know this list for the exam, in the real world, this list is not 100% accurate.

The two standouts that are not on this list are Windows 2000 Professional and Windows XP Professional. (Although I have not tried it, I would also guess Windows NT 4 Workstation should be included.) You can, in reality, install eDirectory on both of these platforms, and they will interoperate just fine with NetWare 6.5 servers. You would not do so in a production environment, but to say that they cannot have eDirectory installed is not accurate.

Having said that, for the exam, know that Windows 2000 Professional and Windows XP Professional are not on the official list of server platforms that interoperate with NetWare 6.5.

Exam Prep Questions

1. Which version of NetWare stored user accounts in a flat-file database?

   A. ○ NetWare 3.12

   B. ○ NetWare 4.11

   C. ○ NetWare 5.1

   D. ○ NetWare 6.5

   Answer A is correct. NetWare 3 and earlier used a flat-file database system called the Bindery to store user accounts. NetWare 4, 5, and 6 use a hierarchical, relational database that is distributed and loosely consistent to store user accounts. Answers B, C, and D are incorrect.

2. Which version of NetWare initially introduced the concept of users logging into a tree, as opposed to a server?

   A. ○ NetWare 3

   B. ○ NetWare 4

   C. ○ NetWare 5

   D. ○ NetWare 6.5

   Answer B is correct. The concept of users logging into a tree, as opposed to a server, was introduced with NetWare 4 and NDS. When users logged into a server and then had to attach to a second or third server, they were using NetWare 3 or earlier versions of the operating system. NetWare 5 and NetWare 6.5 use a more mature version of NDS called eDirectory. With eDirectory, users log into a tree, not a server. Answers A, C, and D are incorrect.

3. Which of the following services are classified as Productivity-Enhancing Services in NetWare 6.5? (Choose two.)

   A. ❑ eDirectory

   B. ❑ File Versioning

   C. ❑ MySQL

   D. ❑ iSCSI-based SAN

   Answers A and B are correct. The productivity-enhancing services that come with NetWare 6.5 are eDirectory, File Versioning, iPrint, eGuide, iFolder, Virtual Teams, Novell Storage Services (NSS), and support for various file protocols that are native to Macs, Unix, Linux, and Windows. MySQL is classified as an Open Source Service, whereas iSCSI-based SANs are classified by Novell as both a Business-Continuity Service and a high-availability solution. Answers C and D are incorrect.

4. Which operating systems can function as a client in a NetWare 6.5 environment? (Choose all that apply.)

A. ❑ DOS

B. ❑ MAC

C. ❑ Windows XP Home

D. ❑ Windows 2003 Server

Answers A, C, and D are correct. DOS, Linux, Windows XP Home and Professional, and Windows 2003 Server can all function as a client in a NetWare 6.5 environment. Answer B is incorrect. The MAC environment is not classified as a NetWare 6.5 client environment.

5. Windows NT 4 Server can _____.

A. ○ Only serve as a client in a NetWare 6.5 environment

B. ○ Only function as an eDirectory server in a NetWare 6.5 environment

C. ○ Function as both a server and a client in a NetWare 6.5 environment

D. ○ Function as neither a server nor a client in a NetWare 6.5 environment

Answer C is correct. Windows NT 4 Server can function as both a client and a server in a NetWare 6.5 environment. You can install eDirectory on a Windows NT 4 server and make it part of an existing tree, or you can create a new tree. The Windows platforms are flexible in a NetWare environment. Answers A, B, and D are incorrect.

6. Which of the following are the boot files that DR-DOS uses? (Choose three.)

A. ❑ Command.com

B. ❑ Io.sys

C. ❑ Msdos.sys

D. ❑ Ibmbio.com

E. ❑ Ibmdos.com

Answers A, D, and E are correct. The DR-DOS boot files are Ibmbio.com, Ibmdos.com, and Command.com. The MS-DOS boot files are Io.sys, Msdos.sys, and Command.com. Answers B and C are incorrect.

7. Which NetWare 6.5 Productivity-Enhancing Service lets your users restore earlier versions of their files without calling you or a help desk technician?

A. ○ PHP

B. ○ File Versioning

C. ○ Virtual Teams

D. ○ NSS

Answers B is correct. File Versioning is a NetWare 6.5 Productivity-Enhancing Service that lets users restore earlier versions of their files without having to call you or one of your help desk technicians. Answer A is incorrect. PHP is classified as a NetWare 6.5 Open Source Service. Answer C is incorrect. Virtual Teams is a Productivity-Enhancing Service that allows users to create a team for real-time collaboration purposes. Answer D is incorrect. NSS is a Productivity-Enhancing Service that provides NetWare 6.5 users with quick file access to large data stores, such as large databases that are common today.

8. Which NetWare 6.5 Web application service provides administrators with a method of deploying standards-based applications that are cross-platform and high-performance?

   A. ○ PHP
   B. ○ Apache
   C. ○ NCS
   D. ○ Novell exteNd Server

   Answer D is correct. The Novell exteNd application server that comes with NetWare 6.5 provides administrators and developers with a method of deploying standards-based applications that are cross-platform and high-performance. Answers A and B are incorrect. PHP and Apache are Open Source Applications and Services that are available with NetWare 6.5. Apache is the Web server, whereas PHP is an open source development language. Answer C is incorrect. NCS is classified as a high-availability solution. NCS is a server-clustering system that provides failback, failover, and load balancing for mission-critical environments.

9. You want to implement NCS in your NetWare 6.5 environment. Which types of shared networks does NCS support? (Choose three.)

   A. ❑ SCSI
   B. ❑ iSCSI
   C. ❑ Fibre-channel
   D. ❑ Token-ring

   Answers A, B, and C are correct. NCS supports SCSI, iSCSI, and fibre-channel environments. It does not support token-ring environments. Answer D is incorrect.

10. You have decided to upgrade your existing NetWare environment because of the open source applications that come with NetWare 6.5. Which of the following is an open source application that comes with NetWare 6.5? (Choose three.)

    A. ❑ Perl
    B. ❑ MySQL
    C. ❑ Open Office 1.1
    D. ❑ Tomcat
    E. ❑ Filer

    Answers A, B, and D are correct. The five open source applications that come with NetWare 6.5 are Perl, PHP, Apache, Tomcat, and MySQL. Answer C is incorrect. Even though Open Office 1.1 is open source, it does not come with NetWare 6.5. It does come with several versions of SuSE Linux Desktop. Answer E is incorrect. Filer is a NetWare-specific utility that is found in the sys:/Public directory. It is not open source now, but stay tuned. Many of Novell's proprietary applications, with the uniting of SuSE Linux and NetWare in Open Enterprise Server (OES), might become open source in the near future.

Installing and Configuring NetWare 6.5

Terms you'll need to understand:

✓ Deployment Manager
✓ DOS Partition
✓ FDISK
✓ FORMAT
✓ CONFIG.SYS
✓ AUTOEXEC.BAT
✓ NET.CFG

✓ Pattern Deployment
✓ Server Console Prompt
✓ NLM
✓ Remote Manager
✓ iManager
✓ OpenSSH

Techniques you'll need to master:

✓ Identify the System, Software, Configuration, and New Server Installation Requirements
✓ Know how to prepare an existing NetWare environment for NetWare 6.5
✓ Know how to prepare your computer/ server for NetWare 6.5
✓ Know the steps involved in a new NetWare 6.5 server installation
✓ Know the load order for the boot files in a NetWare 6.5 server

✓ Identify the three-layer NetWare 6.5 architecture
✓ Identify the most popular NLMs and Console Commands
✓ Identify the function of each NetWare configuration file
✓ Identify the utilities to Remotely Manage a NetWare 6.5 server

Now that you know a little about NetWare 6.5, including its benefits and features, the next step is to install a NetWare 6.5 server. This chapter examines the preparatory steps you must take before installing the server, identifies the procedure for a new server installation, and discusses some basic server-class commands and configuration files. This chapter, unlike the majority of your work as a CNA, concentrates on server-class skills. These are critical to succeeding as a CNA.

Without a good understanding of all of the decisions that impact a server installation and what you can and cannot do at a server console, your ability to efficiently administer your NetWare 6.5 environment will be negatively affected.

Now you can proceed to one of the most critical phases of a NetWare 6.5 server installation: identifying whether the computer you have in front of you has what it takes to become a NetWare 6.5 server. Does it pass muster? Does it meet Novell's laundry list of requirements?

Identify Prerequisite Requirements

Novell breaks down the requirements for installing the NetWare 6.5 operating system on a server-class computer into three categories:

➤ System

➤ Software

➤ Configuration

If this is the first NetWare 6.5 server that you are adding to an existing network, a fourth category can be added to this list: New Server Installation requirements. This is not a Novell category, but it still contains requirements that you must consider when introducing a NetWare 6.5 server into your network.

Before installing the operating system, ensure that all these requirements are satisfied. If not, you might experience an irritating error message after you insert the operating system CD into your computer.

If your system does not have enough disk space or memory, don't try to force the installation, assuming that you can get by until the budget clears. It is a far better idea to wait until all the requirements are satisfied before you begin the actual installation. It will be an easier process.

I must mention two real-world tips at this point. They'll save you a world of time when you consider installing a NetWare 6.5 server on a new computer. First, take time to plan the server installation and prepare a decision table with your responses to each question that will be asked. If you want to see what the installation will look like, before inserting the CD, you can go to **http://www.3wscertification.com/install.html** and select the NW 6.5 Install link in the left navigation bar. Make a list of all the responses you must supply during your install, and write them down. That will definitely shorten the time it takes for your installation.

Second, do your first installation in a test environment, not a production environment. The best assumption you can make, when doing the first installation, is that it will not come out the way you want it to. That's okay. If you do this in a production environment, it's not okay. In a test environment, you can work through the issues of which NetWare 6.5 drivers work with your platform. After you know which drivers work and which requirements must be met, a NetWare 6.5 installation will take you no longer than one hour. The first installation, when you have not met the requirements, do not know the answers to provide, and do not know which drivers will work with your hardware, can take you several hours (on a good day) to complete.

This is not meant to discourage you but to prepare you for reality.

It is imperative not only to know the requirements, but also to know what category each requirement falls under.

The assumption that underlies all of these requirements is that you have a server that has a hard drive with no existing partitions. You need a DOS partition on the primary hard drive, as you will see in the System Requirements, but other than that, you should clean all hard drives of existing partitions.

Numerous utilities are available to accomplish this. The old tried-and-true method of cleaning a hard drive is by using FDISK. If you have existing New Technology File System (NTFS) partitions on your hard drives, in many cases, you cannot remove them with FDISK. You might need to use a third-party solution, such as Partition Magic. Delpart.exe is a utility that Microsoft used to distribute in its Resource Kits that you can employ to remove existing NTFS partitions. However, be careful when you clean a hard drive. Make sure you back up all your data, or you'll lose it.

If you have a new server from one of the major server vendors such as Dell, HP, or IBM, you might have a vendor-installed configuration partition on the primary hard drive. Don't remove that partition. It's there to help you configure a variety of vendor-specific options such as your hardware RAID controller.

The next section looks at the NetWare 6.5 system requirements.

For the exam, you need to know the minimums and recommended requirements. For the real world, these are only base values that will not serve you well in a production environment. You need to examine your environment and your requirements now and for the next 2–5 years for this server. Based on the recommended and optimal values that Novell proposes, you can configure your server to address your needs.

System Requirements

Before you install NetWare 6.5 on a new server-class computer, you must meet the following system requirements. These requirements address the minimum hardware specifications you need to be able to install and run NetWare 6.5:

➤ A PII or later server-class computer. NetWare 6.5 is also supported on a computer with an AMD K7 or later CPU.

➤ If you want to support a multiprocessor computer, you need at least two PIII 700MHz or later processors.

➤ The minimum RAM requirement for NetWare 6.5 is 512MB, but the recommended RAM is 1GB. In a production environment, the more RAM the better.

➤ The video adapter must be Super VGA (SVGA) or higher.

➤ A DOS partition is required. The minimum requirement for the DOS partition is 500MB. The recommended size for the DOS partition is 1GB, but the optimal size for the DOS partition is 500MB plus the amount of installed RAM. This is to provide enough space to accommodate a core dump of the memory in case of an Abend (Abnormal End). For example, if you have 1GB of RAM physically installed, the optimal size of the DOS partition is 1.5GB. If you have 2GB of RAM physically installed, the optimal size of the DOS partition is 2.5GB.

➤ The server hard drive must have a minimum of 2GB of hard drive space above that allocated for the DOS partition. The recommended amount of space is 4GB. This space requirement is for the sys volume. Don't skimp on sys volume space. Although 4GB is recommended, it is not enough for a production server.

➤ The server must have at least one network interface card installed. If you want to do load balancing, need to have network fault tolerance, or want to use the server as a Network Address Translation (NAT) server or a router, you need at least two network interface cards installed.

➤ The server must have at least one CD drive installed. Preferably, your server should be able to boot from the CD drive to perform the server installation.

➤ The server must have a mouse installed. This can be a PS/2 or USB mouse.

These are not difficult hardware minimums for today's high-speed, low-cost computing environments. Most desktop computers in 2004 far exceed these minimums. The next section explains the software requirements.

Software Requirements

The following software is required to install NetWare 6.5 on a server-class computer:

➤ You need two NetWare 6.5 installation CDs: the operating system CD and the products CD.

> The original shipment of NetWare 6.5 included the barebones operating system and products. It did not include any of the support pack fixes that have come out in the past few months. As of December 2004, the latest support pack that is available is SP2 for NetWare 6.5. If you are installing NetWare 6.5 now, you should download the NetWare 6.5 SP2 overlay CDs. There are still two—the operating system CD and the products CD—but all of the support pack fixes have been applied. When you finish your installation, you will have a fully patched operating system. As of this writing, support pack 3 is in beta. To download the NetWare 6.5 overlays, go to **http://support.novell.com/filefinder/18197/index.html**.

➤ You need a NetWare 6.5 license/cryptography disk. You can install the server with a two-user demo license without this disk, but it will have limited capabilities.

➤ A NetWare 6.5 documentation CD is required. You can find most of the up-to-date documentation at
`http://www.novell.com/documentation/nw65/index.html`.

➤ To access the operating system CD on a server that does not boot from the CD, you need the necessary DOS-based CD drivers.

➤ If you are installing your server across-the-wire (which is discussed in the "Prepare the Designated Computer" section), you need either a DOS-based NetWare client disk, or you must be able to access the IP Server Connection utility, which you can find on the Client CD in the SERVINST directory. You can find instructions for setting up a boot disk in the /SERVINST/IPCONN.txt file; the needed boot files are in the /SERVINST/FILES directory.

The next section focuses on the configuration requirements, which define the rights you need if you are installing your server into an existing tree.

Configuration Requirements

The configuration requirements, according to Novell, for installing a NetWare 6.5 server into an existing tree are as follows:

➤ At the [Root]/Tree object of the tree, you must have the Supervisor rights.

➤ At the container where you will install the server, you must have the Supervisor rights.

➤ At the Security container, you must have the Read rights.

In addition to these rights, you must be able to provide the following configuration parameters during a server installation:

➤ If you are installing the TCP/IP protocol, you must be able to provide the IP address, subnet mask, gateway address, and up to three DNS addresses. In addition, you need to know the server name, host name, and domain name for your server.

➤ If you are installing IPX/SPX, you need to know the frame types that are used on your network segment and the network number that is associated with each frame type.

➤ Before you begin the installation, you need the storage and network drivers that work with your hardware. This is often the most difficult part of the server installation. It can also be the easiest. For each of these adapters, you need to know the appropriate slot numbers, interrupts, I/O addresses, and any other essential parameters. If you are using the latest in hardware, you also need to know if a Platform Support Module (PSM) is required. Two are supplied with NetWare 6.5: ACPIDRV.PSM, and MPK14.PSM. These are often used on servers that have XEON processors and on servers that use multiple processors.

New Server Installation Requirements

The new server installation requirements address the real-world introduction of a new NetWare 6.5 server into an existing NetWare environment. If your existing environment consists of some mixture of NetWare 4.x, 5.x, and 6.0 servers, you need to consider these requirements. Three new server installation requirements exist:

➤ Before you install a NetWare 6.5 server into an existing NetWare environment, you must upgrade your version of eDirectory to eDirectory 8 or higher. The current version of eDirectory that ships with NetWare 6.5 with the SP2 overlay is 8.7.3.

➤ Before you install a NetWare 6.5 server into an existing NetWare environment, you must upgrade all NetWare 4.10 servers to NetWare 4.11 or higher. You cannot install a NetWare 6.5 server into a network that has a NetWare 4.10 server in the tree.

➤ Before you install a NetWare 6.5 server into an existing NetWare environment, you must upgrade all existing servers to meet the following support pack levels:

➤ NetWare 4.11 and 4.2 servers must be running SP6a or higher installed.

➤ NetWare 5.0 servers must be running SP4 or higher installed.

➤ NetWare 5.1 servers must be running SP3 or higher installed.

Table 3.1 summarizes these requirements, making it easier for you to prepare for the exam.

Table 3.1 Summary of NetWare 6.5 Installation Requirements			
System Requirements	**Software Requirements**	**Configuration Requirements**	**New Server Requirements**
PII or higher CPU PIII 700 MHz or higher for multiple CPUs	NetWare 6.5 operating system CD NetWare 6.5 products CD	Supervisor to [Root]/Tree object of eDirectory tree	No NetWare 4.10 servers in tree
RAM: 512MB minimum	NetWare 6.5 license disk	Supervisor to server's container	Any NetWare 4.11 or 4.2 servers have SP6a or higher installed
DOS: 500MB minimum	NetWare 6.5 documents disk	Read rights to Security container	Any NetWare 5.0 servers have SP4 or higher installed

(continued)

Table 3.1 Summary of NetWare 6.5 Installation Requirements *(continued)*			
System Requirements	**Software Requirements**	**Configuration Requirements**	**New Server Requirements**
SVGA video card	CD drivers for DOS	IP configuration parameters including: ➤ IP address ➤ Subnet mask ➤ Gateway address ➤ DNS address ➤ Host name ➤ Server name ➤ Domain name	Any NetWare 5.1 servers have SP3 or higher installed
2GB hard drive space above DOS minimum	IP Server Connection utility or earlier Novell Client for Across-the-Wire installation	Driver information including: ➤ Storage adapters ➤ Raid controller ➤ PSM modules ➤ LAN adapters ➤ I/O, interrupts, ports, DMA, and slot numbers for each	
1 or more NICs			
CD drive			
Mouse: USB or PS/2			

Prepare the Existing Network

If you are installing a NetWare 6.5 server into an existing NetWare environment, you need to prepare the environment to accept the NetWare 6.5 server and eDirectory schema changes.

The utility that you use to prepare your environment is Deployment Manager, which you can find at the root of the operating system CD. When you place the operating system CD in your workstation, it runs automatically on most modern Windows workstations and displays the opening screen shown in Figure 3.1.

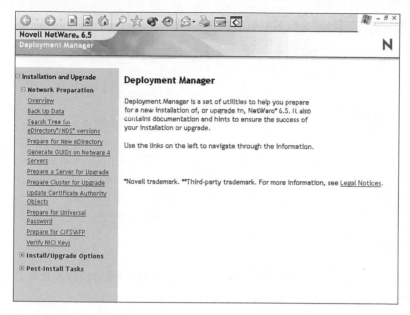

Figure 3.1   Deployment Manager.

Deployment Manager is a set of tools that enable you to prepare your existing network for a NetWare 6.5 server, upgrade to NetWare 6.5, automate an installation, prepare for a variety of NetWare 6.5 components, consolidate servers, migrate to new hardware, create additional volumes, install NetWare 6.5 products, and install a cluster.

If your workstation does not automatically run Deployment Manager when you insert the operating system CD in the CD drive, you can manually launch it by running NWDEPLOY.EXE, found at the root of the CD. If your CD drive is labeled D:, then on a Windows XP Professional Workstation, you could launch Deployment Manager using the following procedure: Start, Run, D:\NWDEPLOY.EXE.

Now you need to prepare the computer that you will install NetWare 6.5 on. This is going to bring back some of the long-forgotten DOS commands that are so useful.

Prepare the Designated Computer

Now that you have a computer that you want to make a new NetWare 6.5 server, you have to prepare it for the installation by creating a DOS partition on it.

Preparing the DOS Partition

You can create a DOS partition with the necessary files to boot the server in three different ways:

➤ Boot the server from the NetWare 6.5 operating system CD.

➤ Create a DOS partition using the tried-and-true DOS Format and FDISK commands.

➤ Create a boot disk, with a version of the Novell Client on it, and access another Novell server where the installation files are stored. After you access the files, you can create the DOS partition using the same steps that you would use if you booted directly from the operating system CD.

The next sections take a brief look at each of these.

Creating a DOS Partition when booting from the NetWare 6.5 Operating System CD

If your server has a clean, unpartitioned hard drive, and you can boot from the NetWare 6.5 operating system CD, you are presented with several opening DOS-based console screens. You're asked to decide the following:

➤ If you want to install a new server or create a boot floppy

➤ If your CD drive is IDE or SCSI

➤ Which method you want to use to restore your floppy to A:

➤ If you want to autoexecute the INSTALL.BAT file that launches the operating system installation or if you want to manually launch it using a variety of options

After the installation has launched, you are presented with four or five screens where you select your language, select your regional and keyboard settings, accept two license agreements, and finally select the type of installation you want to run. The two choices are Default and Manual.

You can then create a DOS boot partition, as shown in Figure 3.2. The default value displayed when you elect to create a DOS boot partition is 500MB, the required minimum. You can increase this, however. Because the version of DOS that comes with NetWare 6.5 is DR-DOS, you can increase the size of the DOS boot partition up 1.5GB.

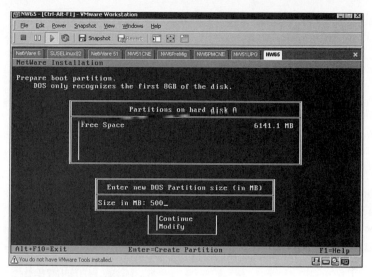

Figure 3.2   Prepare a boot partition.

After you finish configuring the size of the partition, the installation routine creates the partition, formats it, and installs the necessary boot files on the partition. Then you can move on to the rest of the server installation.

This is by far the easiest way to create a DOS partition on a new NetWare 6.5 server. It has its limitations in that you can only create a 1.5GB DOS partition, which for many platforms is not optimal in a production environment. That leads to the old, reliable method of manually creating a DOS partition using FDISK and FORMAT.

Creating a DOS Partition with **FDISK** and **FORMAT**

To create a DOS partition on a new server, you need a DOS boot disk. For universal applications, the best disk you can have is a DOS 6.22 boot disk that has the necessary CD drivers and DOS utilities on it. At a minimum, your DOS disk should have the following DOS utilities on it:

➤ SYS.COM

➤ FDISK.EXE

➤ FORMAT.COM

➤ MSCDEX.EXE

➤ DELTREE.EXE

➤ XCOPY.EXE

You should also have the AUTOEXEC.BAT and CONFIG.SYS files on the disk. If you want the DOS disk to double as a Novell Client, you must have an NWCLIENT directory on it that contains the necessary connection files (covered in the next section).

When you boot your server with this DOS boot disk, you need to create the DOS partition with FDISK.EXE. FDISK is a DOS partition utility that lets you create, delete, view, and activate your partitions. Just follow the menu selections to create a DOS primary partition that has a minimum of 500MB of space.

You can automate this FDISK process, without going through all the menus, by using some command options that are not well documented but will make your life much easier. You can find these options on a variety of Web sites, including http://www.fdisk.com/fdisk/ and http://www.macalester.edu/ ~fines/fdisk.html.

You can also purchase third-party tools or search for shareware and freeware tools on the Internet that will let you create your DOS partition.

After you have created the DOS partition and rebooted your computer, you have to prepare the File Allocation Table on the DOS partition and make the partition bootable. You can accomplish this by using the FORMAT.COM utility with the following switch:

```
A:\FORMAT C: /S
```

This command makes the DOS partition bootable and installs the following files on the C: drive, the first letter assigned to a DOS primary partition:

➤ IO.SYS

➤ MSDOS.SYS

➤ COMMAND.COM

After you format the partition, you can boot the server. You are asked for the correct date and time and land at a C:\> prompt.

You cannot load CDs yet, so you have to create a CONFIG.SYS and AUTOEXEC.BAT file at the root of the C: drive. CONFIG.SYS is a text file that contains system configuration instructions. One of the main commands used is Device, which loads device drivers, such as the CD/DVD driver. The AUTOEXEC.BAT file is a text file that contains configuration, initialization, and application commands.

Following is a basic CONFIG.SYS file, with just the bare minimum configuration parameters:

```
files=50
buffers=30
device=c:\CPQIDECD.SYS /D:IDECD001
```

Next is a basic AUTOEXEC.BAT file:

```
mscdex /d:idecd001
```

Numerous CD drivers are available for the CD and DVD drives that are on the market. The **CPQIDECD.SYS** driver is the only one that I have had success with. It might not work for you, however, especially if you have an SCSI CD or DVD drive in your server. These file samples are provided only as examples, not as definitive universal solutions.

The CPQIDECD.SYS and MSCDEX.EXE files are CD drivers. Note that you load one from the CONFIG.SYS file, using the DEVICE= syntax, but you load the MSCDEX.EXE driver from the AUTOEXEC.BAT file. NetWare 6.5 requires the files and buffers statements. The files statement defines the maximum number of files that can be open simultaneously. The buffers statement defines the number of disk-read buffers.

Using this boot disk, with the properly configured files and CD/DVD drivers, you can boot the server, insert the NetWare 6.5 operating system CD, and launch the installation routine by running INSTALL.BAT from the root of the CD. Because the DOS partition is created, you will not see the screens where you can create and configure a DOS partition.

If you have enough space on your DOS partition, you can **XCOPY** the two installation CDs to different directories on the partition. Then weeks, months, or years up the road, when you want to install an add-on-product and you need the CDs, you will not have to look for them. All of the data will be on the DOS partition.

Now you will learn to take this boot disk a step further in case you do not have a CD/DVD drive on your server. One of the System Requirements is that every NetWare 6.5 server must have a CD/DVD drive. However, what if you have a great server that has a CD/DVD drive but you cannot locate the DOS drivers for it? Can it still be a NetWare 6.5 server? Sure. Here is how.

Creating a DOS Partition During an Across-the-Wire Installation

If you take this DOS boot disk and add a version of the Novell Client to it, you can log in to a NetWare server where your installation files are stored and perform an across-the-wire installation. Initially, your new server acts like a DOS-based NetWare Client. After you copy all of the files from both NetWare 6.5 installation CDs to a NetWare volume on an accessible server, you can log in to that server and launch the installation routine. However, first you must have the correct files on your boot disk. You can create this client boot disk manually or use the IP Server Connection utility, which was mentioned earlier in this chapter.

If you are manually creating the client boot disk, you need to have either a version of Novell Client 32 and all associated files or a copy of the 16-bit Novell Client that was used in NetWare 3 and 4. In either case, you should create a directory on the boot disk called NWCLIENT. In NWCLIENT, you insert all of the necessary client access files. If you are using a 16-bit client, these access files include the following:

➤ LSL.COM—Link Support Layer.

➤ NE2000.COM—Network Adapter Driver. This is only one possible choice.

➤ IPXODI.COM—Internetwork Packet Exchange, Open Datalink Interface.

➤ VLM.EXE—Virtual Loadable Module loader.

If you are using Client 32, you might use the following files:

➤ NIOS.EXE

➤ NBIC32.NLM

➤ LSLC32.NLM

➤ CMSM.NLM

➤ ETHERTSM.NLM

➤ CNE2000.LAN

➤ TCPIP.NLM

➤ TRANNTA.NLM

➤ SRVLOC.NLM

➤ CLIENT32.NLM

Some boot disks that I have utilized use the **NWCLIENT** directory, whereas others use a **NOVELL\CLIENT32** directory. The **NWCLIENT** directory is from the 16-bit days, whereas **NOVELL\CLIENT32** evolved in the late 1990s for the 32-bit DOS Client. It is strictly a matter of preference.

If you use IPX for your Across-the-Wire installation, you will have **IPX.NLM** in the preceding list, not **TCPIP.NLM**. If you are making an IPX connection, you must have IPX loaded and bound to your network adapter on the server where the installation files are located. To avoid dropping the connection during the installation, load IPX on your NetWare 6.5 server. After you've completed the installation, you can remove the **LOAD** and **BIND** statements that reference IPX, while keeping your TCP/IP configuration unchecked.

After you have all the files you need to make a connection, you can create a file called STARTNET.BAT, where the files are called in the correct order. The STARTNET.BAT file is in the NWCLIENT directory, and it is called from the AUTOEXEC.BAT file. You will soon modify the AUTOEXEC.BAT file. The AUTOEXEC.BAT file on the Client boot disk might look like this:

```
mscdex /d:idecd001
A:\NWCLIENT\STARTNET.BAT
```

Soon you will modify the CONFIG.SYS file so that it looks like this:

```
files=50
buffers=30
device=c:\CPQIDECD.SYS /D:IDECD001
LASTDRIVE=Z
```

Notice that the AUTOEXEC.BAT now calls the STARTNET.BAT file, which calls the Novell Client files in the correct order. The CONFIG.SYS file has a LASTDRIVE statement. The Client can now view all the mapped NetWare drives.

The last file that you will insert into the NWCLIENT directory is the NET.CFG file. NET.CFG is a text file that contains configuration parameters and commands that govern how the client interacts with a NetWare server. Following are some of the major sections of the NET.CFG file:

➤ LINK DRIVER—Configures the network adapter

➤ LINK SUPPORT—Configures LSL parameters

➤ PROTOCOL—Configures the communications protocol

➤ NETWARE DOS REQUESTOR—Configures Preferred Server, Preferred Tree, First Network Drive, Name Context, and Cache Size and Level. You can also have a Message Timeout parameter in case an errant message appears during the installation.

The following is an example of a NET.CFG file:

```
Link Support
    Buffers    8 1500
    MemPool    4096
    Max Boards    4
    Max Stacks    4
Link Driver PCNTNW
    Frame    Ethernet_802.2
    Frame    Ethernet_II
Protocol TCPIP
    PATH TCP_CFG    C:\NET\TCP
    ip_address    10.0.0.1 LAN_NET
    ip_netmask    255.255.255.0 LAN_NET
    ip_router    10.0.0.225
    Bind    PCNTNW #1 Ethernet_II LAN_NET
NetWare DOS Requester
    First Network Drive = F
    NETWARE PROTOCOL = NDS BIND
    Preferred Tree = NW65_Tree
    Preferred Server = FS1
    ; PREFERRED SERVER = FS12
    NAME CONTEXT = "O=NW65"
    File Cache Level=0
    Message Timeout=1
    Max Cache Size=5000
```

 You need to know the parameters that are configured in **CONFIG.SYS**, **AUTOEXEC.BAT**, and **NET.CFG**.

You now have a boot disk with the Novell Client on it. When you boot your new NetWare 6.5 server using this disk, you can connect to a NetWare server where the installation files are stored. You can launch the installation routine by running INSTALL.BAT, which is found at the root of the operating system CD files. The installation occurs as if you were booting your server using the NetWare 6.5 operating system CD. You can now create a DOS boot partition on your NetWare 6.5 server, as was explained earlier.

Because you have a DOS partition on the server, and your network and your computer are prepared, you can proceed with the remainder of the NetWare 6.5 installation.

Install NetWare 6.5

Earlier in this chapter when you learned how to create a DOS partition when booting from the operating system CD, you saw a few of the initial steps involved in the installation process. These included the following:

1. Select your language.

2. Select your regional and keyboard settings.

3. Accept two license agreements.

4. Select the type of installation you want to run. Your choices are Default or Manual. If you select Default, several selections are preconfigured:

   ➤ Volume sys is 4GB.

   ➤ Storage and LAN adapters and the mouse are discovered automatically and loaded.

   ➤ The Country Code is 1, the Codepage is 437, and the keyboard is United States.

   ➤ The video adapter is SVGA.

   If you select a Manual installation, you will configure all settings.

5. The next few screens configure and create the DOS boot partition.

NOTE The assumption behind the rest of this installation process is that you will be performing a Manual installation, not a Default.

6. The Server Settings screen is displayed, where you can configure the ServerID number, which used to be called the Internal IPX number. The ServerID number, which is an eight-digit hexadecimal number, only appears in the AUTOEXEC.NCF file if IPX is loaded and bound to a network adapter. In addition to the ServerID, you can configure Server Set parameters, whether you want to have the server automatically reboot, and which video adapter you will use.

7. The initial file copy occurs. During this time, the files that you need to boot the operating system are copied to the c:\NWSERVER directory. This includes the executable SERVER.EXE, which launches the operating system kernel.

8. Select the correct Platform Support Module, Hot Plug Support Modules, and Storages Adapter(s) for your server. Many of these are autodetected, but you must be careful here. NetWare is good about selecting the correct adapters and modules, but every once in a while, it will select the incorrect one, and your installation fails. Always suspect that there is a driver problem if an installation fails. Platform

Support Modules have a .psm extension, whereas Storage Adapters have a.ham (Host Adapter Module) extension.

9. Select the correct drivers for the installed storage devices, such as hard drives and CD drives. These device drivers have a .cdm (Custom Device Module) extension.

10. Select the correct network adapter driver(s). A .lan extension denotes a network adapter driver. You can configure the port, slot, interrupt, and a host of other unique parameters for each installed adapter.

11. The NetWare NSS (Novell Storage Services) Management Utility launches, where you create and configure the initial NetWare 6.5 volume, sys. You must create a sys volume. You can configure the size and type of volume that sys will be. The minimum size for sys is 2GB, but the default is 4GB. You can configure sys to be a Traditional volume or an NSS volume. The default is a 4GB NSS volume. You can also configure a variety of volume properties, including whether compression is enabled at the volume level. At NSSMU, you can create other NetWare partitions, pools, and volumes. These are discussed in Chapters 6, "Introduction to the NetWare 6.5 File System," and 7, "Basic Management Tasks—eDirectory and File System."

12. Files are initially copied to the sys volume, after which the graphical portion of the installation begins.

13. The first graphical screen displayed is the Choose a Pattern screen, shown in Figure 3.3. Here you decide the type of server that you want to install. The installation routine then automatically selects the components that are associated with the pattern. Following are the available patterns:

➤ Customized NetWare Server

➤ Basic NetWare File Server

➤ Premigration Server

➤ DNS/DHCP Server

➤ exteNd J2EE Web Application Server

➤ LDAP Server

➤ NetWare AMP Server

➤ NetWare Backup Server

➤ NetWare Web Search Server

For most installations, you should select the Customized Server option because you have the greatest flexibility in selecting components. That is the choice made for this installation.

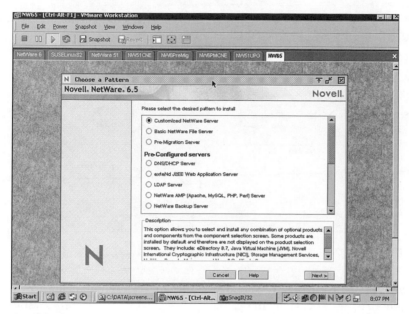

Figure 3.3   Choose a Pattern.

14. If you choose a Customized installation, you see the Components window, shown in Figure 3.4, where you can select the components you want to install. After you have made your selections, a summary window displays, followed by a request for the NetWare 6.5 Products CD. When you change the CDs, the copy process begins.

15. After you copy the necessary files, based on the pattern you selected, the Server Properties screen is displayed. This is where you name the server. The server name can be between 2 and 47 alphanumeric characters. It cannot begin with a period or contain spaces.

Be careful here. Before clicking the Next button on this or any of the subsequent screens, make sure you are entering the value you want for the final installation. When you enter the value, it is written to numerous configuration files. If you get a few screens further in the process and decide you want to change the server name or another value, you can click the Back button and make the change; however, after the server is up, some of the configuration files retain the initial values and do not respond correctly.

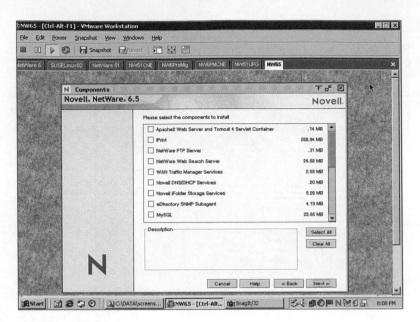

Figure 3.4 Components.

16. After you name the server, you have to select a cryptographic license that has an .nfk extension. You cannot proceed without selecting a valid cryptographic license for NetWare 6.5.

17. Select and configure the protocols for your server. You can select and configure IP, IPX, SLP, SNMP, and IPX Compatibility. You have to configure IP for your server. This includes selecting an IP address, subnet mask, and optional Gateway address for each installed network adapter that you have a driver for. You can also choose to load and bind IPX to your network adapters. If you select IPX, you can select the frame types for each adapter. The default frame type (data packet structure) for NetWare 4.x–6.5 is Ethernet_802.2. When you select a frame type, you can opt to keep the network segment address that is autodetected or randomly generated, or you can change it. Figure 3.5 shows the Advanced Protocols screen, where you can configure the network address for each selected IPX frame. In this figure, the Ethernet_802.2 network address is changed from what was detected, or randomly generated, to the address that is running on the active network, 00000002. Only a 2 is written into the dialog box, but the network address is an eight-digit hexadecimal value. The remaining seven zeros are inserted automatically.

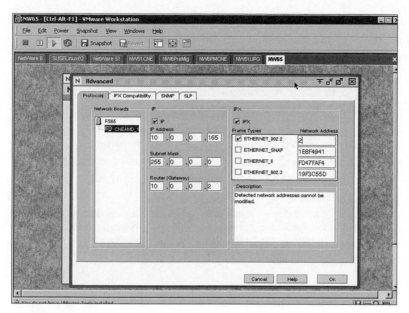

Figure 3.5 Advanced Protocols.

18. After you have the IP protocol configured, you see the Domain Name Services screen, where you provide the server's host name, domain name, and up to three DNS server IP addresses. Take your time when you enter this information, and don't click Next until you are positive that it is correct. The information is immediately written to several configuration files.

19. Configure your time zone, time server type, and time source as needed.

20. You can then configure eDirectory. If this is the first server in the tree, you need to enter the tree name, the container where the server will reside, the container that will hold the admin object, and the admin's password. If you are installing the server into an existing tree, you need to authenticate to the tree before proceeding.

21. Depending on the components you have selected, the remaining screens can include LDAP configuration, NMAS configuration, and many others. After these screens, the final file copy occurs, and you are asked to remove the disks from all drives and reboot your server. If you have not placed the commands to automatically load the server operating system in the AUTOEXEC.BAT file, you can manually load the server by launching SERVER.EXE from the C:\NWSERVER directory.

22. When the server reboots, you have a NetWare 6.5 server that is ready to go to work.

23. If you decide, after your server is up and running, that you want to add components to the server that you did not select during the initial installation, you can install those products using Deployment Manager, the GUI Install, or through NWCONFIG at the server console. NWCONFIG does not have all of the functionality that it had in previous versions of NetWare, but it still is useful when installing a support pack. If you install an add-on component through NWCONFIG, you might see the GUI Install screen, because the two are linked for many products. If you do not have the GUI Install screen up and running on your server, you can launch it by using the STARTX server console command.

 Due to space limitations, I cannot show you all of the screenshots that are displayed during an installation. For your exam preparation, I have created a virtual installation presentation at **www.3WsCertification.com/install.html**. You can select the NW 6.5 Install link and see most of the screens that you would see during a live installation.

The next section explores the server architecture, some useful server commands, configuration files, and utilities for managing the server. Now it is getting good!

Identify the Operating System Components of NetWare 6.5

Now that you have the server installed, you need to know a little about the operating system architecture. Novell has divided NetWare 6.5 and its components into three architectural layers:

➤ Applications/Services

➤ The Kernel

➤ Drivers

Each of these layers has a specific role in the ongoing capabilities of the NetWare 6.5 server.

Protocols and LAN and Storage Adapter drivers are located in the lowest layer of this architecture, the Drivers layer.

The middle layer, the Kernel, is the foundation of the NetWare 6.5 operation system. This is where you find all the fundamental services and capabilities that NetWare offers.

The top layer, Applications and Services, contains the add-on services that NetWare 6.5 can provide. These include DNS/DHCP, iFolder, NSS, Remote Management, and eDirectory.

So much for the architecture. Now what can you do at the server console?

Use Server Console Commands to Manage NetWare 6.5

You can perform a host of management tasks at a NetWare 6.5 server console prompt, as shown in Figure 3.6.

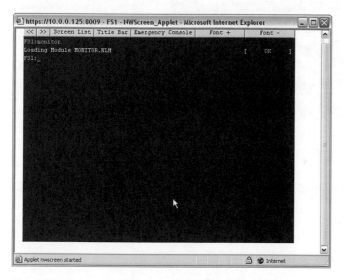

Figure 3.6   Server console prompt.

At the server console prompt, you can run commands; perform a variety of management tasks; load and unload NetWare Loadable Modules (NLMs), which provide a server with added functionality above and beyond what is available in the kernel; reset or restart and down a server; and configure the server environment using SET commands. The tasks that you can perform at the server console prompt involve either console commands or NLMs.

Console Commands

First, you'll learn about some of the most helpful console commands.

The CONFIG command displays your current network adapter configuration, the name of your tree, and the bindery context, as shown in Figure 3.7.

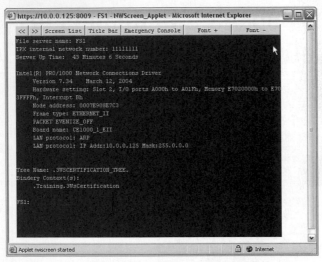

Figure 3.7 The **CONFIG** command.

The HELP command, shown in Figure 3.8, displays all of the server console commands that are available based on your current configuration and installed components.

Figure 3.8 The **HELP** command.

The VOLUMES command, shown in Figure 3.9, displays the volumes that are mounted on your server and the namespaces that have been loaded on each.

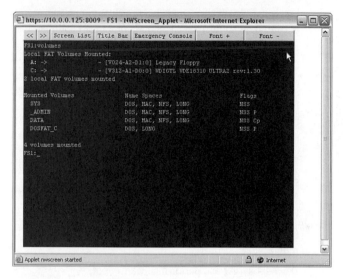

Figure 3.9 The **VOLUMES** command.

Some of the other popular commands are summarized in Table 3.2.

Table 3.2 Server Console Commands	
Server Console Command	**Description**
BIND	Links a network adapter to a protocol.
UNBIND	Unlinks a network adapter from a protocol.
BROADCAST	Sends a message to users who are logged in to a server.
SEND	
CONFIG	Displays configuration information.
CPUCHECK	Displays information about the CPU.
DISMOUNT	Makes a volume unavailable to users.
MOUNT	Makes a volume available to users.
DISPLAY SERVERS	Displays servers using IPX.
DISPLAY SLP SERVICES	Displays SLP services on the network.
DOWN	Graciously powers off a NetWare server.
FILE SERVER NAME	Displays the file server name.

(continued)

Table 3.2   Server Console Commands *(continued)*

Server Console Command	Description
HELP	Displays the available console commands. Can also be used to gain context-sensitive help for a given command. The syntax is **Help command**.
IPX INTERNAL NET	Displays the **SERVERID** defined in the **AUTOEXEC.NCF** file.
LIST DEVICES	Displays a list of storage devices on the server.
LOAD UNLOAD	Plugs an NLM into the kernel or operating system. Unplugs an NLM from the kernel or operating system.
MEMORY	Displays the installed physical memory.
MODULES	Displays all loaded NLMs. Can also be used to see whether a specific module is loaded. Following is an example: MODULES ds.nlm
PROTOCOL	Displays a list of registered protocols.
RESET ROUTER	If your server is acting as a router, this resets the internal router tables.
RESET SERVER RESTART SERVER	Downs a server and performs a warm boot. Downs a server, unloads **SERVER.EXE**, and then reloads it.
SEARCH SEARCH ADD SEARCH DEL	Displays a list of configured search paths, where the server looks for NLMs and NCFs. Adds a path to the current search paths. Deletes a path from the current search paths.
SECURE CONSOLE	Unloads DOS from server memory. Protects a server by allowing only NLMs to be loaded from **SYS:SYSTEM**.
SET	Used to set or view server system parameters. Following are the parameters: Communications, Memory, Traditional File System, Common File System, NSS, Disk, Time, NCP, Miscellaneous, Error Handling, Directory Services, Multiprocessor, SLP, and Licensing Services.
SLP DA	Displays known directory agents.
SPEED	Displays the relative speed of a processor.
SWAP	Displays swap file parameters and adds and removes a swap file from a volume.
TIME	Displays the time and date on a server.
VERSION	Displays the current operating system version and installed support pack.

NLMs

An NLM is a program that adds functionality to the core operating system. You can dynamically load and unload NLMs without downing the server.

Following are the five most common types of NLMs:

➤ NLM—NetWare Loadable Module

➤ HAM—Host Adapter Module

➤ CDM—Custom Device Module

➤ LAN—Local Area Network Module

➤ NAM—Namespace Modules, such as NFS, DOS, LONG, and MAC

The command that you use to plug an NLM into the operating system is LOAD. UNLOAD unplugs an NLM from the operating system.

Following is the syntax to load an NLM, such as MONITOR.NLM:

```
LOAD monitor
```

The syntax to unload MONITOR.NLM is this:

```
UNLOAD monitor
```

The LOAD portion of the command is optional in NetWare 6.5. You can also load an NLM by entering the NLM's name at the server console prompt. For example, monitor does the same thing as LOAD monitor.

That being said, it is a good administrative practice to use the LOAD command to avoid confusion. To unload an NLM, use UNLOAD.

Some of the most popular NLMs are MONITOR.NLM and INETCFG.NLM, shown in Figures 3.10 and 3.11. MONITOR is a management utility where you can monitor utilization, processors, SET parameters, and cache memory status. INETCFG is the tool of choice when you want to modify the network configuration on a server. In INETCFG, you can configure your server as a router, a NAT server, for network load balancing, and for fault tolerance.

The more NLMs that you load, the more screens are available to you on the server. You can use several keystroke combinations, shown in Table 3.3, to navigate through the screens and provide administrative assistance in case a server hangs.

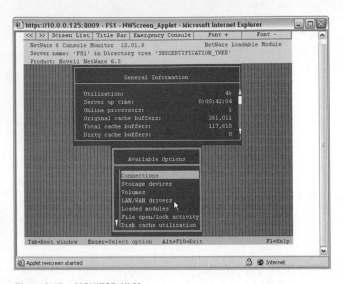

Figure 3.10 MONITOR.NLM.

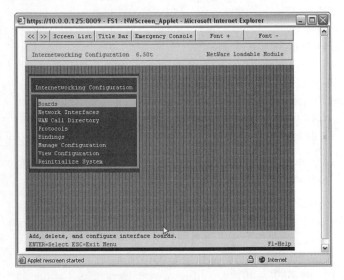

Figure 3.11 NETCFG.NLM.

Table 3.3 Server Keystroke Combinations	
Keystroke Combination	**Description**
Alt+Esc	Toggles from one active screen to the next
Ctrl+Esc	Displays a list of available screens that you can choose from

(continued)

Table 3.3 Server Keystroke Combinations *(continued)*	
Keystroke Combination	**Description**
Ctrl+Alt+Esc	Displays the Emergency Console screen, where you can graciously down a server or cancel a volume mount
Left-Shift+Right-Shift+Alt+Esc	Displays the Debugger, which is great for diagnosing an Abend and graciously downing a server

Now you can identify the most popular server commands and NLMs, but you need to become familiar with the server configuration files that are used when a NetWare 6.5 server boots.

Use Configuration Files

NetWare uses configuration files similarly to other operating systems. An NCF file is a NetWare Configuration File, the equivalent of a batch file, like AUTOEXEC.BAT in DOS. This section examines the key NCF files, their load order, some of the options used when running SERVER.EXE, and the configuration in each of these NCF files.

Five-Step Load Order

Earlier you saw that two configuration files are used to boot a NetWare 6.5 server to DOS. These are CONFIG.SYS and AUTOEXEC.BAT. After you get to DOS, you load SERVER.EXE from the NWSERVER directory on the C: drive. After you launch the server, two other configuration files take over. First is the STARTUP.NCF file followed by the AUTOEXEC.NCF file.

This is the load order for these files:

1. CONFIG.SYS

2. AUTOEXEC.BAT

3. C:\NWSERVER\SERVER.EXE

4. STARTUP.NCF

5. AUTOEXEC.NCF

Both STARTUP.NCF and AUTOEXEC.NCF are text files. STARTUP.NCF is located in C:\NWSERVER on the DOS partition. Its primary function is to load the drivers for your storage adapter(s), storage devices, and platform support modules. It must be on the DOS partition for the drivers to be accessible before NetWare loads. You can find AUTOEXEC.NCF in the SYS:\SYSTEM directory. It configures the following:

➤ SERVERID

➤ File Server Name

➤ Time

➤ LAN Drivers: Load and Bind statements

➤ Protocols

➤ Bindery Context

➤ Search Paths

➤ Applications

Because STARTUP.NCF and AUTOEXEC.NCF are text files, you can create or modify them using any text editor, such as Notepad. On the NetWare 6.5 server, you can also edit these files using EDIT.NLM or NWCONFIG.NLM. EDIT.NLM is a generic text editor that you can use to edit files on the NetWare or DOS partitions. You can use NWCONFIG.NLM to edit STARTUP.NCF or AUTOEXEC.NCF.

Following is a sample STARTUP.NCF:

```
LOAD ACPIDRV.PSM
######## End PSM Drivers ########
LOAD IDECD.CDM
LOAD IDEHD.CDM
######## End CDM Drivers ########
LOAD IDEATA.HAM SLOT=10004
LOAD LSIMPTNW.HAM SLOT=2
######## End HAM Drivers ########
```

Next is a sample AUTOEXEC.NCF file:

```
set Bindery Context = OU=Training.O=3WsCertification
SET Daylight Savings Time Offset = 1:00:00
SET Start Of Daylight Savings Time  = (APRIL SUNDAY FIRST  2:00:00 AM)
SET End Of Daylight Savings Time = (OCTOBER SUNDAY LAST  2:00:00 AM)
SET Time Zone = EST5EDT
# Note: The time zone information mentioned above
# should always precede the server name.
SEARCH ADD SYS:\JAVA\BIN
SEARCH ADD SYS:\JAVA\NWGFX\BIN
SEARCH ADD SYS:\JAVA\NJCLV2\BIN
# WARNING!
FILE SERVER NAME FS1
# WARNING!
# If you change the name of this server, you must update
```

```
# the server name in all the licenses that are assigned
# to it using iManager.
SERVERID 11111111
LOAD IPXSPX
LOAD IPXRTR
LOAD PCNTNW.LAN PCI SLOT=3 MASTER=NO RXEARLY=NO FRAME=ETHERNET_802.2
➥NAME=PCNTNW_1_E82
BIND IPX PCNTNW_1_E82 NET=2
LOAD IPXRTRNM
LOAD CONLOG MAXIMUM=100
LOAD TCPIP
LOAD PCNTNW.LAN PCI SLOT=3 FRAME=ETHERNET_II  NAME=PCNTNW_1_EII
BIND IP PCNTNW_1_EII addr=10.0.0.11 mask=255.0.0.0 gate=10.0.0.125
MOUNT ALL
IPMINIT.NCF
SYS:\SYSTEM\NMA\NMA5.NCF
BSTART.NCF
load nile.nlm
load httpstk.nlm /SSL /keyfile:"SSL CertificateIP"
LOAD PORTAL.NLM
LOAD NDSIMON.NLM
LOAD NICISDI.XLM
LOAD SASDFM.XLM
# -- Added by AFP Install --
AFPSTRT.NCF
# -- End of AFP Install --
# -- Added by CIFS Install --
CIFSSTRT.NCF
# -- End of CIFS Install --
LOAD PKI.NLM
LOAD NLDAP.NLM
# -- Added by Scripting Install --
SCRIPT.NCF
SEARCH ADD SYS:\APACHE2
#ACCESS TO XTIER SOFTWARE
SEARCH ADD SYS:\XTIER
LOAD NCPL
AP2WEBUP
#Apache2 is now the admin server
ADMSRVUP
# tc4admin begin
load perl.nlm
SEARCH ADD SYS:/tomcat/4/bin
tcadmup.ncf
# tc4admin end
# tomcat4 begin
sys:/tomcat/4/bin/tomcat4.ncf
# tomcat4 end
# Storage Management Services components required for Backup
SMSSTART.NCF
#---Added by Native File Access For Unix---
nfsstart
#---Added by Native File Access For Unix END---
# Uncomment the following line after creating DNS Server Object
# LOAD NAMED.NLM
# Uncomment the following line after creating DHCP Server Object
# LOAD DHCPSRVR.NLM
LOAD EMBOX.NLM
#RCONAG6.NLM is required by RConsoleJ
#LOAD RCONAG6 <Your Password Here> 2034 16800 2036
?STARTX
```

IPX/SPX and TCP/IP are configured in this **AUTOEXEC.NCF** file. If you only configure TCP/IP during the server installation you will not see the SERVERID or IPX parameters in the **AUTOEXEC.NCF** file. Novell requires TCP/IP on a NetWare 6.5 server. IPX/SPX is not required. However because of application requirements or backward compatibility issues, some of you will want to configure IPX/SPX after your server is up and running. There are two ways to accomplish this: Novell's way and a very easy way.

Novell's way to configure IPX/SPX on a running NetWare 6.5 server requires you to use the **INETCFG.NLM**. Simply work your way through the Boards, Protocols, and Bindings menu options to configure IPX/SPX. The problem with using the **INETCFG.NLM** is that your LAN configurations are moved to the **INITSYS.NCF**. You can no longer configure your LAN parameters in **AUTOEXEC.NCF** file.

If you want to configure IPX/SPX on your NetWare 6.5 server and still use the **AUTOEXEC.NCF** file, all you have to do is add a few lines of code to it. Using the sample **AUTOEXEC.NCF** file that you just looked at, the lines that configure IPX/SPX are the following:

```
SERVERID 11111111
LOAD IPXSPX
LOAD IPXRTR
LOAD PCNTNW.LAN PCI SLOT=3 MASTER=NO RXEARLY=NO FRAME=ETHER-
NET_802.2
↪NAME=PCNTNW_1_E82
BIND IPX PCNTNW_1_E82 NET=2
LOAD IPXRTRNM
```

The SERVERID parameter is not autogenerated in this case. You can configure it with an eight digit hexadecimal number of your choosing. The SERVERID of 11111111 is strictly provided as an example. I use it only in classroom settings. If you are using registered IPX internal network numbers on your network, you would configure the SERVERID parameter with a registered hexadecimal number.

If you configure IPX/SPX using this sample code, make sure you enter the LAN driver that corresponds to your network adapter, and using a **REM** statement in the **AUTOEXEC.NCF** file, document what this code does, in case you forget. For example, on the line before the SERVERID parameter is configured you might add the following **REM** statement:

```
REM The following section configures IPX/SPX.
```

The next section explores some of the SERVER.EXE options you can use when booting the NetWare operating system.

Server.exe Switches

When you run SERVER.EXE from NWSERVER, you might simply enter the command at the C:\NWSERVER prompt. That works fine for most situations. However, some key options are available that can be a tremendous help when you are faced with a contrary server. Some of these are listed in Table 3.4. Following is the syntax for using these options:

```
C:\NWSERVER>server -ns
```

For a more complete list of SERVER.EXE options, see http://www.salford-software.co.uk/support/kb/SKB62.

Table 3.4 SERVER.EXE Options	
SERVER.EXE Option	Description
-ns	**STARTUP.NCF** is not called. Consequently, neither is **AUTOEXEC.NCF**. That's great when you're trying to troubleshoot storage adapter driver issues.
-na	**AUTOEXEC.NCF** is not called, but **STARTUP.NCF** is. That's great when you're troubleshooting LAN adapter driver issues.
-nl	The initial Novell Splash screen, which hides many of the commands that are being loaded, is *not* displayed. You can actually view all the NLMs and error messages during the server boot.
-a	Use an alternate **AUTOEXEC.NCF** file.
-s	Use an alternate **STARTUP.NCF** file.

It is imperative that you know the **SERVER.EXE** options for the exam.

Identify the Utilities to Remotely Manage NetWare 6.5

Your NetWare 6.5 server is up and running, and you can manage your server locally. Now you need to be able to identify the tools to remotely manage your NetWare 6.5 server. You should be aware of three for this test:

➤ iManager

➤ Remote Manager

➤ OpenSSH

iManager

iManager is the browser-based management tool of choice for most eDirectory tasks. Before iManager, CNAs managed NDS and eDirectory primarily through NetWare Administrator and ConsoleOne. Those tools are still excellent choices for many tasks, but Novell is porting much of its functionality to iManager. This means that regardless of which workstation you are sitting at, you can manage a NetWare 6.5 server.

The URL that accesses iManager is `https://IP_ADDRESSorDNS_Name/nps/iManager.html`.

For example, if your server's IP address is 10.0.0.125, the URL is `https://10.0.0.125/nps/iManager.html`.

The opening iManager screen, as seen in Figure 3.12, shows the wide range of tasks that you can perform. These include managing DNS, DHCP, iPrint, eDirectory, Roles and Tasks, Role Based Service Configuration, NSS Storage devices, licenses, NMAS, Rights, Users, and Virtual Office. Each version of iManager has added functionality. If you have the version of iManager that shipped with NetWare 6.0, you can really only manage five tasks. In version 2.0.2, those five tasks are still available, along with many others.

Remote Manager

If you liked being able to use the commands at the server console, as was discussed earlier, you will love Remote Manager. Remote Manager is a browser-based server management tool. You can monitor your server's health, monitor and mount volumes, run server console commands, load and unload NLMs, partition disks, assign file system rights, create and remove directories and subdirectories, down and restart a server, manage the server's storage and LAN adapters, and access NDS iMonitor and DS Trace. Many of the tasks that you used to have to perform locally at the server can now be performed remotely with Remote Manager.

You can access Remote Manager using three different URLs. If your server's IP address is 10.0.0.125, you can enter the following into your browser's Location bar to access Remote Manager:

`http://10.0.0.125:8008`

`https://10.0.0.125:8009`

`https://10.0.0.125:2200`

The first two URLs, those using port 8008 and 8009, directly access Remote Manager using an unsecured port and a secure port. The last URL accesses Web Manager, where you can select Remote Manager under the Server Management heading in the left navigation bar.

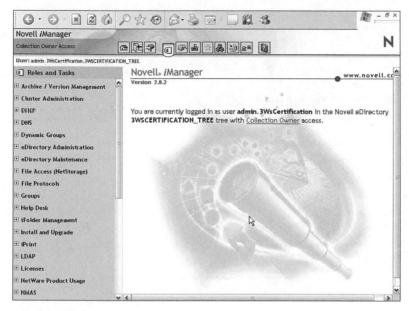

Figure 3.12a   iManager-Top options.

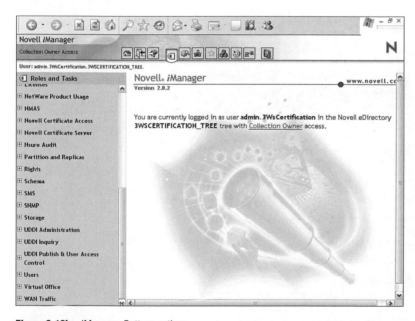

Figure 3.12b   iManager-Bottom options.

The opening screen of Remote Manager, as shown in Figure 3.13, demonstrates the wide range of tasks that you can perform with this tool.

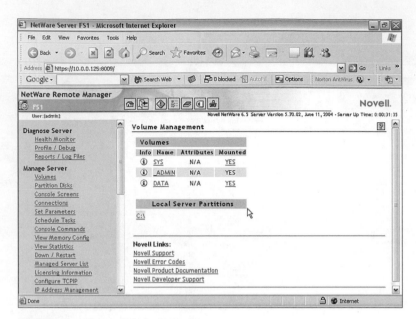

Figure 3.13a Remote Manager-Top options.

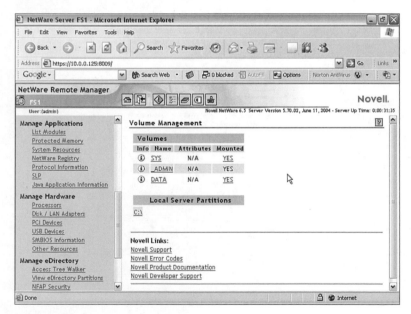

Figure 3.13b Remote Manager-Middle options.

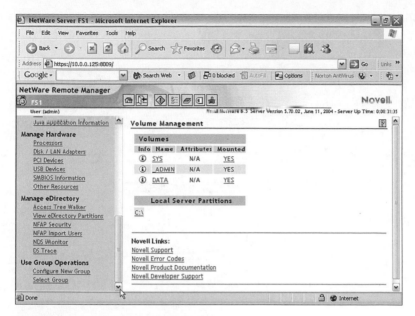

Figure 3.13c   Remote Manager-Bottom options.

You need to know the URLs and tasks that you can perform in iManager and Remote Manager. I strongly encourage you to open each option and explore what is available.

OpenSSH

OpenSSH is an open source technology that enables you to access services on a NetWare 6.5 server securely. OpenSSH comes with ssh, sftp, and scp. These respectively replace Telnet and rlogin, FTP, and rcp. Telnet, rlogin, FTP, and rcp are not secure and transmit data unencrypted, giving hackers easy access. With OpenSSH, data transmission is secure and encrypted.

With OpenSSH, you can shell into a NetWare 6.5 server from another server. You do not have to be at a workstation to start a secure shell. You can work on a server, from another server, as if you were at the first server's console. In addition, you can securely copy and transfer files between a workstation that is running an SSH Client, such as PUTTY or one of the SSH clients on Linux, and a NetWare 6.5 server running OpenSSH.

You can access the OpenSSH Manager shown in Figure 3.14 from Web Manager, by selecting the OpenSSH link under Open Source. You can then select the OpenSSH Simple Administration link to access the OpenSSH Manager. The opening screen of OpenSSH Manager lets you start, restart, or stop your OpenSSH server. You can also launch OpenSSH on your NetWare 6.5 server by loading SSHD.NLM at a server console prompt.

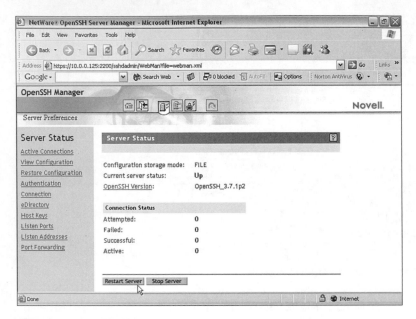

Figure 3.14 OpenSSH Manager.

OpenSSH Manager also allows you to view SSH connections, modify the SSHD Config file, and configure your log preferences. In addition, the OpenSSH implementation on NetWare 6.5 uses a log daemon and LDAP for authentication.

Following is the syntax for launching a secure shell using the ssh utility:

```
ssh user@remote_IP_address
```

Use ssh admin@10.0.0.125 if 10.0.0.125 is the remote server that you want to shell into.

The keystroke combination that exits the remote session is Ctrl+X.

The keystroke combination that changes the displayed screen is Ctrl+F.

To see all of the available keystrokes during an SSH session, go to pages 21 and 22 on the following Novell OpenSSH Web site: **http://www.novell.com/documentation/ nw65/pdfdoc/openssh/openssh.pdf**.

Following is the syntax for launching a secure FTP session:

```
sftp user@remote_IP_address
```

Use `sftp admin@10.0.0.125` if 10.0.0.125 is the remote server that you want to transfer files to or from. After you are connected, you can use any of the traditional FTP commands, such as `get`, `ls`, `lpwd`, `lcd`, `put`, `rm`, and `rmdir`.

The syntax for launching a secure copy session with scp is this:

```
scp local_filename user@remote_IP_address remote_filename
```

Use `scp admin@10.0.0.125` if 10.0.0.125 is the remote server that you want to copy files to or from.

Exam Prep Questions

1. You want to install a new NetWare 6.5 server into your existing tree. The tree has four other servers. Server FS1 is a NetWare 4.2 server with SP8. Server FS2 is a NetWare 5.0 server with SP4. FS3 is a NetWare 5.1 server with SP3. FS4 is a NetWare 4.10 server. You receive an error message when you try to install the new server into the tree. Which server is causing the problem?

   A. ○ FS1

   B. ○ FS2

   C. ○ FS3

   D. ○ FS4

   Answer D is correct. You cannot install a new NetWare 6.5 server into a tree that contains a NetWare 4.10 server. You could upgrade the NetWare 4.10 server to either NetWare 4.11 or 4.2 with at least support pack 6a, and then install the new server, but you cannot install it with a NetWare 4.10 server in the tree. Answers A, B, and C are incorrect. To install a new NetWare 6.5 server into an existing tree that contains NetWare 4 and 5.x servers, the 4.x and 5.x servers must be support packed to a minimum level. According to Novell, this is to guarantee that licensing works correctly. NetWare 4.11 and 4.2 servers must minimally have SP6a installed. NetWare 5.0 servers must minimally have SP4 installed. NetWare 5.1 servers must minimally have SP3 installed. FS1, FS2, and FS3 all meet the minimum SP requirements. They would not cause an installation error.

2. How much RAM does Novell recommend for a new NetWare 6.5 server?

   A. ○ 256MB

   B. ○ 512MB

   C. ○ 1000MB

   D. ○ 2000MB

   Answer C is correct. The recommended amount of installed RAM in a NetWare 6.5 server is 1GB, or 1000MB. The minimum amount of installed RAM in a NetWare 6.5 server is 512MB. Earlier versions of NetWare had a minimum RAM requirement of 256MB. In a production environment, based on the applications you are running, you would probably want to have at least 2000MB, or 2GB, of RAM installed, but that is neither the minimum required nor the recommended amount for a NetWare 6.5 server.

3. You are installing a new NetWare 6.5 server. What is the minimum size you should assign to the DOS partition?

 A. ○ 200MB

 B. ○ 500MB

 C. ○ 1000MB

 D. ○ 100MB

Answer B is correct. The minimum size for a DOS partition on a NetWare 6.5 server is 500MB. Answer C is incorrect. The recommended size is 1000MB, or 1GB. Answers A and D are incorrect. The minimum size for a DOS partition on a NetWare 6.0 server, according to all of Novell's documentation, is 200MB. However, when you install NetWare 6.0, you can configure the DOS partition with a 100MB partition even though Novell does not mention this in its authorized materials.

4. You want to install a new NetWare 6.5 server into your existing network. The network has four other servers. Server FS1 is a NetWare 4.2 server with SP8. Server FS2 is a NetWare 5.0 server with SP4. FS3 is a NetWare 5.1 server with SP3. FS4 is a NetWare 4.11 with SP6a server. What should you do before you install the new server into this network?

 A. ○ Upgrade FS4 to SP8.

 B. ○ Remove FS1 from the network.

 C. ○ Run Deployment Manager.

 D. ○ Install and run iManager.

Answer C is correct. After you have met all the basic requirements for installing a new NetWare 6.5 server, you have to prepare the existing network. The utility of choice to accomplish this is Deployment Manager. Answers A, B, and D are incorrect. You do not need to upgrade FS4 to SP8. That would be nice but is not required. SP6a is the required support pack level for NetWare 4.x servers. You do not have to remove FS2; again, it meets all documented requirements. You would run iManager after installing the NetWare 6.5 server into the network, not before.

5. Which of these lines would you find in the **NET.CFG** file?

 A. ○ **PREFERRED SERVER=FS1**

 B. ○ **C:\MSCDEX /D:IDECD001**

 C. ○ **LOAD IDEATA.CDM**

 D. ○ **DEVICE=C:\CPQIDECD.SYS /D:IDECD001**

Answer A is correct. You use the NET.CFG file when you are connecting to a NetWare server with a boot disk that is set up as a NetWare client. You do this when you are installing a NetWare 6.5 server across-the-wire. In this type of installation, all of the installation files are stored on a NetWare server. You need to access the files using a DOS-based NetWare client on a boot disk. You can also access the installation files using the IP Server Connection utility. In either case, the NET.CFG file serves to configure the DOS-based NetWare client. Some of the parameters configured in the NET.CFG file are PREFERRED SERVER, PREFERRED TREE, and NAME CONTEXT. Answers B, C, and D are incorrect. Answer B is found in an AUTOEXEC.BAT file. Answer C is found in a STARTUP.NCF file. Answer D is found in a CONFIG.SYS file.

6. While you're installing NetWare 6.5 on a new server, you decide to run the Default installation. Which of these parameters is configured correctly for a Default installation?

   A. ○ 2GB **SYS** volume

   B. ○ VGA Plug and Play

   C. ○ PS/2 mouse

   D. ○ Country Code 1

   Answer D is correct. You can install NetWare 6.5 using two possible methods: Default or Manual. If you choose the Default option, many settings are preconfigured. These include a Country Code setting of 1. Answers A, B, and C are incorrect. In addition to the Country Code, a 4GB SYS volume is created, the Codepage is set to 437, LAN and storage drivers are auto-discovered and loaded, the mouse is auto-discovered, video is set to SVGA Plug and Play, and the keyboard is set to United States.

7. In which layer of the NetWare 6.5 architecture would you expect to find iFolder?

   A. ○ Kernel

   B. ○ Drivers

   C. ○ Applications

   D. ○ Services

   E. ○ Applications/Services

   Answer E is correct. The NetWare 6.5 architecture has three layers. The top layer is called Applications/Services. At this layer, you find Applications and Services such as iFolder, eDirectory, and DNS/DHCP. Answers C and D are incorrect because there is no separate Applications layer or Services layer. Answers A and B are incorrect. The Kernel is under the Applications/Services layer and is where you find the NetWare 6.5 operating system. Under the Kernel, you find the Drivers layer, where LAN and Storage drivers reside, and protocols such as TCP/IP.

8. Which of the following drivers would you expect to have an **.nam** extension?

   A. ○ MAC

   B. ○ 3C509

   C. ○ SCSICD

   D. ○ IDEATA

   Answer A is correct. Namespace modules including MAC and NFS have the .nam extension. Answers B, C, and D are incorrect. Storage adapters, such as IDEATA, typically have a .ham extension. Storage devices, such as SCSICD, typically have a .cdm extension. LAN drivers, such as 3C509, typically have a .lan extension.

9. In which configuration file would you find the following lines?
```
FILE SERVER NAME FS1
SERVERID 11111111
BIND IP RTSSRV_1_EII addr=10.0.0.61 mask=255.0.0.0 gate=10.0.0.41
```

   A. ○ **NET.CFG**

   B. ○ **AUTOEXEC.NCF**

   C. ○ **AUTOEXEC.BAT**

   D. ○ **STARTUP.NCF**

   E. ○ **CONFIG.SYS**

   Answer B is correct. The FILE SERVER NAME, SERVERID, and BIND statements are configured in the AUTOEXEC.NCF file located in the SYS:/SYSTEM directory. Answer A is incorrect. The NET.CFG file typically has the PRE-FERRED SERVER, PREFERRED TREE, and NAME CONTEXT parameters configured. Answer C is incorrect. In the AUTOEXEC.BAT file, you find the PATH statement for a workstation and the MSCDEX.EXE file configured as a CD driver parameter. Answer D is incorrect. In the STARTUP.NCF file, you would typically find storage adapters, storage devices, and Platform Support Modules loaded and configured. You typically find STARTUP.NCF in the c:\NWSERVER directory. Answer E is incorrect. In the CONFIG.SYS file, found at the root of the C: drive, you would typically find the CD driver loaded using a DEVICE statement.

10. You are sitting at the server console of server FS10, a NetWare 6.5 server running OpenSSH. FS10 has an IP address of 10.0.0.10. Which command would you enter at your server console if you wanted to authenticate as admin to server FS1, which has an IP address of 10.0.0.1, and run an sftp session?

    A. ○ **ssh admin@10.0.0.10**

    B. ○ **sftp admin@10.0.0.1**

    C. ○ **sftp admin@10.0.0.10**

    D. ○ **ssh admin@10.0.0.1**

Answer B is correct. The correct syntax to launch an sftp session on server 10.0.0.1, from server 10.0.0.10, is `sftp admin@10.0.0.1`. Answer C is incorrect. That is the syntax to launch an sftp session on server 10.0.0.10. Answers A and D are incorrect. The ssh parameter indicates that you are launching a secure shell session, not an sftp session, on the server defined by the IP address.

4

Installing and Configuring the Novell Client

· ·

Terms you'll need to understand:

✓ Novell Client
✓ Client Protocol options
✓ Typical installation
✓ Custom installation
✓ NMAS

✓ NICI
✓ ZENworks for Desktops
✓ Login authenticator
✓ Workstation Manager
✓ /508

Techniques you'll need to master:

✓ Identify the Novell Client features
✓ Identify the Novell Client Protocol options
✓ Identify the four types of Login scripts
✓ Identify the four methods of accessing the Novell Client Login window
✓ Identify the two Novell Client installation methods
✓ Identify the components that are installed by default using each Novell Client installation method
✓ Identify the five tabs that are displayed, and what each is used for, when you select the Advanced option button on the Novell Login window

✓ Identify how to access the Novell Client Properties configuration tabs
✓ Identify how to deploy Novell Client Properties changes to one or more users
✓ Identify the two login authenticator options
✓ Identify the option that is used when launching the Novell Client installation routine that enables special accessibility options

Now that you have your NetWare 6.5 server up and running, you need to tackle the task of installing the Novell Client on your Windows workstation. Most CNAs can do this task in their sleep. With NetWare 6.5, the demand for the Novell Client has declined because you can now authenticate to and access a NetWare server using a variety of methods that do not rely on the Client. Over the years, the main purpose of the Novell Client has been to access and authenticate to a NetWare server/tree. That is still a primary purpose for the Client, but you don't need the Client if all you want to do is file and print sharing. The Client is now designed for Novell power users and administrators who need the full functionality provided by the Client. If you do not fall into one of those categories, one of the smaller, modular, task-specific clients will probably fit the bill. In fact, you might be able to do all of your tasks on a Clientless workstation. However, because the full-blown Novell Client is still in demand and is a hot topic on the exam, you need to look at accessing the Client login screens, some of the Client features, the installation steps, the Client login options, and setting the Client properties for a single user and for numerous users.

Describe the Novell Client

The Novell Client is Novell's opthamological response to workstation myopia. Without the Novell Client, a Microsoft workstation can only see resources and services supplied by Microsoft providers. For the most part, a Microsoft workstation is nearsighted or myopic. The Novell Client is like a fine pair of distance glasses. When you install the Client, you find that there is so much more in the way of Novell resources and services available. You can potentially see up to 26 Novell network drive mappings and 16 Novell search drive mappings. In addition, the Novell Client lets you access and authenticate to a bindery-based Novell server or an eDirectory/NDS-based tree. When it's installed on a Windows workstation, the Novell Client opens the whole realm of Novell possibilities and capabilities. As I noted earlier, even though Novell is moving quickly toward a full Clientless environment, if you're preparing for the NetWare 6.5 Foundations exam, you still need to know what the Novell Client offers to users and administrators. The next section discusses the features of the Novell Client.

Novell Client Features

You should install the Novell Client for several reasons. These reasons include the following seven features:

➤ It is fully integrated with eDirectory.

➤ It is fully integrated with Windows NT/2000/XP. You can view Novell resources through My Network Places, Windows Explorer, and My Computer.

➤ It supports TCP/IP and Internetwork Packet Exchange/Sequenced Packet Exchange (IPX/SPX).

➤ It fully supports NetWare security and authentication models, providing a single point of administration for authentication.

➤ It supports Automatic Client Upgrade (ACU) and Client installation from a networked server.

➤ It provides automatic reconnection to dropped networked services when the services come back online.

➤ Frequently used networked data is cached by the Novell Client.

These are the Novell Client's seven main selling features.

 Make sure you know the seven features of the Novell Client for the exam.

Protocols and Login Scripts

When you install the Novell Client, one of the screens that you encounter is the Protocol Preference screen, as shown in Figure 4.1.

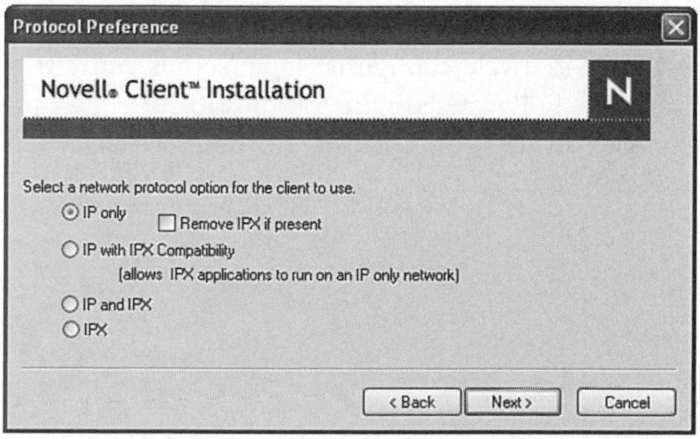

Figure 4.1   Novell Client Protocol Preference options.

At this point in the installation, you have to configure the Client to work with the protocol(s) that you have installed on your workstation and the protocol(s) that you have bound to the network card(s) on your server.

➤ Select IP Only if you are only using TCP/IP on your network and have no need for IPX/SPX.

➤ Select IP and IPX if you are using TCP/IP and IPX/SPX. Perhaps you have a mixed NetWare environment, with NetWare 6.5 and NetWare 4.x servers that are running IPX/SPX and TCP/IP. Or you might have one or more legacy applications that require IPX/SPX, but for all other purposes, you use TCP/IP.

➤ Select IPX (some Client screens show this as IPX Only) if you do not want to have connectivity to the Internet or a wide area network (WAN), if all of your applications and connections are configured for IPX/SPX, or if you simply do not want to transition to TCP/IP because of security concerns.

➤ Select IP with IPX Compatibility if you are in the process of transitioning away from IPX/SPX to TCP/IP but you have not yet transitioned all applications. You can use this option only for a limited time period while you finalize the transition from IPX/SPX to TCP/IP.

With these four options, you can configure your Novell Client based on your current network requirements. This is a real selling feature because you are not locked into a single protocol. Another selling feature of the Novell Client is how it works with login scripts to configure a user's working environment.

When a user logs in to a NetWare 6.5 network using the Novell Client, if configured, a series of administratively configured login scripts run establishing the user's environment. Following are the four possible login scripts that run. They are discussed in detail in Chapter 7, "Basic Management Tasks—eDirectory and File System."

➤ Container script

➤ Profile script

➤ User script

➤ Default script

Having the Novell Client integrated with the NetWare 6.5 login scripts makes your life as an administrator easy to tolerate when things seem to go wrong. When a user decides to completely reconfigure his environment and can no longer access needed NetWare 6.5 resources, you can tell him to log out and log in again. The login scripts that you have configured run and reestablish the user's environment with the needed drive mappings and pointers.

 Make sure you know the four protocol options that are available when you install the Novell Client.

Now that you know the main Novell Client features and protocol options, you will learn how to access the NetWare Login screen.

Client Login Methods

At least four methods provide access to the Novell Client Login screen:

➤ After you install the Client on a workstation, the Novell Client Login screen should appear when you reboot the workstation. The opening screen should look like Figure 4.2 by default. You have the option of selecting the Advanced button. The section titled "Log In to eDirectory and the Workstations" discusses this in greater detail.

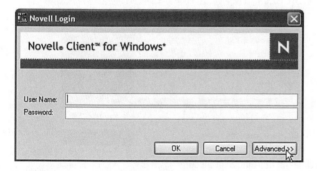

Figure 4.2 Opening Login screen.

➤ Right-clicking the red N in the System Tray (see Figure 4.3) lets you access the Novell Login option (see Figure 4.4).

➤ On a Windows XP Professional Workstation, you can go to Start, All Programs, Novell (Common), Novell Login (see Figure 4.5).

Figure 4.3   Red N in the Windows System Tray.

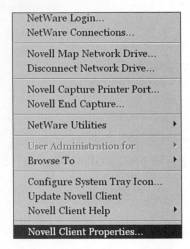

Figure 4.4   Result of right-clicking the red N in the Windows System Tray.

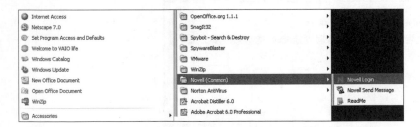

Figure 4.5   Accessing the Novell Login from the Start menu.

➤ From My Network Places, you can select Novell Connections and right-click on the tree you want to log in to (see Figure 4.6).

 NOTE   The Novell Client that is covered in this book and on the exam is the Novell Client 4.90 SP1 for Windows NT/2000/XP. The Novell Client for Windows 9x is not covered in this book or on the exam.

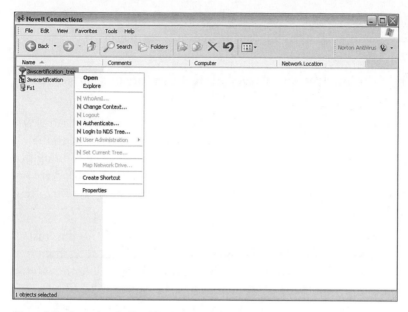

Figure 4.6 Accessing the Novell login from My Network Places.

You must know the four options for accessing the Novell Client Login screen for the exam.

Now that you know the features and how to access the opening Login screen, you need to know how to install the Novell Client on a Windows workstation and which installation types are available.

Install the Novell Client

Installing the Novell Client only takes a few minutes and is an easy process.

The installation steps follow. Due to page space limitations, I cannot show you each screenshot that you will see in the installation. If you want to see the virtual installation presentation that I use in class, go to **http://www.3wscertification.com/ install.html** and select the Client 4.90 SP1 Install presentation from the left navigation bar.

Following are the steps involved in installing the Novell Client:

1. Make sure you have the latest Novell Client for your workstation platform. For the purpose of this book, I am assuming that you are using a

Windows 2000/XP Professional workstation. If you do not have the latest Client, go to `http://download.novell.com/pages/PublicSearch.jsp`.

2. Copy and extract the downloaded file to a directory on your workstation, or insert your Novell Client CD into your CD drive.

3. If your workstation is configured to autorun the Client CD, the installation routine launches automatically. If your computer is not configured to autorun, you can launch the installation routine by running the `WINSETUP.EXE` program. If you have the installation files in a directory on your computer, you can launch the installation routine by running the `SETUPNW.EXE` program.

If your users have special accessibility requirements, you need to install the Novell Client on their computers so that the special accessibility settings are available. You can accomplish this by appending the /508 option to the installation executable. The /508 option is based on Section 508 of the U.S. Federal Government Rehabilitation Act.

Make sure you know that **WINSETUP.EXE** launches the installation routine if the CD does not autorun.

4. After your Client CD is up and running, select the Novell Client 4.90 SP1 for Windows NT/2000/XP option.

5. Select the installation language.

6. Read and accept the Software License Agreement.

7. At the Installation Options screen, you can choose either Typical Installation or Custom Installation. If you select Typical, four Client components are installed by default.

➤ Novell Client for Windows

➤ Novell Distributed Print Services

➤ Novell Workstation Manager

➤ ZENworks Application Launcher

If you select Custom, you can choose these or two others in a following screen. For the purposes of this book and the exam and in a production environment, select Custom.

8. If you select the Custom option, you see the Installation Components screen. Here, you can select any of the four previously mentioned options plus two others: Remote Management and ZENworks Imaging Service. You cannot deselect the Novell Client for Windows component. You must select Custom and the Novell Workstation Manager if you are currently running ZENworks for Desktops with Remote Manager. Workstation Manager is required in this environment.

9. The next screen gives you the option of selecting three additional authentication products: NICI (Novell International Cryptographic Infrastructure) Client, which is selected by default; NMAS (Novell Modular Authentication Service) Client, which lets you explore a wide range of authentication options including SmartCard and Retinal Scans; and NetIdentity Agent, which works with eDirectory to provide authentication to applications that are Web-based and yet require authentication from eDirectory. Examples of applications in which the NetIdentity agent is used are iManager, Remote Manager, and iPrint.

10. Select the protocol(s) that the Client will use on the Protocol Preference screen that was discussed earlier in this chapter (refer to Figure 4.1). At this screen, you can remove IPX if present, when you select the IP Only option. This reduces some "binding" overhead on your workstation.

When you are running multiple clients and multiple protocols on a workstation, you can see a slowdown in authentication and access times. This is often the result of the default bind order. You can reorder the Client (provider) and the protocols. On a Windows 2000/XP workstation, you do this by right-clicking My Network Places and selecting Properties, Advanced, Advanced Settings. There, you can reorder the bind order for each adapter and the provider order. If you have both IPX and IP bound with IPX at the top of the order, but you authenticate with IP, you will experience a slowdown at best. To solve this, if you do not want to remove IPX, move IP above IPX.

11. If you selected the Novell Workstation Manager, you see the Login Authenticator screen, where you can select either NDS or Bindery depending on whether you are logging into a NetWare 4.x or later tree or an earlier NetWare 3.x server.

Make sure you know the two Login Authenticator options.

12. The last screen that you see informs you that you have completed the installation.

Now that you know the installation steps, you need to know what each option tab offers at login.

Log In to eDirectory and the Workstations

After your successful Novell Client installation, reboot your workstation. As was shown in Figure 4.2, the opening Login screen gives you the option of entering your username and password. If you select the Advanced button in the lower-right corner of the dialog box, five tabs appear, one of which has an additional option box.

The five tabs are as follows:

➤ NDS

➤ Script (also has the Variables option box)

➤ Windows

➤ Dial-Up

➤ NMAS

 Make sure you know the five Login tabs and what options are available on each.

NDS

On the NDS tab, shown in Figure 4.7, you can define the tree you want to log in to, your context, or the server where you want to authenticate. If you do not know the exact syntax for each parameter, you can click on the Browse button to the right of each dialog box and browse to the appropriate tree, context, and server. Then you need to enter your username and password. If you do not want to log in to a NetWare tree, you can select the Workstation Only option, which closes all of the tabs except the Windows tab, where you enter your local authentication credentials.

 You can select the Workstation Only option on the NDS tab, but you authenticate to the Windows workstation on the Windows tab.

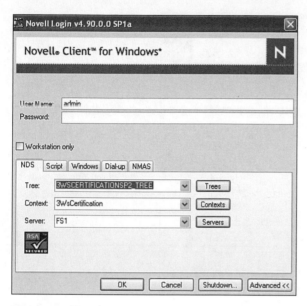

Figure 4.7   NDS tab.

Script

On the Script tab (see Figure 4.8), you can choose whether you want to run login scripts that are associated with your username, whether you want to see a window that displays the results of those scripts, and whether you want the window to close automatically if the script(s) runs without error. As a troubleshooting measure, you can also select an alternate login script or profile script to run in place of those that an administrator defines for you. This is helpful to a CNA who writes a script that is flawed but has trouble breaking out of the script when run due to errors in the code. When this happens, you can select an alternate script to get you into the system, after which you can edit the script with the problem.

Notice the Variables button on the Script tab. Using this button, if a login script is written using a variable, such as %2 (see Figure 4.9), you can define what the variable represents. For example, one user might point %2 to the \Shared\Departmental\Marketing directory, whereas another user might point %2 to the \Shared\Departmental\Sales directory. The use of variables in a login script is helpful in keeping the length of the script reasonable. Employing variables, though, assumes that users have a good grasp of the NetWare login process.

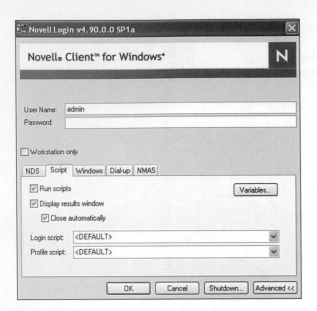

Figure 4.8 Script tab.

Figure 4.9 Variables screen.

Windows

The Windows tab, shown in Figure 4.10, has two functions. It is used when you only want to log in to your Windows workstation or to your Windows domain. The From box defines where the account manager is that will be used for Windows authentication. The Windows tab is also used to store your local authentication credentials. When you log in to your NetWare tree, you also have to log in to your local Windows accounts manager. On this tab, you can enter or change your local login credentials.

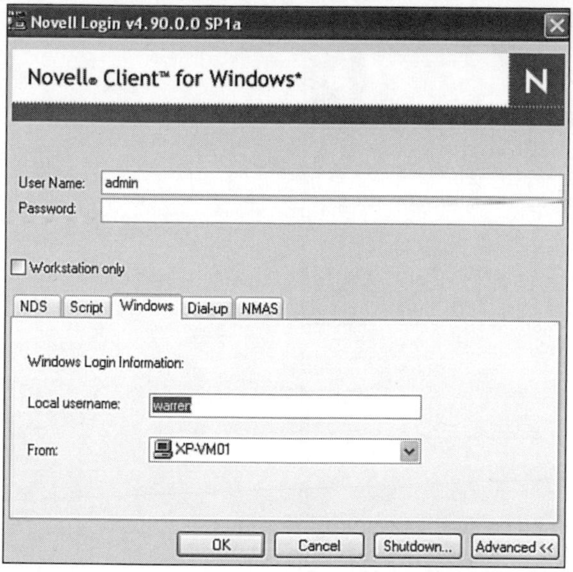

Figure 4.10 Windows tab.

Dial-up

The Dial-up tab, shown in Figure 4.11, is used when you want to log in to your NetWare tree using a dial-up connection. You can choose whether you want to log in using a dial-up connection, which is not chosen by default, and then provide the number to dial and the number you are dialing from.

NMAS

You use the NMAS tab, shown in Figure 4.12, to select the appropriate login sequence that will be used for authentication. With the advent of NMAS and increasing security concerns, you can now elect to authenticate by a host of methods, including biometrics, smart cards, Kerberos, digital certificates, and tokens. You can use these methods either separately or in combination. On the NMAS tab, you can select which authentication sequence to use and provide your clearance level.

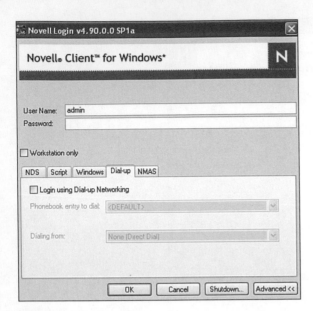

Figure 4.11 Dial-up tab.

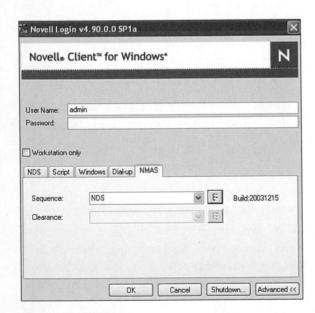

Figure 4.12 NMAS tab.

Set Client Properties

Now that you know what each of the Novell Client login tabs represents and you have logged into your tree successfully, you need to know two additional things to make your users happy.

➤ Which Client properties can be set

➤ How to set Client properties for individuals and for multiple users

Client Properties That Can Be Set

Depending on the version of the Novell Client and the workstation platform, you can set the Client to numerous properties to optimize it. Right-clicking the red N in the System Tray and selecting Novell Client Properties (refer to Figures 4.3 and 4.4) provides access to the Novell Client 4.90 properties. What is then displayed, as shown in Figure 4.13, is a series of configuration tabs that are beyond the scope of this book or this exam. You should take the time, nevertheless, to go through these tabs and examine the parameters that can be configured. Of particular interest to NetWare 6.5 CNAs are the Client, Advanced Menu Settings, and Advanced Settings tabs.

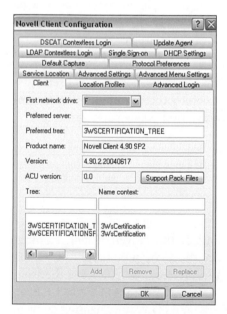

Figure 4.13 Novell Client Configuration tabs.

On the Client tab, you can configure which tree, server, and name context are preferred and which is the first network drive. On the Advanced Menu Settings tab, you can configure which menu settings are displayed in various Windows utilities. On the Advanced Settings tab, you can configure whether File Caching, Autoreconnect, and DOS Long Name Support are on or off.

Setting Client Properties for Individuals and for Multiple Users

You can set Novell Client properties on a station-by-station, user-by-user basis. This is not difficult in a small- to medium-sized environment. However, when you have to do this for hundreds or thousands of users or stations, it becomes more than difficult. Your fun job as a NetWare 6.5 CNA becomes a bear and a bore. To counter this dilemma, Novell suggests two methods of modifying client properties for multiple users:

➤ Dynamic Host Configuration Protocol (DHCP)

➤ ZENworks for Desktops

If you need to modify the IP address, subnet mask, gateway, and DNS information for multiple users, it is best to deploy these parameters network-wide with a DHCP (Dynamic Host Configuration Protocol) server. This is much more administratively efficient than using static addresses.

If you need to modify Client properties, such as First Network Drive, Preferred Tree, Preferred Server, or Name Context, for various users, it is best to use ZENworks for Desktops and deploy these configuration parameters by using a mixture of User and Workstation policy packages.

 If you need to modify Client properties while upgrading the Client, you can accomplish this utilizing the ACU option that is used in conjunction with correctly configured login script directives. This is not one of the testable methods, but it is definitely a real-world option.

You now have a thorough understanding of the Novell Client, features, installation steps, login options, and methods of modifying the Client Properties. In Chapter 5, "Introduction to eDirectory," you leave the wonderful world of installing the Novell operating system and Novell Client. You explore eDirectory, eDirectory objects, and eDirectory naming conventions. Are we having fun yet? I am.

Exam Prep Questions

1. Which Novell Client tab should you select if you want to authenticate only to your local workstation?

   A. ○ NDS

   B. ○ Windows

   C. ○ NMAS

   D. ○ Script

   Answer B is correct. The Windows tab lets you select whether you want to authenticate to your local workstation instead of to the NetWare 6.5 directory services. Answer A is incorrect. The NDS tab is where you can configure the tree, context, and server to be used for authentication. Answer C is incorrect. You use the NMAS tab to select the appropriate login sequence for authentication. Answer D is incorrect. The Script tab lets you select which scripts run during login. It is also a great tab when you have to troubleshoot a login script that needs to be debugged. Using this tab, you can choose to run an alternate script, giving you access to the system and the faulty script.

2. When you attempt to install Novell Client 4.90 on your Windows XP Professional workstation, you have to select the correct protocol. Which of the following are protocol options that you can select from? (Select all that apply.)

   A. ❏ IP Only

   B. ❏ IPX

   C. ❏ IP and IPX

   D. ❏ IPX with IP Compatibility Mode

   Answers A, B, and C are correct. Answer D is incorrect. The four protocol options that are available when you install the Novell Client are IP Only, IPX, IP and IPX, and IP with IPX Compatibility Mode. There is no option for IPX with IP Compatibility Mode.

3. Which Novell Client component must you install if you need to use the Remote Management feature found in ZENworks for Desktops?

   A. ○ Novell Distributed Print Services

   B. ○ ZENworks Application Launcher

   C. ○ Novell Workstation Manager

   D. ○ ZENworks Imaging Services

   Answer C is correct. If you are going to use the ZENworks for Desktops Remote Management feature, you need to install the Novell Workstation Manager client component. Answers A, B, and D are incorrect. You do not need to install Novell Distributed Print Services, ZENworks Application Launcher, or ZENworks Imaging Services if you are using the ZENworks Remote Management feature.

4. You are installing the Novell Client. Which two of the following are installation methods?

A. ☐ Complete

B. ☐ Notebook

C. ☐ Typical

D. ☐ Custom

Answers C and D are correct. The two installation methods available when you install the Novell Client are Typical and Custom. Answers A and B are incorrect. Complete and Notebook are not available options.

5. You are installing the Novell Client. You have chosen the Novell Workstation Manager as one of the components. As a consequence of this, you have to select a login authenticator. What are the two possible login authenticators that are available as a result of your decision?

A. ☐ ADS

B. ☐ Bindery

C. ☐ eDirectory

D. ☐ NDS

Answers B and D are correct. As a consequence of selecting the Workstation Manager component, you have to select a login authenticator. The question that you have to answer is "Will you log in to an NDS/eDirectory tree, or will you log in to a NetWare 3 or earlier bindery-based server?" The two login authenticators that you are presented with during the Novell Client installation are bindery and NDS. Answers A and C are incorrect. ADS (Active Directory Services) and eDirectory are not options at this time. ADS is used on Windows 2000/2003 platforms.

6. You want to install the Novell Client on your Windows XP Professional workstation. Your workstation does not autorun the Novell Client installation CD. What executable can you run to launch the installation routine?

A. ○ **WINSETUP.EXE**

B. ○ **INSTALL.BAT**

C. ○ **SETUP.EXE**

D. ○ **CLIENT.EXE**

Answer A is correct. When the Client CD does not autorun, you can launch the installation routine by running the WINSETUP.EXE program. Answer B is incorrect. INSTALL.BAT launches the NetWare 6.5 server installation routine. Answers C and D are incorrect. SETUP.EXE and CLIENT.EXE do not launch the Client installation routine. SETUP.EXE is the executable that launces the Novell Client 3.4 installation routine on a Windows 9x workstation. There is no CLIENT.EXE executable.

7. Several of your users have special accessibility requirements. You need to install the Novell Client on their computers so that the special accessibility settings are available. Which option should you append to the installation executable to accomplish this?

   A. ○ /443

   B. ○ /508

   C. ○ /631

   D. ○ /2200

   Answer B is correct. The option that you should append to the installation executable for your platform is /508, which is based on Section 508 of the U.S. Federal Government Rehabilitation Act. Answers A, C, and D are incorrect. They are port numbers, not executable options. Port 443 is used for secure Web access. Port 631 is used for nonsecure iPrint printing. Port 2200 is used to access the NetWare 6.5 Web Manager.

8. The Novell Client Login window is displayed when you boot your computer. Which tab should you select if you want to choose the authentication login sequence?

   A. ○ NMAS

   B. ○ NDS

   C. ○ Dial-up

   D. ○ Script

   Answer A is correct. You select the NMAS tab to select the appropriate login sequence for authentication. Answer B is incorrect. The NDS tab is where you can configure the tree, context, and server that will be used for authentication. Answer C is incorrect. The Dial-up tab is used when you want to remotely authenticate over a dial-up connection. Answer D is incorrect. The Script tab lets you select which scripts run during login. It is also a great tab when you have to troubleshoot a login script that needs to be debugged. Using this tab, you can choose to run an alternate script, giving you access to the system and the faulty script.

9. Which of the following is a feature of the Novell Client?

   A. ○ The Novell Client only supports the TCP/IP protocol.

   B. ○ The Novell Client only reconnects to a restored network if the user has admin rights to the tree root.

   C. ○ The Novell Client is fully integrated with all major Unix versions.

   D. ○ The Novell Client can be upgraded using ACU.

   Answer D is correct. The Novell Client gives users one way to access and authenticate to eDirectory. The Novell Client is the tried-and-true means of accessing the full range of NetWare 6.5 services and resources. The features of the Novell Client encompass multiprotocol support, including IPX/SPX and TCP/IP, auto-reconnect capabilities when a connection is lost for all authenticated users, full integration with Windows NT/2000/XP client platforms, and upgrade capability using ACU. Answers A, B, and C are incorrect. You do not have to be an admin to enjoy the auto-reconnect feature. The Novell Client is not yet fully integrated with all major Unix versions. The Novell Client supports more than just TCP/IP.

10. You want to assign the Preferred Server, Preferred Tree, and Name Context to all 1,000 users on your NetWare 6.5 network. Everyone is using the latest Novell Client on Windows XP Professional workstations. What is the most efficient method recommended by Novell to accomplish this?

   A. ○ Deploy all parameters using ZENworks for Desktops 3 or higher.

   B. ○ Send an email to all users detailing the process of configuring the necessary Client properties.

   C. ○ Send a memo to all department heads instructing them on the steps to take to implement the required changes.

   D. ○ At each user's station, right-click the N in the System Tray and make the necessary changes on a station-by-station basis.

   E. ○ Make the necessary changes at the tree object in ConsoleOne. Through the process of replication, all changes are implemented automatically.

   F. ○ Perform an ACU.

Answer A is correct. You can establish client properties on numerous workstations in several ways. The easiest method, if it's available, is to set the needed client properties using DHCP. Novell recommends deploying all parameters using ZENworks for Desktops 3 or higher. Answers B, C, D, E, and F are incorrect. Answers B, C, and D are incorrect because you are making the changes on a station-by-station basis. Even if *you* are not doing it, it is still being done station by station. Answer E is incorrect because you cannot perform this task using ConsoleOne. Answer F is incorrect because you are not asked to upgrade the Client; rather, you are asked to configure the Client. All users are currently using the latest client.

5

Introduction to eDirectory

. . . .

Terms you'll need to understand:

✓ eDirectory
✓ Tree object
✓ Container
✓ Leaf
✓ Object
✓ Property
✓ Value
✓ Schema
✓ Context
✓ Current context
✓ Distinguished Name

✓ Relative Distinguished Name
✓ Typeful
✓ Typeless
✓ Attribute types
✓ CX
✓ Inheritance
✓ Trailing period
✓ Leading period
✓ NetWare Administrator
✓ ConsoleOne
✓ iMonitor

Techniques you'll need to master:

✓ Identify the role and benefits of eDirectory
✓ Identify how eDirectory works
✓ Identify and describe eDirectory components
✓ Identify and describe eDirectory object classes

✓ Identify the flow and design of the eDirectory tree
✓ Identify eDirectory tools and when to use them

Now that you have a server and a client, you need to understand eDirectory, its function and benefits, how it works and how it is organized, how to name and locate objects, and the utilities that are available for management.

Identify the Role and Benefits of eDirectory

eDirectory is the latest iteration of Novell Directory Services (NDS). It can run on a multitude of platforms, including Linux and Windows 2003 Server, and it is LDAP enabled. One of the major benefits of eDirectory is that it is scalable and has an extensible schema. Some Novell documents call eDirectory the most fundamental service that NetWare offers. It keeps track of all network resources through a hierarchical, relational database that is distributed and loosely consistent. eDirectory can be partitioned and replicated.

One-half of your overall administrative duties involve managing eDirectory. The other half of your administrative duties involve managing the file system, which is introduced in Chapter 6, "Introduction to the NetWare 6.5 File System."

Those who come from the Windows NT environment or the NetWare 3.x environment (which were good, solid network operating systems) want to know the benefits of eDirectory before making the transition. Novell cites four major benefits of deploying eDirectory in your environment:

➤ It provides central management of network resources and services.

➤ It uses a standard method to view and manage resources and services. Utilities, such as iManager, ConsoleOne, and NetWare Administrator, are second nature to those of you who administer eDirectory.

➤ It uses a logical organization of network resources that is independent of the physical infrastructure. eDirectory is hierarchically organized. This means that unlike the DOS file system, in which you can place files and directories virtually anywhere you want, in eDirectory, rules govern where you can create objects. Much like the military, where there is a chain of command, eDirectory has a chain of command in the organization of objects. No matter how many wide area network (WAN) links you have, the logical organization is the governing factor in eDirectory object access.

➤ The mapping between an object and the physical resource it represents is dynamic. You can move an object in eDirectory, as you will see in Chapter 7, "Basic Management Tasks—eDirectory and File System," and the link between the physical resource and the eDirectory object is maintained. The relationship is dynamic.

The role of eDirectory is quite simple: It provides a method for users to easily locate and access network resources. When a user logs in to eDirectory, his authentication credentials are validated and his rights are checked. He is given access to those objects where you, as the administrator, have granted him rights. eDirectory acts as the concierge to directory services.

The following basic steps are followed when a user or application requests access to a network resource. These steps are secured with the exchange of public and private keys.

1. After a client requests a network resource, a server that is providing the requested service or resource responds to the request.

2. The resource or service is located in eDirectory and identified.

3. Through several exchanges of digital keys, the client's rights and validity are checked and verified.

4. After extensive checking, the exchange of random numbers, and credential validation, the client is connected to the desired resource or service.

eDirectory provides the environment and means of connecting the client to the resource.

You must completely understand the role of eDirectory in connecting a user or application to a network resource or service.

The eDirectory tree is represented as an upside-down tree, with the top of the tree represented by the Tree object, or in some utilities as the [Root] of the tree. From the Tree object, other objects are organized hierarchically, to the lowest level where network resources and services are found. Some compare the eDirectory tree to the DOS file system, with the Tree object compared to the root of a drive, and resources compared to low-level files. People have also compared the eDirectory tree to the organization used for Domain Name System (DNS), or the Internet domains. The top of the

Internet domains is called the root, the domains under the root—COM, EDU, MIL, INT, and US—are called root domains, and under the root domains are subdomains and then servers providing a host of Web-based services. Whichever comparison works for you is fine. Simply understand that eDirectory is represented, counterintuitively, as an upside-down tree, with the root at the top and the leaves at the bottom.

Before you get too deep into the organization and definition of eDirectory objects, you need to review the features of eDirectory and the platforms that eDirectory runs on.

Identify How eDirectory Works

Some of the features included with the version of eDirectory that ships with NetWare 6.5 include the following:

➤ Index Manager

➤ LDAP support

➤ Import Coversion Export (ICE) utility

➤ iManager for eDirectory management

➤ Merge tool

➤ Linux, Solaris, Tru64, and Unix client libraries

➤ iMonitor for management, monitoring, and diagnosis

To the amazement of many NetWare diehards, eDirectory can run on a variety of non-NetWare platforms. If you have a particular application that must run on a Windows 2000 or 2003 server, you can install eDirectory on that server and manage it and the installed application in your tree. You will have an integrated, multiplatform environment that enables you to expand your capabilities based on the applications that you have to deploy.

Currently, eDirectory runs on Linux, NetWare, Solaris, Tru64 Unix, and Windows NT/2000/2003.

 Know the platforms that eDirectory runs on for the exam.

Now that you know the roles, benefits, and features of eDirectory, you need to understand what makes up eDirectory.

Identify and Describe eDirectory Components

Before you dive into the deep end of the pool, you need to understand a term that governs eDirectory: schema. This is much like understanding the philosophy of an organization. What is the underlying principle that governs how a company is organized and functions? In eDirectory, this is the schema.

The eDirectory schema is the set of rules for object creation and placement. The schema dictates what properties must be assigned values when an object is created and what properties are optional. The schema is composed of two sets of definitions: object class, which defines which objects can be created and what attributes or properties are associated with each object type; and attribute definition, which defines the structure, syntax, and limitations of an attribute. The schema in NetWare 6.5 is extensible, which means that you can introduce new objects and properties into the schema to accomodate other network services and resources. Examples of this include the installation of ZENworks or GroupWise, which each extend the schema and introduce a host of new objects to the base schema that ships with NetWare 6.5. You can extend the schema in NetWare 6.5 using either Schema Manager, found in ConsoleOne under the Tools menu, or iManager. Novell prefers iManager in this version of NetWare.

The three major components of eDirectory are objects, properties, and values. The following list provides definitions for each type of component:

➤ An *object* is a fundamental component of eDirectory that contains information about a network resource. If you compare a traditional database or spreadsheet to eDirectory, a record in a database or a row in a spreadsheet is comparable to an object in eDirectory.

➤ An object has properties. *Properties* are fundamental components of eDirectory. A property is an attribute of an object. If you compare a traditional database or spreadsheet to eDirectory, an object's property is a field in a database or a column in a spreadsheet. Some properties are required, depending on the object, whereas others are optional. Some properties are single-valued, whereas others are multivalued. For example, to create a user object, depending on the utility that you use, you must give the user object a username and a last name. In ConsoleOne, you highlight the object's context to accomplish this, whereas in iManager, you also must provide a context for the user object. All other properties are optional. After you create the user object, you can give the user a description, location, phone number, fax number, and password. The phone number and fax number are multivalued properties to accommodate the many numbers that a user can have. Password, description, and location are single-valued properties. A user can have only one. In the same way, two user objects have the same properties, which are different from the properties that a printer uses. The printer object has a different set of properties that the schema governs. Even though two users have the same properties, the values that are assigned to those properties are different in many cases.

➤ The data that you assign to an object's property is a *value*. If you compare a spreadsheet to eDirectory, a property value is similar to a cell in a spreadsheet.

 Know the difference between a single-valued property and a multivalued property, in addition to those properties that are required and those that are optional. If a property is optional, you can create an object without defining a value for the property. If a property is required, you must define a value for it.

In Table 5.1, you see how a user object with a UserName of Warren, LastName of Wyrostek, and Description of Trainer correlate to records, fields and cells.

Table 5.1	Objects, Properties and Values		
Object	**UserName (Property 1)**	**LastName (Property 2)**	**Description (Property 3)**
User	Warren (Value 1)	Wyrostek (Value 2)	Trainer (Value 3)
Records	**Field 1**	**Field 2**	**Field 3**
Record 1	Value 1	Value 2	Value 3

eDirectory organization is made up of three 3s. The first set of threes is the three major components of eDirectory: objects, properties, and values. You need to learn the second and third sets of three.

➤ The three classes of objects

➤ The three major types of container objects

Identify and Describe eDirectory Object Classes

The three classes of eDirectory objects include the following:

➤ Tree object

➤ Container objects

➤ Leaf objects

The Tree object is the top of the eDirectory tree. In some management utilities, the Tree object is called the [Root] of the tree.

A Container object is a holder of other eDirectory objects. In a sense, a Container logically groups eDirectory objects. Examples of Container objects are the Country object, the Organization object, the Organizational Unit object, the Domain object, the Security container, Role Based Services, and the License container. Some Novell documents also classify the Tree object as a container object. For this exam, consider the Tree object as both a single entity at the top of the tree and as a Container object.

Leaf objects are one of the three major types of eDirectory objects. Network resources are represented in the eDirectory tree by Leaf objects. Examples of Leaf objects are the User object, the Group object, the Server object, the Volume object, the Printer object, and the Organizational Role object.

Figure 5.1 shows examples of each of these object types.

 Be familiar with the icons that represent each type of Container and Leaf object.

Characteristics of the Tree object include the following:

➤ Only one Tree object can exist in an eDirectory tree.

➤ The Tree object is a mandatory object in an eDirectory tree. You cannot have an eDirectory tree without a Tree object.

➤ The Tree object is created when the first NetWare server is installed into the tree.

➤ You cannot move, delete, or rename the Tree object. The name value that you give to an eDirectory tree can be changed, but you cannot change the name of the Tree object.

➤ The Tree object can contain Country and Organization objects or Alias objects to the Country or Organization. The Tree object might also have a Security container.

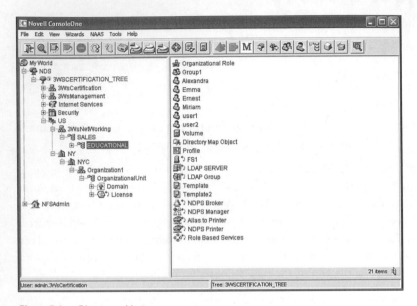

Figure 5.1 eDirectory objects.

When it comes to Container objects, even though NetWare 6.5 has more than three, Novell defines three major types of containers: the Country object, the Organization object, and the Organizational Unit. Following are characteristics of the Country object:

➤A Country object is an optional object. It is generally used for global enterprises, in which the top level of the tree is divided by country.

➤ If you are working in a multiplatform directory services environment that depends on the X.500 standard, you need the Country object. This object is not required on a strictly NetWare-oriented eDirectory network.

➤ A Country object is represented by a two-character country code, such as DE, US, or UK.

➤ The Country object can exist only in the Tree object.

➤ The Country object can contain the Organization object or an Alias object to an Organization. Depending on the version of eDirectory that you are using, you can create other objects under the Country object, but those are not relevant for the exam.

Following are characteristics of the Organization object:

➤ An eDirectory requires at least one Organization object. In the past, Novell recommended that the eDirectory tree have a single Organization object. With the newer versions of eDirectory and NetWare 6.5, that is no longer the case. Novell now suggests that an eDirectory tree can have multiple Organization objects where appropriate.

➤ You use the Organization object to organize the tree into major groups, such as companies, universities, or divisions.

➤ The Organization object can be contained in the Tree object or the Country object.

➤ An Organization object cannot be contained in another Organization object.

➤ An Organization object can contain Organizational Unit objects and Leaf objects.

Following are characteristics of the Organizational Unit object:

➤ An Organizational Unit object is an optional object in eDirectory. Although it is not required, Novell recommends the use of Organizational Units for partitioning the tree.

➤ An Organizational Unit object further subdivides a tree under the Organization object into workgroups, departments, teams, and in some designs, geographical locations.

➤ An Organizational Unit object can be contained in an Organization object or an Organizational Unit object. It cannot be contained in the Country object or the Tree object.

➤ An Organizational Unit object can contain other Organizational Unit objects and all Leaf objects.

Following are the four special types of Container objects:

➤ License Container objects hold license certificate objects and are created when you install a license that is compatible with Novell Licensing Services (NLS).

➤ DNS components are represented by the Domain object, which can exist in an Organization object, Organizational Unit object, Country object, or Locality object.

➤ Security Container objects contain the security policy resources that are applicable to tree resources.

➤ Role-Based Service objects contain the roles and tasks that are assigned to users.

Leaf objects represent the available network resources. Leaf objects include the following:

➤ Alias objects, which are pointers to other objects, generally in a different container. The icon for an Alias object has a dotted quarter circle with a pointer on its right side.

➤ Application objects, which are network-distributable applications. This type of object is available when ZENworks is installed.

➤ Directory Map objects, which are eDirectory objects whose major property is the path to an application.

➤ Group objects, which represent a group of users.

➤ LDAP Groups, which represent one or more LDAP servers.

➤ LDAP Servers, which represent an LDAP server and its configuration information.

➤ NDPS Broker, NDPS Manager, and NDPS Printer, which are NDPS printing objects. These are discussed in detail in Chapter 11, "NetWare 6.5 Printing."

➤ Organizational Role objects, which represent a group of users who have a common task. These are task-oriented objects whose members are defined as occupants.

➤ Print Queue, Print Server, and Printer, which are legacy queue-based printing objects.

➤ Profile objects, which are objects whose major property is a profile login script that is used by groups of users who need the same environmental configuration upon login.

➤ Server objects, which represent a NetWare Core Protocol (NCP) server. These objects are created when a server is installed into the tree.

➤ Template objects, which are objects with properties that can be applied to users, when created, who have properties with the same values.

➤ User objects, which are the most fundamental objects in eDirectory. They represent a person who needs access to network resources. A User object must be created before a user can log in to the network.

➤ Volume objects, which represent a physical amount of storage space on a server. In a variety of NetWare management utilities, you can manage files and directories by opening the Volume object, even though the Volume object does not hold file and directory information.

You have now been introduced to the three 3s: objects, properties, and values; Tree objects, Container objects, and Leaf Objects; Country, Organization, and Organizational Unit. Based on which objects you decide to use in your tree, you can create a variety of tree designs. The simplest design has a Tree object, Organization object, and all Leaf objects in the Organization object. This design is also known as the Bamboo Tree. It looks like and acts like a NetWare 3 environment when only a single server is installed. You can also have a tree with the Tree Object, Organization object, Organizational Unit object, and Leaf objects in the Organizational Unit. This has long been the standard Novell sanctioned tree design. That being said, you can configure different designs based on your needs and the hierarchical rules of eDirectory.

Now that you know what the objects are and what designs they can produce, you need to know how to name objects in the tree.

Identify the Flow and Design of the eDirectory Tree

The eDirectory tree can be as small or as large as you want. The more objects and containers that you include in the design, the more that locating and naming those objects becomes a task.

Objects are named from the Leaf object up to but not including the Tree object. To identify an object in eDirectory, you must be familiar with six concepts:

➤ Context

➤ Distinguished Name

➤ Typeful-using Attribute types

➤ Typeless

➤ Current context

➤ Relative Distinguished Name

An object's context is where the object is located in the eDirectory tree. Context is the full path to an object in eDirectory. In Figure 5.2, Alexandra's context is (starting from the leaf object) Educational-Sales-3WsNetWorking-US, because Alexandra's user object exists in the Educational Organizational Unit, which exists in the Sales Organizational Unit, which exists in the 3WsNetWorking Organization, which exists in the US Country object.

Figure 5.2 eDirectory naming.

A Distinguished Name is a combination of an object's common name and its context, beginning with the object and progressing up to, but not including, the Tree object. You can easily identify a Distinguished Name because it has a leading period, its contextual elements are separated by periods, and it does not have trailing periods.

A Distinguished Name is the best way for you to name objects in map statements, login scripts, and capture statements because you will always include the common name and the context of the object. If you are trying to locate or name an object in a multicontext environment that is not in your context, the best way to do so is with a Distinguished Name.

A Distinguished Name can be typeful or typeless, which means exactly that. In a typeful name, you type more, whereas in a typeless name, you type less. Actually, in a typeful name, you include an Attribute type followed by an equal sign to define what each naming element is. In a typeless name, you do not include the Attribute types.

Following are the four Attribute types:

➤ Country–C

➤ Organization–O

➤ Organizational Unit–Ou

➤ Leaf Object (Common Name)–CN

For the exam, these are the four Attribute types you need to know. Additional Attribute types are part of both the base schema and the schema when extended, but they are beyond the scope of this book.

Alexandra's typeful Distinguished Name is as follows:

.CN=Alexandra.Ou=Educational.Ou=Sales.O=3WsNetWorking.C=US

Following is Alexandra's typeless Distinguished Name:

.Alexandra.Educational.Sales.3WsNetWorking.US

Notice that each Distinguished Name begins with a leading period. That is the indicator of a Distinguished Name. Don't forget that. Also, note the lack of a trailing period at the end of the name. A trailing period indicates a Relative Distinguished Name.

Most NetWare utilities let you use either a typeful or typeless name to authenticate. Some utilities still maintain the need for a typeful Distinguished Name for authentication. The more that you use LDAP, the more you should become comfortable with typeful names.

In LDAP naming, contextual elements are separated by a comma, not a period. When you authenticate to Remote Manager or use ICE to import or export an LDIF file, you need to use LDAP naming conventions.

A workstation's current context is where the workstation is configured to look for objects in the eDirectory. This is called Name Context in some utilities. Current context reflects your current position, at your workstation, in the eDirectory tree.

When you try to authenticate to the tree, if you do not use a Distinguished Name, you have to be aware of your workstation's current context. Based on the container that the workstation is configured to look in, you have to adjust your username to authenticate successfully. In Figure 5.2, if Alexandra's workstation had a current context of Sales.3WsNetWorking.US, and she tried to log in simply as Alexandra, she would fail to authenticate. Her user object is in Educational.Sales.3WsNetWorking.US. If her current context was Educational.Sales.3WsNetWorking.US and she tried to log in simply as Alexandra, she would succeed. Alexandra is her common name, or Relative Distinguished Name.

A Relative Distinguished Name is an object's common name relative to a workstation's current context. A Relative Distinguished Name never has a leading period, but it might have a trailing period. In addition, a Relative Distinguished Name's contextual elements are separated by periods. A trailing period (a period at the end of the name) is used as a shortcut to remove the leftmost such contextual element, as exists in the current context. If more than one trailing period is used, more than one contextual element is removed.

If Alexandra's current context is 3WsNetWorking.US, her typeful Relative Distinguished Name is as follows:

CN=Alexandra.Ou=Educational.Ou=Sales

Following is her typeless Relative Distinguished Name:

Alexandra.Educational.Sales

Neither of these examples has a leading period, which means each is a Relative Distinguished Name.

3WsNetWorking.US (refer to Figure 5.2) has a user named Ronnie. If Ronnie's current context is Educational.Sales.3WsNetWorking.US, Ronnie could authenticate using either a Distinguished Name or a Relative Distinguished Name with trailing periods. Ronnie's typeless Relative Distinguished Name would be this:

Ronnie ..

The two trailing periods remove the two leftmost such contextual elements as exist in the current context. In this case, those two trailing periods remove Educational and Sales from the current context. That would leave the current context as 3WsNetworking.US, where Ronnie's User object exists.

From this discussion, you can see that the following is true:

Relative Distinguished Name + Current Context = Distinguished Name

There's one important point that you shouldn't overlook: Every object in eDirectory has a Relative Distinguished and Distinguished Name. This includes Volume objects, Server objects, and Container objects. The rules that apply to naming a User object also apply to all other objects. In addition, the simplest name that users can log in with is their username with no trailing or leading periods. That is their Relative Distinguished Name when their current context is pointing to their context.

You must know the difference between Distinguished and Relative Distinguished Names, typeful and typeless, and Context and Current context. Practice naming the objects you see in Figure 5.2. Be sure you know which has a leading period and which does not.

One cool utility that you can use with your current context is CX. CX is a NetWare command-line utility that allows you to view or change your current context.

To see all of the possible options that are available with CX, at a command prompt, enter the following (see Figure 5.3):

```
CX /?
```

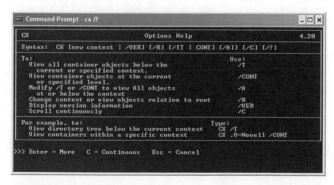

Figure 5.3   CX Help screen.

Following are the most widely used CX options:

➤ /R to change your current context to the Root of the tree

➤ /T to view all containers in your current context

➤ /A to view all objects in your current context

Enter the following:

```
CX /T /A /R
```

You will see all objects in all containers up to and including the Root of the tree.

You can also move from Container to Container either by entering a sub-container's name or by using a trailing period to move up the tree. See Figure 5.4 for some examples of what you can do with CX.

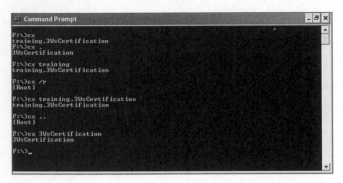

Figure 5.4 CX examples.

The last concept that is worth noting under this objective is inheritance. You will hear much more about inheritance in Chapters 8, "File System Security," and 9, "eDirectory Security," but because this objective deals with the flow and design of eDirectory, it's necessary to mention inheritance in passing.

When you design your eDirectory tree, with all of its Containers and Leaf objects, and you know how to name all of them, you need to take into consideration how the design affects both eDirectory security and file system security. Inheritance in this context is a security concept. It's the process of rights flowing down from a higher level to a lower level in both the eDirectory tree and the NetWare 6.5 file system. Consider how inheritance impacts security as you design your tree.

Now that you know how to name and locate eDirectory objects, you need to be able to identify four tools that will become your best friends when it comes to managing eDirectory.

Identify eDirectory Tools and When to Use Them

Your four best friends when it comes to managing eDirectory are as follows:

➤ NetWare Administrator

➤ ConsoleOne

➤ iManager

➤ iMonitor

NetWare Administrator is a Windows-based eDirectory management utility for creating, deleting, moving, and renaming objects. In NetWare 6.5, it is also valuable for configuring printing and licensing. In addition, you can use it to manage the NetWare 6.5 file system. In Figure 5.5, you can see three windows open in NetWare Adminsitrator for managing the tree, the file system, and one of the many containers in the 3WsCertification tree.

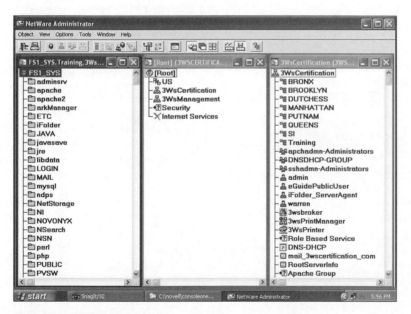

Figure 5.5 NetWare Administrator.

Following is the path to the NetWare Administrator executable
`NWADMN32.EXE`:

`SYS:\PUBLIC\WIN32`

Although NetWare Administrator is not the fair-haired child of Novell as it was in the mid to late 1990s, it is still one of the best eDirectory tools around. Novell is no longer making NetWare Administrator snap-ins available for many of the tasks that are now performed in eDirectory. For those, Novell wants people to use ConsoleOne or iManager.

Versions of NetWare Administrator that used to run on Windows 95 and Windows NT were found in the **PUBLIC\Win95** and **PUBLIC\WINNT** directories, respectively. You can still find those directories in the NetWare 6.5 file system.

ConsoleOne is a Java-based eDirectory management utility for managing large eDirectory trees. You can use it for creating, deleting, moving, and renaming objects; extending the schema; configuring partitions and replicas; managing the file system; and assigning rights. Early in this chapter in Figure 5.1, you saw an example of ConsoleOne's interface. Because ConsoleOne is Java based, it can run on a host of non-Windows platforms. Up to NetWare 6, ConsoleOne was the tool of choice for eDirectory management. You can find the ConsoleOne executable, `CONSOLEONE.EXE`, on a NetWare 6.5 server at `SYS:\PUBLIC\MGMT\CONSOLEONE\1.2\BIN`.

With the dawn of NetWare 6 and now NetWare 6.5, Novell is moving many of the ConsoleOne and NetWare Administrator tasks to iManager, as shown in Figure 5.6.

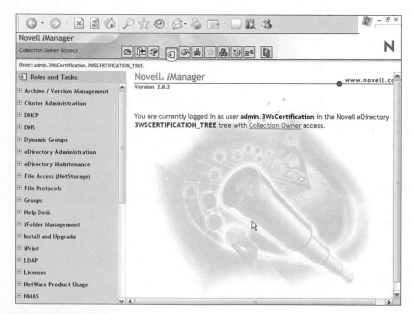

Figure 5.6　iManager.

iManager is a browser-based management tool that is the tool of choice for most eDirectory tasks. The opening iManager screen shows the wide range of tasks that you can perform. These include managing DNS, DHCP, iPrint, eDirectory, Roles and Tasks, Role Based Service configuration, NSS storage devices, licenses, NMAS, Rights, Users, and Virtual Office.

The URL to access iManager is `https://server_ip_address/nps/ iManager.html`.

iMonitor, shown in Figure 5.7, is one of the Web Services tools that ships with NetWare 6.5. You can monitor and diagnose servers in your eDirectory tree from any computer that has a compatible browser installed. Traditional NetWare diagnostic tools such as DSTRACE, DSBROWSE, DSDIAG, and DSREPAIR are incorporated into iMonitor. You can still use many of these server-based tools, although much of their functionality is now built into the workstation-based iMonitor.

Following are some of the iMonitor tasks that you can perform:

➤ DSREPAIR

➤ Health summary, including synchronization information

➤ Health check

➤ Agent configuration and information

➤ Partitions

➤ DirXML monitor

➤ Reports and error information

What you are able to do in iMonitor is based on who you are logged in as and what rights you have been granted. If you are a user without Supervisor object rights to the server object, you cannot run DSREPAIR. You can use iMonitor to keep an eye on the following server platforms:

➤ NetWare 4.11 and higher

➤ Windows NT/2000/2003

➤ Linux, Unix, Tru64 Unix

You can access iMonitor by using either of the following URLs:

`https://server_ip_address:8009/nds`

`http://server_ip_address:8008/nds`

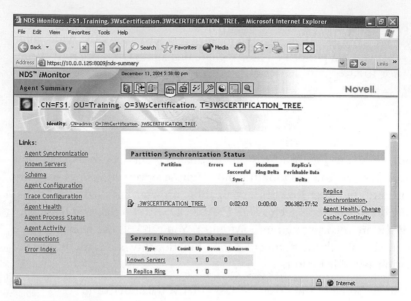

Figure 5.7 iMonitor.

Exam Prep Questions

1. You need to launch NetWare Administrator to manage eDirectory on your NetWare 6.5 server. Which of the following is the correct path to the NetWare Administrator executable?

A. ○ **SYS:\PUBLIC\MGMT\NETWARE ADMINISTRATOR\NWADMN32.EXE**

B. ○ **SYS:\SYSTEM\NWADMN32.EXE**

C. ○ **C:\NWSERVER\NWADMN32.EXE**

D. ○ **SYS:\PUBLIC\WIN32\NWADMN32.EXE**

Answer D is correct. Answers A, B, and C are incorrect. The correct path to the NetWare Administrator executable, on a NetWare 6.5 server, is SYS:\PUBLIC\WIN32\NWADMN32.EXE. The other options do not exist on a NetWare 6.5 server.

2. You need to launch ConsoleOne to manage eDirectory on your NetWare 6.5 server. Which of the following is the correct path to the ConsoleOne executable on your server?

A. ○ **SYS:\PUBLIC\BIN\CONSOLEONE.EXE**

B. ○ **SYS:\SYSTEM\MGMT\CONSOLEONE\1.2\BIN\CONSOLEONE.EXE**

C. ○ **SYS:\PUBLIC\MGMT\CONSOLEONE\1.2\BIN\CONSOLEONE.EXE**

D. ○ **SYS:\MGMT\CONSOLEONE\1.2\BIN\CONSOLEONE.EXE**

Answer C is correct. Answers A, B, and D are incorrect. The correct path to the ConsoleOne executable on a NetWare 6.5 server is SYS:\PUBLIC\MGMT\CONSOLEONE\1.2\BIN\CONSOLEONE.EXE. The other options are not the default location for ConsoleOne.

3. An object's location in the eDirectory tree is called the object's

_____.

The correct answer is context. An object's context in eDirectory is the object's location in the tree.

4. The _____ defines the types of objects that you can create in the eDirectory tree, where you can create them, and what properties you need to create them.

The correct answer is schema. The eDirectory schema is the set of rules governing object creation and placement in the tree. It also defines the required and optional properties of an object.

5. Based on Figure 5.8, the typeful distinguished name for Emma is_____.

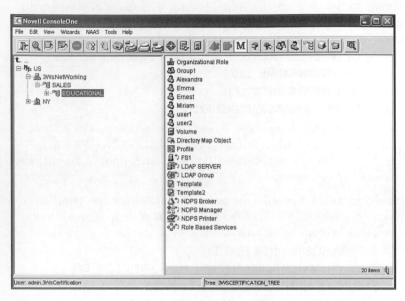

Figure 5.8

The correct answer is the following: .CN=EMMA.OU= EDUCATIONAL.OU=SALES.O=3WsNetWorking.C=US

Remember that a distinguished name has a leading period, period separators between contextual elements, and no trailing period(s). A typeful name includes an object's attribute with an equal sign in each contextual element.

6. Which command can you run at a command prompt if you want to change your workstation's current context to the top of the tree?

A. ○ **CX**

B. ○ **CX /T**

C. ○ **CX /A /T**

D. ○ **CX /R**

Answer D is correct. To change your current context to the top, [Root], of the tree, you can run the cx /R command. Answers A, B, and C are incorrect. Answer A displays your current context. Answer B displays containers in your current context. Answer C displays all objects and containers in your current context.

7. In Figure 5.9, circle the eDirectory container object.

Figure 5.9

The correct response is to circle Role Based Services. All other objects in Figure 5.9 are Leaf objects.

8. Which of the following are Leaf objects? (Select all that apply.)

A. ❑ Domain

B. ❑ Group

C. ❑ Server

D. ❑ Country

Answers B and C are correct. A Group and a Server are eDirectory Leaf objects. Answers A and D are incorrect. Domain and Country are Container objects.

9. Which objects can the Tree object contain? (Select all that apply.)

A. ❑ Organization

B. ❑ Country

C. ❑ User

D. ❑ Organizational Unit

Answers A and B are correct. Answers C and D are incorrect. The Tree object can contain the Country object, the Organization object, the Security container, or Alias objects to the Country object. It cannot contain an Organizational Unit object or a User object. An Organization object can contain an Organizational Unit and all Leaf objects.

10. Which Leaf object represents users who are called occupants?

    A. ○ Group

    B. ○ Alias

    C. ○ Organizational Role

    D. ○ LDAP group

Answer C is correct. Users who are part of an Organizational Role object are called occupants, unlike users who are part of a Group, who are called members. Answers A and B are incorrect. Leaf objects, like the Alias object, do not hold occupants or members. Answer D is incorrect, because the members of an LDAP Group are Server objects. In ConsoleOne, the Members tab is labeled Server List.

Introduction to the
NetWare 6.5 File System

Terms you'll need to understand:

- ✓ Volume
- ✓ Directory
- ✓ Traditional volume
- ✓ **SYS**
- ✓ **DATA**
- ✓ **APPS**
- ✓ **ADMIN**
- ✓ NSS volume
- ✓ Partition

- ✓ Pool
- ✓ Logical volume
- ✓ Overbooking
- ✓ **SYSTEM** directory
- ✓ **PUBLIC** directory
- ✓ **LOGIN** directory
- ✓ Mirroring
- ✓ Duplexing

Techniques you'll need to master:

- ✓ Identify network file service components
- ✓ Identify types of NetWare volume storage
- ✓ Identify the guidelines for planning Network volumes
- ✓ Identify the content and purpose of NetWare **SYS** directories

- ✓ Identify the types of directories used for organizing a file system
- ✓ Evaluate directory structures

You have tackled the eDirectory side of NetWare 6.5 administration. Now you need to begin looking at file system administration. Managing the network file system is the point at which most admins begin interacting with NetWare. The only difference between managing the NetWare 6.5 file system and the file system in earlier versions of NetWare is that now there is a bit more to manage. Other than that, the tasks and skills are the same.

In this chapter, you learn what makes up the file system after a default installation, the types of volumes in NetWare 6.5, some basic guidelines for creating and organizing data using NetWare 6.5 volumes, the directories that the system creates, directories that Novell suggests you create for management purposes, and evaluating whether your file system design is good or bad.

Identify Network File Service Components

The NetWare 6.5 file system is much like the DOS and Linux file systems. It is hierarchical, meaning that data can be organized in a series of directories, subdirectories, and files. The only unique component to the NetWare file system is the fundamental unit of storage called the volume. When compared to DOS, a volume is similar to what you might call the C: drive. The C: drive might be a complete hard drive or a partition on a hard drive that holds directories, subdirectories, and files.

When you installed the NetWare 6.5 operating system, you were asked to create a single volume: SYS. This is the default storage volume created on a NetWare server. You can create other volumes, but the SYS volume is the only unit of storage that is required on a NetWare server, and it is the first volume that is created.

When you create a storage group and Novell Storage Services (NSS) volume, such as the **SYS** volume, during the operating system installation, the **_ADMIN** volume is created automatically. This is a read-only volume that holds a dynamic list of objects that NSS uses. At the server console when you display the mounted volumes, you see that the **_ADMIN** volume has the **P** attribute, which indicates that you cannot delete it. In NetWare 6.5, **files.cmd** was added to the **_ADMIN** volume for applications such as NetStorage, which use it to communicate with the server. Unlike past versions of NetWare, the **_ADMIN** volume is visible to users. The content of the **_ADMIN** volume on a NetWare 6.5 server with support pack 2 installed is shown in Figure 6.1.

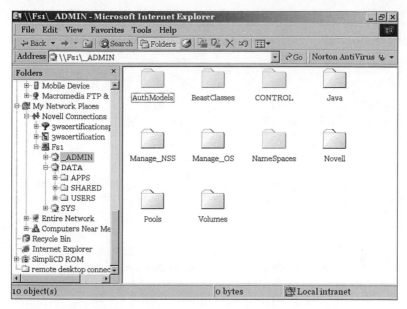

Figure 6.1   The **_ADMIN** volume.

A volume can be all of the space on a hard drive, the space spanned across multiple hard drives, the space on a CD or DVD, or the free space on several storage devices combined. A hard drive, depending on the type of volumes being considered, can hold multiple volumes. Just remember that a volume is the most fundamental unit of NetWare storage.

A volume contains directories, subdirectories, and files. A directory can hold files or subdirectories; it is a file system container. A subdirectory is a subcontainer of a directory that can hold files and other subdirectories. Files are the actual data and application units that are stored in directories, subdirectories, and at the root of a volume. It is worth noting that you do not, technically, need directories or subdirectories on a volume. You can store all your data and application files at the root of a NetWare volume, but it would be difficult to manage security and locate your data. Develop an organizational design for your file system that works best for your environment.

Perhaps you have not fully migrated to a paperless method of data collection. If you still use the old, reliable file cabinet, Table 6.1 might help you understand the NetWare 6.5 file system.

Table 6.1 Traditional File Cabinet and the NetWare 6.5 File System	
Traditional File Cabinet	**NetWare 6.5 File System**
File cabinet	File server
File cabinet drawer	Volume
Hanging file folder	Directory
Manila file folder inside a hanging file folder	Subdirectory
Paper files and documents	Files

As elementary as Table 6.1 seems, it is great fodder for proving conceptual understanding of NetWare storage components.

You can name volumes using one of two conventions: a physical volume name or a volume object name. This is covered in more detail in Chapter 7, "Basic Management Tasks—eDirectory and File System." A physical volume name is denoted by a backslash between the name of the file server and the volume. A volume object name is denoted by an underscore between the name of the file server and the volume. All volume names have a colon (:) at the end of the name, regardless of whether you use a physical name or volume object name. Following is an example of a physical volume name and a volume object name for the SYS volume:

Physical Volume Name

FS1\SYS:

Volume Object Name

FS1_SYS:

Now you know the basic file system components and how to name NetWare volumes. In earlier versions of NetWare, only one type of volume was available. NetWare 5 and, most importantly, NetWare 6.x have two major types of volumes. You need to be familiar with these two storage types.

Identify Types of NetWare Volume Storage

The two types of NetWare volumes in NetWare 6.5 are as follows:

➤ Traditional

➤ NSS

Unlike earlier versions of NetWare, the default volume type in NetWare 6.5 is the NSS volume. During server installation, you can configure the SYS volume as a Traditional volume, but by default, it is an NSS volume.

Traditional Volumes

A Traditional volume is the fundamental unit of storage used prior to NetWare 5.1. It is provided in NetWare 6.5 for those who need or want to store data on Traditional volumes, using the Traditional File Services technology. Traditional File Services is a 32-bit system. A Traditional volume is a fixed amount of storage space that can be part of a single drive, take up a complete drive, or span multiple drives.

With Traditional volumes, you first create a NetWare partition on a drive. Then you create the volume or volumes that will store data in that partition.

You can have up to 63 Traditional volumes on a NetWare 6.5 server in addition to a traditional SYS volume. The maximum Traditional volume size is 1TB, spanned over a maximum of 32 segments.

When you mount a Traditional volume, its File Allocation Table (FAT) and Directory Entry Table (DET) are loaded into server memory. The more Traditional volumes you mount, the more server memory you will use.

 When a volume is mounted, it is available to users for data storage. When a volume is dismounted, it is no longer available to users.

NSS Volumes

The NSS file system is Novell's answer to the current need for storing large databases, numerous files, or huge volumes, and being able to mount them quickly. NSS is a 64-bit file storage technology. An NSS volume has a maximum size of 8TB and can store up to 8 trillion files. A NetWare 6.5 server can have a maximum of 255 NSS and Traditional volumes, in addition to the SYS volume, mounted at the same time. If all volumes are NSS, an unlimited number of NSS volumes can be mounted on a NetWare 6.5 server.

One unique, highly marketable feature of NSS volumes is that they do not have to scan the entire file system when mounted, as Traditional volumes do. Rather, NSS volumes use a Journaling File System, which does not need to scan the entire file system to load the FAT and DET into memory and allows large volumes to mount quickly, store huge amounts of data, and avoid corruption. Only when files are accessed are they entered into the FAT, not when the volume is mounted. Because of this feature, NSS volumes do not require additional memory to mount.

Unlike Traditional volumes, which use a NetWare partition and volume architecture, NSS uses partitions, storage pools, and logical volumes.

A NetWare partition is a defined amount of hard disk space that is dedicated to the NetWare operating system.

A storage pool is free space that is gathered from the storage devices in your NetWare 6.5 server.

A logical volume is similar to a Traditional volume in that it can store data in directories and subdirectories. However, it is different because an NSS volume can have a defined amount of space allocated to it or be allowed to grow dynamically as the need arises.

Following is the order of NSS component creation:

1. Partitions

2. Pools

3. Logical Volumes

There is a reason that I have repeated this order of component creation several times over the course of this text. You should know this order like you know your own name. It is that important in NetWare 6.5.

First you create a partition. After that, you can create one or more storage pools based on the storage space available from the installed storage devices. In those pools, you can then create one or more logical volumes.

Following are some key NSS points to remember:

➤ A partition can only be tied to a single pool.

➤ A pool can have one or more logical volumes.

➤ If a pool has a single logical volume, the volume cannot grow to be larger than the pool.

➤ If a pool has multiple logical volumes, the volumes can be set to grow dynamically, or the sum of the volumes can be set to be larger than the size of the NetWare partition. This lets a volume borrow space from the pool as the need arises. Overbooking is the NSS feature that allows the sum of the volume sizes to be larger than the defined size of the partition they are in.

➤ Unlike Traditional volumes that you repaired when they crashed, in NSS, you repair the pool, not the volume. This lets you potentially repair multiple volumes at the same time when you repair the pool, if the pool has multiple logical volumes.

For a summary comparison of Traditional and NSS volumes, look at http://www.novell.com/documentation/nw65/index.html?page=/ documentation/nw65/sdiskenu/data/akimeps.html#akimeps.

Now that you are familiar with the types of NetWare storage options, it is time to explore Novell's design recommendations for the NetWare 6.5 file system.

Identify the Guidelines for Planning Network Volumes

The key guidelines for planning your NetWare 6.5 network, server, file system, and eDirectory can be summarized in the following three points:

➤ Make it easy to use for the end users.

➤ Make it easy for you to administer.

➤ Make it secure.

Remember: If it is not easy to use, your users will complain, and you will be miserable. Also, if it is not easy to administer, you will be miserable. If the design is not easily secured, you will definitely be miserable and be looking for a career change.

Some of you might be wondering if you have read this already in this book. You have. I am not suffering memory lapses. In every aspect of design, these three points continue to show up, so they need to be repeated. They are especially critical when planning the file system.

Those are the guidelines for the overall file system. Novell encourages you to consider additional guidelines when planning your volumes. These guidelines include the following:

➤ Keep the SYS volume for the operating system files and files that the server requires. This includes any support packs that you might have to install. Do not store volatile data on the SYS volume. If the SYS volume

runs out of space, the server ceases to function. For those of you who
have had the pleasure of seeing the SYS volume crash because of lack of
space, it is an ugly sight that you do not want to experience again.
Novell recommends that you create a file system that has multiple volumes. One that is highly regarded is shown in Figure 6.2. When you are
planning your NetWare 6.5 file system or any networked file system,
design the system with a minimum of two major halves: DATA and
Programs/Applications/Executables. On a NetWare server, also take
into account the system files on SYS.

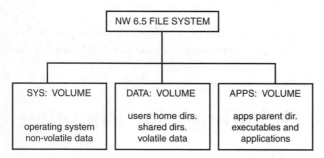

Figure 6.2   A NetWare 6.5 file system design.

➤ NSS volumes have all namespace capabilities on by default. By default,
an NSS volume supports DOS, Long, Macintosh and Unix namespace
requirements. This is unlike what happens on a Traditional volume,
which by default only supports the DOS namespace. You must take this
consideration into account when planning the types of volumes you
want on your server.

➤ When you plan your file system, provide meaningful, recognizable
names for the volumes. Do not do what Novell used to recommend, and
name your volumes Vol1, Vol2, and so on. Give the volumes names that
you will be able to recognize. One of my former students, who still uses
print queues, sets aside a whole volume for them and calls it QUEUES. In
his environment, that is a great idea. He has set an attribute on the
QUEUES directory on this volume that purges all deleted files immediately. You will learn how to set this attribute in Chapter 8, "File System
Security." The result is he has no maintenance on this volume that he
clearly can identify.

➤ When you are planning your file system, use one drive per volume if
your major concern is fault tolerance and not performance. One example of this is to put the SYS volume on one drive, the DATA volume on

another drive, and the APPS volume on a third drive. If any one drive fails, you still have the other two and only need to perform a restore to be back up and running. If performance is your major concern, span the volume over several drives. The problem with spanning a volume over several drives is that if any one of the drives fails, you lose the volume and all other data on that drive.

➤ You can protect your data using one of the low-level RAID (Redundant Array of Inexpensive Disks) technologies. The two that are most often mentioned are Mirroring and Duplexing. In a mirror, you have identical data being written to two drives on the same channel. If one of the drives fails, the other drive automatically takes over. In a duplex configuration, you have identical data being written to two drives that are on separate channels. Each channel has its own storage controller and cable. In a mirror configuration, if the channel or cable fails, you could still lose your data because you do not have access to either drive. In a duplex configuration, if one channel fails, you have a redundant channel to access your mirrored drive. The downside to mirror and duplex configurations is that you have access to only 50% of the overall installed storage capacity. If you have two 100GB drives in a mirror or duplex configuration, you really only have 100GB of storage capacity. The other 100GB is an online identical backup.

Now that you know what you should do with the file system, you need to know what the installation gave you in the file system on the SYS volume.

Identify the Content and Purpose of NetWare **SYS** Directories

You need to know what you get when you do a clean install of the NetWare 6.5 operating system. Novell used to call these system-created directories. The only confusing aspect to that term is that not all directories that are system created are created at the time of server installation. Some are created by the system after some event, such as when all files in a directory are deleted along with the directory. Some of the directories found on the SYS volume, shown in Figure 6.3, that you should be aware of include the following:

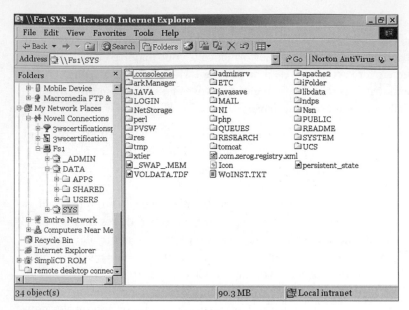

Figure 6.3 System-Created Directories on the **SYS** volume.

➤ **apache2**—This contains files for the Apache Web Server.

➤ **adminsrv**—This contains files for the Apache Server that manages iManager, iFolder, and other Web-based utilities.

➤ **ETC**—This contains TCP/IP sample and configuration files.

➤ **JAVA and javasave**—These contain Java-related files.

➤ **LOGIN**—This is the only directory that a user can see before authenticating to the tree. This directory contains the various iterations of LOGIN.EXE and CX.EXE for changing your current context.

➤ **MAIL**—This is a legacy directory that contains old hexadecimal mailboxes used in earlier versions of NetWare. One such program that used the MAIL directory was Pegasus. MAIL was also used for bindery-based user login scripts and print job configurations. Newly created eDirectory users will not have or need the MAIL directory.

➤ **ndps**—This contains files related to Novell Distributed Print Services, such as printer definition files and drivers.

➤ **NI**—This directory is a mystery to many NetWare users. It contains files related to the server installation. It also contains response files generated during the server install that document all of your responses during the installation. These response files are covered in depth in Appendix D, "Sample Response File."

➤ **Nsn, perl, and php**—These contain Novell Script-, Perl Script-, and PHP-related files, respectively.

➤ **PVSW**—This contains license and client files used by the Pervasive SQL Server components.

➤ **PUBLIC**—This is an important directory for all Novell users. It contains a host of NetWare utilities that users and administers rely on. You can find utilities such as MAP.EXE, NDIR.EXE, FLAG.EXE, FILER.EXE, CONSOLEONE.EXE, and NETWARE ADMINISTRATOR in the PUBLIC directory. All admins should carefully analyze the PUBLIC directory. By default, all users can access utilities such as FILER and ConsoleOne. This can potentially cause a major security gaff. Only leave those utilities in this directory that users absolutely need access to. Move other utilities, such as FILER, to a directory such as SYSTEM, which only admins have access to.

Many new admins are not familiar with **FILER**, which was a staple in the NetWare 3 and 4 days. **FILER** is a powerful file system utility for creating, modifying, and deleting directories and files. You can also use it to modify attributes and grant rights. **FILER** does bring a potential danger to a NetWare environment. If a user is mistakenly granted excessive rights, he could permanently delete the entire file structure on the **SYS** volume with a single keystroke. The likelihood of this happening is remote, but it can and has happened. When I demonstrate this danger in class, admins of school systems especially are taken back. Forewarned is forearmed. I strongly suggest you move **FILER** from the **PUBLIC** directory to the **SYSTEM** directory for administrative use only. This is not Novell's position, but it's mine based on experience.

➤ **QUEUES**—This is a directory that is created for backward compatibility with queue-based printing requirements. It's created by default on the SYS volume, but you should move it to another volume because of its volatility.

➤ **SYSTEM**—This contains most of the NLMs that control the NetWare 6.5 operating system, including utilities and administrative applications. This directory should be available only to admins and the operating system, not to the public.

➤ **tomcat**—This contains important files that the Tomcat servlet engine uses. This engine works in cooperation with Apache to provide many of the Web-based management tools that are used in NetWare 6.5.

➤ **DELETED.SAV**—This is system created but not at the time of server installation. This directory is created when all files in a directory on a Traditional volume are deleted but not purged from the system. Then the directory that was holding those files is subsequently deleted. DELETED.SAV holds those files for future salvage operations. By default,

DELETED.SAV is not used on current versions of NSS volumes. You can manually create a DELETED.SAV directory on an NSS volume. Figure 6.3 shows a default set of directories on the SYS volume, which is an NSS volume. Because SYS is an NSS volume, DELETED.SAV is not present.

NOTE

Novell has a good Technical Information Document (TID) titled "Salvaging Files in Subdirs of an NSS Volume." It explains how **DELETED.SAV** is used on NSS volumes and Traditional volumes. You can find this document at **http://support.novell.com/cgi-bin/search/searchtid.cgi?/10061387.htm**.

Despite this, you must know about the **DELETED.SAV** directory for the exam.

This brings up a major point for those of you from NetWare 4 and 5 environments. Some management features that you take for granted with Traditional volumes are different on NSS volumes. For example, **MONITOR.NLM** is the standard tool for managing cache on Traditional volumes. You cannot manage cache on an NSS volume using **MONITOR.NLM**. NSS volumes are managed at the server console with a host of commands. Some that you should be aware of, not for the exam, but for your everyday management duties, are the following:

NSS HELP

NSS STATUS

NSS CACHESTATS

NSS POOLS

NSS VOLUMES

CDDVD.NSS

DOSFAT.NSS

NSS /ZLSSVOLUMEUPGRADE=

Two other NSS commands that are noteworthy are **/POOLREBUILD** and **/POOLVERI-FY**. These replace the **VREPAIR** command used on Traditional volumes. Only use them under extreme conditions. Only use **/POOLREBUILD** as a lastditch option to save a pool.

Take a close look at **NSS HELP** to see what each command is used for. You will be amazed at the NSS capabilities available using just these few server console commands.

If you want to convert a Traditional volume to an NSS volume, use **VCU.NLM**. The default syntax for **VCU.NLM** is this:

VCU *Traditional_volume NSS_pool*

Look at the following article for information on tuning NSS volumes: **http://developer.novell.com/research/appnotes/2002/july/01/a0207015.htm**.

For information on purging and salvaging files on an NSS volume, see **http://www.novell.com/documentation/nw65/index.html?page=/documentation/nw65/nss_enu/data/bqq4w30.html**.

For a complete overview of NSS volumes on a NetWare 6.5 server, see **http://www.novell.com/documentation/nw65/nss_enu/data/hn0r5fzo.html**.

One last cautionary note regarding NSS volumes: If you are running a NetWare 6 server, you should minimally install SP3 and SP2 on a NetWare 6.5 server. NSS has gone through a long maturation process. It has not always performed according to published documentation. NetWare 6 SP3 and NetWare 6.5 SP2 resolved many of the published problems and have proved to offer stable NSS environments for their respective operating systems.

These are some of the directories that NetWare 6.5 creates automatically. Now you will learn some of the key directories that you have to create to set up a top-notch NetWare 6.5 environment.

Identify the Types of Directories Used for Organizing a File System

Now that you know what the system gives you, you need to know what directories you should create after installation. Novell strongly recommends these four:

➤ **USERS or HOME parent directory**—This is a directory found at the root of a volume where you will store your users' individual home directories for their private files. The purpose of this directory is to prevent users from having their home directories at the root of a volume where security becomes an issue. To avoid this, you create a USERS or HOME directory. Then when you create a user, the system creates the user's home directory, if you choose for it to do so, under this parent directory. That gives users a file system hierarchy to work with. You can create a user account manager, who will be responsible for just this branch of the file system. Users are not given rights to the parent directory, only to their personal directory. Only a users account manager or admin is given rights to the USERS directory. This USERS parent directory should (when possible) not be on the SYS volume. This is a great candidate for a DATA volume because the data in this directory is highly volatile. Also, by placing this on a separate volume, backups of only user data become simplified.

➤ **SHARED parent directory**—This is a directory found at the root of a volume where groups of users can store collaborative data. This should not be on the SYS volume because of its volatility. A good candidate for this parent directory is the DATA volume. A good design for the subdirectories under SHARED consists of a General and a Departmental directory. In the SHARED\General directory, users in an organization can share upcoming events, policy statements, and company vacation days. In the SHARED\Departmental directory, you could create a tree of departments, where users in each department could share data that is only for their people. For example, in Shared\Departmental\Sales, those in the Sales department would store collaborative data that is unique to their users.

➤ **APPS parent directory**—This directory is found at the root of a volume where you would install your network installed applications. This should not be on the SYS volume because of the large amount of space it could potentially require. A good candidate for this parent directory is the APPS volume mentioned earlier. In the APPS parent directory, you might have subdirectories of WP, SS, DB, Prst, and PDFviewers. Under each of these, you would create a directory structure required by your applications.

➤ **CONFIGURATION directories**—These are directories (note that more than one is possible) that are often placed in users' home directories or in the applications' directories that they pertain to. These might simply be a configuration file or .ini file that governs how an application should react when a user launches it. One example that Novell cites for these directories is ZENworks profile directories. In the education sector, if you are using a gradebook program, you might need some type of configuration directory in each teacher home directory for the gradebook program to display correctly.

On a server that only has a SYS volume and a DATA volume, you can place the USERS, SHARED, and APPS parent directories on DATA. This is shown in Figure 6.4.

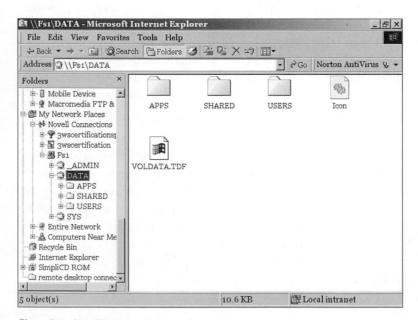

Figure 6.4 Novell's suggested parent directories.

To summarize, Novell suggests that you create USERS, SHARED, and APPS parent directories and some type of configuration directories for the applications that require them.

You now have a solid understanding of what a good file system design looks like. It's time to pull all of this knowledge together so that you can evaluate a NetWare 6.5 file system structure.

Evaluate Directory Structures

On the exam, you have to look at a directory structure and evaluate it for its strengths and weaknesses. To do this, you need to be keenly aware of the design guidelines discussed in this chapter and some additional ones. The following summarizes those points you should take with you into your production environment and into the exam:

1. Reserve the SYS volume for operating system files and nonvolatile files.

2. Create USERS, SHARED, and APPS parent directories. Do not store applications or data on the root of a volume.

3. Whenever possible, create multiple volumes that are distinctively named. This enables you to split administrative duties between those managing data, those managing applications, and those managing the operating system.

4. Do not have multiple USERS parent directories on different volumes. This drives a sane admin nuts trying to figure out where users' data is stored.

5. Keep the design simple and straightforward. Any admin walking into your shoes should be able to immediately identify the role and purpose of each volume and directory. Do not name volumes Vol1 and Vol2 or something unrecognizable like this.

6. If you have to create a one-volume structure, with just the SYS volume, keep data and applications separate from the operating system files.

7. Never store the QUEUES directory on the SYS volume. Print queues are volatile and can occupy a lot of space, even after being deleted but not purged.

8. It is a best practice to periodically check your volume space usage on the SYS volume, especially after you install a support pack, and purge any deleted files that you no longer need.

9. Consider whether you are most interested in fault tolerance or performance, and set up your volumes accordingly.

10. Last but not least, design the file system to be easy to use, easy to administer, and easy to secure.

Knowing these 10 guidelines will get you well on your way to being able to determine whether a file system structure is good or bad.

Exam Prep Questions

1. When compared to a traditional filing cabinet and its organization, which NetWare 6.5 file system component is most like a hanging folder in one of the file cabinet drawers?

   A. ○ Volume
   B. ○ File
   C. ○ Directory
   D. ○ Subdirectory

   Answer C is correct. Novell loves to compare the NetWare file system to a traditional filing cabinet. In this analogy, a NetWare volume is a file cabinet drawer, a directory is a hanging folder in a drawer, a subdirectory is a manila folder inside a hanging folder, and a file is the paper documents inside a manila folder. Answers A, B, and D are incorrect.

2. Which of the following represents a NetWare 6.5 volume with a physical volume name?

   A. ○ **FS1_DATA**
   B. ○ **FS1-DATA**
   C. ○ **FS1:DATA**
   D. ○ **FS1\DATA**

   Answer D is correct. The indicator of a physical volume name is a backslash between the server name and the volume name. Answer A is incorrect. This is volume object name, indicated by the underscore between the server name and the volume name. Answers B and C are not valid volume names in NetWare.

3. What is an NSS pool?

   A. ○ The most fundamental unit of storage in NetWare 6.5
   B. ○ An NSS feature that permits the sum of multiple units of storage to exceed the size of the partition
   C. ○ Free space obtained from one or more storage devices
   D. ○ A unit of storage that can be set to dynamically grow as the need arises

   Answer C is correct. An NSS pool is the free space obtained from one or more storage devices in a server. Answer A is incorrect. This is the default definition of a Traditional volume. Answer B is incorrect. This is the definition of overbooking. Answer D is incorrect. This is the definition of an NSS Logical volume.

4. Which volume should you reserve for operating system files?

   A. ○ **SYS**
   B. ○ **DATA**
   C. ○ **APPS**
   D. ○ **_ADMIN**

Answer A is correct. You should reserve the SYS volume for operating system files and administrative files that are nonvolatile. If the SYS volume runs out of space, the server cannot function. You must protect SYS. Answers B and C are incorrect. These are used for applications and private data that can be volatile. Answer D is incorrect. The operating system creates the _ADMIN volume automatically for communication with Web-based applications.

5. You are designing your NetWare 6.5 file system. Your CIO has informed you that your design should give fault tolerance a much higher priority than performance. Which NetWare 6.5 file system guideline should you follow?

A. ○ Create multiple volumes per disk.

B. ○ Create one volume per disk.

C. ○ Create multiple pools per disk.

D. ○ Create one NetWare partition per disk.

Answer B is correct. When your file system design dictates that fault tolerance is more important that performance, you should have one volume per disk. Answers A, C, and D are incorrect. None of these is appropriate if fault tolerance is more important than performance.

6. In which NetWare 6.5 directory do you find the FILER, FLAG, NetWare Administrator, MAP, NDIR, and ConsoleOne utilities?

A. ○ **SYSTEM**

B. ○ **LOGIN**

C. ○ **PUBLIC**

D. ○ **ETC**

Answer C is correct. The PUBLIC directory on the SYS volume holds NetWare utilities such as FLAG, FILER, MAP, NDIR, ConsoleOne, and NetWare Administrator. Answers A, B, and D are incorrect. These do not hold publicly accessible NetWare utilities. The LOGIN directory executables LOGIN.EXE and CX.EXE are publicly available for login, but they do not hold the other mentioned utilities.

7. Which NetWare 6.5 directory is only created on a Traditional volume when all files in a directory are deleted, but not purged, along with the directory that held them?

A. ○ **LOGIN**

B. ○ **NI**

C. ○ **DELETED.SAV**

D. ○ **QUEUES**

Answer C is correct. The DELETED.SAV directory is system created on Traditional volumes when all files in a directory are deleted but not purged, along with the directory that held them. Answers A and B are incorrect. The LOGIN and NI directories are created when the server is installed. Answer D is incorrect. QUEUES is not created when the system is installed, but is system created when the first print queue is created and configured.

8. Which of the following is a directory that Novell suggests that you, the CNA, create after the server has been installed?

   A. ○ **NSN**

   B. ○ **ZENWORKS**

   C. ○ **GROUPWISE**

   D. ○ **SHARED**

   Answer D is correct. Novell suggests that you create a SHARED parent directory as part of your overall file system design. Answer A is incorrect. The NSN directory is system created. Answers B and C are incorrect. These are suggested directories when and if you install GroupWise or ZENworks.

9. Which two parent directories does Novell suggest that you, the CNA, create after you've installed the server? (Select two.)

   A. ❑ **APPS**

   B. ❑ **USERS**

   C. ❑ **SYS**

   D. ❑ **CONFIG**

   Answers A and B are correct. Novell suggests that you create a USERS parent directory for your users' home directories, and an APPS parent directory for your installed applications. Answer C is incorrect. SYS is the first volume created when a server is installed. Answer D is incorrect. Novell does not suggest a CONFIG directory. Rather, it suggests that you create subdirectories either under your APPS hierarchy or in the users' home directories as needed for any application configuration files or .ini files.

10. Which guidelines should you follow when evaluating a NetWare 6.5 file system design? (Select three.)

    A. ❑ It is easy to use.

    B. ❑ It is easy to administer.

    C. ❑ It is easy to modify.

    D. ❑ It is easy to secure.

    Answers A, B, and D are correct. The file system should be easy to use for your users, easy to administer for you, and be easily secured. Answer C is incorrect. There is no guideline that a file system should be easy to modify.

Basic Management Tasks—eDirectory and File System

Terms you'll need to understand:

- ✓ Container login script
- ✓ Profile login script
- ✓ User login script
- ✓ Default login script
- ✓ Map
- ✓ REM
- ✓ Admin object

- ✓ Regular drive mapping
- ✓ Search drive mapping
- ✓ Template object
- ✓ eDirectory Administration
- ✓ Users
- ✓ GUID
- ✓ Hot Fix Redirection Area

Techniques you'll need to master:

- ✓ Describe the Admin object
- ✓ Create, delete, modify, and move User objects
- ✓ Create NSS volumes
- ✓ Create Traditional volumes

- ✓ Access volumes and applications using regular drive mappings and search drive mappings
- ✓ Identify the four major types of login scripts

The most fundamental administrative task that you have as a NetWare 6.5 CNA is managing User objects and the file system. In this chapter, you learn about the only User object that was created when your NetWare 6.5 environment was set up; the steps to create, modify, move, and delete User objects; the steps to create a Traditional and a Novell Storage Services (NSS) volume; and the steps for accessing those volumes using the MAP command and its options. Notice that you are dealing with the two faces of NetWare 6.5 administration in this chapter: eDirectory administration and file system administration. The next section looks at the Admin User object.

Describe the Admin Object

In earlier versions of NetWare, when you installed the operating system, a superuser, called Supervisor, was automatically created. Supervisor was impervious to attack. You could not delete or rename Supervisor, and you could not remove its rights.

In NetWare 6.5, when you install a NetWare server into a new eDirectory tree, you create a single User object called Admin. Admin is the only User object that is created in the new tree. No Guest User object or Group objects are created. Admin is given Supervisor rights to the Tree object and to the new server. That is where the similarity between Admin and Supervisor ends. Following are some of the major characteristics of Admin:

➤ Admin initially has rights to manage all aspects of an eDirectory tree, including the ability to create, delete, and modify objects.

➤ You can delete Admin from the tree.

➤ You can rename Admin, which is a good administrative practice to avoid hacking.

➤ Admin can lose its Supervisor rights to both the Tree and server objects.

➤ You can have multiple Admin objects with the same rights in the tree in different containers. This is a good administrative practice to prevent loss of control of the tree and its branches. If you have only a single Admin object, and that object is deleted, you lose complete control of the tree.

If your Admin object is deleted and it's the only one you have, you can still regain supervisor control of the tree using a custom NLM called **MAKESU.NLM**, available from DreamLan Network Consulting, LTD., at **http://www.dreamlan.com**. It's not free, but its cost is minimal when compared to having to rebuild an eDirectory tree from scratch.

As Admin with a new NetWare 6.5 server in a new eDirectory, you now must begin creating User objects so that your users can log in and utilize the services and resources that are available to them.

Create User Objects

You can use numerous utilities and procedures to create User objects. Depending on which you are comfortable with, you can create User objects with any of the following:

➤ NetWare Administrator

➤ ConsoleOne

➤ iManager

➤ Third-party utilities

> If you need to create multiple User objects, the most efficient way is to use one of the third-party utilities. Some of the best are available from JRB Software at **http://www.jrbsoftware.com/** and Wolfgang's Tools Network at **http://www.geocities.com/wstools/**.

For this exam, you need to know the steps to create a User object with iManager. You can use two links on the opening iManager screen to begin the process of creating a User object:

➤ eDirectory Administration

➤ Users

The Create Object link found under eDirectory Administration (see Figure 7.1) can be used to create most eDirectory objects, whereas the Create User link found under Users (see Figure 7.2) can only be used to create User objects.

> Do not confuse eDirectory Administration with eDirectory Maintenance. Under eDirectory Administration, you can create, delete, modify, move, and rename eDirectory objects. Under eDirectory Maintenance, you can configure backups, use the Import Conversion Export (ICE) Wizard, merge and rename a tree, repair a replica and a replica ring, and repair a server.
>
> The exam focuses on using the Create User link under Users in iManager.

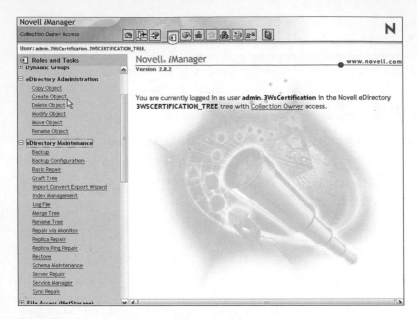

Figure 7.1 iManager: eDirectory Administration links.

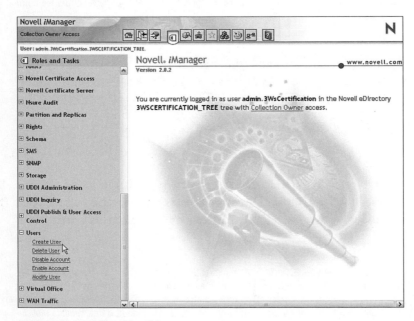

Figure 7.2 iManager: Users links.

Following are the steps to create a User object in iManager:

1. Under iManager, Users, select Create User.

2. You must provide the user with a Last Name, Username, and Context (see Figure 7.3).

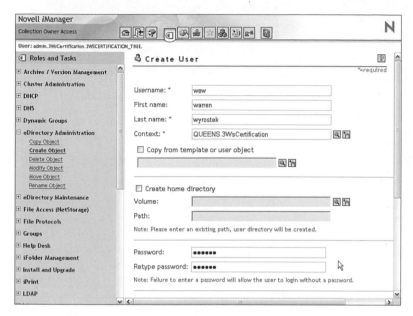

Figure 7.3   iManager: Create User.

3. Optionally, you can use a template object to create the user. A template is an eDirectory object that enables you to assign similar property values to multiple users. For example, if 50 users are being hired for the Science department, all having the same phone and fax numbers, you can create a template object called Science, fill in the Department, Telephone, and Fax Number fields, and then assign the template to each user by checking the Copy from Template or User Object box in the Create User screen. All users that you create then have those property values upon creation.

a. You can create a template object under eDirectory Administration, Create Object, Template Object, which results in the screen shown in Figure 7.4.

b. You assign values to a template object under eDirectory Administration, Modify Object, Select Your Template Object, which results in the screen shown in Figure 7.5.

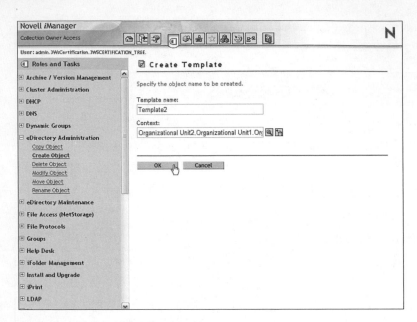

Figure 7.4 iManager: Create Template object.

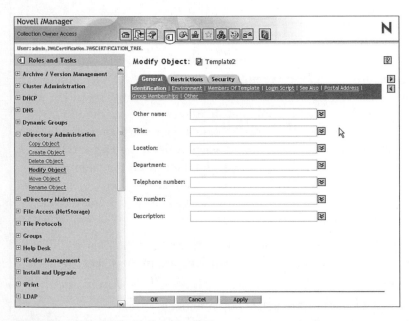

Figure 7.5 iManager: Modify Template object.

4. While creating a User object, you can automatically create a home directory on a NetWare 6.5 server, for a user's private files. You can do this by clicking on the Create Home Directory option and browsing to the correct volume and path.

5. You should initially assign the user a password for security purposes. This is optional, but it is a good administrative practice.

6. You can optionally provide values for the user's title, location, department, telephone, fax number, email address, and description, in addition to a Simple Password if you are using NetWare File Access Protocols.

7. When you have made all of your selections, create the User object by clicking on OK.

Now that you have your User object created, you need to know how to modify its properties.

Modify User Objects

You can modify properties of a User object in iManager by selecting Users, Modify User, which results in the screen shown in Figure 7.6.

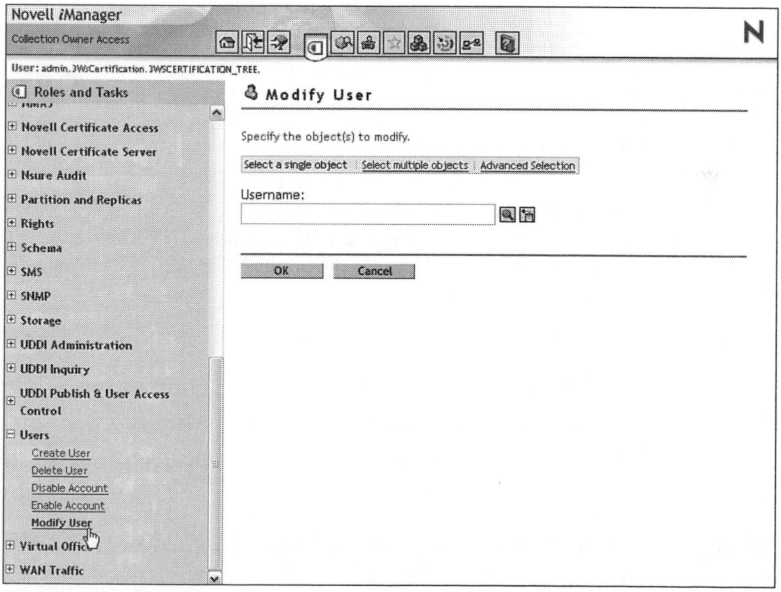

Figure 7.6   iManager: Modify User.

You have the option in the Modify User window to modify a single User object, to modify multiple User objects, or to perform an advanced search. To modify multiple User objects, select Users, Modify User, Select Multiple Objects.

In the template example shown in Figure 7.5, if you wanted to change the department for the 50 users from Science to Pharmacology, you could select the 50 users and make a single change that would apply to all 50. Figure 7.7 shows the result of selecting multiple objects (2) in the Modify User window.

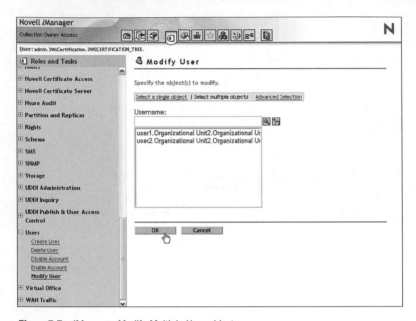

Figure 7.7 iManager: Modify Multiple User objects.

In past versions of NetWare, you could modify multiple objects using NetWare Administrator or ConsoleOne. You can still use those utilities in NetWare 6.5, but for this test, Novell prefers that you understand the capabilities of iManager for this task.

If you want to modify the property values for a single user, click on the Select a Single Object option, browse for the User object in the Modify User window, and select OK. The Modify User Details window appears, as shown in Figure 7.8.

You can change the property values that you initially assigned during User object creation, in addition to many more.

The next administrative task you have to tackle is moving a User object.

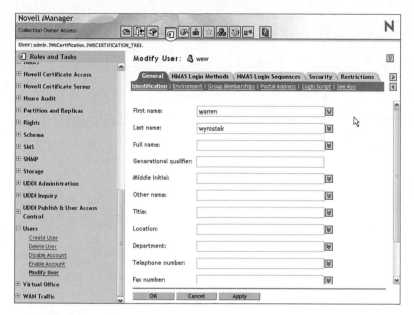

Figure 7.8   iManager: Modify User Details.

Move Objects

User objects are no different from the people they represent. Just as people move, so you must occasionally change the context of a User object. In other words, you must move the object in the tree from one Container to another. This is a simple, straightforward process using iManager. Following are the steps to move a User object in iManager:

1. In iManager, select eDirectory Administration, Move Object.

Just as you can modify a single object or multiple objects, you can move a single object or multiple objects simultaneously.

Be aware of the fact that you are moving a User object using the Move Object link under eDirectory Administration, not under Users. Users has no Move User link.

2. In the Move Object window (see Figure 7.9), select the object or objects that you want to move and the container where you will move them.

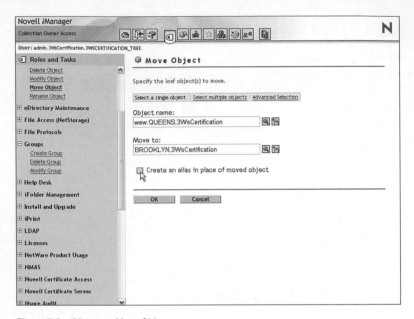

Figure 7.9 iManager: Move Object.

3. After you have selected the object and the object's destination, you can choose to have an alias object placed in the User object's original location. This is an important option. By placing an alias object, a pointer object, in the original User object's location, you do not interrupt applications, resources, or services that depend on this location.

4. After you have selected the User object, its new location, and whether you want to create an alias object in place of the moved object, select OK to move the object.

Now you can create,modify, and move a User object, but you still have to learn how to delete one.

Delete User Objects

Most novice network administrators are quick to delete User objects when a user is fired, quits, is laid off, or is transferred. However, it is not the best administrative practice to delete a User object until some time has passed, unless security is threatened. If a user leaves, it is a best practice to disable the user account until you are absolutely sure that the user will not return. All rights assignments, group memberships, and so on travel with the User object. If you delete a User object, you not only delete the object but also the

Global User ID (GUID). The GUID is the number assigned to the User object upon creation that is associated with the rights and memberships you have assigned to the user. You permanently lose the User object and all assignments. If you re-create the User object using the same name, the object gets a new GUID, and you have to reassign all rights and memberships from scratch. Be patient when considering whether you want to delete a User object.

The steps to delete a User object are simple, if you decide that is what you want to do. Just keep in mind that the decision is irreversible. Following are the steps for deleting a User object in iManager:

1. You can either use the eDirectory Administration link or the Users link in iManager to delete a User object. Using the eDirectory Administration link, you can select Delete Object and select one or more objects to delete (see Figure 7.10). Using the Users link, you can select Delete User and select one or more User objects to delete (see Figure 7.11). The first choice allows you to delete any eDirectory objects, whereas the second option allows you to delete only User objects.

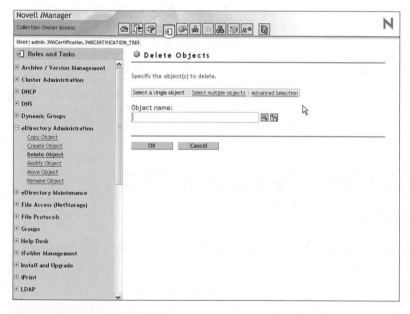

Figure 7.10   iManager: Delete Object.

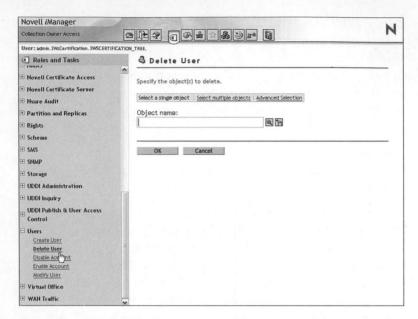

Figure 7.11 iManager: Delete User.

2. When you have selected the user or users you want to delete, click OK. The User objects are permanently deleted from the eDirectory tree, along with their GUID and the rights and memberships that are assigned to the GUID.

You now know how to create, modify, move, and delete User objects, tasks that are associated with eDirectory administration. It's time to learn the steps for creating traditional and NSS volumes.

Create Traditional and NSS Volumes

According to Novell, you can use one of four utilities to create traditional and NSS volumes:

➤ ConsoleOne

➤ NSSMU (Server-based utility)

➤ Remote Manager

➤ iManager

The four utilities are shown in Figures 7.12 through 7.15, respectively.

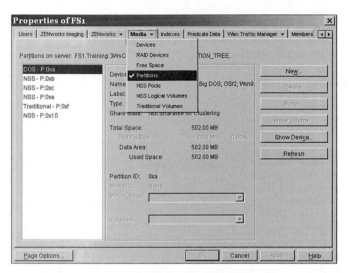

Figure 7.12 ConsoleOne: Media tab.

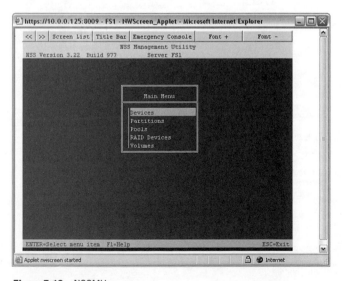

Figure 7.13 NSSMU.

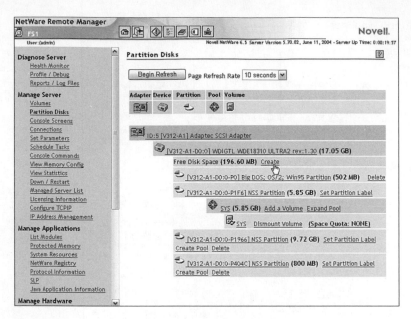

Figure 7.14 Remote Manager: Opening screen to create a volume.

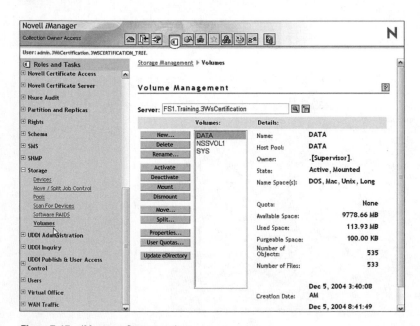

Figure 7.15 iManager: Storage options.

You must be aware of these four options. In addition, you must know the steps to create a Traditional volume and an NSS volume using Remote Manager.

Not all versions of ConsoleOne let you create, delete, or modify a Traditional or NSS volume. Version 1.3.3, which was used for Figure 7.12, can be used for this purpose. You cannot use the versions of ConsoleOne that ship with NetWare 6.5, including 1.3.6 and 1.3.6c, for this purpose. If you click on the NCP file server object, Properties, Media tab, and any of the options, you get the error message shown in Figure 7.16. For the exam, you should know that ConsoleOne is an accepted tool, but in the real world, this function is being ported away from ConsoleOne.

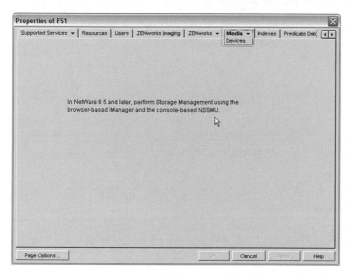

Figure 7.16   ConsoleOne error message.

As part of your file system administration skillset, you need to know the steps to create a Traditional volume using Remote Manager.

Create Traditional Volumes

Following are the steps to create a Traditional volume in Remote Manager:

1. Select Partition Disks under the Manage Server heading in the left navigation bar. You do not create a volume using the Volumes link. Using the Volumes link, you create a directory at the root of a volume or a subdirectory under a directory on a volume.

2. On the Partition Disks screen (refer to Figure 7.14), select the Create link to the right of Free Disk Space.

3. You see the File System Creation Operations window, where you select NetWare Traditional File System in the Partition Type drop-down list. You see the two links below the drop-down list change to Create a New Partition and Create a New Partition and Volume (see Figure 7.17).

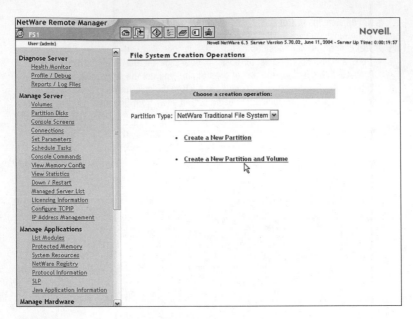

Figure 7.17   File System Creation Operations.

4. Select Create a New Partition and Volume (see Figure 7.18).

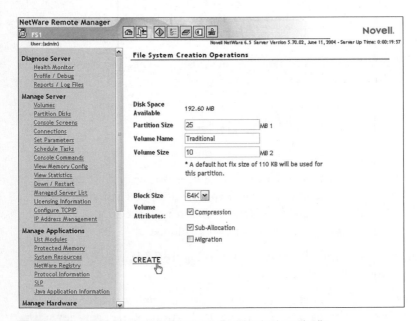

Figure 7.18   File System Creation Operations: Traditional volume details.

5. Enter a size for the new partition, a name for the Traditional volume, and the size of the volume. You do not have to use all of the partition size for the volume if you want to create additional volumes in the partition. Notice on this screen, Figure 7.18, that you can choose to select or deselect the three attributes for the volume, depending on the hardware installed in your server, besides defining the block size. The three attributes are Compression, Sub-Allocation, and Migration. You can only define these when you create the volume. If you want to change this after you create the volume, you have to delete the volume and re-create it. This could mean loss of data, so be careful at this point in the creation process. Notice on this screen that a Hot Fix Area is defined automatically. This is 2% of the available disk space. The Hot Fix Redirection Area automatically stores data in a safe area on a drive in case one or more blocks becomes corrupt. The data is moved from the bad block to the Hot Fix area.

You should monitor the number of blocks used in the Hot Fix Redirection Area with Monitor.NLM. If the number of blocks used begins to increase rapidly, immediately back up all data and replace the hard drive. A rapid increase in the number of blocks used in the Hot Fix area is a sign that the drive is failing.

6. When you have finished configuring the Traditional volume parameters, click Create and OK. You can then return to the Partition Disks link and see the new volume. It is dismounted by default. If you click on the Mount link next to it, it will be available for your users.

Next you'll learn the steps to create one of the new-and-improved NSS volumes.

Create NSS Volumes

As you learned in Chapter 6, the broad steps to create an NSS storage area are as follows:

1. Create a partition.

2. Create a pool.

3. Create a volume.

Even though I am repeating what I said in Chapter 6, you need to know the partition-pools-volumes progression well—in that order!

Now that you know the broad steps, you're ready to take the practical steps to create an NSS volume using Remote Manager:

1. Select Partition Disks under the Manage Server heading in the left navigation bar. You do not create a volume using the Volumes link. Using the Volumes link, you create a directory at the root of a volume or a subdirectory under a directory on a volume.

2. On the Partition Disks screen (refer to Figure 7.14), select the Create link to the right of Free Disk Space.

3. You see the File System Creation Operations window, where you select Novell Storage Services in the Partition Type drop-down list. The two links below the drop-down list are Create a New Pool and Create a New Pool and Volume (see Figure 7.19).

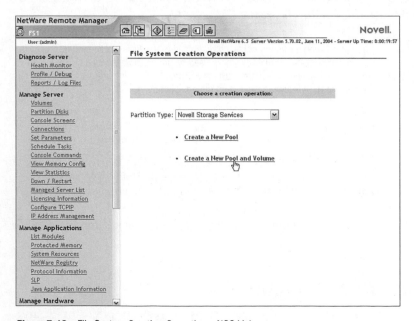

Figure 7.19 File System Creation Operations: NSS Volume.

4. Select Create a New Pool and Volume because it is the most efficient. When you create the pool, you also create a partition that is the same size as the pool. After you select the option, you see the NSS Volume Create window (see Figure 7.20).

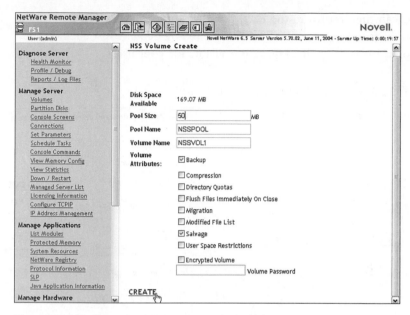

Figure 7.20   File System Creation Operations: NSS Volume Create window.

5. In the NSS Volume Create window, you can define the size of the pool, give the pool and logical volume a name, and define the attributes for the volume. You must consider nine attributes when creating an NSS volume, unlike when you create a Traditional volume, in which you must consider only three. Following are the nine NSS volume attributes:

a. Backup

b. Compression

c. Directory Quotas

d. Flush Files Immediately on Close

e. Migration

f. Modified File List

g. Salvage

h. User Space Restrictions

i. Encrypted Volume

6. You can also assign a password on the volume for security purposes. After you have made your selections, click on Create and OK.

7. You can then return to the Partition Disks link and see the new NSS volume (see Figure 7.21). It is dismounted by default. Just click on the Mount link next to it to make it available for your users.

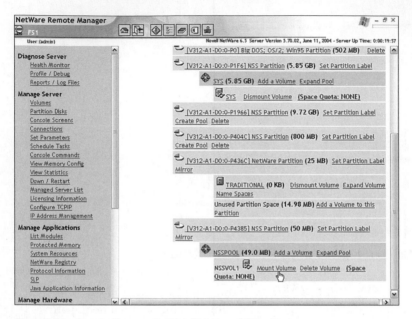

Figure 7.21 Remote Manager: Partition Disks, new NSS volume.

After you have created an NSS volume and a Traditional volume, you can check their status by entering the Volumes command at a server console prompt. The result is a list of all mounted volumes, their name spaces, and flags, as shown in Figure 7.22. CP represents the compression attribute, and Sa represents block suballocation on a Traditional volume. The P flag on the _Admin NSS volume is a flag indicating that the volume cannot be deleted.

Now that you have mounted Traditional and NSS volumes, you need to know how to easily access those volumes using NetWare drive mappings.

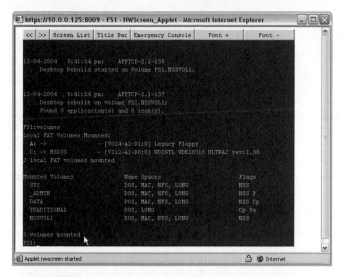

Figure 7.22   The result of the Volumes command after creating an NSS volume and a Traditional volume.

Access Volumes Through Mapped Network Drives

A drive mapping is simply a volatile pointer to a place in the NetWare file system. It is volatile because it exists in workstation memory as a function of the Novell Client, and it can be easily reassigned or lost when a user exits the network. Instead of having a user enter a ridiculously long path to his data or application every time he needs to access it, you as the CNA create a drive mapping to this path and configure the user's environment to have that pointer when he logs in to the network. Instead of the long path, the user simply enters a single drive letter, such as H:.

Types of Drive Mappings

Two types of NetWare drive mappings exist:

➤ Regular or network drive

➤ Search drive

The regular or network drive mappings traditionally are pointers to data. Search drive mappings are traditionally pointers to applications and executables that are inserted or appended to the workstation's path statement. A search drive mapping allows a user to run an application from anywhere in the file system. The most frequently used applications should be at the top of the search drive mapping list—in other words, at the front of the path.

Some texts reference a drive mapping to private data as a regular drive mapping, whereas others call this a network drive mapping. It has been my practice to call it a regular or network drive mapping to make sure my students are prepared for either occurrence on an exam. It is a little longer, but better to be safe than sorry!

You can have a maximum of 26 regular or network drive mappings, with the assumption that the first four or five drive letters are mapped to local workstation resources. The mappings traditionally begin with the letter E or F and end with the letter Z.

You can have a maximum of 16 search drive mappings. Search drive mappings begin with the letter Z and end with the letter K. The first search drive mapping is called S1 and uses letter Z. The last search drive mapping is called S16 and uses letter K.

Depending on the reference that you look at, some have the first four drive letters point to local hardware resources, such as your floppy drive, your first and second hard drive, and your CD/DVD drive. Others have the first five drive letters point to local resources. I have seen Novell's literature reference both. There is little or no consistency.

After logging in to your server, when you enter the map command at a workstation command prompt, the current drive mappings are displayed. The regular or network drive mappings are at the top of the list, whereas the search drive mappings are at the bottom of the list, as seen in Figure 7.23.

Figure 7.23 The result of the map command.

Notice that Figure 7.23 is a result of the current context being training.3WsCertification. If you change your current context to [Root], for example, the resulting map display (see Figure 7.24) changes to reflect it. The Relative Distinguished Names are modified based on your workstation's current context.

Figure 7.24   The result of the map command with a changed current context.

Soon you will learn the fundamental syntax for composing map statements, but before you do, you need to be aware that you can map a drive not only with a Windows GUI, but also by selecting the Novell Map Network Drive option when you right-click the red N in the Windows System Tray. That launches the Novell Map Drive window (see Figure 7.25), where you can dynamically map a regular or search drive.

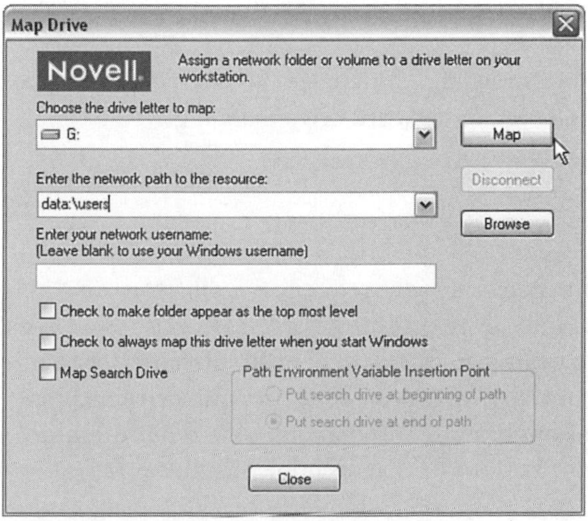

Figure 7.25   Novell Map Drive GUI window.

Map Syntax

When you reference a NetWare volume in a map statement, you can use either a physical volume name or a volume object name. The difference is subtle but significant for real-world reasons and for the exam.

A physical volume name can be used at a command prompt and is recognized by DOS. A volume object name is an eDirectory name for the volume and is not recognized by DOS. In terms of syntax, the difference between the two is one character. In the following example, using the FS1 server and the DATA volume, a physical volume name is represented with a backslash between the server and volume names:

```
FS1\DATA:
```

A volume object name is represented with an underscore between the server name and the volume name:

```
FS1_DATA:
```

To map a regular or network drive to a directory or subdirectory, use the following syntax with a physical volume name:

```
Map [options]drive letter:=Server\Volume:\directory\subdirectory\
```

You can use forward slashes or backslashes when entering a map command.

You can write the same command using a volume object name, as seen in the following syntax:

```
Map [options]drive letter:=Server_Volume:\directory\subdirectory\
```

The following two examples show the difference between two ways of composing map statements for regular network drive mappings:

```
Map H:=FS1\DATA:\Users    [Using a Physical Volume Name]

Map H:\FS1_DATA:\Users    [Using a Volume Object Name]
```

In each of these examples, the map statement references a directory on a volume. You can also map to a volume by omitting the \Users portion of each statement. Simply stated, you can map to a volume or to directory or subdirectory on a volume. You can also map a drive to an existing drive mapping. You do this to satisfy some application installations that require multiple drive letters to the same path. Following is an example of this:

```
Map H:=I:
```

The syntax for a search drive mapping is much the same, as far as physical volume and volume object names, but with a difference in the basic syntax. Following is the syntax for search drive mappings:

```
Map [options] S#:=Server\Volume:\directory\subdirectory
```

Next is an example of a search drive mapping:

```
Map ins S1:=FS1\Public
```

This is a standard search drive mapping that should be in every container login script to give users access to the directory where NetWare utilities are stored.

 Some of you might be wondering about all this fuss over map syntax when you can easily do mappings from a Windows GUI. Novell expects every CNA to know the syntax for writing map statements, which are used heavily in login scripts to configure a user's environment. You should also know how to map a drive using a GUI for the exam and for real-world use, besides knowing the syntax.

Map Options

Note in the syntax statements just covered that right after the map command is an options box for both types of drive mappings. The regular or network drive mapping options shown in Table 7.1 are powerful and worth knowing.

Table 7.1 Regular or Network Drive Mapping Options	
Option	**Description**
map N or **map Next**	This maps to the next available drive letter. This cannot be used in a login script and is generally not used with search drive mappings.
map del	This deletes a drive mapping. You can use this with regular or network drive mappings and search drive mappings.
map root	The **root** option used with the **map** command makes a directory appear to users as the topmost directory on a volume. Users cannot use the DOS **CD** command to move back up the file system hierarchy to the root of the volume.

Now look at the search drive mapping options shown in Table 7.2.

Table 7.2 Search Drive Mapping Options	
Option	**Description**
map c H:	This changes a drive mapping from a search drive mapping to a regular or network drive mapping. You can also use this to change a regular or network drive mapping to a search drive mapping.
map del	This deletes a drive mapping. You can use this with regular or network drive mappings and search drive mappings.
map root S1:	The **root** option used with the **map** command makes a directory appear to users as the topmost directory on a volume. Users cannot use the DOS **CD** command to move back up the file system hierarchy to the root of the volume.
map ins S1:	This inserts a search drive mapping into the first place of the current path statement. It does not overwrite the pointer that currently occupies the first place. This is the best method of creating a search drive mapping. It does not alter the workstation path statement; it simply adds to it.
map S16:	This appends a search drive mapping at the end of the current path statement. You can have multiple **S16** statements, one right after the other in a login script, and they each append to the path statement until 16 search drive mappings exist. Then any others that are added force the first one that was appended to be removed.
map S1:	This creates a search drive mapping that overwrites the pointer that currently occupies the first place in the path statement. This works by deleting that first pointer. It is not the best administrative practice to use this syntax.
map ins root S1:	This both inserts a search drive mapping and makes it appear as the topmost directory in a volume.

Now that you know some of the most popular map commands and options, you need to know where these map statements can help you as a CNA.

NetWare 6.5 Login Scripts

As a NetWare 6.5 CNA, one of your main responsibilities is to make the network easy for your users. One of the ways you make the NetWare 6.5 network a user-friendly environment is by strategically using login scripts.

A login script is a simple text file that uses Novell login script syntax to configure a user's environment when he logs in. One of the main components of a login script is the map statements that you incorporate into the script. Four login scripts are used in NetWare 6.5. A user does not necessarily have all four scripts run when he logs in. That depends on how you configure the scripts. The four scripts are listed in Table 7.3.

Table 7.3	NetWare 6.5 Login Scripts
Script	**Description**
Container	This is the first script that runs for a user. It is a property of the Container object. Only users in the Container are impacted by a Container script. Users in subcontainers are not impacted by a Container script that is not immediately configured for their container.
	A Container script is the easiest way to establish an environment for the maximum number of users simultaneously.
	If a Container script is not configured, the login process checks whether a Profile script is configured.
Profile	This script runs after a Container script if it is configured and associated with a user. You generally use a Profile script for groups of users who are in different containers. You can also use it for users who are in the same container and have similar job functions.
	The Profile script is a property of a Profile object. A Profile script is not associated with a group object but with each individual in a group. You must configure each User object that is supposed to have a Profile script on a user-by-user basis.
	A user can only be associated with one Profile script at a time. If a user is in multiple groups, he or she cannot be associated with multiple Profile scripts.
	If a Profile script is not configured, the login process checks whether a User script is configured.
User	This is a script that establishes an environment for a single user. The User login script is a property of the User object. If a user has a User script configured for him, this script runs after the Container and Profile scripts. Any map statements in a User script that are the same but pointing to other locations in the file system than previously configured in the Container or Profile scripts overwrite those pointers. Because **map** statements are volatile and in workstation RAM, the last in wins.
	If a User script exists, the Default login script does not run.
	If possible, avoid using User login scripts. Try to accomplish as much as possible with Container and Profile scripts. It is a good CNA practice.

(continued)

Table 7.3	NetWare 6.5 Login Scripts *(continued)*
Script	**Description**
Default	This script is hard-coded into **LOGIN.EXE** and creates a basic network environment by establishing a search drive mapping to the **Public** directory and a first network drive mapping. You cannot edit this script. If you have a User script configured, the Default script does not run.
	If you do not have a User script configured, this script runs automatically and overwrites any similar drive pointers. The way to avoid this is by having a **NO_DEFAULT** statement in either the Container or Profile script.

Now that you know the four types of login scripts, you need to see how map statements are used in a sample login script.

Login Script Syntax

This section presents a sample login script in which different map statements are used. Notice that a REM statement documents what each statement does. There are four ways to include REM statements in a NetWare login script. A REM statement does not execute. It is simply a means of providing documentation in a script. Following are the four ways of including REM statements in a NetWare login script:

➤ REMARK

➤ REM

➤ *

➤ ;

The login script is presented in Listing 7.1.

Listing 7.1   Sample Login Script with Commenting

```
Rem This is a sample container script.
*This next statement welcomes the user who logs in
➥using his username.
WRITE "Good %GREETING_TIME, %LOGIN_NAME!"
;This next statement prevents the login script from being echoed
➥to the screen.
MAP DISPLAY OFF
*This is a search drive map statement, using a physical volume name,
➥to the Public directory.
MAP ROOT INS S1:=FS1\SYS:PUBLIC
;This is a regular drive mapping to the user's home directory.
```

(continued)

Listing 7.1   Sample Login Script with Commenting *(continued)*

```
MAP ROOT H:=%HOME_DIRECTORY
REMARK This is a regular or network drive mapping, using a volume
➥object name, to the gradebook data.
MAP ROOT J:=.FS1_DATA.TRAINING.3WsCertification\Shared\Gradebook
;This next statement prevents the Default login script from launching.
NO_DEFAULT
REM  This next statement fires 3 phasers so you will know
➥when the user logs in.
FIRE PHASERS 3
*These next statements display the configured drive mappings.
MAP DISPLAY ON
MAP
```

Exam Prep Questions

1. What is the name of the only User object that is created when you install your first NetWare 6.5 server into a new eDirectory tree?

   A. ○ Supervisor

   B. ○ Administrator

   C. ○ Admin

   D. ○ Root

   Answer C is correct. The only User object created when the first NetWare 6.5 server is installed into a new eDirectory tree is the Admin object. Answer A is incorrect. Supervisor is the user superuser created when a NetWare 3 and earlier server is installed. Answer B is incorrect. Administrator is the default user created on Windows NT/2000/2003 server. Answer D is incorrect. Root is the superuser created on a Linux or Unix workstation or server.

2. Which of the following is a characteristic of the User object that is created when you install your first NetWare 6.5 server into a new tree?

   A. ○ It cannot have its Supervisor rights to the Tree object deleted.

   B. ○ It cannot have its name changed.

   C. ○ You can only have one such object in the tree.

   D. ○ You can delete this object.

   Answer D is correct. Unlike many superuser objects, you can delete the Admin object. You can change its name. It can lose all if its rights, including Supervisor rights to the Tree object. You can have multiple Admin User objects, in different containers, with the same Supervisor rights. This is a good administrative practice. Answers A, B, and C are incorrect.

3. You want to create an eDirectory User object in your new NetWare 6.5 tree. Which two links can you use in iManager to accomplish this? (Select two.)

   A. ❏ eDirectory Maintenance

   B. ❏ Groups

   C. ❏ Users

   D. ❏ eDirectory Administration

   Answers C and D are correct. The two opening screen links on iManager 2.0.2 that you can select to begin the process of creating a User object are Users and eDirectory Administration. Answers A and B are incorrect. eDirectory Maintenance gives you access to a wealth of maintenance tools such as backup, ICE, merging a tree, and renaming a tree. The Groups link allows you to create, delete, and modify group objects.

4. You are creating a User object in iManager for your NetWare 6.5 network. Which of the following values must you supply to successfully create the User object? (Select all that apply.)

A. ❑ First name

B. ❑ Last name

C. ❑ Context

D. ❑ Username

E. ❑ Home directory

Answers B, C, and D are correct. In iManager, to create a User object, you must supply the object with a Last Name, Username, and Context. Answers A and E are incorrect. You do not have to supply a home directory or First Name. Those are optional properties.

5. You want to create a template object using iManager. Which option should you initially select to begin the process?

A. ○ Users

B. ○ Storage

C. ○ eDirectory Administration

D. ○ eDirectory Maintenance

Answer C is correct. You create eDirectory objects, including User objects and template objects, under the eDirectory Administration link in iManager. Answer A is incorrect. You can create a User object using the options under this link, but you cannot create a nonuser object, such as a template object. Answers B and D are incorrect. You do not create eDirectory objects with the options found under these links in iManager.

6. You want to move User object wew1 from the Brooklyn container to the Training container using iManager. What type of eDirectory object can you have created in the Brooklyn container in case you have applications that require the wew1 User object to be in Brooklyn after the move?

A. ○ Profile object

B. ○ Alias object

C. ○ Directory Map object

D. ○ Template object

Answer B is correct. You can have eDirectory automatically create an Alias object, a Pointer object, when you are moving an object from one context to another. This Alias object points to the object's new context in case applications or services depend on the object's initial context. Answers A, C, and D are incorrect. You are not given the option of automatically creating these objects during an object move.

7. You want to modify several User objects using iManager. Can you do so efficiently? How?

   A. ○ Yes, by selecting Users, Modify User, Select Multiple Objects.

   B. ○ Yes, by modifying the User objects one at a time.

   C. ○ No, you can only modify multiple User objects in ConsoleOne.

   D. ○ No, you can only modify multiple User objects by using NetWare Administrator.

   Answer A is correct. Just as you could in NetWare Administrator and ConsoleOne, you can modify multiple eDirectory objects, including User objects, at the same time. You can do this by selecting Users, Modify User, Select Multiple Objects. You can also do the same thing using eDirectory Administration, Modify Object, Select Multiple Objects. Answers B, C, and D are incorrect. You can modify users one at a time, but this is not efficient. Although you can still modify multiple users simultaneously with NetWare Administrator and ConsoleOne, you can also do the same now in iManager.

8. Which NetWare 6.5 login script can't you edit or delete?

   A. ○ System

   B. ○ Container

   C. ○ Profile

   D. ○ User

   E. ○ Default

   Answer E is correct. The only login script that you cannot edit or delete is the Default script, which is hard-coded into LOGIN.EXE. Answer A is incorrect. The System script is the login script that is used on NetWare 3.x servers. Answers B, C, and D are incorrect. They can all be edited and deleted.

9. Which map option should you use if you want to have a directory appear to a user as the topmost directory on the volume?

   A. ○ **Insert**.

   B. ○ **Root**.

   C. ○ **Top**.

   D. ○ There is no such option.

   Answer B is correct. The root option used with the map command makes a directory appear to users as the topmost directory on a volume. Answers A, C, and D are incorrect. The insert option is used with search drive mappings to insert a map into the existing path statement. The map command does not have a top option. Answer D is simply false.

10. What is the maximum number of drive letters that you can assign to regular drive mappings on a NetWare 6.5 server?

    A. ○ 26

    B. ○ 10

    C. ○ 12

    D. ○ 16

    Answer A is correct. You can have a maximum of 26 letters assigned as regular or network drive mappings. Answer D is incorrect. You have a maximum of 16 drive letters assigned to search drive mappings. Answers B and C are incorrect. These are neither maximums or minimums for regular or search drive mappings.

File System Security

. . . .

Terms you'll need to understand:

✓ Universal Password
✓ Trustee
✓ Rights
✓ ACL
✓ IRF
✓ Inheritance
✓ Explicit Assignment
✓ Inherited Assignment
✓ Effective rights
✓ RIGHTS command
✓ FLAG
✓ FILER
✓ NDIR
✓ Access Control List
✓ Remote Manager

Techniques you'll need to master:

✓ Identify the types of network security provided by NetWare
✓ Identify how NetWare file system security works
✓ Plan file system rights
✓ Identify directory and file attributes

You now have a working NetWare 6.5 server and a default file system with some admin-created directories, but how do you secure this top-notch server? The universal response that is preached these days is security. You have to secure your system.

In this chapter, you learn the fundamental concepts that govern file system security. As you will see when you get to Chapter 9, "eDirectory Security," the concepts covered in this chapter also apply to eDirectory security. It's the same hymn, just a different verse. It's crucial that you sit back and get comfortable, because what you learn in this chapter can be the difference between having a comfortable life as a NetWare admin or having to keep pulling out that résumé to find another job. Security is ultimately the NetWare admin's responsibility. You can't pass the buck or blame someone else if a user accesses data that he should not be accessing.

In this chapter, you learn the types of security used in NetWare, how file system security works, how you should design your file system security, and how attributes contribute to file system security. It's time to secure that server.

Identify the Types of Network Security Provided by NetWare

Depending on the vendor you are supporting, the term *security* evokes many thoughts and emotions. NetWare security is just as evocative, but Novell has done a good job of classifying the types of security that the CNA is responsible for. No single security branch addresses all security issues. To fully secure a NetWare environment, all security branches must be in place. Most Novell references historically cite five classes of NetWare security, with one addendum for NetWare 6.x:

➤ Login security

➤ File system security

➤ eDirectory security

➤ Printing security

➤ Server console security

➤ Universal password (the addendum)

Although this might sound condescending, the point must be made that security, in the eyes of most vendors including Novell, is ultimately the responsibility of the network administrator, which means you as the CNA.

Login security, which is discussed in Chapter 10, "NetWare 6.5 Network Security," addresses who can log in to the network, when a user can access resources, and what the authentication restrictions are, if any.

File system security, which is discussed in this chapter, addresses the capabilities that a user has in the NetWare file system when he is logged in. As an example, file system security governs whether students in a school system have access to the teacher's gradebook so that they can change their grades without the teacher knowing, or whether employees have access to the office payroll database and can change their salaries without their employer knowing about it. Who can go where in the file system and what they can do when they get there is the thrust of file system security.

eDirectory security, which is discussed in Chapter 9, addresses the capabilities that a user has in the eDirectory tree when he has logged in. Following are some questions that are addressed in eDirectory security:

➤ Can a user access a Controlled Access printer?

➤ Can a user control a Container object?

➤ Can a user create or delete objects in his Container?

Printing security, which is briefly mentioned in Chapter 11, "NetWare 6.5 Printing," addresses a user's control over the printing environment. Following are some issues that are governed in printing security:

➤ Can a user print to a given printer?

➤ Can a user control his print jobs?

➤ Can a user control all users' print jobs?

Server console security, also called physical security, which is discussed in Chapter 10, addresses the measures that you must take to secure the server from physically being attacked. Many of the issues that fall under this category are common-sense issues that many environments ignore because they seem too simple.

Universal password is a NetWare 6.5 feature that enables you to integrate and manage different types of passwords and systems of authentication into a single common or universal password. This feature is *not* turned on by default. Its benefit comes into play when you have users who must log in to systems using different authentication mechanisms, or when you are using Native File Access Protocol (NFAP) in a NetWare 6.5 environment. Instead of having to remember multiple passwords, the user can authenticate to all systems with a single password.

> Some might argue that there is another security class in NetWare 6.0 and 6.5: the security capabilities that are available through Role Based Services. The user cannot perform several tasks until he is configured as a member who is capable of performing a task found under a role. Role Based Services are configured in iManager. If, after you have granted a user the rights you think he needs to perform a task, a user still cannot work, look in iManager, Configure and see if the user has been configured. If he has, what tasks has he been configured for? This can be a real issue for new NetWare 6.5 CNAs.
>
> This is not historically listed as a security class in NetWare documentation, but it can be just as important as any of those listed earlier.

It is now time to secure the file system. It is all about rights!

Identify How NetWare File System Security Works

As a CNA, your goal in file system security is to grant users only the rights to the files and directories that they need to perform their jobs. Don't give users too many rights and later have to troubleshoot why files and directories are being changed or deleted. Likewise, don't give users too few rights because then they can't do their jobs.

To adequately explore file system security, you need to be able to answer the following questions:

➤ What are rights, and what are the NetWare file system rights?

➤ What are the default assignments granted in NetWare 6.5?

➤ What are trustees, ACLs, and inheritance?

➤ What are the two ways to change a trustee assignment?

➤ What are effective rights?

➤ What are the rules of NetWare 6.5 file system security?

After you learn the answers to these questions, you will be able to tackle some practice questions in which you calculate a user's effective rights based on a scenario.

What Are Rights, and What Are the NetWare File System Rights?

Rights control access to network resources, including file system resources and eDirectory objects. They are granted to Users, Groups, Container objects, Organizational Role objects, or the [Public] trustee. Novell defines rights as "system flags."

NetWare 6.5 has eight file system rights:

➤ **Supervisor**—If you have the Supervisor right, you have all eight rights. You have complete control over a given level of the file system.

➤ **Read**—If you have the Read right, you can open a file, read its contents, or run an executable.

➤ **Write**—If you have the Write right, you can write to a file or directory.

➤ **Create**—If you have the Create right, you can create and write to a file and create new directories and subdirectories.

➤ **Erase**—If you have the Erase right, you can delete a file or directory.

➤ **Modify**—If you have the Modify right, you can rename a file or directory and change a file or directory's attributes. You'll read more about attributes in the section "Identify Directory and File Attributes," later in this chapter.

➤ **File Scan**—If you have the File Scan right, you can see a file or directory in a directory scan, such as when you run DIR at a command window.

➤ **Access Control**—If you have the Access Control right, you can create a trustee assignment or an inherited rights filter (IRF).

You need to know these rights in this order for your upcoming CNA exam.

As a tool for learning the rights, but not in order, you can use the mnemonic SCREAM W/Fear, which is what many students do when they think about NetWare file system security. Notice that the *ear* in *Fear* is lowercase. Those letters are not representative of one of the eight rights.

The rights are often noted by their first letter. Someone who has all eight rights would have the notation SRWCEMFA. If a user has been granted all rights except the Supervisor right, the notation would be RWCEMFA. If a user has Read and File Scan to an executable, the notation would be RF. Throughout the rest of this chapter, rights assignments are conventionally referenced using only the first letter of the right.

The greatest temptation for a new CNA is to either grant the Supervisor right to a user or to grant all eight rights, SRWCEMFA. Only grant the user the minimum rights needed. You should only grant users the Modify and Access Control rights when they absolutely need them. These two rights are powerful; users who have them can cause havoc on your network.

In addition, unless you have your résumé ready for a new job, *never* grant a user the Supervisor right unless you trust them with your job. A user who has the Supervisor file system right has full control at the file system level granted and all levels beneath that level. As you will see in a few pages, this right has power beyond all the other file system rights. This user has full control and all that that term means. Only give the Supervisor right to someone you trust with your job.

As a CNA, you grant users rights so that they can have a certain level of control in the file system. To be able to perform certain tasks, you must grant a user or group of users more than one file system right. It is not adequate to grant a user only the Read right if the user needs to open and write to a file.

Following are some of the most common rights assignments you will make:

➤ WCEM if a user needs to open and write to an existing file and either rename it or change its attributes

➤ RF if a user needs to run an executable or copy files from a directory

➤ CF if a user needs to copy files to a directory

➤ RF on a file and C on a directory if a user needs to salvage a file

File system rights are unique to the file system. A different set of rights governs eDirectory security. As a CNA, as I have mentioned earlier in this book, you have two administrative hats to wear: the eDirectory hat and the file system hat. The same holds true when it comes to security. These two, with one exception, never come into contact. The one exception, for many of you the one "gotcha," is the eDirectory Server object. If, as you will see in Chapter 9, you grant a user the Supervisor object eDirectory right to the Server object, the user automatically has the Supervisor file system right, and you cannot remove it, overwrite it, or filter it in the file system. In fact, the user has, in this case, the Supervisor file system right to all volumes on the file server. This is the exception and something to watch out for. It's the only link between file system rights and eDirectory rights, but as you know, a chain is only as strong as its weakest link. If you are not watchful when granting eDirectory rights to users, your weakest link to file system security might be the Server object.

It's essential that you understand the implications of granting the Supervisor object right to the Server object and its implications for the file system. You must know this for the exam for questions revolving around file system rights and eDirectory rights, but apart from that, you must be watchful on your production networks when troubleshooting users who have too many rights in the file system. Unknown to you, they could be coming from rights granted to the Server object.

The only right that you can grant to the Server object that has this implication is the Supervisor object right. No other eDirectory rights create this link to the file system.

Knowing what the file system rights are, it is time to look at some of the default file system assignments.

What Are the Default Assignments Granted in NetWare 6.5?

When you created a user earlier in this book, you had a chance to automatically create a home directory for the user in the file system. The user is automatically granted a set of rights to his home directory. This is one example of the operating system automatically creating a file system security assignment. You need to be familiar with the most common default rights assignments in the file system:

➤ **User's home directory**—The user is granted RWCEMFA—all but S— to his home directory.

➤ **The Server object**—The user who created the eDirectory Server object is granted the S right to all volumes on the server. Any user who has the eDirectory Supervisor object right to the Server object has the S right to all volumes on the server.

➤ `SYS:\Public` **directory**—All users in the same Container as a `Volume` `SYS` object receive RF access to the `Public` directory and all utilities in that directory.

What Are Trustees, ACLs, and Inheritance?

You've heard a good bit of NetWare security language up until now. To fully understand it, you need to be able to answer several key questions:

➤ What utilities are used to manage file system security?

➤ What is a trustee? What is an explicit assignment? What is an access control list (ACL)?

➤ How do you add users to the ACL? How do you delete users from an ACL?

➤ What is inheritance and what is an inherited assignment?

For all examples in this chapter, you will be using the file system hierarchy shown in Figure 8.1. Written out, the structure is Data, Certification, NW65CNA, FileSyst, EffRghts.txt.

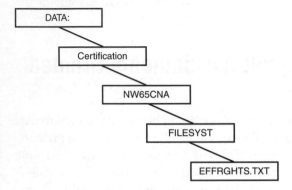

Figure 8.1 Sample file system.

What Utilities Are Used to Manage File System Security?

With the release of NetWare 6.5, Novell has attempted to move all NetWare administrators to Web-based management tools, as this book has discussed in various chapters. You can use one of these tools to manage file system security. However, certain tried-and-true utilities are still the workhorses of file system security management. For both the exam and the real world, you need to know all of them and then make a decision regarding which interface you like the best. As you explore file system security, you will be introduced to the following utilities:

➤ **Remote Manager**—This is the fair-haired child of Novell with the release of NetWare 6.5 for file system security management. This utility is the most heavily weighted on the exam, so become familiar with the interface, as shown throughout this chapter.

➤ **ConsoleOne**—This is what many from the NetWare 5.x days are comfortable with on a Windows-based workstation. It's a tried-and-true Java utility that Novell put a lot of energy into in the late 1990s and the early part of this century.

➤ **NetWare Administrator**—This utility is still the favorite of those who grew with it from the NetWare 4.x days. It does a great job with file system security issues, but it lacks plug-in support for many objects.

➤ **RIGHTS**—This is a workstation-based executable that is run from a command prompt. It displays your current rights to a file or directory, or it displays those objects that are on the ACL for a file or directory.

➤ **FILER**—This is a powerful workstation-based menu-driven utility for managing the NetWare 6.5 file system, rights, and attributes. Those who grew up during the NetWare 3.x days love this tool. It also has some power that the other GUI-based tools do not.

➤ **Windows Explorer**—This is not a NetWare utility per se, but you can use it when the Novell Client has been installed to manage file system security. As you will see later in Figure 8.5, you can view and make changes to a file or directory's ACL.

What Is a Trustee? What Is an Explicit Assignment? What Is an ACL?

The key to understanding NetWare file system and eDirectory security is understanding what a trustee is. In the file system, this is a User, Group, Organizational Role object, Container, or [Public] trustee that is explicitly granted rights to a directory or file by being added to the directory or file's ACL.

An explicit assignment is one in which a User, Group, Organizational Role object, Container, or [Public] trustee is added to the ACL of a file, directory, or eDirectory object and granted explicit rights at that point in either the file system tree or the eDirectory tree.

When you are added to a resource's ACL and given one or more of the eight file system security rights, you are said to have been made a trustee of that directory or file and granted those rights. You are made a trustee through an explicit assignment.

The ACL is a property of every file, directory, and eDirectory object. Objects that you add to an ACL are granted explicit rights to that file, directory, or eDirectory at that point in the hierarchy. Every object has an ACL.

Figures 8.2, 8.3, 8.4, 8.5, and 8.6 show examples of file system ACLs in Remote Manager, ConsoleOne, NetWare Administrator, Windows Explorer, and with the Rights command, respectively. Some show trustees at the directory level, some at the file level, and others are empty. All are based on the file structure shown in Figure 8.1.

To view an ACL in Remote Manager, access Remote Manager using `https://server_IP_address:8009` or `http://server_IP_address:8008`.

Under Volumes, select your volume and then select the INFO button next to the directory or file whose ACL you want to display. The ACL is displayed under the section titled Trustee Information.

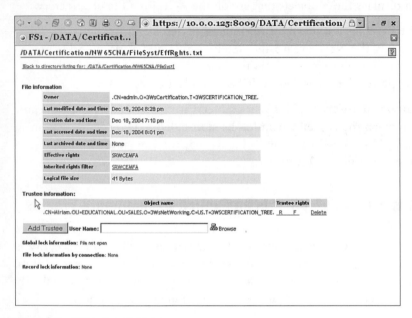

Figure 8.2 ACL in Remote Manager.

To view an ACL in ConsoleOne, double-click the volume you want to expand and scroll to the directory or file whose ACL you want to display. Highlight the directory or file, right-click it, and select Properties, Trustees.

To view an ACL in NetWare Administrator, double-click the volume you want to expand and scroll to the directory or file whose ACL you want to display. Highlight the directory or file, right-click it, and select Details, Trustees of this File/Directory.

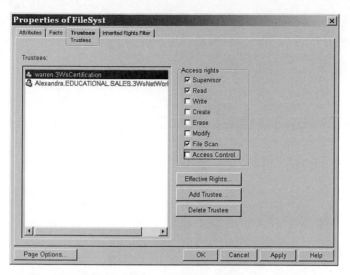

Figure 8.3 ACL in ConsoleOne.

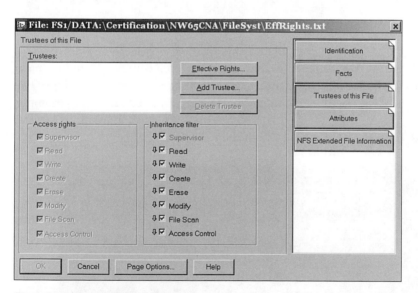

Figure 8.4 ACL in NetWare Administrator.

To view an ACL in Windows Explorer, right-click the NetWare directory or
file and select Properties, NetWare Rights. You can access a similar screen
by right-clicking the red N in the Windows System Tray and selecting
NetWare Utilities, Trustee Rights and then scrolling to the directory or file
whose ACL you want to display.

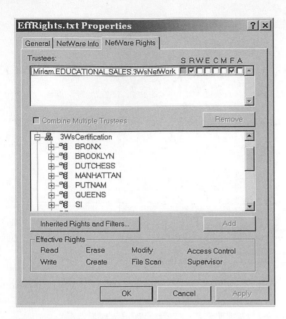

Figure 8.5 ACL in Windows Explorer.

To view an ACL with the Rights command, open a command window, navigate to the file or directory, and then enter Rights /T. Figure 8.6 shows two examples of the Rights /T command being used. By itself, in the top example, you see the ACL for the directory Filesyst. In the bottom example, you see the ACL for the EffRghts.txt file in the FileSyst directory.

```
C:\WINNT\system32\cmd.exe                                            _ □ X

J:\CERTIF~1\NW65CNA\FileSyst>rights /t
FS1\DATA:\CERTIF~1\NW65CNA\FILESYST
User trustees:
     warren.3WsCertification                        [SR    F ]
     Alexandra.EDUCATIONAL.SALES.3WsNetWorking.US    [ R    F ]
----------
No group trustees have been assigned.


J:\CERTIF~1\NW65CNA\FileSyst>rights *.* /t
FS1\DATA:\CERTIF~1\NW65CNA\FILESYST\EFFRGHTS.TXT
User trustees:
     Miriam.EDUCATIONAL.SALES.3WsNetWorking.US       [ R    F ]
     Alexandra.EDUCATIONAL.SALES.3WsNetWorking.US    [ RWCEMF ]
----------
No group trustees have been assigned.


J:\CERTIF~1\NW65CNA\FileSyst>
```

Figure 8.6 ACL Using **Rights /T**.

The following eDirectory objects can be trustees on a directory or file ACL:

➤ Users

➤ Groups

➤ Organizational role object

➤ Container objects

➤ [Public] trustee

You can grant explicit assignments to any of these, but it is more administratively efficient to grant rights to as large a group of users, who have similar file system security requirements, as possible. You can do this because when you grant rights to a Group, Organizational Role object, or Container, all users who respectively are members, occupants, or reside in those objects, because they are considered security equivalent to those objects, receive the rights assigned to the containing object.

The [Public] trustee is a unique object in eDirectory in that it represents all authenticated and nonauthenticated users, in essence everyone. The [Public] trustee is represented with square brackets, is used only in trustee assignments, functions like any other trustee, and by default is granted the RF rights when added to an ACL.

How Do You Add/Delete Objects To/From the ACL?

The steps to add an object to or delete an object from a directory or file's ACL are as follows, depending on the utility used:

➤ **Remote Manager**—View the ACL as described earlier, and then browse for the object you want to add to the ACL, assign the appropriate rights, and select Add Trustee to add a trustee to the list. To delete an object, click the Delete link next to the trustee you want to remove from the ACL.

➤ **ConsoleOne**—View the ACL as described earlier, click Add Trustee, browse for the object you want to add to the ACL, and assign the appropriate rights. To delete an object, hightlight the object and select Delete Trustee.

➤ **NetWare Administrator**—View the ACL as described earlier, select Add Trustee, browse for the object you want to add to the ACL, and assign the appropriate rights. To delete an object, highlight the object and select Delete Trustee.

➤ **Windows Explorer**—View the ACL as described earlier, and in the bottom window, scroll for and highlight the object you want to add to the ACL, select Add, and then assign the appropriate rights. To delete an object, highlight the object in the ACL and select Remove.

What Is Inheritance, and What Is an Inherited Assignment?

Up to this point, you have only heard about trustees and explicit assignments. NetWare security also has an administrator-friendly concept that uses those explicit trustee assignments and lets them follow the trustee to lower levels in the given hierarchy.

In Chapter 5, "Introduction to eDirectory," you briefly heard about inheritance. In this chapter and in Chapter 9, inheritance comes into focus.

As you remember, inheritance is the process of rights flowing down from a higher level to a lower level in both the eDirectory tree and the NetWare 6.5 file system. Looking at the sample file system structure shown in Figure 8.1 (Data, Certification, NW65CNA, FileSyst, EffRghts.txt), if you make Jill a trustee of Certification and grant her RWCEF, by inheritance she will have RWCEF in NW65CNA, in FileSyst, and in EffRghts.txt. Her explicit assignment is at Certification, but she has an inherited assignment at NW65CNA, FileSyst, and EffRghts.txt.

If you had made Jill a trustee of Data and granted her RF, then at Certification, she would also have an inherited assignment of RF. But you just made Jill a trustee of Certification with an explicit trustee assignment. In this case, the explicit assignment overwrites the inherited assignment. At Certification, Jill's rights are RWCEF, not RF.

An explicit trustee assignment, in the file system and in eDirectory, overwrites an inherited assignment.

Another way that an object can receive rights is through security equivalence. You can make one eDirectory object security equivalent to another eDirectory object, such as by making Warren security equivalent to Monk. All rights assignments, explicit or inherited granted to Monk, are in turn granted to Warren through security equivalence. NetWare 6.5 has two problems with security equivalence:

➤ If Monk's User object is deleted, Warren loses all rights and capabilities that he had through being security equivalent to Monk.

➤ If Monk is a Supervisor, then making Warren security equivalent to Monk is making Warren a Supervisor whether you want to or not. It's almost impossible to track the source of Warren's rights. It is far better to grant Warren an explicit assignment and do away with the notion of security equivalent. It is easier when you are under the gun or being lazy to use security equivalent, but it will come back to bite you later on.

After you grant a user a trustee assignment, the next issue is how to change it at a lower level in the structure?

What Are the Two Ways to Change a Trustee Assignment?

You can change a trustee assignment in both the file system and in eDirectory in two ways.

The preferred method and the most granular/specific way to change an object's trustee assignment is to grant the object a new assignment that is lower in the branch. The example I cited earlier shows how Jill received a new assignment at Certification. That new assignment overwrites any inherited assignment that she has at the given level of the tree.

Globally inherited rights can be filtered using an IRF. Some of you from the NetWare 3 days will remember these being called inherited rights masks (IRMs). An IRF is really a filter. Every level of the file system and the eDirectory tree has an IRF. The file system default IRF allows all rights to flow down the file system hierarchy. No rights are filtered. You can change the filter using any of the previously mentioned utilities by clearing the rights that you do not want to be inherited. In Figure 8.4, you see the ACL in NetWare Administrator. On the right side of the screen, you see the IRF for the EffRghts.txt file. Notice that all rights are checked, which means that all inherited rights are allowed to flow down the branch through this level. If a right is cleared, anyone who has that inherited right loses it from that point down the branch.

The default IRF is represented as [SRWCEMFA] with all rights displayed. If a right is filtered, it is missing. For example, [SRWCE F] filters the MA inherited rights. The MA rights cannot be inherited from that point down the branch of the tree.

Following are some key points to remember about IRFs:

➤ IRFs do not affect an explicit trustee assignment at the level that the IRF is implemented. If a user is granted RWCEMFA at the same level where the IRF is [SRW   ], the user does not lose rights because an IRF filters only inherited rights.

➤ You cannot filter the Supervisor (S) right with an IRF. You will never see the S right missing in an IRF. The stumbling point for students is when the S right is in the IRF. Does that mean that the user receives the S right? No, it does not. The S in the IRF only means that if a user has the Supervisor right higher in the tree, that right flows down through the IRF. If the user does not have an inherited assignment with S, the S in the IRF is a moot point.

➤ IRFs globally filter inherited rights. All users who have an inherited assignment lose the rights that an IRF filters. The only exception, as just mentioned, is that the S right cannot be filtered in the file system.

Notice I said *in the file system.* An IRF in the file system cannot filter the Supervisor right, but as you will see in Chapter 9, in eDirectory security, you can filter the Supervisor rights. That is a major point to remember.

➤ The default IRF in the file system is [SRWCEMFA]. All directories, subdirectories, and files have this IRF by default. Unless you want a lot of work, don't change it. You don't need to use IRFs in the file system. They are an annoyance to troubleshoot and can cause more harm than good. Whenever possible, grant a new trustee assignment instead of using an IRF. A new trustee assignment gives you far more control that is specific, granular, and easy to troubleshoot and track.

You have trustees, explicit trustee assignments, inherited rights, and inherited rights filters. In the end, after all of that, what can you actually do at a given level of the file system? That is where effective rights come in. What can you effectively do?

What Are Effective Rights?

Effective rights are what a user or group can actually do at any given level of the file system or eDirectory tree, after any IRFs.

The NetWare 6.5 operating system automatically calculates a user's effective rights at any given level of the file system. It does the same thing for you in eDirectory, as you will see in Chapter 9.

For your CNA purposes, you need to know three things about effective rights:

➤ How to display a user's effective rights in each management utility

➤ The rules that govern file system security

➤ How to calculate a user's effective rights based on the rules that govern file system security

 You can expect to see several questions on the CNA exam asking you to predict a user's effective rights at a level in the file system or in the eDirectory tree. Our focus in this chapter is the file system. The fact that the operating system does this automatically for you is insufficient for Novell to consider you a good CNA. A good CNA must be able to predict what impact a rights assignment will have before granting that assignment. Therefore, you must be able to calculate a user's effective rights.

In this section, you are introduced to the utilities for displaying a user's effective rights. In the next two sections, you are introduced to all the rules, some of which you have already encountered, and you learn how to calculate effective rights.

You can display a user's effective rights in Remote Manager, ConsoleOne, NetWare Administrator, with the red N in the Windows System Tray, and with the Rights command.

To display a user's effective rights in Remote Manager, access the directory or file's ACL, as discussed earlier. On this screen are your effective rights, shown in Figure 8.7. To see another user's effective rights, you have to authenticate as that user. You cannot simply browse for that user and display his effective rights. This is a weakness of using Remote Manager. Notice that you can see the IRF that is in place at that level of the file system.

To display a user's effective rights in ConsoleOne, access the directory or file's ACL, as discussed earlier. This screen has an Effective Rights button. When you click that button, an Effective Rights window, shown in Figure 8.8, appears showing your effective rights. You can click the Browse button to the right of the Trustee field and browse for another trustee. When you select the trustee, his effective rights are displayed in the Effective Rights box.

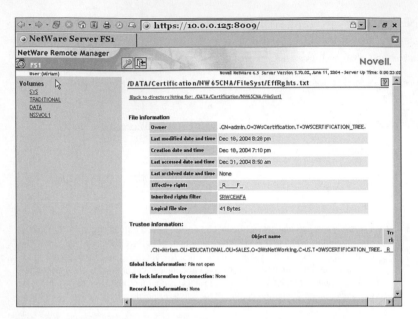

Figure 8.7 Effective rights using Remote Manager.

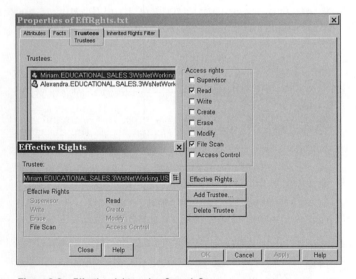

Figure 8.8 Effective rights using ConsoleOne.

To display a user's effective rights in NetWare Administrator, access the directory or file's ACL, as discussed earlier. This screen has an Effective Rights button. When you click that button, an Effective Rights window, as shown in Figure 8.9, appears with your effective rights. You can click the Browse button to the right of the Trustee field and browse for another trustee. When you select the trustee, his effective rights are displayed in the Effective Rights box.

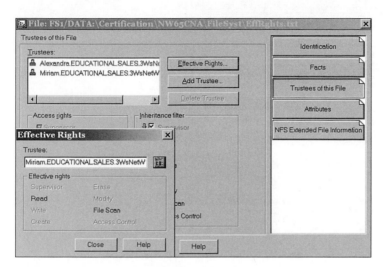

Figure 8.9 Effective rights using NetWare Administrator.

To display a user's effective rights with the red N in the Windows System Tray, right-click the red N and select NetWare Utilities, Trustee Rights. Browse to the file or directory and view the effective rights for the logged-in user in the lower portion of the window, as shown in Figure 8.10. In this example, the logged in user is admin, with effective rights of SRWCEMFA.

To display a logged-in user's effective rights with the Rights command, at a command prompt, navigate to the file or directory that you want to query. At the appropriate prompt, enter Rights, as shown in Figure 8.11. The logged-in user's effective rights are displayed. In this case, because the logged in user is the admin, his effective rights are SRWCEMFA.

The Rights command is a useful tool. So far in this chapter, you have learned only about the command and the /T option. To view the other options that are available, at a command prompt, run Rights /?. You see a screen similar to Figure 8.12.

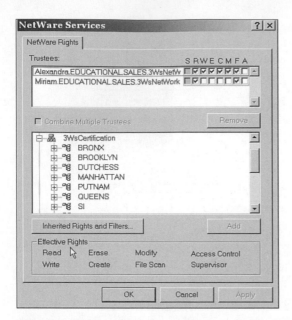

Figure 8.10 Effective rights using the red N in the Windows system tray.

Figure 8.11 Effective rights using the **Rights** command.

Figure 8.12 **Rights** command options.

What Are the Rules of NetWare 6.5 File System Security?

As you have noticed in this chapter, many parameters govern file system security. The easiest way to digest them is with a list.

➤ The file system rights in order are Supervisor, Read, Write, Create, Erase, Modify, File Scan, and Access Control.

➤ A user's default right to his home directory is [RWCEMFA].

➤ The Supervisor right grants a user all rights.

➤ You cannot overwrite or filter the Supervisor right, and you can only remove it at the file system level at which it is granted. If an admin grants you the S right at the Certification level, he cannot change it at the NW65CNA level. He can only change it where he made the initial assignment, at the Certification level.

➤ Users who are in the same Container as the file server are automatically granted [RF] to the Public directory.

➤ You can globally change rights with an IRF, or you can specifically filter them by making a new trustee assignment.

➤ The best way to block rights is to grant a new trustee assignment.

➤ IRFs are used only as a last resort in the file system, but you will see them on the exam.

➤ An explicit trustee assignment to a user or group overwrites a user or group's inherited assignment respectively at a given level of the file system.

➤ Rights can be granted to Users, Groups, Organizational Roles, Containers, and the [Public] trustee. A user can receive rights from multiple eDirectory objects at a given level in the file system.

➤ Rights that are granted to users and groups are cumulative. If a user has individual rights and rights from his Container, those rights, inherited or explicit, are added together.

➤ Effective rights are calculated, as shown in Figure 8.13, by adding group rights to individual rights (inherited or explicit) and subtracting any IRFs in the file system that are encountered.

   GROUP RIGHTS
      +
  <u>INDIVIDUAL RIGHTS</u>
      -
<u>ANY IRFs ALONG THE WAY</u>

  =EFFECTIVE RIGHTS

Figure 8.13 Calculating effective rights.

Effective Rights Practice

Now that you know the rules governing file system security, it's time for you to calculate a user's effective rights based on a scenario. You will see two scenarios: one that is easy, and one that is a bit more complex. The file system structure that is used in these two is the same that has been used throughout this chapter (refer to Figure 8.1), which is Data, Certification, NW65CNA, FileSyst, EffRghts.txt. Based on the scenarios, fill in the blanks with the rights that the user has at each level of the file system. Don't cheat and look at the answers before tackling these on your own.

 On the exam, you are given a file structure and a scenario. For instructional purposes, I am using a table format to show you how rights, explicit and inherited, follow the rules that were just presented. On the exam, you will *not* be given a table like I am using here. You can create your own, if you have time, but the best strategy is to visualize the flow of rights based on the examples used in this book.

Scenario 1

If Alexandra has been granted the RWCEMFA trustee assignment to the Certification directory and has been granted the RWCF trustee assignment to the EffRghts.txt file, what are her effective rights at each level of the file system?

Fill in the blanks in Table 8.1.

Table 8.1	Calculating Effective Rights: Simple Inheritance	
Folder/File	**Rights**	**Alexandra**
Certification	IRF	[SRWCEMFA]
	Trustee assignment	RWCEMFA
	Effective	
NW65CNA	IRF	[SR F]
	Inherited	
	Trustee assignment	
	Effective	
FileSyst	IRF	[SRWCEMFA]
	Inherited	
	Trustee assignment	
	Effective	
EffRghts.txt	IRF	[SR F]
	Inherited	
	Trustee assignment	RWCF
	Effective	

The correct response to Scenario 1 is shown in Table 8.2. Alexandra has her initial trustee assignment at Certification filtered in NW65CNA, so effectively she has only RF at that level and at FileSyst. In EffRghts.txt, she is granted a new explicit assignment that overwrites her inherited assignment, so her new effective rights in EffRghts.txt are RWCF.

Table 8.2	Calculating Effective Rights: Simple Inheritance Answer	
Folder/File	**Rights**	**Alexandra**
Certification	IRF	[SRWCEMFA]
	Trustee assignment	RWCEMFA
	Effective	RWCEMFA

(continued)

Table 8.2	Calculating Effective Rights: Simple Inheritance Answer *(continued)*	
Folder/File	**Rights**	**Alexandra**
NW65CNA	IRF	[SR F]
	Inherited	RF
	Trustee assignment	—
	Effective	RF
FileSyst	IRF	[SRWCEMFA]
	Inherited	RF
	Trustee assignment	—
	Effective	RF
EffRghts.txt	IRF	[SR F]
	Inherited	—
	Trustee assignment	RWCF
	Effective	RWCF

Scenario 2

Jill has been granted the RWCEFA individual trustee assignment to the Certification directory. As a member of the Trainers group, she has been granted the WCEM assignment to the NW65CNA directory. In the FileSyst directory, Jill is granted an individual assignment of S, whereas in EffRghts.txt, the trainers are granted a new group assignment of RF. What are Jill's effective rights at each level of the file system? Fill in Table 8.3.

Table 8.3	Calculating Effective Rights: Complex Inheritance	
Folder/File	**Rights**	**Jill**
Certification	IRF	[SRWCEMFA]
	Individual trustee assignment	RWCEFA
	Group trustee assignment	
	Effective	
NW65CNA	IRF	[SR F]
	Inherited	
	Individual trustee assignment	
	Group trustee assignment	WCEM
	Effective	

(continued)

Table 8.3	Calculating Effective Rights: Complex Inheritance *(continued)*	
Folder/File	**Rights**	**Jill**
FileSyst	IRF	[SRWCEMFA]
	Inherited	
	Individual trustee assignment	S
	Group trustee assignment	
	Effective	
EffRghts.txt	IRF	[SR F]
	Inherited	
	Individual trustee assignment	
	Group trustee assignment	RF
	Effective	

The answers for Scenario 2 are presented in Table 8.4.

Table 8.4	Calculating Effective Rights: Complex Inheritance Answer	
Folder/File	**Rights**	**Jill**
Certification	IRF	[SRWCEMFA]
	Individual trustee assignment	RWCEFA
	Group trustee assignment	—
	Effective	RWCEFA
NW65CNA	IRF	[SR F]
	Inherited	RF
	Individual trustee assignment	—
	Group trustee assignment	WCEM
	Effective	RWCEMF
FileSyst	IRF	[SRWCEMFA]
	Inherited	RWCEMF
	Individual trustee assignment	S
	Group trustee assignment	—
	Effective	SRWCEMFA
EffRghts.txt	IRF	[SR F]
	Inherited	SRF
	Individual trustee assignment	—
	Group trustee assignment	RF
	Effective	SRWCEMFA

Jill's effective rights at Certification are RWCEFA, which is based on the individual assignment received at Certification. Coming through the IRF at NW65CNA, Jill inherits RF but also receives a new Group trustee assignment of WCEM. Effectively at NW65CNA, she now has RWCEMF. After the IRF at FileSyst, Jill inherits the same rights because all rights are allowed through. At FileSyst, she receives a new individual assignment of S and no new group assignment. Effectively at FileSyst, she has all rights because of S. Coming through the IRF at EffRghts.txt, Jill inherits SRF and receives a new group assignment of RF. Effectively, because of the S right inherited from FileSyst, she has all rights at EffRghts.txt.

For more examples and practice, see Appendix B, "NetWare 6.5 File System: Effective Rights Practice Scenarios."

The table format used in Tables 8.1 through 8.4 is based on Novell's earlier presentation of these types of examples. This table format has changed over the years, with some preferring this method and others the newer method, which is a compilation of two tables, one for individual rights and the other for group rights. It does not matter which is preferred; on the exam, no table is given to you. To differentiate between individual rights and group rights on the exam, use your scratch paper to draw a circle around rights coming from Groups, Containers, Organizational Role objects, or the [Public] trustee, and leave the individual assignments uncircled. Do whatever works for you.

Plan File System Rights

Two Novell guidelines are available for implementing all these rules and concepts for file system security:

➤ Plan your file system rights from the top down. Only give the minimum rights needed where they are needed in the structure. Don't give rights at the root of the volume, especially the S right. Take into account the role of inheritance and that the S right cannot be blocked or IRFed. Also don't give rights too close to the root of the volume. Give them as close to the file system resource as possible.

➤ Give rights to the largest contingent of users who have similar needs as possible. Give rights first to the [Public] trustee when possible, then to Container objects, then to Group objects and Organizational Role objects, and then to individual users. Only when absolutely necessary should you use security equivalence.

If you follow these two guidelines, your chances of having success with NetWare 6.5 file system security are good.

Identify Directory and File Attributes

When implemented, one additional level of file system security can override trustee assignments. This level involves the use of directory and file attributes. An attribute is a property of a directory or file that dictates how users can manage it. It has global impact. If a file is flagged read-only, that RO attribute impacts all users, even those that have the S right to the file.

Directories and files have different attributes. Just as with other file system tasks, you can manage attributes by using a variety of utilities.

In Remote Manager, you can manage both directory and file attributes by selecting the attribute link next to the file or directory that you want to manage. Figures 8.14 and 8.15 respectively show the available directory attributes and file attributes that you can manage using Remote Manager.

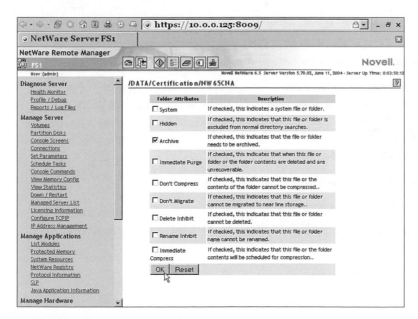

Figure 8.14   Remote Manager: Directory attributes.

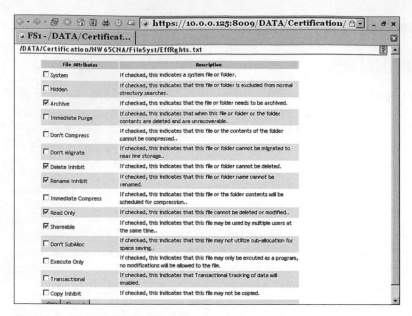

Figure 8.15   Remote Manager: File attributes.

Following are the directory attributes in NetWare 6.5:

➤ Sy for System, which prevents a directory from being seen if the DIR command is run. It also prevents it from being copied or deleted.

➤ Ri for Rename Inhibit.

➤ P for Purge immediately upon deletion.

➤ N for Normal, in other words, no attributes.

➤ Ic for Immediate compress.

➤ H for Hidden for directories that should not be displayed when a DIR command is run.

➤ Dm for Don't Migrate.

➤ Di for Delete Inhibit.

➤ Dc for Don't Compress.

➤ All to specify Di, H, Ic, P, Ri, and Sy as a group.

Next are the file attributes:

➤ A for Archive to show that you need to back up a file.

➤ Ci for Copy Inhibit.

➤ Dc for Don't Compress.

➤ Di for Delete Inhibit.

➤ Dm for Don't Migrate.

➤ Ds for Don't Suballocate; used on traditional volumes.

➤ H for Hidden.

➤ Ic for Immediate Compress.

➤ P for Purge immediately upon deletion.

➤ Ri for Rename Inhibit.

➤ Ro for Read-Only. You cannot write to or delete this file.

➤ Rw for Read-Write.

➤ Sh for Shareable. Many network-based applications that are for multiple users require this.

➤ Sy for System, which prevents a file from being seen if the DIR command is run, and prevents it from being copied or deleted.

➤ T for Transactional, which protects the file using the Transaction Tracking System.

You can manage these attributes with ConsoleOne and NetWare Administrator, respectively, accessing the Properties or Details page of the file or directory and then respectively selecting the Attributes tab or the Attributes button.

Three other tools are useful for managing attributes:

➤ FILER

➤ FLAG

➤ NDIR

All of these are command-line utilities, although FILER is launched from the command line and has a menu-driven interface. All three tools have their roots in earlier versions of NetWare but are still useful in file system security management.

FILER is one of the most powerful and dangerous publicly available utilities in NetWare 6.5. It is in the Public directory. You can use it to manage attributes and rights. In the wrong hands, with a single keystroke, FILER can obliterate a file system hierarchy. Be careful with it. You might want to move

FILER from the Public directory to the System directory, where users cannot readily access it. FILER's attribute abilities are shown in Figure 8.16. A caution regarding FILER is shown in Figure 8.17. In this figure, all directories are highlighted on the SYS volume and the Delete key has been pressed. Notice the menu that appears.

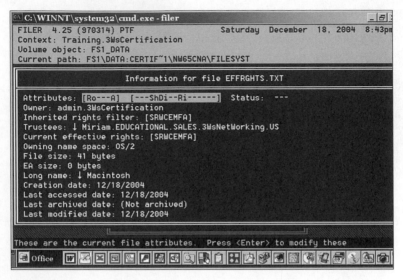

Figure 8.16 FILER's attributes options.

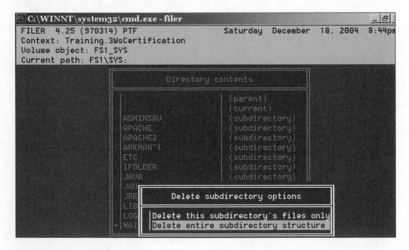

Figure 8.17 A FILER caution.

FLAG, shown in Figure 8.18, is a workstation-based executable that is run from a command prompt to display or modify a directory or file's attributes. For all of FLAG's options, run FLAG /? at a command prompt.

Figure 8.18   The **FLAG** command.

NDIR, shown in Figures 8.19 and 8.20, is one of the most overlooked work-station-based executables, run from a command prompt. It displays information on files, directories, or volumes. You can display rights, attributes, IRFs, last time accessed, last time modified, and much more. For all of NDIR's options, run NDIR /? at a command prompt.

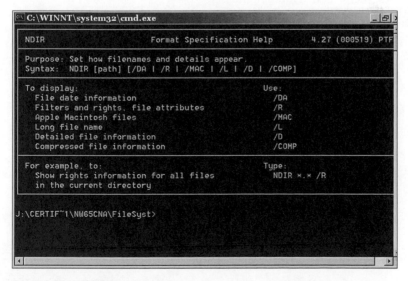

Figure 8.19   The **NDIR** /? command.

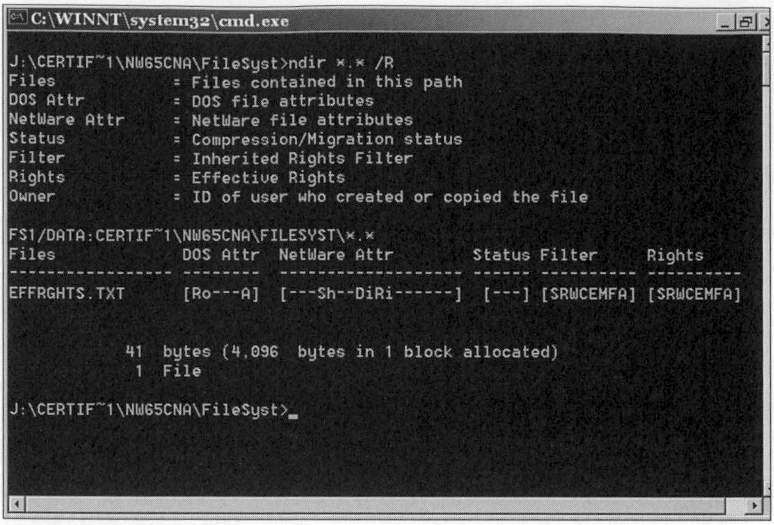

```
C:\WINNT\system32\cmd.exe                                    _ 8 >

J:\CERTIF~1\NW65CNA\FileSyst>ndir *.* /R
Files              = Files contained in this path
DOS Attr           = DOS file attributes
NetWare Attr       = NetWare file attributes
Status             = Compression/Migration status
Filter             = Inherited Rights Filter
Rights             = Effective Rights
Owner              = ID of user who created or copied the file


FS1/DATA:CERTIF~1\NW65CNA\FILESYST\*.*
Files            DOS Attr  NetWare Attr        Status Filter     Rights
---------------- --------  ------------------- ------ ---------- ----------
EFFRGHTS.TXT     [Ro---A]  [---Sh--DiRi------]  [---] [SRWCEMFA] [SRWCEMFA]



        41  bytes (4,096  bytes in 1 block allocated)
         1  File

J:\CERTIF~1\NW65CNA\FileSyst>_
```

Figure 8.20   The **NDIR** /**R** Command.

Become familiar with FILER, FLAG, and NDIR for day-to-day tasks on
your production network. Remember: FLAG is useful when you want to
update a directory that is full of Ro files. You can flag all files as Rw for a
moment, make the necessary updates, and reflag all the files as Ro. You can
do this with three simple commands. In a GUI, you have to change attributes on each file, which is inefficient.

Exam Prep Questions

1. Which type of NetWare 6.5 security governs who can access a Volume object?

   A. ○ Login

   B. ○ File system

   C. ○ eDirectory

   D. ○ Printing

   Answer C is correct. eDirectory security controls who can access objects in the eDirectory tree, such as Volume objects. Answer A is incorrect. Login security controls who can gain access to the network resources. Answer B is incorrect. File system security controls who can access files and directories and what capabilities a user has at any given place in the file system. Answer D is incorrect. Printing security controls who can print to any given printing device and who can mange printer devices and print jobs.

2. What NetWare 6.5 feature is not on by default but is helpful for users who must authenticate to many different types of systems?

   A. ○ Universal Password

   B. ○ Native File Access Protocol

   C. ○ Virtual Office

   D. ○ Simple Password

   Answer A is correct. The Universal Password feature enables you to integrate and manage different types of passwords and systems of authentication into a single common password. This feature is *not* turned on by default. Its benefit comes into play when you have users who must log in to systems using different authentication mechanisms, or when you are using Native File Access Protocol in a NetWare 6.5 environment. Instead of having to remember multiple passwords, the user can authenticate to all systems with a single password. Answers B and C are incorrect. They do not provide a unified method of authentication. Answer D is incorrect. In earlier versions of NetWare, this would be a possible correct response. It is the password that is used in NetWare 6.0 for clientless environments using the Native File Access Protocol.

3. What is a User, Group, Organizational Role object, or Container that is explicitly granted rights to a directory or file by being added to the directory or file's ACL?

   A. ○ Admin

   B. ○ Supervisor

   C. ○ Trustee

   D. ○ Administrator

Answer C is correct. A trustee is a User, Group, Organizational Role object, or Container that is explicitly granted rights to a directory or file by being added to the directory or file's ACL. Answers A, B, and D are administrative users in various network operating systems.

4. Which file system rights do you need to grant to a user if he has to copy files to a directory? (Select two.)

A. ❑ R

B. ❑ F

C. ❑ C

D. ❑ W

Answers B and C are correct. To copy files to a directory, you need the Create and File Scan rights. Answers A and D are incorrect. You do not need Read and Write to copy files to a diretory.

5. What is the only file system right that you need to grant to a user if all he needs to do is rename a directory?

A. ◯ M

B. ◯ S

C. ◯ A

D. ◯ E

Answer A is correct. The Modify right is the only right you need to grant to a user if all he needs to do is rename a directory. Answers B, C, and D are incorrect. The Supervisor right lets the user rename files and directories and a lot more. The user does not need Access Control or Erase to rename a file or directory.

6. The **NW65CNA** directory has an IRF of [SRWF]. Alexandra has been granted [RWCEMF] at **NW65CNA**. What rights does she have at the **NW65CNA** directory?

A. ◯ [SRWCEMFA]

B. ◯ [SRWF]

C. ◯ [CEM]

D. ◯ [RWCEMF]

Answer D is correct. An explicit assignment overwrites an inherited assignment and is not affected by an IRF. Alexandra's rights at NW65CNA are the rights she has been explicitly granted at that level, [RWCEMF]. Answers A, B, and C are not correct. They do not follow the rules governing file system rights.

7. You want to globally block the [MA] rights, and only those rights, at the **NW65CNA** directory. Which IRF should you configure for this directory?

   A. ○ [MA]

   B. ○ [RWCEF]

   C. ○ [SMA]

   D. ○ [SRWCEF]

   Answer D is correct. With IRFs, you have to think backward. What you see in the IRF is what is allowed to filter through. If you do not see it, it is blocked. Also, you must remember that the Supervisor right cannot be filtered; it is always displayed. The only IRF that only blocks [MA] is [SRWCEF]. Answers A, B, and C are incorrect and do not follow the rules governing the file system.

8. You want to display all objects on the **NW65CNA** ACL at the command prompt. Which of the following should you use to accomplish this?

   A. ○ **RIGHTS** /T

   B. ○ **FILER /T**

   C. ○ **NDIR /T**

   D. ○ **FLAG /T**

   Answer A is correct. The RIGHTS /T command displays a directory or file's ACL. Answers B, C, and D are incorrect. These are file system utilities for displaying file, directory, and volume information, and changing attributes.

9. You want to begin granting rights to your NetWare 6.5 users. In what order should you assign the following rights?

   1. [Public] trustee

   2. User

   3. Security equivalence

   4. Organizational unit

   5. Organizational Role object

   A. ○ 1, 5, 4, 2, 3

   B. ○ 1, 4, 5, 3, 2

   C. ○ 2, 5, 4, 1, 3

   D. ○ 1, 4, 5, 2, 3

   Answer D is correct. When you are assigning rights, you assign them from the largest group to the single user, and only when necessary do you use security equivalence. In this case, you would first assign rights to the [Public] trustee, then a Container object such as an Organizational Unit, then Organizational Role objects or groups, then users, and only as a last resort would you use security equivalence. No other answer follows this order of assignment.

10. You do not want anyone to see your administrative directory on the **DATA** volume on your NetWare 6.5 server, if that person uses the **DOS DIR** command. You do not want to delete it either. Which attributes can you assign to this directory so that it will be protected? (Select two.)

A. ❏ Dc

B. ❏ N

C. ❏ P

D. ❏ H

E. ❏ Sy

Answers D and E are correct. You can either assign a directory the Hidden attribute or the System attribute if you do not want someone to see the directory when he uses the DOS DIR command. Answers A, B, and C are incorrect. Dc is for Don't Compress a directory, N is for Normal (no attributes are enabled), and P is to purge a directory immediately when files are deleted.

9

eDirectory Security

. . . .

Terms you'll need to understand:

✓ NetAdmin

✓ IRF

✓ ACL

✓ Trustee

✓ Effective rights

✓ Selected property rights

✓ All property rights

✓ Object rights

✓ Entry rights

✓ Property rights

✓ Attribute rights

Techniques you'll need to master:

✓ Describe eDirectory security

✓ Determine how rights flow

✓ Block inherited rights

✓ Determine eDirectory effective rights

✓ Troubleshoot eDirectory security

You have come a long way toward your NetWare 6.5 CNA. The previous chapter was surely a baptism by fire. Before you dive into this chapter, please be absolutely sure that you are comfortable with all of the concepts discussed in Chapter 8, "File System Security." If you are not, stop and go back over that chapter. When you are thoroughly comfortable with file system concepts, you are ready to take that information and apply it to eDirectory security.

In this chapter, you learn to describe eDirectory security, including what rights are used to secure network resources, how rights flow and are blocked, how to determine effective rights, and how to troubleshoot when an object has too many or too few rights.

Describe eDirectory Security

eDirectory security addresses the capabilities that a user has in the eDirectory tree when he has logged in. Can a user access a Controlled Access printer, control a Container object, or create or delete objects in his container? These questions are addressed in eDirectory security.

As was discussed in Chapter 8, the concepts of trustees, rights, access control lists (ACLs), inherited rights filters (IRFs), inheritance, explicit and inherited assignments, and effective rights apply both to file system security and eDirectory security. There are a few differences, but the major one is that now instead of looking at files and directories in a file system hierarchy, you are looking at objects in the hierarchical eDirectory tree. One point can be confusing for new CNAs when working in ConsoleOne: When you are working in file system security, you are looking at yellow folders and files. When you are working in eDirectory security, you are looking at little people-like objects and Container objects.

The fact that NetWare has both file system security and eDirectory security gives the CNA one potential design option. You could have an admin who is completely in control of file system security, and another admin could control eDirectory security. It's a division of labor. In eDirectory security, you can even take that a step further and design your eDirectory administration motif around a centralized administration plan or distributed administration plan, in which each container has its own admin. In a centralized scheme, one admin at the top of the tree controls everything. In distributed administration, one top-level admin controls high-order tree tasks, and container admins take care of the day-to-day tasks.

File system security and eDirectory security in NetWare 6.5 are different in three other ways:

➤ Rights do not flow from the file system to eDirectory with one exception. That exception, as mentioned in Chapter 8, is at the Server object. Any eDirectory object that has the Supervisor object right to the Server object automatically receives the Supervisor file system right to all volumes on the Server object. This is the only link between file system and eDirectory rights.

➤ The file system has a single set of eight rights. eDirectory has two sets of six rights each. One set of rights is called object or entry rights, and the other set of rights is called property or attribute rights. Each set has two names depending on the utility used to manage the rights. There has been little consistency in this regard over the years. Up to NetWare 5, the rights were always called object and property. With NetWare 5, Novell tried to move everyone to the entry and attribute names primarily because they were going to be visible in ConsoleOne. With NetWare 6.x, Novell has regressed and gone back to using both naming conventions. This chapter sticks with object and property except where the utility being looked at varies.

➤ Both object and property rights have a Supervisor right. In the file system, you noted that the Supervisor right cannot be blocked, removed, or overwritten except at the point where the right was initially given. In eDirectory security, that is not the case. Both the Supervisor object and Supervisor property rights can be blocked, filtered, removed, or overwritten in the tree. The Supervisor eDirectory rights can be revoked, which could potentially be a disaster for a tree administrator who has not explicitly granted another User object the same rights to the Tree object. This is a time when having one or more backup admins is critical. The Admin object could potentially lose supervisory control of the complete tree. As mentioned in an earlier chapter, Dr. Peter Kuo of http://www.dreamlan.com has developed a get-out-of-jail tool if this should happen. The tool is called MAKESU.NLM. Instead of purchasing this tool, it is best to realize that the Supervisor eDirectory rights can be revoked and take proactive steps to avoid such a disaster.

As you can see, for you to be a top-notch CNA, you need to explore eDirectory security. This section introduces you to the following:

➤ The 12 default eDirectory rights and the eDirectory ACL

➤ The utilities that you can use to administer eDirectory security

➤ The default eDirectory rights assignments

➤ The rules and guidelines for eDirectory rights

For all examples in this chapter, the eDirectory hierarchy that will be used is shown in Figure 9.1.

Figure 9.1 Sample eDirectory branch.

Now you'll learn about the rights.

eDirectory Rights and the eDirectory ACL

eDirectory rights control access to eDirectory objects. The following objects are potential trustees in eDirectory security:

➤ Users

➤ Groups

➤ Container objects

➤ Organizational Role objects

➤ The Tree object or trustee

➤ The [Public] trustee

Users who are members of groups, occupants of Organizational Role objects, or reside in a container automatically receive the rights that are assigned to those containing objects. All authenticated users in the tree receive rights assignments when the Tree object, sometimes called the Tree trustee, is made a trustee of an object. All authenticated and nonauthenticated objects receive rights assignments when the [Public] trustee is made a trustee of an object. Rights, just like the file system, can also be assigned through the security equivalence option.

Two sets of eDirectory rights exist: object and property. Object rights govern an object's extrinsic attributes. Object rights address the following types of questions: Can the object be seen, created, deleted, or renamed? Property rights govern an object's intrinsic attributes. They include questions such as these: Can the object's properties be read and compared to other objects, and can a user modify those properties if he has the rights to do so?

Following are the default object rights:

➤ **Supervisor**—If you have the Supervisor object right, you have all object rights and all property rights. The Supervisor right grants you complete eDirectory control over eDirectory rights because you are granted all object and all property rights.

➤ **Browse**—If you are granted the Browse object right, which a user is granted by default when made a trustee of an object, you can see the object in the tree.

➤ **Create**—If you are granted the Create object right, you can create objects in a container. The Create object right can be granted only at the container level. Through inheritance, this right can filter down to Leaf objects, but it has no effect on Leaf objects because you cannot create an object in a Leaf object.

➤ **Delete**—If you have been granted the Delete object right, you can delete an eDirectory object.

➤ **Rename**—If you have been granted the Rename object right, you can rename an eDirectory object.

➤ **Inheritable**—If you have been granted the Inheritable object right, the object rights you have been granted can be inherited to objects and sub-containers in the container. The Inheritable object right can be granted only at the container level. It is not applicable to Leaf objects. The Inheritable object right is granted automatically to a trustee of a container. If the Inheritable right is revoked or cleared, the trustee's rights cannot be inherited in subcontainers or objects in the container.

 In the iManager screens that you will see later in this chapter, you will notice a Dynamic object right and a Dynamic property right. These rights exist in iManager but not ConsoleOne. They apply only to Dynamic Group objects that you have created. If you create a Dynamic Group object in iManager and make it a trustee of another object, the Dynamic check boxes are enabled. The discussion of Dynamic Groups is beyond the scope of this book. For further information, check out Peter Kuo's book *Novell's Guide to Troubleshooting eDirectory*. Because this is not historically considered a default object or property right, it is not covered on this exam.

Following are the default property rights:

➤ **Supervisor**—If you are granted the Supervisor property right, you have all property rights. The Supervisor right grants you complete eDirectory control over eDirectory property rights.

➤ **Read**—If you are granted the Read property right, you can read an eDirectory object's property values. When the Read property right is granted, the Compare property right is automatically granted at the same time.

➤ **Compare**—If you are granted the Compare property right, you can compare property values. When two property values are compared, the result is a Boolean TRUE or FALSE. All that is visible is whether the properties are the same or different. The actual properties are invisible. This property right is granted automatically when the Read property right is granted.

➤ **Write**—If you are granted the Write property right, you can write a value to a property. You can add, change, or delete a value. When you are granted this property right, you are also automatically granted the Add/Remove Self property right. Granting the Write property right under certain conditions is a good business decision. However, if it is granted through the All Properties option, which will be discussed next, a user could potentially abuse his power, write himself into a trustees list, and take control of an object.

➤ **Add/Remove Self**—If you are granted the Add/Remove Self property right, you can add or remove yourself as an object's property value. A user who has this right can add himself to an object's trustees list. This right is granted automatically when the Write property right is granted.

➤ **Inheritable**—If you have been granted the Inheritable property right, the property rights you have been granted can be inherited to objects and subcontainers in the container. The Inheritable property right can only be granted at the container level. It is not applicable to Leaf objects. The Inheritable property right is granted automatically to a trustee of a container when the All Properties option is selected. The Inheritable property right is not granted automatically if the Selected Properties option is selected. If the Inheritable right is revoked or cleared, the trustees rights cannot be inherited in subcontainers or objects in the container.

The property rights are further divided into two types:

➤ All Property Rights, also known as the All Attribute Rights option

➤ Selected Property Rights option

When a User object, for example, is granted the default property rights to a Container object, he is granted the RC rights through the All Properties option. This means that the user has Read and Compare rights to all of the properties associated with that Container object, regardless of whether the user needs access to all of the properties. This is the default method of assigning property rights. It is not the most secure or the one that Novell recommends, but it is the easiest to administer for a new CNA.

Instead of granting property rights through the All Properties option, you can grant property rights through the Selected Properties option. In this case, the user is granted property rights only to those properties that he needs access to. For example, a user is granted property rights to a Container object so that he can change the phone number for all users in the container. That is all he needs to do. Instead of granting the Write property right at the container level to the user, which would grant the user Write access to all properties, you select Selected Properties. Then you choose the Telephone Number property and grant the user the Write property right. In this case, you grant the user the RCW property rights to the Telephone Number property. This way, the user can change only the telephone numbers. In this example, the user is granted the RC to all properties of the Container object, including the telephone number. However, when you grant a Selected Property assignment, as you did to the Telephone property, the Selected Property assignment overwrites the All Properties assignment. Therefore, through All Properties, the user has RC to the telephone number, and through Selected Properties, he has RCW. His effective rights for the Telephone Number property are RCW. You can see an example of choosing a Selected Property in NetWare Administrator in Figure 9.2. NetWare Administrator is shown because it presents the clearest depiction of this task. Choosing a Selected Property in iManager is shown in Figure 9.3.

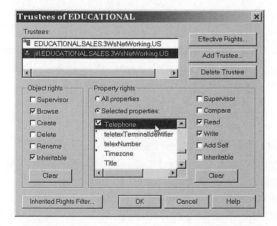

Figure 9.2 Selected Properties option in NetWare Administrator.

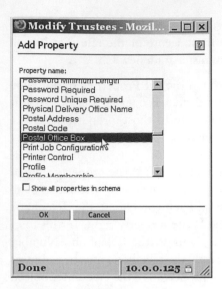

Figure 9.3 Selected Properties option in iManager.

One word of caution about Selected Properties and All Properties. When you select All Properties, they are inheritable by default. When you choose Selected Properties, they are not inheritable by default. You can choose to have them inheritable, but if you don't specify, they apply the Selected Property rights assignment only to the eDirectory Container object and go no lower in the tree.

Granting eDirectory Rights: The Utilities

With the release of NetWare 6.5, Novell has attempted to move all NetWare administrators to Web-based management tools, as you learned in Chapter 8. You can use one of these tools to manage eDirectory security. However, some tried-and-true utilities are still the workhorses of eDirectory security management. For both the exam and the real world, you need to know all of them and then make a decision about which interface you like the best. As you explore eDirectory security, you will be introduced to the following utilities:

➤ **iManager**—This is the utility that is most heavily weighted on the exam, so you need to be familiar with the interface, as shown throughout this chapter. This is the latest and greatest tool for managing eDirectory rights. Four options are available for managing rights, shown in Figure 9.4. Notice in iManager that you can manage IRFs, trustee assignments, and rights to other objects, and you can view effective rights. To view an object's ACL, select Modify Trustees under Rights, and select the object whose ACL you want to display. The ACL is displayed, as shown in Figure 9.5. You can click the Assigned Rights link next to the trustee you want to query to view a trustee's rights. You can also add and delete trustees in this screen.

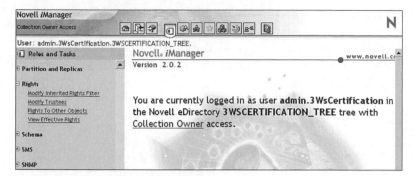

Figure 9.4   iManager: Rights.

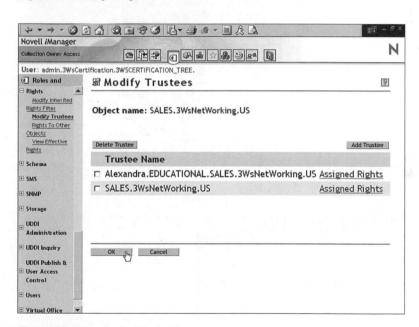

Figure 9.5   iManager: An object's ACL.

➤ **ConsoleOne**—This is what many from the NetWare 5.x days are comfortable with on a Windows-based workstation. This is a reliable Java utility where much of Novell's energy was spent in the late 1990s and early part of this century. For many CNAs, this is where the lion's share of eDirectory security is managed. You can access an object's ACL by right-clicking the object, selecting Trustees of This Object, NDS Rights tab, Trustees of This Object, as shown in Figure 9.6. Notice on the NDS Rights tab that you can also manage IRFs and effective rights, add or delete a trustee, and view a trustee's assigned rights. If you want to view an object's effective rights, click the Effective Rights button, and a screen similar to Figure 9.7 is displayed. On this interface, properties are called attributes, and object rights are called entry rights. Also note the difference between All Attribute Rights and those rights that are grayed out, the Selected Attribute Rights. To display an object's Effective Selected Attribute Right, scroll down to the attribute. The effective rights are displayed in the Rights dialog box.

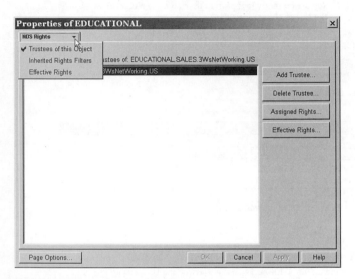

Figure 9.6   ConsoleOne: An object's ACL.

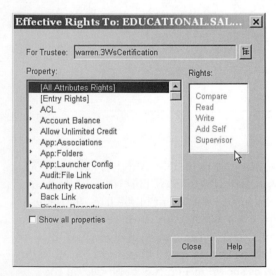

Figure 9.7   ConsoleOne: An object's effective rights.

➤ **NetWare Administrator**—This is still the favorite of those who grew
with it from the NetWare 4.x days. It does a great job with eDirectory
security issues, but it lacks plug-in support for many objects. Just as with
ConsoleOne, you can view an object's ACL by right-clicking it and then
selecting Trustees of This object, as shown in Figure 9.8. Notice on this
interface that you can add or delete a trustee, view an object's effective
rights, and manage an object's IRF. Also notice the All Properties and
Selected Properties buttons.

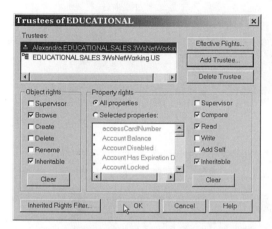

Figure 9.8   NetWare Administrator: An object's ACL.

➤ **NetAdmin**—This is a menu-driven command-line utility that is no
longer packaged with NetWare. It was a staple in the NetWare 4.x days,
and if you can find it, it still works in NetWare 6.5. It is a simple tool
that enables you to manage eDirectory rights, IRFs, and effective rights.
Its opening screen is shown in Figure 9.9, and its eDirectory security
menu is shown in Figure 9.10.

 A couple of cautionary notes are necessary when it comes to NetAdmin. If you want
to use NetAdmin because of its simplicity, you must be sure that you have all the necessary .MSG, .HEP, .IDX, .XLT, and .OVL supporting files in the directory with
NETADMIN.EXE; otherwise, the utility does not run.

Also be aware that NetAdmin has not been supported since NetWare 4. The schema
in NetWare 6.5 has been extended significantly since the days of NetWare 4.x. User
objects and the like can be managed in NetAdmin, but the newer objects generate
some error messages and might cause you fits. It works for some tasks, but not all.

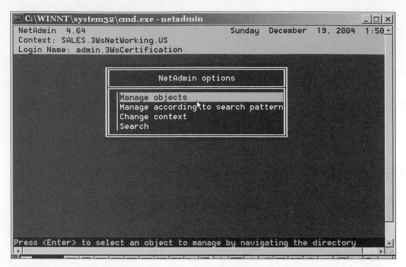

Figure 9.9 NetAdmin: Opening screen.

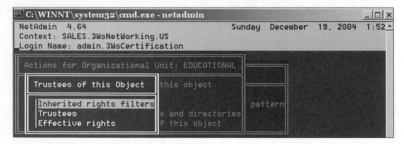

Figure 9.10 NetAdmin: eDirectory security menu.

Default Rights

It is time to explore the default eDirectory rights assignments that are system generated. These rights assignments work great on a new NetWare 6.5 server. Use them and judiciously modify them. Be careful that you do not give too many or too few rights for your users to be able to work.

The rule of thumb when it comes to eDirectory rights is to give rights only where they are needed as low down in the tree as possible, and only assign those rights that are needed. Do not overassign rights to make things easy for you in a pinch.

The following default eDirectory assignments are worth noting:

➤ Admin is granted the Supervisor object right to the Tree object when the tree is created.

➤ Admin is granted the Supervisor object right to the Server object, which means that the admin has the Supervisor file system right to all volumes on the Server object.

➤ The [Public] trustee is granted the Browse object right to the Tree object so that users can see the tree before logging in.

➤ The Tree object has the Read property right to the host server name and host resource properties for all Volume objects on the server.

The Rules and Guidelines for eDirectory Rights

Now you can take your knowledge of the 12 eDirectory rights and compile a list of rules and guidelines that govern them:

 You will probably encounter many questions on eDirectory security on the CNA exam. Some will be derivatives from these rules and guidelines, whereas others will present a scenario to you and ask you to apply these rules in an attempt to calculate an object's effective rights, much as you did in file system security. It is imperative that you know the rules and guidelines of eDirectory security.

➤ The Supervisor object right gives all object and all property rights.

➤ Supervisor property rights give all property rights.

➤ When the Read right is granted, Compare is granted automatically. Compare evaluates two values and returns a TRUE or FALSE.

➤ The Admin user is granted Supervisor object rights to the Tree object when the tree is created.

➤ All users are granted the Browse object right to the tree through the [Public] trustee.

➤ A Selected Property rights assignment overrides an All Property assignment.

➤ Supervisor rights can be overwritten, revoked, and can be IRFed.

➤ When you assign Supervisory rights, do not just assign the S right. Instead, assign all of the object and property rights in case the S right is revoked, overwritten, or IRFed.

➤ The Security Equal property can be a nightmare to troubleshoot; only use it as a last resort.

➤ Use the Organizational Role object for task-oriented positions, such as backup administrators.

➤ Rename your admins so they are not targets for hackers.

➤ A new explicit assignment overwrites an inherited assignment. Furthermore, a new object assignment overwrites an inherited object assignment, and a new property assignment overwrites an inherited property assignment. A new property assignment does *not* overwrite an inherited object assignment.

➤ Any object that has an explicit or inherited Supervisor object rights assignment to the Server object automatically receives the Supervisor file system right to all volumes on the server, and the file system right cannot be revoked, overwritten, or IRFed.

➤ The Create and Inheritable rights only apply to Container objects. If you grant these rights to a Container object, Leaf objects have these rights grayed out when you display their effective rights. You cannot create another object in a Leaf object, and Leaf objects contain no other objects. Therefore on Leaf objects, the inheritable right is a moot right.

➤ The Inheritable right at the container level is not enabled by default if Selected Property rights are used. It is enabled by default if All Property rights are used at the container level.

➤ Give rights only where they are needed as low down in the tree as possible, and only assign those rights that are needed. Do not overassign rights to make things easy for you in a pinch.

➤ If you have a new container with no objects in it, and you want a user to supervise that container and all of the objects in it (including Server objects), the only eDirectory right you have to assign to that user is the Create object right at the container level. He then owns any object he creates in that container. He is the supervisor of all objects he creates. This is an easy way to give the minimum rights assignment for the maximum productive output from a user. You do not have to worry about the user crawling out of the container with too many rights and hacking another container.

Determine How Rights Flow

For the third time in this book, the discussion comes back to inheritance. In Chapters 5, "Introduction to eDirectory," and 8, you heard about this vital security concept. Once more, it is the backbone of eDirectory security.

As you remember, inheritance is the process of rights flowing down from a higher level to a lower level in both the eDirectory tree and the NetWare 6.5 file system. Looking at the sample eDirectory structure shown in Figure 9.1—US, 3WsNetWorking, Sales, Educational—if you make Alexandra a trustee of the 3WsNetWorking Organization object and grant her B object and RC property rights, by inheritance, she will have B and RC in the Sales and Educational OUs. Her explicit assignment is at 3WsNetWorking, and she has an inherited assignment at the Sales and Educational OUs.

If Alexandra had been made a trustee of the US Country object and been granted the Supervisor object right, then at 3WsNetWorking, she would also have an inherited assignment of the Supervisor object. However, you just made Alexandra a trustee of 3WsNetWorking, with an explicit trustee assignment of B and RC. In this case, the explicit assignment overwrites the inherited assignment, even though the inherited assignment is the Supervisor object right. At 3WsNetWorking, Alexandra's effective rights are B and RC, not S. Remember: The Supervisor object and property rights can be overwritten, revoked, deleted, and IRFed.

An explicit trustee assignment, in the file system and in eDirectory, overwrites an inherited assignment. Also, the Supervisor object and property rights can be revoked, overwritten, deleted, or IRFed.

The only issue with inheritance comes into play with the Create object right and the Inheritable rights. These rights apply only to Container objects.

If you grant Alexandra the Create and Inheritable object rights to the Sales OU, she will inherit C and I in the Educational OU. However, when it comes to Leaf objects in the Educational OU, such as the Server object or a Printer object, she will not have the C and I rights. The Server and Printer objects are Leaf objects, and you cannot inherit the C and I rights in a Leaf object. If you grant Alexandra the SBCDRI object rights to the Sales OU, she will inherit all those rights in the Educational OU (assuming that the default IRF is in place) and will only inherit SBDR in the Server object and the Printer object in the Educational OU.

Block Inherited Rights

Just as in the file system, inherited rights can be blocked in one of two ways:

➤ Grant a new trustee assignment

➤ Apply an IRF

The preferred method and the most granular or specific way to change an object's trustee assignment is to grant the object a new assignment lower in the tree. The example just cited showed how Alexandra received a new assignment at 3WsNetWorking, and that the new assignment overwrites any inherited assignment that she has at the given level of the tree.

A key point to remember is that a new object assignment overwrites an inherited object assignment, and a new property assignment overwrites an inherited property assignment. A new property assignment does *not* overwrite an inherited object assignment.

You can globally filter inherited rights by using an IRF. Every level of the eDirectory tree has an IRF. The eDirectory default IRF allows all rights to flow down the tree, without filtering rights. You can change the filter using any of the previously mentioned utilities by clearing the rights that you do not want to be inherited. In Figures 9.11 and 9.12, you see the IRF screens in NetWare Administrator and iManager, respectively. Notice that all rights are checked, meaning that all inherited rights are allowed to flow down through this branch of the tree. If a right is cleared, anyone who has that inherited right loses that right from that point down the branch.

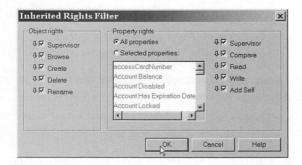

Figure 9.11   NetWare Administrator: IRF configuration options.

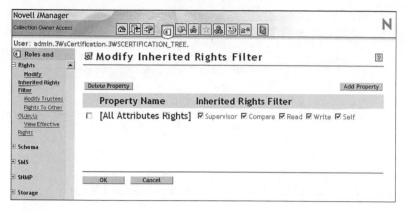

Figure 9.12   iManager: Modify IRF window.

The default eDirectory object IRF is represented as [SBCDRI] with all rights displayed. The default eDirectory property IRF is represented as [SRCWAI] with all rights displayed. If a right is filtered, it is missing. For example, [S CDRI] filters the B object inherited rights, which means the object cannot be seen in the tree. The B object right cannot be inherited from that point down the branch of the tree.

The following points are important to remember about IRFs:

➤ IRFs do not affect an explicit trustee assignment at the level that the IRF is implemented. If a user is granted SBCDRI at the same level where the IRF is [BCD], the user does not lose rights because an IRF filters only inherited rights.

➤ The Supervisor rights can be filtered with an IRF. You can see the S rights missing in an IRF, unlike what happens in the file system.

➤ IRFs globally filter inherited rights. All users who have an inherited assignment lose the rights that an IRF filters. This includes the Supervisor right. Blocking the Supervisor object right to a container establishes that Container object as an Exclusive container for high security issues. To avoid losing control over the container, it is best to create an admin in the container with Supervisor object rights to the container and when needed to the Tree object.

I am not a big advocate for IRFs in the file system. Neither is Novell. However, IRFs can be useful in eDirectory. Here's something that might help. When you create a backup Admin object in the tree, put a B object IRF on the new Admin object so that users who do not have supervisor rights to the tree cannot see the backup admin if they are looking at the tree with a utility that they should not be using. This is a type of Ghost user.

Another good administrative use for an IRF is blocking the B object right to a highly secure Container object that users should not be able to see. Be careful here, though; a nefarious intruder can use this to hack your tree. The B object IRF can be used for both good and bad.

Determine eDirectory Effective Rights

Effective rights are what a user or group can actually do at any given level of the eDirectory tree, after any IRFs.

The NetWare 6.5 operating system automatically calculates a user's effective rights at any given level of the tree.

For your CNA purposes, you need to know two things about effective rights:

➤ How to display a user's effective rights.

➤ How to calculate a user's effective rights based on the rules that govern eDirectory security.

 You can expect to see several questions on the CNA exam asking you to predict a user's effective rights at a level in the eDirectory tree. The fact that the operating system does this automatically for you is not sufficient for Novell to consider you a good CNA. A good CNA must be able to predict what impact a rights assignment will have before granting that assignment. Therefore, you must be able to calculate a user's effective rights.

You can display a user's effective rights in iManager by clicking the View Effective Rights link under the Rights heading. Then select the trustee you want to query and browse for the target object for which you want to display the object's effective rights. This displays a screen similar to that shown in Figure 9.13.

You can view a user's effective rights in ConsoleOne by displaying the object's ACL, as discussed earlier in this chapter, and clicking the Effective Rights button. Doing so displays a screen similar to Figure 9.7. Here, you can click the Browse button next to the For Trustee field and browse for any object you want to query. The effective rights are displayed in the Rights panel on the right side of the screen.

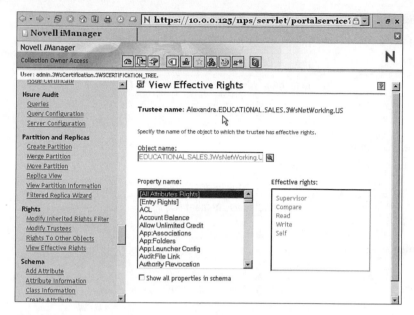

Figure 9.13   iManager: Viewing effective rights.

Even though it is easy to display an object's effective rights, Novell expects CNAs to be able to predict a user's effective rights before granting them. Following is the rule of thumb for calculating a user's effective rights:

User rights + group rights + container rights + Tree object + [Public] trustee rights (explicit or inherited) + security equivalences – any IRFs along the way = effective rights

Now you will look at two eDirectory scenarios in Tables 9.1 and 9.3 based on the eDirectory branch shown in Figure 9.1, US 3WsNetWorking, Sales, Educational, FS125, where FS125 is a Server object in the Educational OU. Tables 9.2 and 9.4 provide the correct answers. Don't cheat and look at the answers until you have worked through it yourself.

Scenario 1

If Anna has been granted the B RC trustee assignment to the US Country object and the S object trustee assignment to the Educational OU, and the [Public] trustee has been granted RCW All Property rights to the Sales OU, what are her effective rights at each level of the tree?

Fill in the blanks in Table 9.1.

Table 9.1   Calculating Effective Rights: eDirectory Security

Tree Object	Rights	Anna	
C=US	IRF	[SBCDRI][SRCWAI]	
	Individual trustee assignment	B	RC
	Group trustee assignment		
	Effective		
O=3WsNetWorking	IRF	[SBCDRI][SRCWAI]	
	Inherited		
	Individual trustee assignment		
	Group trustee assignment		
	Effective		
OU=Sales	IRF	[SBR][SI]	
	Inherited		
	Individual trustee assignment		
	Group trustee assignment	RCW	
	Effective		
OU=Educational	IRF	[BCDRI][RCWAI]	
	Inherited		
	Individual trustee assignment	S	
	Group trustee assignment		
	Effective		
CN=FS125	IRF	[SBCDRI][SRCWAI]	
	Inherited		
	Individual trustee assignment		
	Group trustee assignment		
	Effective		

Answers follow in Table 9.2.

Table 9.2   Calculating Effective Rights: eDirectory Security Answer

Tree Object	Rights	Anna	
C=US	IRF	[SBCDRI][SRCWAI]	
	Individual trustee assignment	B	RC
	Group trustee assignment	—	
	Effective	B	RC

(continued)

Tree Object	Rights	Anna	
O=3WsNetWorking	IRF	[SBCDRI][SRCWAI]	
	Inherited	B	RC
	Individual trustee assignment	—	
	Group trustee assignment	—	
	Effective	B	RC
OU=Sales	IRF	[SBR][SI]	
	Inherited	B	
	Individual trustee assignment	—	
	Group trustee assignment		RCW
	Effective	B	RCWA
OU=Educational	IRF	[BCDRI][RCWAI]	
	Inherited	B	RCW
	Individual trustee assignment	S	
	Group trustee assignment	—	
	Effective	SBCDRI	SRCWAI
CN=FS125	IRF	[SBCDRI][SRCWAI]	
	Inherited	S	
	Individual trustee assignment	—	
	Group trustee assignment	—	
	Effective	SBDR	SRCWA

Table 9.2   Calculating Effective Rights: eDirectory Security Answer *(continued)*

Answer Explanation

Because Anna has been granted the B RC trustee assignment to the US
Country object, her effective rights at US are B and RC. She inherits those
rights in the 3WsNetWorking organization where the default IRF exists. Those
are also her effective rights. In Sales, because Anna is security equivalent to
the [Public] trustee, she receives a new group assignment of RCW property
rights. The IRF at the Sales OU blocks her RC inherited assignment from
3WsNetWorking. Effectively at Sales, she has the B object right through inheritance and the RCW property rights from the [Public] trustee. However,
because the Write right is automatically linked to the Add/Remove self, she
effectively has the RCWA property rights. In the Educational OU, Anna
receives the S object trustee assignment. This new assignment overwrites her
inherited assignment; therefore, at the Educational OU, she effectively has all
object and property rights. Because the FS125 Leaf object has the default IRF,
she inherits all rights in the Server object. However, effectively she loses the

CI and I rights because they do not apply to a Leaf object. At FS125, she has SBDR object rights and SRCWA property rights.

Scenario 2

Marty has been granted B and RC, the default rights, at 3WsNetWorking. She receives a new trustee assignment in the Educational OU for changing only users' phone numbers. The Selected Property assignment to the Telephone property is RCWA. No other property options have been enabled. What are Marty's effective rights at each level of the tree? Fill in the blanks in Table 9.3.

Table 9.3 Calculating Effective Rights: eDirectory Security		
Tree Object	**Rights**	**Marty**
C=US	IRF	[SBCDRI][SRCWAI]
	Individual trustee assignment	
	Group trustee assignment	
	Effective	
O=3WsNetWorking	IRF	[SBCDRI][SRCWAI]
	Inherited	
	Individual trustee assignment	B RC
	Group trustee assignment	
	Effective	
OU=Sales	IRF	[SBR][SI]
	Inherited	
	Individual trustee assignment	
	Group trustee assignment	
	Effective	
OU=Educational	IRF	[BCDRI][RCWAI]
	Inherited	
	Individual trustee assignment	RCWA-Selected
	Group trustee assignment	
	Effective	
CN=FS125	IRF	[SBCDRI][SRCWAI]
	Inherited	
	Individual trustee assignment	
	Group trustee assignment	
	Effective	

Answers are presented in Table 9.4.

Table 9.4	Calculating Effective Rights: eDirectory Security Answer	
Tree Object	**Rights**	**Marty**
C=US	IRF	[SBCDRI][SRCWAI]
	Individual trustee assignment	—
	Group trustee assignment	—
	Effective	—
O=3WsNetWorking	IRF	[SBCDRI][SRCWAI]
	Inherited	B RC
	Individual trustee assignment	—
	Group trustee assignment	—
	Effective	B RC
OU=Sales	IRF	[SBR][SI]
	Inherited	B
	Individual trustee assignment	—
	Group trustee assignment	—
	Effective	B
OU=Educational	IRF	[BCDRI][RCWAI]
	Inherited	B
	Individual trustee assignment	RCWA-Selected
	Group trustee assignment	—
	Effective	B and RCWA-Selected for Telephone property
CN=FS125	IRF	[SBCDRI][SRCWAI]
	Inherited	B
	Individual trustee assignment	—
	Group trustee assignment	—
	Effective	B

Answer Explanation

Because Marty has been granted the B RC trustee assignment to 3WsNetWorking, effectively at 3WsNetWorking, those are her rights. She has no rights at the US Country object. Because of the IRF in the Sales OU, effectively she has only the B object right to the Sales OU. She inherits the B object right in the Educational OU but is granted a new Selected Property assignment for the Telephone property. Effectively at the Educational OU, Marty has the B object right to the container, and the RWCA Selected Property rights only to the Telephone property. She has no other property rights in the Educational OU. Nothing else has been enabled, including the Inheritable right. In the FS125 Server object, Marty only inherits the B object right, because Selected properties are not inheritable by default. At the FS125 Server object, she can only see the Server object.

Have you had enough yet? There's just one more little bit to consider. What if a user has too many or too few rights? What do you do?

Troubleshoot eDirectory Security

When you're troubleshooting users who have too many or too few rights, you have to proceed from the lowest level where the right is found and backtrack up the tree, looking at group memberships, Organizational Role occupancies, Containers, and security equivalences. You might well have to start in the file system and trace all links. You also have to pay special attention to IRFs and security equivalences.

Start by looking at a user's effective rights at each level of the tree. When you find the level that is flawed, start backpedaling.

It is always a good thing to avoid IRFs and security equivalences in your file system and tree design because troubleshooting rights issues is not a matter of *if* they are going to happen, but *when*. Remember, Murphy was an optimist. You will have to troubleshoot eDirectory security when you have the least amount of time and patience.

Troubleshooting rights issues is half science and half art. The CNA artist is the one who designs the system so that troubleshooting it takes the least amount of time and effort.

Exam Prep Questions

1. What is the default eDirectory rights assignment that is granted to the [Public] trustee to the Tree object when the first NetWare 6.5 server is installed into a new tree?

   A. ◯ Supervisor object to the Server object

   B. ◯ Supervisor property to the Tree object

   C. ◯ Browse object to the Tree object

   D. ◯ Read property to the Server object

   Answer C is correct. The [Public] trustee is given the Browse object right to the Tree object when the first NetWare 6.5 server is installed into a new tree. Answers A, B, and D are incorrect. These are not the rights assignments granted to the [Public] trustee to the Tree object.

2. Which object that represents all authenticated users to the eDirectory tree can you grant rights to?

   A. ◯ Tree object

   B. ◯ [Public] trustee

   C. ◯ Organization object

   D. ◯ Everyone group

   Answer A is correct. The Tree object represents all authenticated users in the tree. This object can be made a trustee of an object if the admin wants all users in the tree to have access to an object. Answer B is incorrect. The [Public] trustee represents all users, including those who have not authenticated to the tree. This object is a special trustee object that is designed to allow users to see the tree before logging in. Answers C and D are incorrect. The Organization object does not necessarily represent all authenticated users in the tree, especially if the tree has more than one Organization object. The Everyone group is a legacy group from the NetWare 3.x days that can still be created in NetWare 6.5, but for the most part has been replaced by Container objects.

3. Which eDirectory object right, when granted, only lets a user remove an object from the tree?

   A. ◯ B

   B. ◯ C

   C. ◯ I

   D. ◯ D

   Answer D is correct. The delete object right lets a user remove an eDirectory object from the tree. Answers A, B, and C are incorrect. The Browse right lets you see the object, the Create right lets you create objects, and the Inheritable right lets rights flow down from a Container object to Leaf objects and subcontainers in the container.

4. Which eDirectory right is automatically granted if the Read property right is granted to an object?

A. ○ C

B. ○ W

C. ○ A

D. ○ S

Answer A is correct. When the Read property right is granted to an object, the Compare right is granted automatically. Answers B, C, and D are incorrect. These rights are not granted automatically when the Read property right is granted.

5. Which of the following statements regarding eDirectory rights are true? (Select two.)

A. ❑ An All Property assignment overrides a Selected Property assignment.

B. ❑ The Supervisor object right implicitly grants the Supervisor property right and all object and property rights.

C. ❑ The Browse object right to the Server object automatically grants a user [RF] to the file system.

D. ❑ The Create object right is only applicable to the Container objects.

Answers B and D are correct. The Supervisor object right implicitly grants the Supervisor property right and all object and property rights, and the Create object right is applicable only to the Container objects. Answers A and C are incorrect. A Selected Property assignment overrides an All Property assignment. The Supervisor object right to the Server object automatically grants a user the Supervisor file system right to the root of the file system.

6. Which of the following are eDirectory object rights? (Select two.)

A. ❑ Browse

B. ❑ Write

C. ❑ Add-self

D. ❑ Create

Answers A and D are correct. The eDirectory object rights are Supervisor, Browse, Create, Delete, Rename, and Inheritable. Answers B and C are incorrect. These are not object rights.

7. What is another term for eDirectory object rights?

A. ○ Property rights

B. ○ Attribute rights

C. ○ Extrinsic rights

D. ○ Entry rights

Answer D is correct. Another term for eDirectory object rights is entry rights. Answers A and B are incorrect. These are terms for eDirectory property rights. Answer C is incorrect. Extrinsic rights is not another term for object rights.

8. In your eDirectory tree, you have the following structure:

O=3WsNetWorking, OU=Sales, OU=Educational, CN=Printer1

Each level of the tree has the default IRF. You grant Alexandra the default eDirectory rights at the **Sales** OU. What object right does Alexandra have at **Printer1**?

A. ○ Supervisor

B. ○ Browse

C. ○ Create

D. ○ Delete

E. ○ Rename

Answer B is correct. The default object right granted to a user is Browse. By inheritance, Alexandra has the Browse object right to Printer1. Answers A, C, D, and E are incorrect. All of these are object rights that can optionally be granted to a user, but are not the default rights granted.

9. In your eDirectory tree, you have the following structure:

O=3WsNetWorking, OU=Sales, OU=Educational, CN=Printer1

Each level of the tree has the default IRF. Emma has been granted [SBCDRI] at **3WsNetWorking**. What rights does Emma have at **Printer1**?

A. ○ [SBCDRI]

B. ○ [SBCDR]

C. ○ [SBDR]

D. ○ [SBCI]

Answer C is correct. Emma, by inheritance, has all rights to Printer1. The only issue is that Printer1 is a Leaf object. Therefore, Emma only has [SBDR] to Printer1, because [CI] are applicable only to Container objects. Answers A, B, and D are incorrect because they do not take into account the fact that the Create and Inheritable rights do not apply to Leaf objects.

10. In your eDirectory tree, you have the following structure:

O=3WsNetWorking, OU=Sales, OU=Educational, CN=Printer1

Each level of the tree has the default IRF. Emma has been granted the Browse object right and all property rights to **3WsNetWorking**. She receives a new assignment at **Educational** of [BDR]. What are Emma's effective rights at **Printer1**?

A. ○ [SRCWAI]

B. ○ [BDR] AND [SRCWAI]

C. ○ [B] [RC]

D. ○ [BDR]

Answer D is correct. At 3WsNetWorking, Emma has [B] and [SRCWAI]. She inherits those at Sales. At Educational, she is granted a new assignment that overwrites her inherited assignment. Her effective rights at Educational are [BDR]. She inherits [BDR] at Printer1. Answers A, B, and C are incorrect. They do not follow the rules of eDirectory rights.

NetWare 6.5 Network Security

Terms you'll need to understand:

- ✓ Security policy
- ✓ **SCRSAVER.NLM**
- ✓ **Burglar.NLM**
- ✓ NAAS
- ✓ Hidden Object Locator
- ✓ Firewall
- ✓ Packet-filtering firewall
- ✓ NAT
- ✓ Circuit-level gateway
- ✓ Application proxy
- ✓ VPN
- ✓ Caching server

Techniques you'll need to master:

- ✓ Internally secure a network
- ✓ Troubleshoot common internal security problems
- ✓ Identify how to provide external network security with a firewall

In the previous two chapters, you explored, in depth, file system security and eDirectory security, respectively. This chapter exposes you to the broad strokes of securing a network. This chapter is a compilation of guidelines for network security that Novell has emphasized in virtually every admin class ever taught. For the most part, this chapter is the do's and don'ts of security. You learn what a security policy is, a bit about login security, some additional guidelines about file system and eDirectory security, and some common-sense network don'ts. To cap it off, you learn about firewalls.

Internally Secure a Network

As few as 10 years ago, network security was a concern of network administrators, but it was taken for granted. It was important to protect the network, which meant following some common-sense guidelines that Novell presented. Since 9/11, security has been raised in importance to a level never before imagined. Whole courses and certifications are offered that deal with nothing more than how to hack a network and, conversely, how to secure it internally and externally. For this test, your concern is internally securing your network. In Chapters 8, "File System Security," and 9, "eDirectory Security," you learned many of the best practices for internally securing the file system and eDirectory. However, before you can secure those two NetWare 6.5 services, you must have a corporate security policy.

A security policy is a corporate document detailing your practices and procedures for implementing a secure overall environment for your employees and infrastructure. This document addresses in detail your proactive and reactive measures for dealing with network security and security breaches. Your security policy is implemented and enforced by the management and those in charge of corporate security. It addresses how to secure your resources while allowing employees to efficiently do their jobs. One of the temptations for those drafting a security policy is to go overboard and impose restrictions that are irrational and prevent users from being productive. This is where experience and balance come into play.

When designing a security policy, you must assess what resources need protecting and how much protection is necessary. To do this, you need to do the following:

➤ List the resources that need to be secure.

➤ List the possible external and internal attacks that your resources are susceptible to.

➤ Perform a threat analysis, prioritizing which resources are most susceptible and which are least susceptible.

➤ Define appropriate actions for protecting your resources.

➤ Communicate your security plan to your employees, educating them so that they can assist you in protecting your resources.

➤ Document your plan, detail the security measures that are appropriate on a resource-by-resource basis, and continually review the plan's effectiveness and how to improve it.

➤ Assign a security administrator who will implement the policy.

In terms of network security, specifically, you need to detail in the security policy what rights users receive, what rights admins receive, who is the tree admin, and who makes security policy for the network.

Following are a couple of real-world examples of security policy issues that are wrestled with today. One of the most time-consuming and sensitive issues in network security, especially in healthcare networks, is how to deal with HIPPA regulations and patient records in a secure yet private manner on an enterprise network. This same security issue is pervasive in educational environments when it comes to student records and student health information. For example, should the network admin (the tree admin) have access to student health records, or should a health professional be set up as a container admin for the server where this data is stored, while filtering the network admin from this context? In other words, should the records be for healthcare eyes only? Also, if this is the policy implemented, what happens if the healthcare professional/container admin decides to abort his professional standards and corrupts the data? A policy must be in place so that the network admin can intervene before irreversible damage is done and private data is released to the public.

Following are network security guidelines that must be addressed in a good security policy:

➤ Guidelines for physically securing the server

➤ File system security guidelines

➤ Login security and intruder lockout guidelines

➤ Password guidelines

➤ eDirectory rights guidelines

➤ Administrative access guidelines

➤ Virus protection guidelines

The next section examines Novell's guidelines on each of these issues.

 You must know Novell's guidelines for physically securing the server. Novell loves this material on its CNA exams.

Guidelines for Physically Securing the Server

Following are Novell's guidelines for physically securing a NetWare 6.5 server:

➤ Place the server in a locked room that is not easily accessible.

➤ Remove the mouse and keyboard and any other input devices from the server so that console access is not locally available.

➤ Use the server screen saver, SCRSAVER.NLM, on the server so that anyone who is accessing the server console screen must provide admin authentication credentials.

➤ Execute Secure Console on the server. Secure Console can have a major impact on what you can do on a NetWare 6.5 server. You cannot access the system debugger from the server keyboard. Secure Console also prevents you from changing the server's date and time. Furthermore, you cannot load NetWare Loadable Modules (NLMs) from anywhere but SYS:\SYSTEM or C:\NWSERVER. You can still down the server, but Secure Console forces you to reboot it.

File System Security Guidelines

When it comes to file system security, this is somewhat of a repeat of the material in Chapter 8, but it's worth repeating to drive home the point. For the experienced NetWare 6.5 admin, these guidelines are second nature.

➤ Only give users the rights they absolutely need to do their jobs. It's a mistake to grant users more rights than they need.

➤ You can block inheritance with an IRF or with a new trustee assignment. Whenever possible, use a new trustee assignment and do not rely on inheritance. Avoid file system IRFs. They are a nightmare to troubleshoot. Explicit trustee assignments are much easier to troubleshoot.

➤ Let file and directory attributes be your friend. Don't be afraid to flag an executable as read-only to prevent users from deleting it or corrupting it.

> Novell documents love to advocate the Execute-only attribute. Over the past 10 years, this attribute has been praised and cursed by many who have assigned it to an executable. I've seen it work well, but I've also had trouble removing it at times so that I could update an executable. I would caution you to consider the System and Read-only attributes and not the Execute-only attribute, despite what Novell documents say. You will save yourself a world of uncertainty.
>
> Also, be aware that this annoying attribute is one that Novell might ask you an obscure, ridiculous question on. The Execute-only (X) attribute works, but just be careful in the real world.

➤ Don't put users' private files, their home directories, or any kind of volatile data on the SYS volume. Set up a multiple volume environment and keep the SYS volume pristine and reserved for the operating system files. Don't store volatile data on the SYS volume, because if the volume runs out of space, the server ceases to function.

Login Security and Intruder Lockout Guidelines

Login security addresses who has access to the network and what information a user must provide to authenticate to the tree. You should keep the following guidelines in mind when designing the section on login security in your security policy. Figure 10.1 shows the account restriction options available in iManager when you choose to modify an object.

> On earlier Novell CNA exams, Novell expected you to know what options were available and how to restrict a user's access. For this exam, Novell simply wants you to know the guidelines.

➤ When a user account has not been used for a considerable period of time, disable it, as shown in Figure 10.2. Also, if you hire a network contractor to perform some task on your network, and you have to create a user account for him, disable it after he has finished his task. Some might say delete it altogether, but that is not a good strategy especially if you have to bring him back at a later date to perform some maintenance tasks. Don't delete the User object until you are absolutely sure you will never need that object/user again. Otherwise, you will have to re-create all memberships and make all new assignments when the user returns.

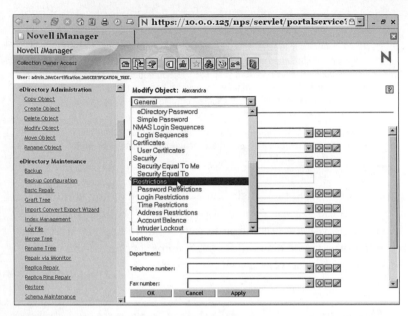

Figure 10.1 Account Restrictions menu in iManager.

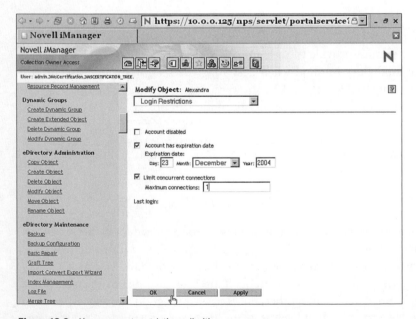

Figure 10.2 User account restrictions: limiting access.

NOTE

Figure 10.2 shows some of the user account restrictions that you can set by using iManager, eDirectory Administration, Modify Object. You can also set account restrictions at the Container object. When setting restrictions at the Container object, you are globally setting the restrictions. You can also set account restrictions using either ConsoleOne or NetWare Administrator. In addition, you can set some of the restrictions with NetAdmin if you have moved it from your earlier NetWare environment to your NetWare 6.5 environment. The option you choose to use in your production environment is a matter of preference. For this exam, you should be familiar with the iManager screens.

Also, note in Figure 10.2 that after you select the options, the default values are displayed.

➤ It is a best practice to assign nonpermanent employees, who have a User object in the tree, an expiration date as shown in Figure 10.2.

➤ Users should not be able to have multiple connections simultaneously. Limit the number of connections that a user can have open (refer to Figure 10.2). Notice that when Limit Concurrent Connections is selected, the default number of user connections allowed is one.

➤ When a user is created, by default, he can access the tree 24 hours a day, 7 days a week. This can be a major security issue. As shown in Figure 10.3, you can limit the hours and days that a user can log in to the network. In Figure 10.3, all users in the 3WsNetWorking container can access the network 7 days a week from 6 a.m. to 6 p.m. They cannot access the network from 6 p.m. to 6 a.m.

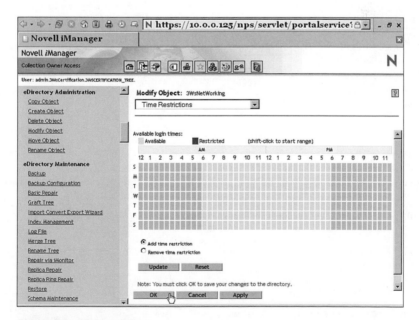

Figure 10.3 Time restrictions.

➤ If you have help desk employees or container administrators who need limited capabilities to impose login restrictions, the maximum number of property rights you need to assign is three: Read, Write, and Inheritable. For some tasks, you only need the Read and maybe the Inheritable rights. Don't assign too many rights where they are not needed and can pose a security risk.

➤ It is a good practice to enable Intruder Lockout measures at your Container objects. Intruder Lockout measures prevent users from trying to hack your network with bogus usernames and passwords until they come onto a workable pair. With Intruder Lockout, as shown in Figure 10.4, a user by default can only unsuccessfully attempt to log in 7 times in 30 minutes. After unsuccessfully attempting to authenticate, the user is locked out for 15 minutes. Each of those parameters is configurable based on your security policy. After a user is locked out, you as the admin must unlock his account if he needs to get in before the lockout period is over (see Figure 10.5).

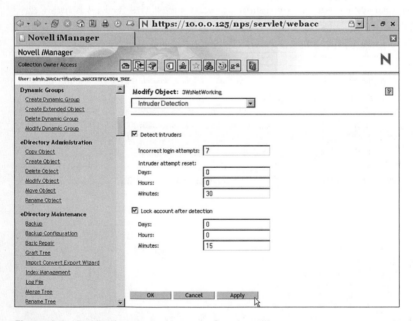

Figure 10.4 Enabling Intruder Lockout at the Container object.

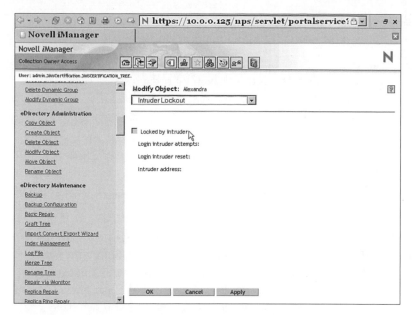

Figure 10.5   Unlocking a user account that was locked by Intruder Lockout.

Be aware that Intruder Lockout is enabled or disabled at the Container object, but unlocking a user account that was locked as a result of Intruder Lockout is done at the User object level.

Also note that you can lock out the Container object by Intruder Lockout. Using ConsoleOne, the Container object has two menu options, which can be confusing to new administrators. On the General tab, you can configure Intruder Lockout using the Intruder Detection option. On the Restrictions tab, you can unlock a container that has been locked out by using the Intruder Lockout option.

The defaults that are displayed when you enable Intruder Lockout on a Container object are not good choices for a production environment. You do not want a potential hacker to have 7 shots at you in 30 minutes. A better choice is 3 attempts in 5 minutes and then lock the hacker out for at least 30 minutes until you can locate him. When a user is locked out by Intruder Lockout, you receive a message on the server console screen telling you the date and time of the lockout and the MAC address of the station. This is helpful in tracking down mischievous users.

Password Guidelines

Password security guidelines dictate your rules and regulations for implementing, using, and changing passwords. The available password options in NetWare 6.5 (shown in Figure 10.6) include the following:

➤ Allow the user to change his password. It is a good practice to enable this because you do not want the responsibility or the headache of remembering everyone's password.

➤ By default, passwords are not required. It is a best practice to require users to enter a password during authentication.

➤ When you require a password, you must define the minimum password length. The default is 5 characters, which by today's standards is a weak password. A minimum of 7–8 characters should be used. Passwords can be up to 128 characters long.

➤ It is a good practice to force users to change their passwords periodically. Users get sloppy and often tell others their passwords, which they should never do. Having users change their passwords adds a layer of security that prevents someone from impersonating a user because he has a password that has not been changed.

➤ If you force users to change their passwords, you should also have in your security policy the number of days that can pass before they have to change their password. You need to set a balance here. You can set this up to 365 days, which is as good as not setting this parameter. If you force users to change their passwords too frequently, you will have a rebellion on your hands. Every 30 to 40 days is a good balance for an environment that is not a high security area. If you are in a high security environment, you might want to have the passwords changed every 15 days. But again, you need to strike a balance between productivity and security.

➤ You can also set when a password expires. Some use this parameter for nonpermanent or contract workers.

➤ One of the options that is available when configuring password restrictions is to require unique passwords. This forces users to periodically use a different password than they have been using. In fact, the password must be different from any of the eight previously used passwords. Earlier versions of NetWare kept track of the previously used 20 passwords. This number has been reduced since NetWare 5.

➤ Several options deal with grace logins. A grace login permits a user to log in a defined number of times if his password has expired. You can enable grace logins and set the number of grace logins permitted. The third parameter, monitored by eDirectory, is remaining grace logins. You can change this if a user has been lax in resetting his password and has run out of grace login attempts.

➤ The final password restriction option available is to change the user's password. When the user has forgotten his password or simply needs to have his password changed, you can accommodate him by using this option.

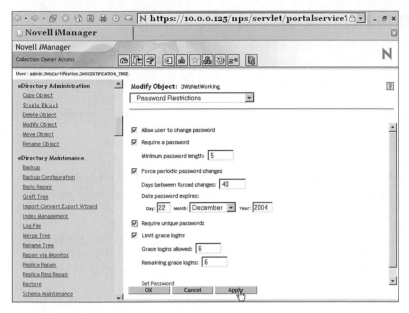

Figure 10.6   Password restrictions.

eDirectory Rights Guidelines

As discussed in Chapter 9, eDirectory rights control what a user can do with resources in the tree. Novell emphasizes several eDirectory rights guidelines that should be on the minds of all NetWare 6.5 administrators.

➤ NetWare 6.5 works out of the box. Don't overwrite the default rights. These rights are granted to allow users and administrators to work efficiently.

➤ When assigning eDirectory property rights, whenever possible avoid granting rights with the All Properties option. Instead, grant property rights with the Selected Properties options. Rights that are granted with the Selected Properties option give you granular control over your users' capabilities.

➤ Assign the Write property right only to users who absolutely need it. The Write property right allows a user to add his User object as a trustee to an eDirectory object's access control list (ACL) and potentially grant himself additional, and generally unnecessary, rights.

➤ When you want to assign rights to all users in the same container, assign the rights to the Container object. All users in the container are security equivalent to the container and have the same rights as assigned to the container.

Administrative Access Guidelines

Depending on the design of your tree, you might be using a centralized model with a single tree admin, or you might be using a distributed model with an enterprise admin and multiple container admins. Just as you have to establish a security policy for users, you must also consider admins as a potential security consideration. Consider the following guidelines for admins when drafting security policy.

➤ If you have multiple admins in your tree, and you need to assign uniform rights to them, make the admins occupants of an Organizational Role object. This is a task-oriented eDirectory object that is designed for situations like this.

➤ When assigning Supervisor rights to admins, don't just assign the Supervisor eDirectory right. Assign all rights in case the Supervisor right is IRFed or overwritten.

➤ Unless absolutely necessary, do not make a user Security Equal to an admin. Grant explicit rights to the user instead of using this feature. Remember: You can overwrite, remove, or block the Supervisor right in eDirectory. This is not like the Supervisor file system right. The Supervisor eDirectory right is susceptible to removal.

➤ It is a good practice to have multiple admins in the tree all with the same explicit assignments. This prevents a major issue should the Admin object be deleted. This is also a good practice to maintain tight control over highly secure containers and servers. Do not name each of these admins "admin." In fact, rename the original admin so that it is not a vulnerable point in the tree. Also, do not let all administrative users use the single Admin object for authentication. Create unique User objects for each user who will be an admin. Require these admins to authenticate using their own User object, who will have his own distinct rights assignments.

➤ Do not permit admins to do day-to-day tasks with their Admin User object. Rather, create at least one other User object for each admin. Give these new User objects default user assignments, without administrative rights. Require admins, when doing normal user tasks, to use their nonadministrative User object. This prevents a host of security vulnerabilities and inadvertent administrative gaffs.

➤ In your security policy design, if you decide to go with a distributed administrative model, you must decide if there will be one or more eDirectory admins and one or more file system admins. Alternatively, will the admins be responsible for both the file system and eDirectory?

Do you want to have a division of labor? Based on your design, you could set up exclusive container admins for highly secure environments.

➤ One trick that you can use if you are creating a new container and want to assign an admin to the container, granting him the minimum rights, is to only grant him the Create object right to the container. Then he will own and have the Supervisor object right to every object he creates in the container—including all object and property rights. He is the superuser of that container. You also do not have to worry about that user having too many rights and causing havoc elsewhere in the tree.

➤ Remember: If an admin has the Supervisor object right to the Server object, either explicitly or by inheritance, that admin has Supervisor file system rights to every volume on the Server object, and the Supervisor file system rights cannot be IRFed or overwritten. Do not assign Supervisor object rights to the Server object unless you trust this user completely.

➤ Only use eDirectory IRFs when necessary. They are useful if you want to set up a ghost admin account that users cannot see in the tree, but they can be difficult to troubleshoot. The Supervisor eDirectory rights can be IRFed.

Virus Protection Guidelines

Regardless of how tight your security policy is, someone will always try to cause problems. One of the biggest security issues for network administrators today is the number and types of virus attacks. A virus is a program that is designed to cause problems for networks and standalone computers. Some are dormant until a user performs an action, whereas others are time dependent. On an enterprise network, virus protection can be a full-time job. Novell's guidelines for virus protection include the following:

➤ Do not ignore the possibility of virus attacks in your security policy. Whether you are connected to the Internet or not, if you have a computer, you are susceptible.

➤ Purchase and install good virus protection software on your workstations and your servers. If you are running specialty servers, such as e-mail servers, also protect them.

➤ After installing the virus protection software, configure it for your needs and environment. Do not assume that it is configured for your environment out of the box.

➤ Keep the virus signatures up-to-date, not a week or two behind. The day you least expect to be infected is the day you are vulnerable.

➤ Configure the virus protection software to automatically delete or quarantine infected files so that they are isolated and users cannot access them.

Troubleshoot Common Internal Security Problems

It is one thing to impose a security policy that protects your network environment from external attacks. It is a completely different can of worms to protect your environment from attacks that are launched from inside your corporate infrastructure. In the ideal world, you should not have to protect yourself from co-workers, employees, or even employers. But in the real world, everyone is suspect. Trust, in much of the rest of the world, is a good thing. In network security, trust can compromise your environment. Based on trust, many admins open gaping holes in their environments. Following are a few network security don'ts:

➤ Don't give anyone, unless your job depends on it, Supervisor object rights to the Tree object, to the Server objects, or to any mission-critical environments. This is like giving the keys to your house and car over to a thief and telling him to take what he needs. It gives me chills thinking about it because it happens so often and is justified as an easy way to give a user the rights he needs to do his job without taking up your valuable time. Take the time to give explicit assignments, and don't assign the Supervisor object rights.

➤ Don't give anyone the admin's password. If you think that someone has the admin password, change it immediately and make it difficult to crack. Certain utilities, such as SETPASS.NLM, can be used to change an admin's password. Monitor your logs for nefarious NLMs being loaded.

➤ Don't assume that a backdoor has not been created in the eDirectory tree. Users have a host of programs available to them on the Internet, such as BURGLAR.NLM, that create an admin user for use as a backdoor. This type of user is often hidden and called a rogue admin.

Be aware of the previous two bullets. Both cite NLMs as ways to hack your tree/server. One uses **SETPASS.NLM** and the other uses **BURGLAR.NLM**. These are not loaded from the workstation but on the server. Remember back to earlier guidelines in this chapter, where physically protecting the server was encouraged. If a user can easily access the server console, and **Secure Console** has not been launched, he can run NLMs such as **SETPASS** and **BURGLAR**. If the server console is inaccessible, it is much more difficult for a user to launch these attacks. A user can launch these NLMs remotely from a workstation using Remote Manager, as an example, but it is a bit more of a challenge.

Following are three time-tested tools for monitoring and tracking security breaches:

➤ HOL (Hidden Object Locator)

➤ NAAS (Novell Advanced Audit Services)

➤ BindView Solutions for Novell

These three utilities are not only a valuable security asset, but they are also worth knowing for the exam.

You need to know about NAAS for the exam, but in the NetWare 6.5 SP2 Overlay release, you can install the Nsure Audit 1.0.1 Starter Pack for auditing.

You can find the HOL on Novell's Cool Solutions at `http://www.novell.com/coolsolutions/tools/1098.html`.

NAAS is a product that you can install during the server operating system installation or after the fact through the NetWare graphical user interface (GUI).

BindView Solutions for Novell is a third-party solution. Information is available at `http://www.bindview.com/Products/VulnMgmt/PlatformManagement/bv-Control_NDSeDirectory.cfm` and `http://www.bindview.com/Products/VulnMgmt/PlatformManagement/bv-Control_NetWare.cfm`.

Having reviewed network security guidelines, it is time to take a brief look at firewalls. If you can protect your network from external attacks, you are well on your way to having a secure environment.

Identify How to Provide External Network Security with a Firewall

One of the best ways to protect your network is with a firewall solution. A firewall is software/hardware technology that protects a network from outside attacks. It is not designed to protect your interior network from internal attacks, virus attacks, or newly released attacks. You must update firewalls, their software configuration, and ACLs at regular intervals, which leaves a firewall open to newly generated means of attack.

A firewall can do the following:

➤ Add a layer of security that reinforces your security policy's desired outcome

➤ Provide a single gateway in and out of your network, which helps to limit the type of traffic you allow into and deny access to your environment.

➤ Provide a central point for monitoring inbound and outbound traffic

➤ Provide a means of detecting intruders and limiting the scope of an attack

Firewall technologies come in several types, such as the following:

➤ Packet filtering

➤ Network Access Translation (NAT)

➤ Circuit-level gateway

➤ Application proxy

➤ Virtual private network (VPN)

➤ Caching server

A packet-filtering firewall permits or denies access to packets based on the rules configured. Packets can be filtered based on source or destination IP address, port number, service type, or interface. This is a network layer firewall technology.

Network Address Translation (NAT) is a gateway found at the network layer of the Open System Interconnection (OSI) model. NAT is primarily used to translate a private IP address to an IP address that is suitable for the Internet—the public network. Private IP addresses are IP addresses that are used primarily for private networks, or intranets. A NAT server provides a gateway to the public network for those on a private network and vice versa.

A NetWare 6.5 server that is configured with NAT has two interfaces: one on the private network and one on the public network. Those on the private network who want to access the public network send data through the NAT server. The NAT server routes that information through the public interface, translating the private IP address to its public IP address. The only IP address that is visible on the public network is the public IP address on the NAT server. No other nodes on the private network can be accessed directly. Data sent from the public network to the private network is translated and routed back through the NAT server.

A circuit-level gateway is similar to a NAT server, in that it translates private addresses to or more pubic addresses. Circuit-level gateways function at the session layer of the OSI model. The circuit-level gateway does not care about upper-level issues. It is concerned only with source and destination addresses.

A proxy server is a middleman between a private network and a public network. Much like a NAT server, a proxy server shows the public network a single registered address, while protecting all nodes on the private network. Many types of proxy servers exist.

An application proxy is a proxy server that is protocol specific. For example, a Simple Mail Transfer Protocol (SMTP) proxy server only accepts SMTP packets and either transports them or drops them based on the rules that are configured. This is also called an application gateway, or application-level proxy.

A virtual private network (VPN) is a private network that uses the public network infrastructure for secure communication between private nodes.

A caching server is a feature of some firewall packages, such as Novell's BorderManager. A caching server, also called a Web caching server or a Web proxy, locally stores frequently contacted URLs so that client access time to Internet data is shortened. Frequently accessed data is retrieved from the server's cache, as opposed to having to go out to the Internet source and download it each time it is needed.

Exam Prep Questions

1. You have decided to run Secure Console on your NetWare 6.5 server. Which of the following results from your action? (Select all that apply.)

   A. ❑ You can't load NLMs from anywhere but the **SYS:\PUBLIC** directory.

   B. ❑ You can't access the system debugger from the server keyboard.

   C. ❑ You can't change the server's date.

   D. ❑ You can't down the server.

   Answers B and C are correct. Secure Console can have a major impact on what you can do on a NetWare 6.5 server. It is a great security tool, but it has significant ramifications. First, you cannot access the system debugger from the server keyboard. Also, you can't change the server's date and time. Answers A and D are incorrect. You cannot load NLMs from anywhere but SYS:\System or C:\NWSERVER. With Secure Console, you can still down the server, but you are forced to reboot it.

2. You want to limit physical access to your NetWare 6.5 server as part of your overall security plan. Which of the following are measures you should take to implement this part of your plan? (Select all that apply.)

   A. ❑ Load **SCRSAVER.NLM** on your server.

   B. ❑ Remove the keyboard from the server.

   C. ❑ Locate the server in a room that is easily accessible to administrators.

   D. ❑ Remove the monitor from the server.

   Answers A and B are correct. Two of the four measures that Novell recommends for securing the file system include loading SCRSAVER.NLM at the server console and removing the keyboard and mouse from the server. Answers C and D are incorrect. The server should be located in a locked room that is not easily accessible. There is no reason to remove the monitor from the server. The monitor is an output device, not an input device.

3. You want to secure a NetWare 6.5 server file system as part of your overall security plan. Which of the following are measures you should take to implement this part of your plan? (Select all that apply.)

   A. ❑ Use IRFs whenever possible to globally restrict access.

   B. ❑ Locate users' private directories on the **SYS** volume.

   C. ❑ Grant users only the minimum rights needed to perform their jobs.

   D. ❑ Assign file attributes to strengthen file system security.

   Answers C and D are correct. Security on a NetWare 6.5 file system requires you to use file attributes to strengthen your security and to grant users the minimum rights needed as low down in the file system tree as possible. Answers A and B are incorrect. Avoid the use of IRFs in the file system whenever possible. If you can, place users' private, volatile, directories on a volume other than SYS.

4. Which of the following are password properties that you can configure on a NetWare 6.5 server? (Select all that apply.)

A. ❑ Require a Password

B. ❑ Grace Logins Allowed

C. ❑ Maximum Password Length

D. ❑ Date Password Commences

Answers A and B are correct. A host of configuration parameters is available for NetWare 6.5 passwords. These include Require a Password and Grace Logins Allowed. Answers C and D are incorrect. There is a Minimum Password Length parameter and a Date Password Expires option, but Answers C and D do not exist in NetWare 6.5.

5. You have decided as part of your overall NetWare 6.5 password policy to require unique passwords. How many passwords does NetWare 6.5 keep track of when this option is selected?

A. ○ 1

B. ○ 8

C. ○ 20

D. ○ 255

Answer B is correct. Password requirements are essential ingredients in securing a NetWare 6.5 network. One of the options that is available when configuring password requirements is Require Unique Passwords. This forces users to periodically use a different password than they have been using. In fact, the password must be different from any of the eight previously used passwords. Earlier versions of NetWare kept track of the previously used 20 passwords. This number has decreased since NetWare 5. Answers A, C, and D are incorrect.

6. As part of your overall NetWare 6.5 security plan, you decide to use container administrators. Which of the following is a measure you should take to successfully implement this security option?

A. ○ Assign only the Supervisor right to container administrators.

B. ○ Use an Organizational Role object to consolidate multiple container administrators.

C. ○ Use the Security Equal property to efficiently grant rights to container administrators.

D. ○ Rely on inherited rights for container administrators.

Answer B is correct. If you are using container administrators, group these admins with an Organizational Role object for efficient administration of rights. Answers A, C, and D are incorrect. You should assign all rights, not just the Supervisor right, to container administrators. The Supervisor eDirectory right can be blocked or overwritten. Avoid using the Security Equal property. It can cause you an administrative nightmare when troubleshooting inadequate or excessive access capabilities. Do not rely on inherited rights. Always use explicit assignments for container administrators. Inherited eDirectory rights can be IRFed or overwritten.

7. As part of your overall NetWare 6.5 security plan, you need to protect your admin user. Which of the following is a measure you should take to successfully implement this security option?

A. ○ Allow users who need administrative access to use the Admin object for authentication.

B. ○ Grant all users who need administrative access the Supervisor object right to the Server objects in the tree.

C. ○ Make sure the admin for the tree only uses the Admin object for all tasks.

D. ○ Rename the Admin object.

Answer D is correct. One of the first things you should do to secure your NetWare 6.5 environment is rename the Admin User object. Answers A, B, and C are incorrect. Admins should have at least two User objects: one for administrative tasks and one for day-to-day tasks. The Admin object should be protected from being used by too many users. Each user who needs administrative access should have his own object and not be allowed to use the Admin object. Users who need administrative access should not be granted the Supervisor object right to the Server objects. If that right is granted, these users will have the Supervisor file system right to all volumes on the server, and that right cannot be overwritten or blocked in the file system. That is a major security design flaw.

8. Which of the following tools can you use to monitor NetWare 6.5 security breaches? (Select all that apply.)

A. ❑ Burglar

B. ❑ NAAS

C. ❑ HOL

D. ❑ BindView Solutions for Novell

Answers B, C, and D are correct. You can use NAAS, BindView Solutions for Novell, and HOL to monitor security breaches in a NetWare 6.5 environment. Answer A is incorrect. Burglar.NLM is a hacker's tool, available on the Internet, for creating a rogue admin on a server. If you forget your admin password or someone changes it on you, this tool gives you access to the tree.

9. Which of the following are limitations of a firewall? (Select all that apply.)

A. ❑ It cannot protect your network from malevolent outside attacks.

B. ❑ It cannot protect your network from malevolent inside attacks.

C. ❑ It cannot protect your network from virus attacks.

D. ❑ It cannot protect your network from threats that are recently released.

Answers B, C, and D are correct. Firewalls can protect your inside network from a host of external attacks, but they have certain limitations. They cannot protect from malevolent inside attacks, virus attacks, or recently released threats. Answer A is incorrect. A firewall can protect from malevolent outside attacks.

10. Which type of network layer firewall technology should you deploy if you want to filter transmitted data based on source or destination IP address, port number, service type, or interface?

    A. ○ NAT

    B. ○ Packet filtering

    C. ○ Circuit-level gateway

    D. ○ Application proxy

    Answer B is correct. A packet-filtering firewall permits or denies access to packets based on the rules configured. Packets can be filtered based on source or destination IP address, port number, service type, or interface. This is a network layer firewall technology. Answers A, C, and D are incorrect. None of these satisfy all the criteria defined in the question.

NetWare 6.5 Printing

Terms you'll need to understand:

✓ NDPS
✓ Public Access printer
✓ Controlled Access printer
✓ Printer agent
✓ NDPS Manager
✓ Printer Gateway
✓ Printer Broker
✓ ENS
✓ SRS
✓ RMS
✓ RPM configuration
✓ iPrint
✓ IPP

Techniques you'll need to master:

✓ Identify the features of NDPS
✓ Identify the types of printers
✓ Describe NDPS components
✓ Set up NDPS
✓ Manage NDPS
✓ Implement iPrint

One of the heaviest responsibilities for a CNA is efficiently managing printing in a NetWare environment. One of my former CNE students estimated that 75% of his time was taken up with printing issues. Despite the fact that we are moving toward a so-called paperless society, everyone still wants a hard copy for business, personal, and legal reasons. Printing is the responsibility of the CNA.

NetWare has traditionally been known as a queue-based printing environment. With the release of NetWare 5.x, Novell positioned NetWare to change its printing focus. With NetWare 5.x, Novell shifted away from queue-based printing to Novell Distributed Print Services (NDPS). NDPS is a printer-based environment. Users submit jobs, not to a queue, but directly to a printer. Novell has combined the functionality of the printer, print queue, and print server from queue-based printing into one software entity known as a printer agent.

NDPS is the default printing service in NetWare 6.5. Queue-based printing is still available for users who either prefer or require that earlier technology.

In queue-based printing, administrators are required to create and link printers, queues, and print servers. A print queue is a directory on a NetWare server that holds print jobs waiting to be routed by a print server to a printer. A printer is a printing device that is directly connected to a network cable, a workstation running a remote program that makes the printer available for network sharing, or a server. A print server is a NetWare Loadable Module (NLM) that can service up to 255 printers and whose function is to route print jobs from a print queue to the desired printer. The utility of choice in queue-based printing was and to this day still is NetWare Administrator. You can create and link these three key objects under the Tools menu using the Print Services Quick Setup option shown in Figure 11.1. You can also manually create queue-based print objects by using the Create Object option in NetWare Administrator, shown in Figure 11.2.

Queue-based printing configuration is not covered on the NetWare 6.5 CNA exam. It is briefly covered here in case you are a reader trying to prepare for the NetWare 6.0 CNA exam, 050-677. Queue-based printing is covered on that exam. This is not an exhaustive description of the process, but you should be aware that in case you are using this book to prepare for the 6.0 CNA exam, queue-based printing is a topic you need to study.

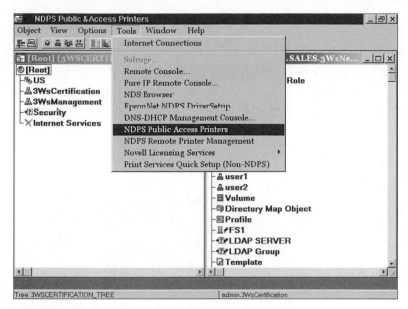

Figure 11.1 NetWare Administrator: Tools menu.

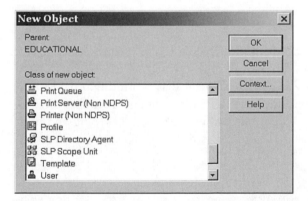

Figure 11.2 NetWare Administrator: Create queue-based (Non-NDPS) printing objects.

NetWare Administrator is not the tool of choice for managing print services, even NDPS, according to Novell. iManager, shown in Figure 11.3, is the preferred tool. Know that you can still use NetWare Administrator to manage many of the NDPS tasks that iManager now manages. For many of you, it's a matter of preference. However, you must know how to perform these tasks and understand the series of steps to take in iManager for the NetWare 6.5 CNA exam.

iPrint/NDPS options

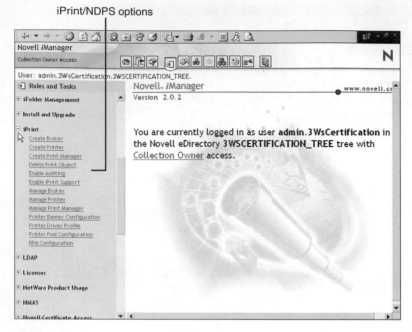

Figure 11.3   iManager: iPrinttasks.

In NDPS, the administrator (theoretically) only has to create a printer agent. In queue-based printing, users submit jobs to a queue, whereas in NDPS, jobs are submitted directly to a printer. Queue-based printing provides unidirectional communication, whereas NDPS offers full bidirectional communication. NDPS has an extensible architecture and has plug-and-print options available. Queue-based printing is not extensible and is not plug-and-print compliant.

In this chapter, you are introduced to the features of NDPS, the types of NDPS printers, the major NDPS components, setting up a printing environment, and using NDPS to leverage iPrint so that users can print from anywhere in the world to their office printers.

Identify the Features of NDPS

Some of the features of NDPS include the following:

➤ Administration is centralized and uses an easy-to-understand view of your network.

➤ It is closely integrated with eDirectory.

➤ You can automatically download and install print drivers.

➤ It provides a much more user-friendly printing environment than what is available in queue-based printing.

➤ You can use NDPS on both Internetwork Packet Exchange/Sequenced Packet Exchange (IPX/SPX) and Transmission Control Protocol/Internet Protocol (TCP/IP) networks. Non-NetWare clients can print to NetWare printers through TCP/IP.

➤ Printers can have multiple configurations.

➤ Without Service Advertising Protocol (SAP), NDPS can communicate directly with printers, reducing network traffic.

➤ You can schedule print jobs based on desired criteria, such as job size or print medium required.

➤ Event notification is configurable.

➤ Printer and print job feedback and control occur in real time and are bidirectional.

➤ NDPS is fully backward compatible with queue-based printing.

➤ You can remotely install printers on workstations without the user intervening.

➤ NDPS is compatible with the Internet Printing Protocol (IPP).

Now you need to learn the two types of NDPS printers.

Identify the Types of Printers

NDPS printers come in two types:

➤ Public Access

➤ Controlled Access

Public Access printers are available to everyone on a network, have no eDirectory object or security, require little or no administrative action, and provide true plug-and-print capabilities. Public Access printers are created in NetWare Administrator through the Details page of the NDPS Manager, shown in Figure 11.4, which is covered in the next section titled "Describe NDPS Components."

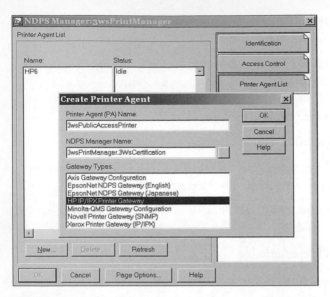

Figure 11.4 Creating a Public Access printer in NetWare Administrator.

Controlled Access printers have an eDirectory object, provide full administrative control, and include a full range of eDirectory security options. Only users who have sufficient eDirectory rights can access a Controlled Access printer.

 The task involved in creating and managing Public Access printers is not a focus of this exam. You must know the features of both Controlled Access and Public Access, and you must know how to create, configure, and manage Controlled Access printers. This topic is covered in the remainder of this chapter.

Now that you know the features and NDPS printer types, you need to learn the components that make up the NDPS environment.

Describe NDPS Components

Following are the four components that make up the NDPS printing environment:

➤ Printer agent

➤ NDPS Manager

➤ Printer Broker

➤ Printer Gateway

Printer Agent

A printer agent, on a one-to-one basis, represents each printer. The agent can represent only a single printer. It can be software running on a server that represents either a network-attached printer or a server-attached printer, or it can represent an NDPS-capable printer that is physically attached to the network.

The printer agent manages print job processing and responds to client queries about print jobs.

NDPS Manager

The NDPS Manager is an eDirectory object that manages printer agents. One NDPS Manager can be loaded on a NetWare 6.5 server. An NDPS Manager theoretically can manage an unlimited number of agents. The NDPS Manager NLM is NDPSM.NLM.

The NDPS Manager and the printer agents that the Manager controls should be on the same network segment. It is best not to keep all printer agents on the same server with a single NDPS Manager. This produces a single point of failure (SPOF) scenario. It is good practice to have multiple NDPS Managers, distributed in your tree, controlling a subset of printer agents to avoid the SPOF possibilities. Remember, though, that only one instance of the NDPSM.NLM can be loaded on a server.

Printer Broker

A Printer Broker provides three services: Service Registry Services (SRS), Resource Management Services (RMS), and Event Notification Services (ENS). By default, a Broker is installed on a network every three hops. The SRS enables users to advertise and discover public-access printers. The ENS enables printers to send users and operators messages about printer events. The RMS enables resources to be centrally located. Those resources, such as printer drivers, banners, fonts, and definition files, can be accessed, downloaded, and installed easily.

Printer Gateway

A Printer Gateway provides a means to use NDPS printing with printers that are not NDPS compliant. Gateways also enable printing to queue-based printers. A Printer Gateway is a translation device that converts NDPS queries to a printer-specific language. The primary gateway supported in

NetWare 6.5, when using iManager, is the Novell Gateway. It is a generic gateway that supports even older dot-matrix printers in an NDPS environment. A host of third-party gateways is available. You will see some of them if you create a printer agent using NetWare Administrator or the NDPS Manager server menus, as shown in Figures 11.4 and 11.5.

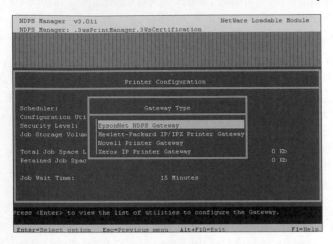

Figure 11.5 NDPS Manager on a NetWare 6.5 server: Gateway options.

Now that you have been introduced to the four NDPS components, you need to learn the steps for installing NDPS; creating and loading each of the components; and configuring the environment to download printer drivers automatically to users' workstations.

Set Up NDPS

You can install NDPS on a NetWare 6.5 server in several ways. The easiest way is to install it when you are initially installing the operating system on your server. The second most common method is to install it after you have installed the operating system by using the NetWare 6.5 Server GUI install. Following are the steps to accomplish this:

1. Mount the NetWare 6.5 Products CD on your server as Volume.

2. Start the Server GUI by entering STARTX at a server console prompt.

3. In the Server GUI, select Novell, Install.

4. Select Postinst.ni on the Products CD, and then select Clear All.

5. Select the iPrint product option, Next, Copy Files.

6. Then either reboot your server or reload the Apache Web server by selecting Reset Apache. Now you're ready to configure NDPS for your printing environment.

After you have NDPS installed on your NetWare 6.5 server, launch iManager from your administrative workstation, and expand iPrint to display the options available (refer to Figure 11.3). The steps to set up a working NDPS environment are as follows:

1. If a Broker does not exist within three hops of your server, or if you are on a side of a WAN link where a Broker is not currently active, from iManager, create and load a Broker on your server.

> Remember: You should create a Broker if one is not within three hops or if you are on a side of a WAN link where an NDPS Broker is not active.

2. Create and load an NDPS Manager.

3. Create printer agents for each of your printers. You can create Public Access printers or Controlled Access printers. For the purposes of iPrint, discussed later in this chapter, and for the CNA exam, you will be learning the steps for a Controlled Access printer.

4. Finally, configure your environment so that workstations are automatically configured for the correct printer.

The next sections look at each of these steps in detail.

Set Up the Broker

To create the Printer Broker from iManager, select iPrint, Create Broker.

Following is the information you have to provide to create a Broker:

➤ Print Broker's name and context.

➤ From SRS, ENS, and RMS, select the services you want to be enabled.

➤ If RMS is selected, provide the volume name that you want the Resource Management Service to be accessed from. This is the volume where you installed NDPS.

When you have created the Broker, load it on the server using the
BROKER.NLM. Following is the syntax to load the BROKER.NLM on a NetWare
6.5 server:

```
LOAD BROKER <DISTINGUISHED NAME OF PRINT BROKER OBJECT>
```

Here's an example:

```
LOAD BROKER .3WSBROKER.3WSCERTIFICATION
```

You can automatically load the Broker on your server if you enter the correct
syntax in the AUTOEXEC.NCF file.

If you want to manually load the Broker each time you boot the server, you
can enter

```
LOAD BROKER
```

at the server console, and then select the Broker object you want to load from
a menu like the one shown in Figure 11.6.

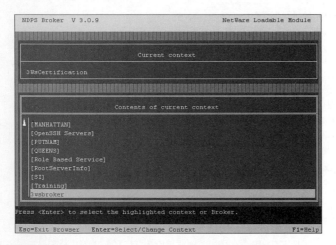

Figure 11.6 Broker selection menu on a NetWare 6.5 server.

After you load the Broker on your NetWare 6.5 server, you will have an
NDPS Broker screen active on your server, as shown in Figure 11.7. This
screen shows the Broker services that are enabled.

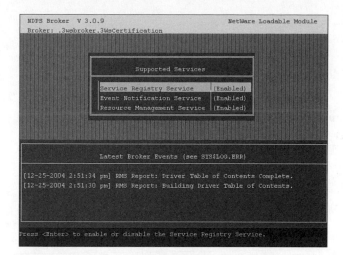

Figure 11.7 NDPS Broker screen on a NetWare 6.5 server.

Set Up the NDPS Manager

After you've created and loaded the Broker object, you need to create the NDPS Manager.

> Depending on the resource that you look at, the NDPS Manager is also referred to as the Print Service Manager, or Print Manager. All refer to the same eDirectory object.

To create the NDPS Manager from iManager, select iPrint, Create Print Manager.

Following is the information that you have to provide to create a Print Manager:

➤ The name and context for the Print Manager

➤ The name of the volume where you want to create the Print Manager's database

After you have created the Print Manager, load the Manager on the server using the module NDPSM.NLM. Following is the syntax to load the module NDPSM.NLM on a NetWare 6.5 server:

```
LOAD NDPSM <DISTINGUISHED NAME OF PRINT MANAGER OBJECT>
```

This is an example:

```
LOAD NDPSM .3WSPRINTMANAGER.3WSCERTIFICATION
```

You can automatically load the Manager on your server if you enter the correct syntax in the AUTOEXEC.NCF file.

If you want to manually load the Print Manager each time you boot the server, you can enter

```
LOAD NDPSM
```

at the server console, and then select the Print Manager object you want to load from a menu like the one shown in Figure 11.8.

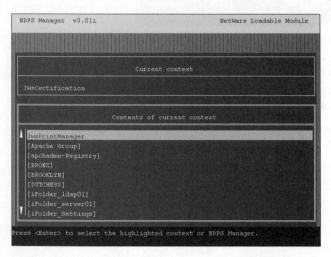

Figure 11.8   Print Manager selection menu on a NetWare 6.5 server.

After you've loaded the Print Manager on your NetWare 6.5 server, you will have an NDPS Manager screen, as shown in Figure 11.9, active on your server. This screen shows the printer agents that are available and their status. Those printers that are up and available for printing display their status as IDLE.

Set Up the Printer Agents

After you have a Broker and a Print Services Manager loaded on your NetWare 6.5 server, you can create printer agents (printer objects) for each printer that you want to be available in your environment.

To create a printer from iManager, select iPrint, Create Printer.

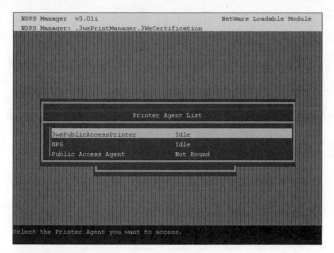

Figure 11.9   NDPS Manager screen on a NetWare 6.5 server.

You must provide the following information to create a printer:

➤ The name of the printer. This is the name of the eDirectory printer object in the tree.

➤ The context for the object.

➤ The name of the NDPS Print Service Manager that will manage this printer.

➤ The Gateway that is appropriate for this printer. In iManager, you have two choices: the Novell Gateway or the Axis LPR Gateway. You can change gateways after you create the printer object.

➤ If you select the Novell Gateway you are asked to supply either the IP address for the printer or the host name/DNS name of the printer.

➤ You can then select the default drivers for the printer for the Windows XP, Windows 2000, Windows NT 4, and Windows 95/98 platforms. You can also choose not to select drivers at this time. You can add the vendor-appropriate drivers to the RMS Broker Service at a later time and then configure the default driver for the printer.

 This is the procedure if you are using the Novell Gateway in iManager. If you are creating a print object in NetWare Administrator using a different gateway, the steps are a bit different. For example, if you select an HP IP/IPX Printer Gateway, you can select the IPX address for the printer.

You now have a Broker, an NDPS Print Service Manager, and a printer object with its Gateway up and running. All that is left to do is deploy the drivers, as easily as possible, to your users. You no longer have to run to users' offices with the print driver CD and ask for permission to sit at their computer to install the drivers. You can do all of it automatically without the user even knowing it is happening.

Set Up RPM (Remote Print Management)

To automatically install an NDPS printer to your users' workstations, in iManager, select iPrint, RPM Configuration and select the object that you want to deploy the printers to. This object can be a user, a group, or a container. If you select a container, all users in the container have the printer installed. After you have selected the object for deployment, the screen shown in Figure 11.10 is displayed.

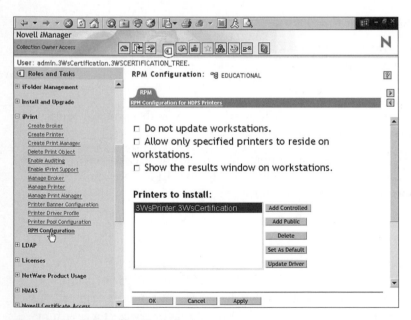

Figure 11.10   RPM Configuration options.

In the RPM Configuration window, you can elect to automatically install Public Access or Controlled Access printers, show or hide the results of the installation on the users' screens, update the workstations, update the installed drivers if a new driver has been released, and select which printer is the default printer for the user, group, or container. You can also decide if only certain printers should be on users' computers, thereby removing printers that are cluttering up the workstation environment.

After the users log back in to the NetWare environment, depending on your selections, you can automatically install the printers without the users' knowledge. When users opt to print a document to a new printer that you have selected as their default, the job is automatically directed to that printer, like magic. With NDPS, your printer headaches are significantly reduced.

At this point, you need to explore some management tasks so that you can make printing both user and administrator friendly.

Manage NDPS

With iManager, you can manage your Brokers, NDPS Print Service Managers, and printers by selecting the corresponding iPrint manage option, as shown in Figure 11.3.

You need to be familiar with four Manage Printer options:

➤ Configuring the default security setting for printers

➤ Reordering print jobs

➤ Modifying the spool location

➤ Configuring client support for iPrint

These options are testable, but you should take the time to explore the myriad of Manage Printer options that are available under the tabs shown in Figures 11.11 and 11.12. Also explore the Manage Broker and Manage Print Manager options.

To configure the default security setting for printers, in iManager, iPrint, select your printer and then the Access Control tab and the Security link, shown in Figure 11.11. Here, you can restrict access to your printers based on a default security setting. The default setting is Medium, which allows client applications to govern nonprint operations and NDPS to govern print operations. A Low setting allows client applications to govern all print and nonprint operations. A High setting allows NDPS to govern all print and nonprint operations.

To reorder print jobs, in iManager, iPrint, select your printer, and then on the Printer Control tab, select the Jobs link, shown in Figure 11.12. Here, you can reorder print jobs, promoting those that must be printed first. This is where you can go when your employer demands that his print job be printed immediately even though it is far down in the spool.

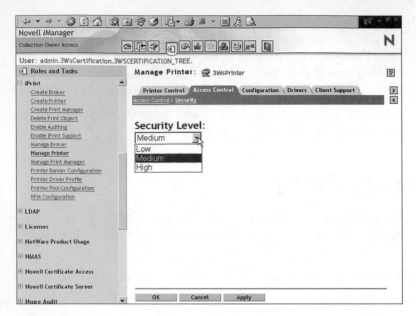

Figure 11.11 Printer access control.

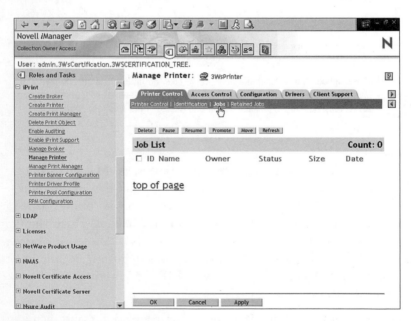

Figure 11.12 Print job management.

To modify the location of the print spool, where jobs are held when they are waiting to be printed, in iManager, iPrint, select your printer. Then on the Configuration tab, select the Spooling link, shown in Figure 11.13. Here, you can reconfigure the volume that will serve the print spool, restrict the amount of space allocated to the spool, and define the scheduling option that the spool uses.

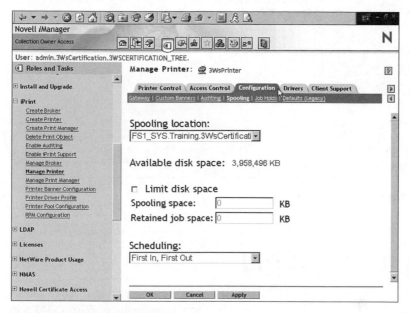

Figure 11.13   Print spool management.

To configure client support for iPrint, in iManager, iPrint, select your printer. Then on the Client Support tab, select the iPrint Support link, shown in Figure 11.14, and either enable or disable iPrint support for this printer. You can also configure the URL that is used for accessing this printer.

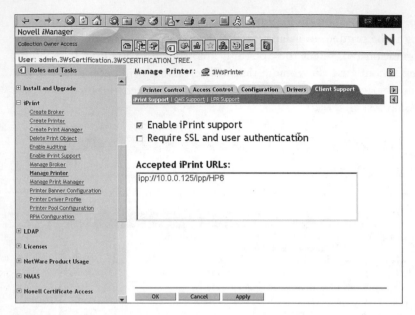

Figure 11.14 Client Support management.

Implement iPrint

Now that you have explored NDPS and seen how to enable iPrint support on a printer, it is time to expand your horizons and see how to use NDPS in conjunction with IPP to print to an iPrint printer from anywhere in the world.

iPrint is a NetWare 6.5 feature that facilitates printing over the Internet with reduced costs, customized printer views, and unified management. You can now access printers using a standard Web browser.

Some of the features of iPrint include the following:

➤ Access to printers from anywhere in the world. Secure access across the Internet to printers in your office is possible with iPrint.

➤ iPrint, because of its integration with eDirectory, awards access only to authorized users.

➤ Printing to high-end printers for remote users came at a significant price before iPrint. iPrint dramatically reduces the cost of printing to high-end printers.

➤ iPrint includes a Map tool that enables administrators to create floor plans or other graphics and place printers on those graphics so that users can click on a graphical link to access a printer of choice. Users can access administrator-created floor plans or maps via a Web browser.

Now that you know the features of iPrint, you need to be introduced to the iPrint components and configuration steps.

The two major iPrint components are NDPS and IPP.

For iPrint to work, you must load and configure NDPS. You must also configure the NDPS Broker, Manager, and agent. In addition, Novell's iPrint requires that you load IPPSRVR.NLM on a NetWare server. This occurs automatically when you configure the first iPrint printer. You must also install several browser plug-ins on the Windows workstation for Novell's implementation of iPrint. You can install an optional iPrint client on a Windows workstation, but it is not required.

iPrint uses IPP to enable secure, Web-based printer access from anywhere in the world. Novell's implementation of iPrint is based on NDPS and its printing infrastructure. IPP is a simple, TCP/IP-based printing protocol that has been accepted as an industry standard. It has broad support from vendors, works over LANs and WANs, supports encryption of data, and can be used on multiple platforms, including Unix, Linux, Macintosh, and Windows.

You must take two iPrint configuration steps after you set up NDPS:

1. You have to configure a DNS "A" record for each server on which you want to load the NDPSM.NLM. This allows clients to access your iPrint printers using common names in a Web browser. Configure this before you enable support for iPrint printers. After you have configured the DNS record, you can load the NDPSM.NLM with the /dnsname option. Use this syntax:

```
LOAD NDPSM <Manager's_eDirectory_ Distinguished_Name>
/dnsname=Manager's_DNS_Name
```

Following is an example of this:

```
LOAD NDPSM .3WSMANAGER.3WSCERTIFICATION /dnsname=3WSMANAGER.MAIL.3WSCER-
TIFICATION.COM
```

2. Next, you have to enable iPrint support on each printer that you want to be available. You accomplish this in iManager, iPrint. Select your printer, and then on the Client Support tab, select the iPrint Support link, shown in Figure 11.14. Next, enable iPrint Support for this printer. You can also configure the URL that is used for accessing this

printer, and choose to require SSL and user authentication for access to the printer.

Note that step 2 repeats the last Manage Printer task discussed in the "Manage NDPS" section earlier in this chapter. This is not a mistake. It is important enough that I repeated it to make sure you know it for the exam.

After your servers and printers are set up and your NDPS environment is ready to go, you need to install the iPrint client on the client workstations so that you can access and download the printers either through the default printer list or a location-based map. If you have not installed the iPrint client when you select an iPrint printer, you are given the option of saving the client or installing it directly from the server. After the client is installed and you select a printer, a link is displayed enabling you to install the printer.

The default printer list, with a link to install the iPrint client, is available at `http://iPrintServer_IPAddress_or_DNS_Name:631/IPP`.

An example of the default printer list is shown in Figure 11.15, as a result of entering `http://10.0.0.125:631/IPP`.

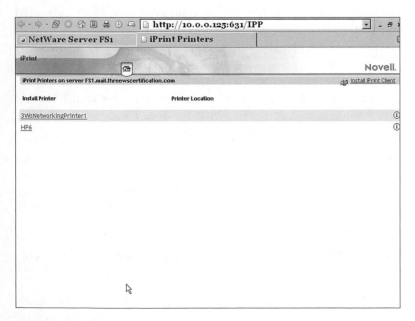

Figure 11.15 Default printer list.

If you have to print through a secure port, substitute port 443 for port 631 in the URL. You can do this with either of the following URL examples:

```
http://10.0.0.125:443/IPP
```

or

```
https://10.0.0.125/IPP
```

One of the iPrint capabilities that makes printing user friendly is that you can create location-based maps that show users in a graphical format where printers are located. These are the requirements for creating a map:

➤ Internet Explorer 5.5 or later. If you try a non-IE browser, you get an error message.

➤ The iPrint client installed.

➤ A mapped drive to volume SYS.

➤ Windows 9x/Me/NT/2000/XP.

➤ Graphics or floor plans that are representative of your facility. Copy these to SYS:\APACHE2\HTDOCS\IPPDOCS\IMAGES\MAPS. By default, this location has two maps: Office.gif and Office2.gif. These maps can be .bmp, .gif, or .jpg graphics.

After you have met these requirements, you can open Maptool.htm, which is located in SYS:\APACHE2\HTDOCS\IPPDOCS in Internet Explorer. This opens the iPrint Map Designer shown in Figure 11.16.

NOTE This discussion is predicated on the idea that you have the Novell Client installed on your workstation. Otherwise, you cannot map a Novell drive to volume **SYS**. If you do not have the Novell Client installed, you can still open **Maptool.htm** in Internet Explorer using **http://server_IP_address:631/IPPDOCS/Maptool.htm**.

After you have the iPrint Map Designer opened, select a background graphic and a printer icon. Then drag the icon to the correct location on the graphic, the corresponding printer from a drop-down list, a printer URL, mouse-over text, and a printer caption. You can save this graphic by default to the SYS:\APACHE2\HTDOCS\IPPDOCS directory. Users can then access the map through the defined URL and print to their office printer, for example, from anywhere in the world.

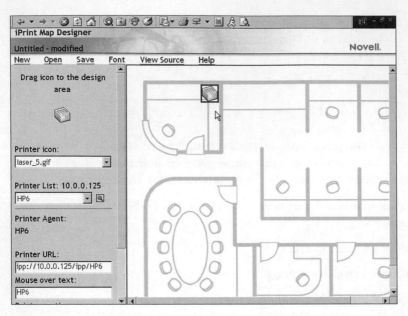

Figure 11.16 iPrint Map Designer.

This chapter contains numerous file system locations and sample URLs. I encourage you to familiarize yourself with these paths and URLs. Realize that you can substitute your own IP address where I have used 10.0.0.125 or a DNS name when you have DNS configured and the necessary records configured.

Exam Prep Questions

1. Which of the following are features of NDPS? (Select all that apply.)

   A. ❑ NDPS can automatically detect printers and download drivers.

   B. ❑ NDPS requires TCP/IP.

   C. ❑ Printing is tightly integrated with eDirectory.

   D. ❑ NDPS can be administered centrally.

   Answers A, C, and D are correct. Some of the features of NDPS are that printers can be automatically detected and drivers downloaded, printing is tightly integrated with eDirectory, and NDPS can be centrally administered. Answer B is incorrect. NDPS works with TCP/IP and IPX/SPX.

2. Which type of NDPS printer has no object in the eDirectory tree?

   A. ○ Public Access

   B. ○ Controlled Access

   C. ○ Queue-based

   D. ○ Line printer

   Answer A is correct. Two categories of NDPS printers exist: Public Access and Controlled Access. Public Access printers are available to everyone on a network, have no eDirectory object, have low security, and provide true plug-and-print capabilities. Answer B is incorrect. A Controlled Access printer has an object in the eDirectory tree. Answers C and D are incorrect. Neither is a type of NDPS printer.

3. Alexandra wants to deploy NDPS in her NetWare 6.5 environment. She uses HP IV laser printers on her network. The HP IV laser printers are not NDPS aware. Which NDPS object is designed to assist Alexandra with the deployment?

   A. ○ Gateway

   B. ○ Broker

   C. ○ Printer agent

   D. ○ NDPS Manager

   Answer A is correct. A Printer Gateway provides a means to use NDPS printing with printers that are not NDPS compliant. Gateways also enable printing to queue-based printers. Answers B, C, and D are incorrect. These are all components of NDPS, but they do not provide the functionality required by the question.

4. Marion wants to load the NDPS Manager on her NetWare 6.5 server. The server's name is FS1. The Manager's name is NDPSManager. The Manager exists in the same context as FS1. What command should Marion enter at the FS1 server console prompt to launch the NDPS Manager, without selecting the printer from a menu?

A. ○ **NDPSManager**

B. ○ **NDPSM Manager**

C. ○ **NDPSM NDPSManager**

D. ○ **NDPSManager NDPSM**

Answer C is correct. The server console command that loads the NDPS Manager on FS1 is NDPSM NDPSManager or LOAD NDPSM NDPSManager. Answers A, B, and D are incorrect. They do not use the correct syntax.

5. Which NDPS Broker service enables users to advertise and discover public-access printers?

A. ○ SRS

B. ○ ENS

C. ○ RMS

D. ○ RPM

Answer A is correct. The SRS enables users to advertise and discover public-access printers. Answers B, C, and D are incorrect. ENS and RMS are Broker services, but they do not provide the required functionality. RPM is the Remote Printer Management option that allows print drivers to be downloaded automatically when a user logs in to the network.

6. Which of the following NDPS components are required on a network that primarily uses iPrint? (Select all that apply.)

A. ❑ Gateway

B. ❑ Broker

C. ❑ NDPS Manager

D. ❑ Printer agent

Answers B, C, and D are correct. iPrint requires the configuration of the Broker, NDPS Manager, and printer agent. Answer A is incorrect. iPrint does not require the Gateway component of NDPS.

7. Which of the following are features of IPP? (Select all that apply.)

A. ❑ It works well over LANs.

B. ❑ It runs over TCP/IP networks.

C. ❑ It has limited support from vendors.

D. ❑ It is a simple printing protocol.

E. ❑ It supports data encryption.

Answers A, B, D, and E are correct. IPP is a simple, TCP/IP-based printing protocol that has been accepted as an industry standard. IPP has broad support from vendors, works over LANs and WANs, supports encryption of data, and can be used on multiple platforms, including Unix, Macintosh, and Windows. Answer C is incorrect.

8. You want to configure an iPrint map to support printing based on printer location. Which of the following is the location where you should copy your map to enable this type of printing?

    A. ○ **SYS:\APACHES\IMAGES\HTDOCS\PPDOCS\MAPS**

    B. ○ **SYS:\APACHE2\IMAGES\PPDOCS\MAPS**

    C. ○ **SYS:\APACHE2\PPDOCS\IMAGES\HTDOCS\MAPS**

    D. ○ **SYS:\APACHE2\HTDOCS\PPDOCS\IMAGES\MAPS**

    Answer D is correct. To configure iPrint printing based on printer location, you should copy all of your images, or maps, to SYS:\APACHE2\HTDOCS\IPPDOCS\IMAGES\MAPS. All other responses are incorrect because they do not represent the correct path to the map images for location-based printing.

9. You have deployed iPrint on your NetWare 6.5 network. You want your users to access the default printer list that iPrint generates. They can find it on a NetWare 6.5 server that has an IP address of 10.0.0.125, using the default nonsecure port. What URL do your users have to enter into the browser Address field if they want to access the default printer list?

    A. ○ **http://10.0.0.125:631/IPP**

    B. ○ **http://10.0.0.125:443/IPP**

    C. ○ **https://10.0.0.125:2200**

    D. ○ **http://10.0.0.125:8008**

    Answer A is correct. Users who want to take advantage of iPrint need to install the iPrint client and the printer they want to use. They can use this same address to access the default printer list that iPrint generates. To access the default printer list on a server that has an IP address of 10.0.0.125, users enter http://10.0.0.125:631/IPP in the browser location bar. Port 631 is used for nonsecure access. Answer B is incorrect. If users need to access the URL with a secure port, the default URL is http://10.0.0.125:443/IPP. Answers C and D are incorrect. Answer C points to the Web Manager on server 10.0.0.125, whereas Answer D points to Remote Manager on the same server.

10. Which NetWare 6.5 utility should you use if you want to change the default security level of a printer from Medium to High?

    A. ○ iMonitor

    B. ○ iManager

    C. ○ Remote Manager

    D. ○ ConsoleOne

    Answer B is correct. The NetWare 6.5 utility that you should use to manage NDPS printers is iManager. In iManager, under iPrint, Manage Printer, *Printer*, Access Control, Security, you can change a printer security level from Medium to High. Answers A, B, and C are incorrect. These tools are not capable of managing NDPS printers. It seems odd that you cannot manage printers in ConsoleOne, but Novell never ported that functionality to ConsoleOne. You can perform some NDPS management tasks in NetWare Administrator, but not ConsoleOne.

iFolder and Virtual Office

Terms you'll need to understand:

✓ Startx
✓ iFolder Management Console
✓ Passphrase
✓ Virtual Office
✓ NetStorage
✓ Virtual Teams

Techniques you'll need to master:

✓ Implement iFolder
✓ Describe Virtual Office
✓ Install Virtual Office
✓ Configure Virtual Office

This chapter introduces you to two powerful NetWare products that permit users to securely share files and to collaborate in real time over the Internet. These products are iFolder and Virtual Office. They enable users, regardless of their location, to share data and work together. The virtual office is a reality in business today. It is your job as a CNA to enable users to efficiently function in this virtual marketplace using iFolder and Virtual Office.

 At this point in this book, you might be a bit tired from information overload. However, don't dismiss this chapter. As both a potential NetWare 6.5 CNA and a NetWare 6.5 admin in a production environment, you need to understand how iFolder and Virtual Office are installed and configured and what their benefits and features are. This chapter contains enough potential exam questions to make the difference between your becoming a CNA and your being ever so close.

Implement iFolder

iFolder 2.1, which ships with NetWare 6.5, lets users have secure access to their files from home, the office, or on the road. Without copying files back and forth to a floppy disk, users can access the latest version of their data when and where they need it with an Internet connection and a browser that is Java enabled.

In this section, you are introduced to the features and benefits of iFolder, learn how to install the server-side and client-side components, and discover how to configure iFolder using the Web-based iFolder Management Console.

iFolder: Its Benefits and Features

Some of iFolder's features and benefits include the following:

➤ A user's data can seamlessly follow him wherever he goes. Data is stored and synchronized so that a user's data is available as he expects it to be regardless of where he is sitting.

➤ Any changes that a user makes to his data offline are tracked, logged, and synchronized when the user reconnects to the network.

➤ Because data is stored on a NetWare server, it can be easily backed up and protected.

➤ Data is secure from unauthorized access because of the encryption algorithm used in iFolder. Before being transmitted across the Internet, data is encrypted, avoiding data compromise in transit. The iFolder Passphrase is an option that encrypts data on an iFolder Server or when transmitted to a workstation. This option ensures that data is secure and private. An admin can recover a user's passphrase in iFolder 2.1.

➤ User productivity is increased because users do not have to upload files to their laptop before going on the road. When a user has the iFolder Client installed on his laptop, data is automatically synchronized to his laptop when he connects to the Internet from his destination.

➤ iFolder works with the Apache Web Server, IIS, and because of its LDAP support, eDirectory and Active Directory.

➤ An iFolder Server can manage up to 10,000 user accounts, and the possible number of iFolder Servers on your network is unlimited.

➤ Data access is available either with or without the iFolder Client. If the iFolder Client is not used, a Web browser is required. You can also use handheld devices with a Web browser and without the iFolder Client to access iFolder data.

➤ End-user training requirements are dramatically reduced. A user simply stores his data in a local iFolder directory, and the contents of that directory are synchronized when he authenticates to the iFolder Server. If a user can save a file in the correct local folder, iFolder takes care of the rest.

➤ Users can connect to multiple iFolder accounts simultaneously using Novell's NetDrive product.

➤ Thinclients are supported through Novell's NetDrive product, Windows 2000 Terminal Server, and ZENworks OnDemand Services.

Installing iFolder and the iFolder Client

Now that you know the benefits and features of iFolder, you need to know the prerequisites of installing it.

Following are the iFolder installation prerequisites:

➤ Minimum 450MHz CPU

➤ Minimum 512MB RAM

➤ Minimum 15MB space on volume sys and enough space for user data on a volume of your choice, preferably not sys

➤ Minimum support pack levels for the following NetWare versions:

    ➤ NetWare 5.1 SP5

    ➤ NetWare 6.0 SP2

    ➤ NetWare 6.5

➤ Minimum eDirectory 8.6.2

➤ Minimum Apache Web Server 1.3.26

After you have met the server requirements, you can install iFolder in any of five ways:

➤ During the operating system installation, you can select Custom Install and the iFolder product.

➤ During the operating system installation, iFolder is automatically installed by selecting a Virtual Office Server preconfigured server installation.

➤ During the operating system installation, iFolder is automatically installed by selecting a Novell iFolder Storage Services Server preconfigured server installation.

➤ During the operating system installation, iFolder is automatically installed by selecting an exteNd J2EE Web Application Server preconfigured server installation.

➤ After operating system installation, you can use the Novell Server graphical user interface (GUI). If you do not have the Novell Server GUI loaded, you can launch the GUI from the server console using the STARTX command. After the GUI is up, follow these installation steps:

    1. In the Server GUI, select Novell, Install, Add.

    2. Select Postinst.ni on the Products CD, which you have previously mounted as a volume, and then select Clear All.

    3. Select the iFolder product option, Next, Copy Files.

    4. After you authenticate as the Admin object, configure iFolder by confirming or changing the LDAP Host Name or IP Address, LDAP Port, LDAP Context for Admin, iFolder Server Host Name or IP Address, iFolder Admin name, and User Database Path.

    5. After you select Next and all files are copied, reboot your server.

Now that you have the server-side iFolder component installed, you should, although you don't have to, install the iFolder Client on every workstation (laptops and desktops) that users will use for iFolder access. iFolder supports Windows 98 SE, 2000 Professional, and XP Home and Professional. You can install the iFolder Client with the following steps:

1. Authenticate to the local workstation as an Administrative user.

2. Using Internet Explorer, enter the following URL in your browser's location bar: `http://server_ip_address/iFolder`.

 Use Internet Explorer 5.0 or later for all of your iFolder tasks. You can perform many of the Web-based NetWare management tasks with any browser. iFolder is compatible with Internet Explorer. Some of Novell's documentation specifically says Internet Explorer 5.0 or later, but other documents are not as clear.

3. Click the iFolder Windows Client Download link, shown in Figure 12.1. You can either save the client to a local directory or run the client install from the server.

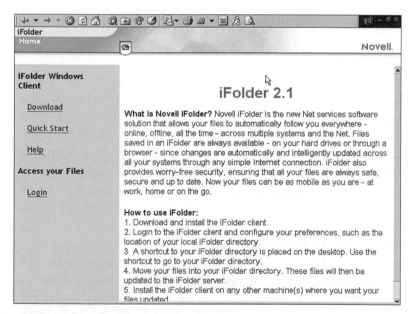

Figure 12.1   iFolder Windows Client Download link.

4. During the client install, you configure the language, accept the iFolder license agreement, copy files to the default location, and complete the installation by rebooting your workstation.

5. After reboot, you have a desktop icon, shown in Figure 12.2. The same icon appears in your System Tray which you can right-click to access an iFolder configuration menu, shown in Figure 12.3. After the iFolder Client is configured with your authentication credentials and passphrase, whenever you place data in the desktop folder, it is synchronized with your iFolder Server based on the time delays you have configured, as shown in Figure 12.4. You can access your files without the iFolder Client by going to `http://server_ip_address/iFolder` and clicking the Login link, under Access Your Files, shown in Figure 12.1.

Figure 12.2   iFolder icon.

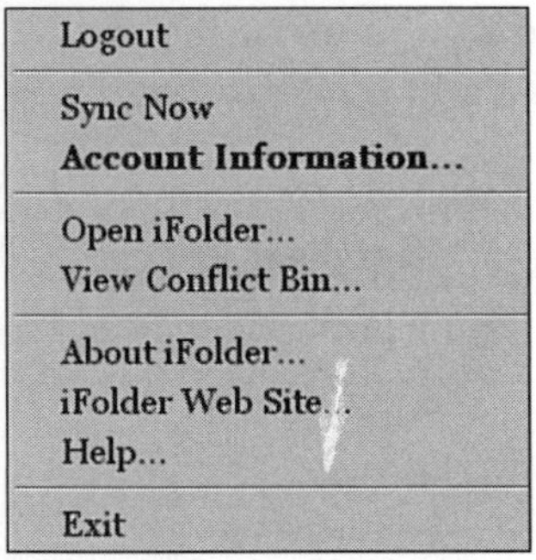

Logout
Sync Now
Account Information...
Open iFolder...
View Conflict Bin...
About iFolder...
iFolder Web Site...
Help...
Exit

Figure 12.3   iFolder Client configuration menu.

Now that you have the iFolder Server-side component installed and can access your iFolder storage folder using the iFolder Client, you need to configure the iFolder Server using the iFolder Management Console.

Configuring iFolder

The utility of choice for managing and configuring the iFolder Server is the iFolder Management Console, shown in Figure 12.5. You can access the iFolder Management Console by typing `https://server_ip_address/iFolderServer/Admin` in the location bar of your Internet Explorer browser.

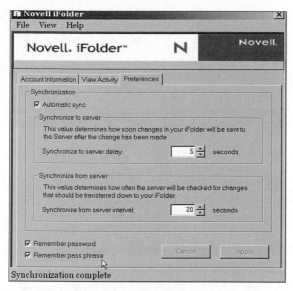

Figure 12.4   iFolder Client synchronization preferences.

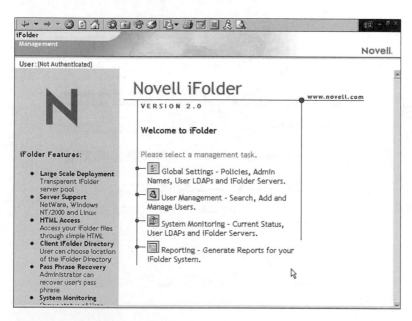

Figure 12.5   iFolder Management Console.

Notice on the opening screen of the iFolder Management Console the four major configuration options:

➤ Global Settings

➤ User Management

➤ System Monitoring

➤ Reporting

Under each of these links is a series of iFolder Server configuration options.

Take some time to thoroughly review this opening screen and the tasks you can perform under each major configuration option.

Global Settings

The configuration links are shown in Figure 12.6 and in the following list. They are available when you select the Global Settings option.

➤ General Info

➤ Global Policies

➤ Admin Names

➤ User LDAPs

➤ iFolder Servers

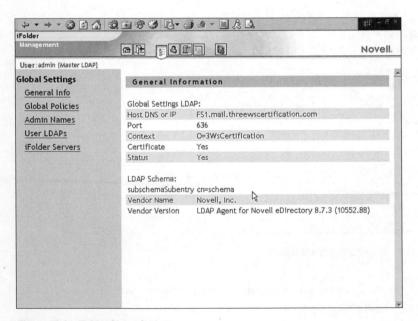

Figure 12.6 iFolder Global Settings.

On the General Information page, you see iFolder Server information, such as the Host IP, Context, and Port number. You cannot modify this information on this screen.

On the Global Policies page, shown in Figure 12.7, you can configure Client and Server policies.

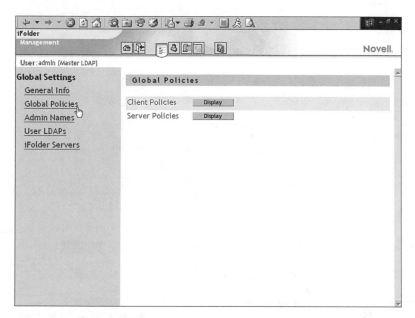

Figure 12.7   iFolder Global Policies.

On the Client Policies page, shown in Figure 12.8, you can enable or disable several client policies and configure whether the policies are enforced or visible to the user. If a policy is enforced, it is grayed out in the iFolder Client so that a user can see the setting but not change it. If a policy is not enabled, a user can change the setting. iFolder users cannot view or modify a policy that is hidden. By default, a hidden policy is enforced.

On the Server Policies page, shown in Figure 12.9, you can configure the initial amount of storage space that is available to a user.

When you return to the Global Settings page, you can configure User LDAPs (Lightweight Directory Access Protocols), where you can configure the contexts that are searched when a user authenticates (shown in Figure 12.10) or add a User LDAP (shown in Figure 12.11). You can also select Admin Names, where you can change the admin's name or add other names to the admin list. In iFolder Servers, you can configure the default iFolder Server if more than one exists in your environment.

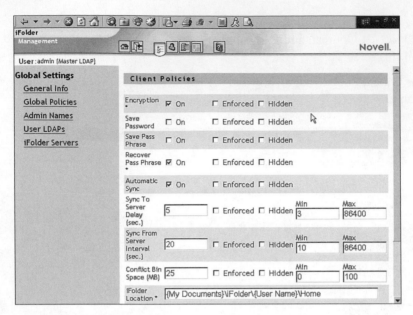

Figure 12.8 iFolder Client Policies.

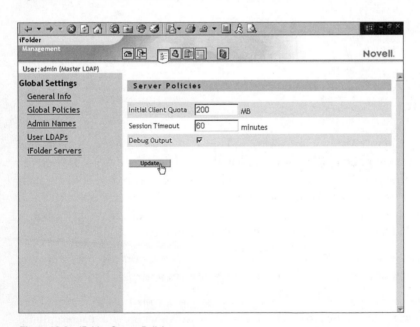

Figure 12.9 iFolder Server Policies.

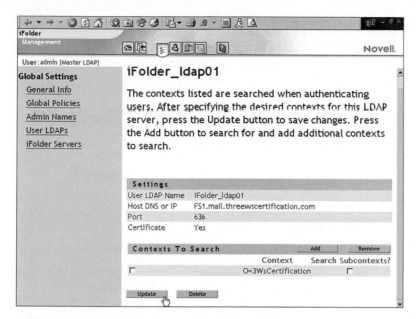

Figure 12.10 iFolder: Changing user context with User LDAPs.

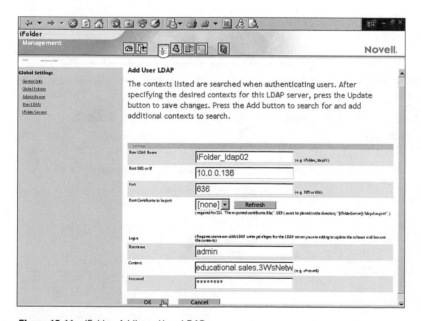

Figure 12.11 iFolder: Adding a User LDAP.

User Management

When you select User Management from the opening iFolder Management Console page, you can add, search, or manage iFolder users, as shown in Figures 12.12 and 12.13.

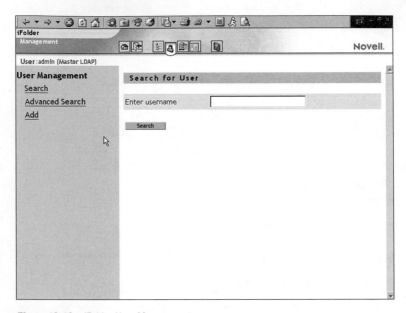

Figure 12.12   iFolder User Management.

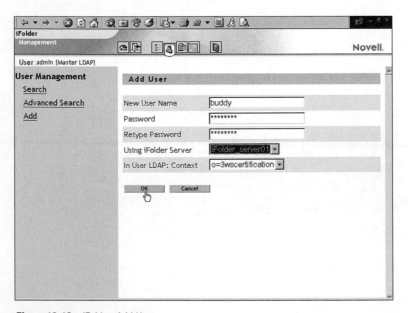

Figure 12.13   iFolder: Add User.

System Monitoring

When you select System Monitoring from the opening iFolder Management Console page, you can monitor User LDAPs, iFolder Server current sessions, and Stop Sync, as shown in Figure 12.14.

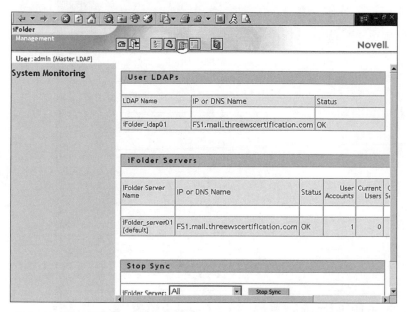

Figure 12.14   iFolder System Monitoring.

Reporting

When you select Reporting from the opening iFolder Management Console page, you can access General Info and display or export information on User Accounts, User LDAPs, and iFolder Servers, as shown in Figure 12.15.

Novell recommends three configuration steps to optimize iFolder:

1. Increase the amount of server RAM. The more iFolder users, the more memory the server needs. The rule of thumb is 16KB of memory for each iFolder session, and 1GB of RAM if you have more than 4,000 users.

2. If you have thousands of users, increase the sync delay parameters.

3. Increase the number of Apache threads. The maximum number of threads on a NetWare server is 2,048, and the default is 150. Depending on the speed of your network interface card, Novell

recommends increasing the Apache threads to either 312 on a 100Mbps network or 2048 on a 1000Mbps network. You can configure the Apache threads in the HTTPD.CONF file. You can find this file in various places in NetWare 6.5 depending on the installed support pack.

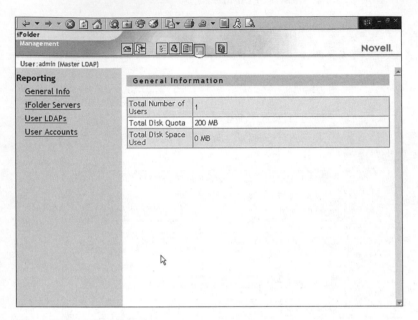

Figure 12.15   iFolder Reporting.

You have been introduced to the features and benefits of iFolder, installing the server-side and client-side components, and configuring iFolder using the Web-based iFolder Management Console. Now you're ready to move on to Virtual Office and working with people you might never meet in person. Wow!

Describe Virtual Office

Virtual Office is a collaboration and information-sharing portal for remote users who work as part of a virtual team. Virtual Office allows users to communicate in real time, publish a personal Web page, back up information, manage passwords, access a team calendar and contact list, and access stored files through NetStorage. A sample Virtual Office home page, with a Woodworkers Virtual Team, is shown in Figure 12.16. A Virtual Team is a location in Virtual Office where a group of linked users can share data, exchange files, keep a calendar, and update each other in real time.

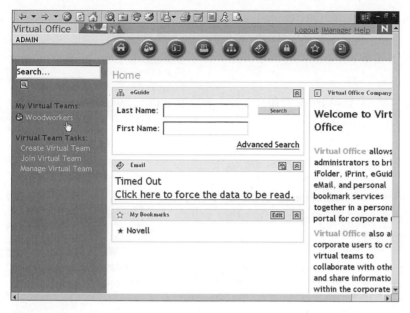

Figure 12.16   Virtual Team sample home page.

Install Virtual Office

Now that you know a bit about Virtual Office, you can install it on your NetWare 6.5 server. Just as with the other products discussed until now, you have a variety of options for installing Virtual Office on a NetWare 6.5 server:

➤ You can install it when installing the server operating system using a Custom Install.

➤ During the operating system installation, you can select a Virtual Office Server preconfigured server installation.

➤ You can perform a post-operating system installation using the Novell Server GUI. If you do not have the Novell Server GUI loaded, you can launch the GUI from the server console using the START command. After the GUI is up, follow these installation steps:

    1. In the Server GUI, select Novell, Install, Add.

    2. Select `Postinst.ni` on the Products CD, which you have previously mounted as a volume, and then select Clear All.

    3. Select Novell Virtual Office Framework, Next, Copy Files.

4. After the files are copied, authenticate as the admin from your tree, providing a username, password, and context.

5. A dialog box appears informing you that the installation is complete.

6. Access the Virtual Office home page from your workstation using the following URL in your browser: `http://server_ip_address/vo`.

   You can also use the server's DNS name if you have DNS configured on your network.

If you want to have access to eGuide, iPrint, and NetStorage from Virtual Office, you need to install them either before or when you install Virtual Office on your server.

 Remember: You need to install eGuide, iPrint, and NetStorage when you install Virtual Office if you want to have those capabilities. If you do not install them, these capabilities will not be available to your Virtual Teams.

Also be sure you know the URL to access Virtual Office.

You are now ready to configure Virtual Office using two different utilities. Then your users, who will never meet, can work together in harmony! How great is that?

Configure Virtual Office

Just as you configured iFolder using a host of screens, Virtual Office requires a good bit of configuration. The only difference is that with iFolder, you did 90% of the configuration in the iFolder Management Console. With Virtual Office, the configuration is split between iManager and the Virtual Office interface.

Virtual Office Configuration Using iManager

As shown in Figure 12.17, iManager has two links, under Virtual Office, for configuring Virtual Office:

➤ Services Administration

➤ Environment Administration

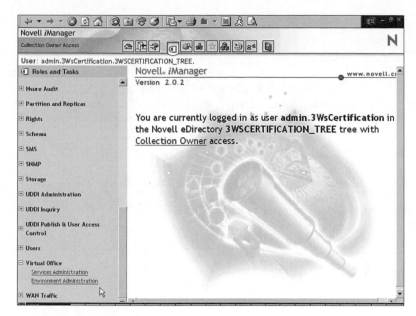

Figure 12.17   Virtual Office configuration links in iManager.

You need to be familiar with the tasks that you can perform under each option. First you'll learn the tasks that you can perform under the Services Administration link.

In case you have forgotten, the URL for iManager is **https://server_ip_address/ nps/iManager**.

If you do not see the Virtual Office link in iManager because you installed it after the operating system was initially installed and configured, you can reconfigure iManager to display Virtual Office. You can accomplish this by clicking the Configure button at the top of iManager. Then select iManager Configuration, Modules, Install. Browse to the **VirtualOffice.npm**, which is found in **SYS:\TOMCAT\4\WEBAPPS\NPS\PACK-AGES**. After you install the module in iManager, you have to restart the Tomcat Servlet Engine. Following are the server console commands to accomplish this:

➤   TC4STOP

➤   AP2WEBDN

➤   AP2WEBUP

➤   TOMCAT4

Be patient when Tomcat is stopping. Don't proceed until it's completely stopped. Check the Console Logger to verify this.

Virtual Office Configuration Using iManager: Services Administration Link

In Figure 12.18, you can see 10 configuration tasks that you can perform under the Services Administration link.

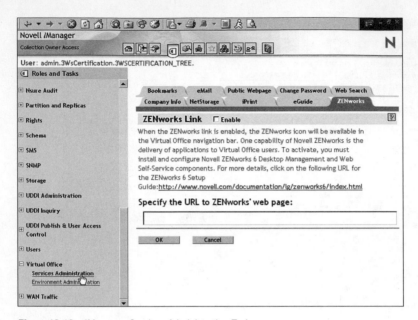

Figure 12.18 iManager: Services Administration Tasks.

These include the following:

➤ Bookmarks

➤ E-mail (including GroupWise and NetMail, depending on which is installed)

➤ Public Webpage

➤ Change Password

➤ Web Search

➤ Company Info (displayed on the opening Virtual Office page)

➤ NetStorage

➤ iPrint

➤ eGuide

➤ ZENworks

ZENworks shows up in this list if you have previously installed it. The server that I am using for this book has ZENworks for Desktops 4.01 installed. If you do not have ZENworks installed, this tab might not be displayed.

On the Company Information tab, shown in Figure 12.19, you can enable Company Info on the Virtual Office home page. Then you can insert information that will be displayed in the Virtual Office News field on the far right side of the opening Virtual Office page, shown in Figure 12.16. You can enter this information in HTML or in plaintext.

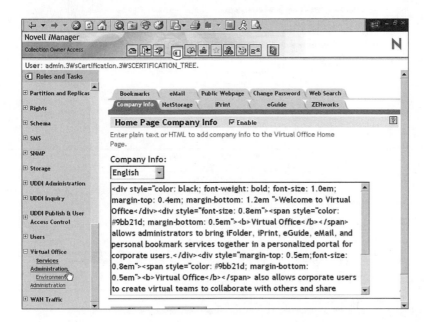

Figure 12.19   iManager: Company Info tab.

On the NetStorage page, shown in Figure 12.20, you can enable NetStorage capabilities for Virtual Office users. If you do enable it, you can configure the URL that is used for NetStorage.

The other tabs that are displayed in iManager-Services Administration also let you either enable or disable their link for Virtual Office users. If the link is enabled, the tabs allow you to configure the URL that should be used for that link and other pertinent parameters.

Virtual Office Configuration Using iManager: Environment Administration Link

You can use the iManager: Environment Administration link, shown in Figure 12.21, to configure the following:

➤ Team Configuration

➤ Portal Configuration

➤ Logging

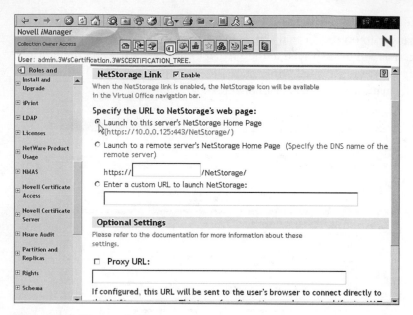

Figure 12.20 iManager: NetStorage page.

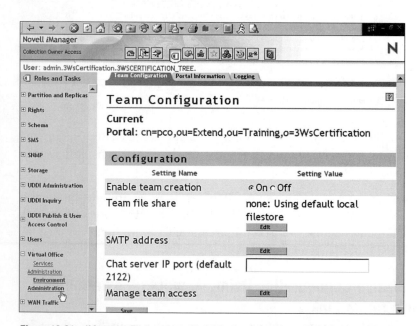

Figure 12.21 iManager: Environment Administration link options, Team Configuration tab.

On the Team Configuration tab, shown in Figure 12.21, you can enable or disable the creation of teams. If you enable the option, you can configure the Team File Share, SMTP Address, Chat Server IP Port, and Manage Team Access.

On the Portal Information tab, shown in Figure 12.22, you can add or remove portal containers and display portal locations and the Virtual Teams found by iManager.

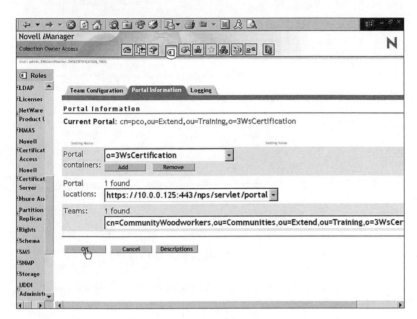

Figure 12.22 iManager: Environment Administration link options, Portal Information tab.

On the Logging page, shown in Figure 12.23, you can configure a host of logging options, including the following.

➤ Enable or disable logging.

➤ Set the logging level. By default, the level is set to High.

➤ Configure the logging modules you want to include. If nothing is displayed, all modules are included.

➤ Enable or disable logging to standard error, which logs by default to the Tomcat logger screen on the server.

➤ Enable or disable logging to standard out, which logs by default to the Tomcat logger screen on the server.

➤ Log to a file. The default location for the log file is SYS:\TOMCAT\4\ WEBAPPS\NPS\WEB-INF\DEBUG.XML. You can also select to view all log messages or clear all log messages.

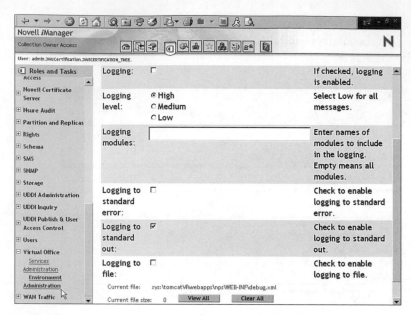

Figure 12.23 iManager: Environment Administration link options, Logging page.

Be acutely aware of the configuration options, paths, and URLs that are part of the iManager interface for Virtual Office.

You can complete certain Virtual Office configuration tasks in iManager. The next section focuses on the tasks that you can accomplish using the Virtual Office interface.

Virtual Office Configuration Using the Virtual Office Interface

Most of the configuration tasks that you can perform in the Virtual Office interface (see Figure 12.16) are accomplished using the Quick Link buttons at the top of the interface. The Quick Links across the top of the Virtual Office home page, from left to right, are the following:

➤ **Home**—Provides access to the Virtual Office home page.

➤ **Virtual Teams**—Provides access to a list of the Virtual Teams. This is also where you can join or decline an invitation to join a Virtual Team.

➤ **Files**—Provides access to files and folders through NetStorage. NetStorage provides users with secure access to files with nothing to install or download as long as the user has an Internet connection. Users can access data with a browser or Microsoft's Web Folders.

➤ **iPrint**—Provides access to the default list of iPrint printers.

➤ **eGuide**—Opens a search box where you can use eGuide to search configured contacts. This is a corporate contact list.

➤ **E-mail**—Opens a window where you can authenticate to the configured e-mail program. In NetWare 6.5, this is NetMail by default.

➤ **Password** —Opens a window where you can change your password.

➤ **View and Manage My Bookmarks** —You can manage your list of favorite Web sites and publish them to your Virtual Office home page.

➤ **View and Edit My Web Page**—Opens a window where you can edit the sections that appear on your opening Virtual Office page, including User Information, Team Members, Published Favorites, and Files.

In addition to these configuration tasks, you can manage your Virtual Team from the Virtual Teams page. From the Virtual Office opening page, you can click on your team in the left navigation bar to display a screen similar to Figure 12.24.

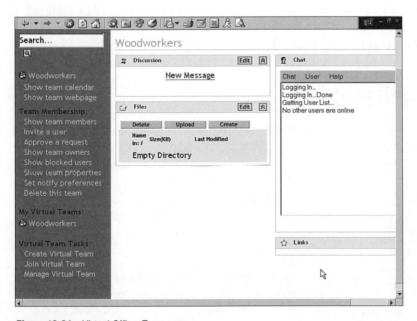

Figure 12.24 Virtual Office: Team page.

On your Virtual Team page, you can do the following:

➤ Show Team Calendar

➤ Show Team Web Page

➤ Show Team Members

➤ Invite a User

➤ Approve a Request

➤ Show Team Owners

➤ Show Blocked Users

➤ Show Team Properties

➤ Set Notify Preferences (includes preferences for new discussion posts, created events, and uploaded files)

➤ Delete This Team

➤ Display your Virtual Teams and a Virtual Team Inbox, managing your Teams' membership

From the Team home page, you can exchange messages with other members of the team in the Discussion box, chat with users in the Chat panel, share files with team members in the Files panel, and display Web page links that are of interest to team members in the Links panel.

Conclusion

This concludes your journey toward the NetWare 6.5 CNA exam, "Foundations of Novell Networking: NetWare 6.5." Take a breath! Go over the practice questions at the end of this book, and be sure you review the Cram Sheet. If you have followed this book's guided tour and are diligent in your study, you will be well on your way to enjoying the benefits of becoming a Novell NetWare 6.5 CNA. When you have completed your study, if you find that you would like some hands-on practice, go to www.3WsCertification.com/65CNA.html.

Thank you for allowing me to be your virtual teacher. Let me know how you do. Feel free to contact me with questions or comments at wyrostekw@msn.com. I wish you all the best.

—Warren E. Wyrostek, M.Ed., MCNI

Exam Prep Questions

1. You need to manage several iFolder user accounts on your NetWare 6.5 server. What is the correct URL for the iFolder Management Console if the IP address of your NetWare 6.5 server is **10.0.0.125**?

    A. ○ **http://10.0.0.125/Admin/iFolderServer**

    B. ○ **http://10.0.0.125/iFolder/Admin**

    C. ○ **https://10.0.0.125/iFolderServer/Admin**

    D. ○ **https://10.0.0.125/iFolderAdmin/Server**

    Answer C is correct. The iFolder Management Console is the tool of choice to manage iFolder user accounts. If the IP address of the iFolder Server is 10.0.0.125, the default URL for the Management Console is https://10.0.0.125/iFolderServer/Admin. Answers A, B, and D are incorrect.

2. You did not install iFolder or Virtual Office when you installed the NetWare 6.5 operating system on the **FS1** server. Your CIO has asked you to install both products on **FS1**. You insert the NetWare 6.5 Products CD in the server DVD drive. Which of the following commands do you enter at the server console prompt to launch the server GUI interface so that you can continue with the installation?

    A. ○ **Novell**

    B. ○ **Install**

    C. ○ **NWCONFIG**

    D. ○ **STARTX**

    Answer D is correct. The command to launch the NetWare 6.5 server GUI interface is STARTX. At the server GUI interface, you can select Novell, Install and install both products. Answers A, B, and C are incorrect. There is no Novell server console command. Install.NLM was the interface for installing NetWare products prior to NetWare 5. NWCONFIG.NLM is still used in NetWare 6.5 to install some products. The curious thing about NWCONFIG is that if you try to install some products, NWCONFIG redirects you to the server GUI interface. NWCONFIG is not as powerful or admin friendly as it was in previous versions of NetWare.

3. During the installation of NetWare 6.5 on server **FS1**, you want to install iFolder as one of the additional products. You do not want to perform a Custom Installation. Rather, you want to select one of the available Preconfigured server patterns. Which of the following Preconfigured server patterns include iFolder as part of the installation? (Select all that apply.)

    A. ❏ exteNd J2EE Web Application Server

    B. ❏ LDAP Server

    C. ❏ Virtual Office Server

    D. ❏ NetWare AMP Server

Answers A and C are correct. iFolder is installed automatically if you select the Virtual Office Server or the exteNd J2EE Web Application Server Preconfigured server option. iFolder is also installed if you select the Novell iFolder Storage Services Server option. You have the option of selecting iFolder if you do a Custom install. Answers B and D are incorrect. iFolder is not part of a NetWare AMP Server installation or an LDAP Server installation.

4. Which of the following servers complies with the server requirements for an iFolder Server?

A. ○ NetWare 5.0 SP3 with 1024MB RAM and eDirectory 8.7.3

B. ○ NetWare 6.0 with 256MB RAM and Apache Web Server 1.3.26

C. ○ NetWare 6.0 SP1 with eDirectory 8.6.1

D. ○ NetWare 6.5 with 512MB RAM and 15MB on the **SYS** volume

Answer D is correct. The only option that meets iFolder Server requirements is the NetWare 6.5 server with 512MB RAM and 15MB of space on volume SYS. Answer A is incorrect. A NetWare 5 server must be NetWare 5.1 with at least SP5. Answer B is incorrect. A NetWare 6.0 server must have at least SP2 installed and have 512MB RAM. Answer C is incorrect. This server must have SP2 installed and have eDirectory 8.6.2 or later.

5. You want to configure your iFolder Client policies so that they are hidden from the iFolder users. Circle the option in Figure 12.25 that you should initially select to accomplish this.

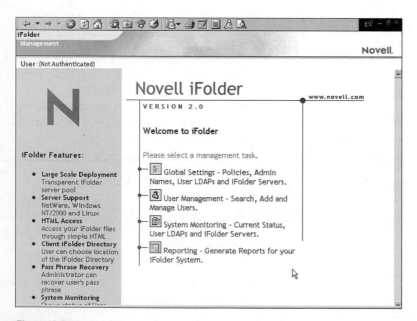

Figure 12.25

You should have circled Global Settings. One of the options under Global Settings is Global Policies, where you can set Client and Server policies. One of the Client policies is to hide a user policy setting from an iFolder user.

6. You want to install the iFolder Client on your Windows XP Professional workstation. What URL should you enter into your Internet Explorer browser to accomplish this, if the iFolder Server's IP address is **10.0.0.125**?

   A. ○ **https://10.0.0.125/iFolderServer/Admin**

   B. ○ **http://10.0.0.125/iFolder**

   C. ○ **http://10.0.0.125/iFolderClient**

   D. ○ **https://10.0.0.125/iFolderClient/Admin**

   Answer B is correct. The correct URL to access the iFolder Client on an iFolder Server with an IP address of 10.0.0.125 is http://10.0.0.125/iFolder. Answers A, C, and D are incorrect. Answer A directs the user to the iFolder Management Console. Answers C and D are not valid iFolder URLs.

7. You are installing Virtual Office on your NetWare 6.5 server. Which additional products should you install so that you can access them from Virtual Office? (Select all that apply.)

   A. ❑ Remote Manager

   B. ❑ NetStorage

   C. ❑ eGuide

   D. ❑ iPrint

   Answers B, C, and D are correct. You can access your files with NetStorage, your corporate contact list with eGuide, and print to corporate printers with iPrint. Answer A is incorrect. You cannot access Remote Manager from Virtual Office.

8. In Figure 12.26, circle which Virtual Office: Services Administration tab in iManager you should access if you want to post breaking news on the Virtual Office home page.

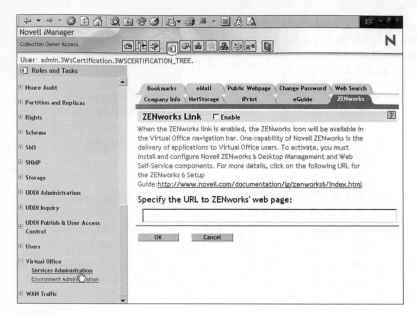

Figure 12.26

You should have circled the Company Info tab. After you have enabled Company Info shown in Figure 12.19, you can enter breaking news in the News field.

9. A location in Virtual Office where users can collaborate in real time, share a calendar, and exchange files is called a

_____.

The correct response is a Virtual Team. The creator of a Virtual Team is the team owner and a member of the team.

10. You want to maintain Virtual Office logs by storing them in a file. What is the default location for Virtual Office log files?
   A. ○ **SYS:\VIRTUALOFFICE\DEBUG.XML**
   B. ○ **SYS:\APACHE2\LOGS\DEBUG.XML**
   C. ○ **SYS:\SYSTEM\DEBUG.XML**
   D. ○ **SYS:\TOMCAT\4\WEBAPPS\NPS\WEB-INF\DEBUG.XML**

Answer D is correct. The default location for Virtual Office logs sent to file is SYS:\TOMCAT\4\WEBAPPS\NPS\WEB-INF\DEBUG.XML. Answer A is incorrect. This is not a system-created path in NetWare 6.5. Answer B is incorrect. The Apache error and access logs are saved in SYS:\APACHE2\LOGS. Answer C is incorrect. The server error log, SYS$ERR.LOG, is stored in SYS:\SYSTEM.

Practice Exam 1

Other than years of hands-on experience, the best way to prepare for the Foundations of Novell Networking CNA certification test is by taking practice (or sample) exams. It is critical that you learn to approach Novell's certification tests thinking like Novell wants you to. If you have taken hundreds of certification tests from other vendors, you will have a tendency to answer the way other vendors deem correct. That might or might not be correct on a Novell exam. Therefore, take these practice tests and start thinking like a Novell NetWare 6.5 CNA. I have included two sample tests in this book, in addition to the practice questions provided at the end of each chapter. You can find the answers to these questions in Chapter 14, "Answers to Practice Exam 1."

The current format of the actual Foundations of Novell Networking exam is form based, as presented in the practice questions and sample tests in this book. Novell might change the actual test to an adaptive format without notice. Continue to monitor Novell's Test Data Web site for up-to-date information. You can find that at `http://www.novell.com/training/testinfo/testdata.html`.

1. Many of the documents you work on while at the office, you also have to work on while you are home. Before NetWare 6.5, you had to save these documents to a floppy disk and then copy them to your laptop at home. Which NetWare 6.5 feature allows you to access your documents from home, the office, or while on the road, without copying the files back and forth to a floppy disk?

   A. ○ Novell Cluster Services

   B. ○ Novell iFolder

   C. ○ NetWare Web Access

   D. ○ NetWare Remote Manager

2. You are considering NetWare 6.5 because it comes with Novell Cluster Services (NCS). What is the maximum number of servers that you can configure with NCS?

   A. ○ 2

   B. ○ 16

   C. ○ 32

   D. ○ 64

3. Your NetWare 6.5 server is having trouble communicating on the network. You suspect that it is a driver issue. Which NetWare 6.5 driver should you investigate if the driver is the one that controls the network interface card?

   A. ○ CDM

   B. ○ DSK

   C. ○ HAM

   D. ○ LAN

4. Which statements are true concerning the role of DOS in NetWare 6.5? (Choose two.)

   A. ❑ NetWare 6.5 does not require a DOS partition.

   B. ❑ NetWare 6.5 requires a DOS partition after the Network operating system is up and running.

   C. ❑ NetWare 6.5 requires a DOS partition to boot the server but does not require DOS to be available after the server is up and running.

   D. ❑ NetWare 6.5 requires a DOS partition to boot the server, and requires a DOS partition after the server is up and running.

   E. ❑ NetWare 6.5 stores the folders and files that boot the network operating system on the DOS partition.

   F. ❑ NetWare 6.5 stores the folder and files that boot the network operating system on the SYS volume, and stores the files that launch Deployment Manager on the DOS partition.

5. Which other operating systems can function as a server in a NetWare 6.5 environment? (Choose two.)

A. ❑ Linux

B. ❑ Windows 2000 Professional

C. ❑ Windows NT Workstation

D. ❑ DOS

E. ❑ Windows Me

F. ❑ Windows 2000 Advanced Server

6. A senior Novell engineer has told you that you have a problem with the executable that launches the NetWare 6.5 operating system. What is the correct name and path of this executable?

A. ○ **SYS: SETUP.EXE**

B. ○ **C:\LAUNCH.EXE**

C. ○ **C:\SERVER.EXE**

D. ○ **C:\NWSERVER\SERVER.EXE**

7. You are installing a new NetWare 6.5 server. The server has 1024MB of physical memory installed. What is the minimum size required for your DOS partition?

A. ○ A DOS partition is not required.

B. ○ 200MB.

C. ○ 500MB.

D. ○ 1024MB.

E. ○ 1224MB.

8. You are installing a new NetWare 6.5 server. Which of the following is one of the configuration requirements for a NetWare 6.5 server?

A. ○ 500MB DOS partition

B. ○ NetWare 6.5 license/cryptography disk

C. ○ Supervisor object rights to the Tree root

D. ○ Supervisor object rights to the Security container for the eDirectory tree

9. Your network currently consists of 30 NetWare 5.1 servers and 10 NetWare 4.2 servers. You want to add one NetWare 6.5 server to your tree. Which tool do you need to use before adding the server to your current environment?

A. ○ Deployment Manager

B. ○ Remote Manager

C. ○ iManager

D. ○ iMonitor

10. You need to update your network before installing a NetWare 6.5 server into your tree. What is the correct name and path to the executable that will enable you to accomplish this?

    A. ○ **SYS:\SYSTEM\DEPLOY.EXE**

    B. ○ **C:\NWSERVER\NWDEPLOY.EXE**

    C. ○ **C:\DEPLOY.EXE**

    D. ○ **NWDEPLOY.EXE** at the root of the NetWare 6.5 operating system CD

11. Which NetWare 6.5 Productivity-Enhancing service is a Web-based address book, enabling users to find the names, addresses, and phone numbers that are stored in eDirectory?

    A. ○ File Versioning

    B. ○ iFolder

    C. ○ eGuide

    D. ○ eDirectory

    E. ○ iPrint

    F. ○ NSS

12. You need to know which Support Pack has been installed on your NetWare 6.5 server. Which server console command displays this information?

    A. ○ **MODULES**

    B. ○ **INETCFG**

    C. ○ **CONFIG**

    D. ○ **VERSION**

13. Which NetWare 6.5 configuration file do you need to edit if you want to change the SERVERID number?

    A. ○ **CONFIG.SYS**

    B. ○ **AUTOEXEC.BAT**

    C. ○ **STARTUP.NCF**

    D. ○ **AUTOEXEC.NCF**

14. You want to create a role that will only allow an assigned user the capability to change users' passwords. Which NetWare 6.5 utility allows you to accomplish this?

    A. ○ iMonitor

    B. ○ Web Manager

    C. ○ Remote Manager

    D. ○ iManager

15. You need to access the NetWare 6.5 Web Manager. Your server's IP address is 10.0.0.125. Which URL should you use to access this utility?

    A. ○ **http://10.0.0.125**

    B. ○ **http://10.0.0.125:8008**

    C. ○ **http://10.0.0.125:631/IPP**

    D. ○ **https://10.0.0.125:2200**

16. You are installing the Novell Client 4.90 on your Windows XP Professional workstation. When you insert the Client CD in your workstation, it does not launch automatically. Which executable can you run to launch the client installation routine?

    A. ○ **INSTALL.EXE**
    B. ○ **WINSETUP.EXE**
    C. ○ **CLIENT.EXE**
    D. ○ **SETUP.EXE**

17. During the installation of the Novell Client 4.90 on a Windows XP Professional workstation, you decided on a Typical installation. Which features are installed by default? (Choose all that apply.)

    A. ❑ Remote Management
    B. ❑ Novell Distributed Print Services
    C. ❑ Novell Workstation Manager
    D. ❑ ZENworks Application Launcher

18. Which eDirectory objects are classified as Container objects? (Choose two.)

    A. ❑ Server
    B. ❑ Directory Map
    C. ❑ Organizational Role
    D. ❑ Organizational Unit
    E. ❑ LDAP Server
    F. ❑ Role Based Service

19. Which of the following is an example of a typeless Relative Distinguished Name?

    A. ○ **admin.NW65**
    B. ○ **.CN=admin.O=NW65**
    C. ○ **CN=admin.O=NW65**
    D. ○ **.admin.NW65**

20. **CN=EMMA.OU=TRAINING.** is an example of which of the following?

    A. ○ A typeful Distinguished Name
    B. ○ A typeless Distinguished Name
    C. ○ A typeful Relative Distinguished Name
    D. ○ A typeless Relative Distinguished Name

21. What is Current Context?

    A. ○ The full path to an object in eDirectory
    B. ○ The location in the tree where your workstation is currently positioned, or pointing
    C. ○ An object's full name and path, distinguished by a leading period
    D. ○ An object's common name relative to a workstation's name context

22. The NetWare 6.5 Productivity-Enhancing service that lets users create a group for real-time collaboration purposes is called _____.

23. You want to assign eDirectory rights to multiple users to make your administrative life simple. Which objects allow you to accomplish this? (Choose all that apply.)

    A. ❑ Organizational Role
    B. ❑ Server
    C. ❑ Tree
    D. ❑ [Public]
    E. ❑ Country
    F. ❑ Computer
    G. ❑ Group

24. In iManager, which Virtual Office task should you select if you want to configure the location for Virtual Office log files?

    A. ○ **Services Administration**
    B. ○ **Environment Administration**
    C. ○ **Global Settings**
    D. ○ **System Monitoring**

25. You have decided to install the IPX protocol during your NetWare 6.5 server installation. To which frame type is IPX bound by default?

    A. ○ Ethernet_SNAP
    B. ○ Ethernet_802.2
    C. ○ Ethernet_II
    D. ○ Ethernet_802.3

26. What eDirectory trustee includes all non-authenticated users?

    A. ○ Tree
    B. ○ Country
    C. ○ [Public] trustee
    D. ○ Organization

27. You are planning to create a new eDirectory tree for your company. What are the characteristics of the eDirectory Tree object? (Choose three.)

    A. ❑ An eDirectory tree can have a maximum of 32 Tree objects.
    B. ❑ An eDirectory Tree object can hold Country, Organization, and User objects.
    C. ❑ An eDirectory Tree object can be created during server installation and post-server installation by using Deployment Manager.
    D. ❑ An eDirectory Tree object cannot be moved.
    E. ❑ An eDirectory Tree object cannot be deleted.
    F. ❑ An eDirectory Tree object sits atop the eDirectory tree.

28. You are configuring file system rights on a NetWare 6.5 server. Using the following list of eDirectory objects, you should grant rights through trustee assignments in a specific order.

    1. Tree object

    2. Security Equivalent

    3. User Object

    4. [Public] trustee

    5. Groups and Organizational Roles

What is the correct order for assigning trustee assignments?

    A. ○ 1, 4, 3, 5, 2

    B. ○ 4, 1, 5, 3, 2

    C. ○ 4, 1, 5, 2, 3

    D. ○ 3, 2, 5, 1, 4

29. An eDirectory Country object can be a child to which eDirectory object?

    A. ○ Organization

    B. ○ Organizational Unit

    C. ○ Domain

    D. ○ Tree object

30. During the installation of your new NetWare 6.5 server, an Admin object is created. Which of the following is one of the characteristics of this object?

    A. ○ It cannot be deleted.

    B. ○ It cannot be renamed.

    C. ○ It can have its Supervisor object rights to other objects overwritten.

    D. ○ An eDirectory tree can only have one Admin object.

    E. ○ It is one of three user objects created during the initial installation. The others are Guest and Supervisor.

31. Your NetWare 6.5 server is named **SERVER6**. You have a **DATA** volume on **SERVER 6**. The **DATA** volume has a root directory that you have called **SHARED**. The **SHARED** directory has a subdirectory that you have called **GENERAL**. You want to map the G: drive to the **GENERAL** directory using a volume object name. Which command accomplishes this?

    A. ○ **MAP G:=SERVER6\DATA:GENERAL\SHARED**

    B. ○ **MAP G:=SERVER6:\DATA\SHARED\GENERAL**

    C. ○ **MAP G:=GENERAL**

    D. ○ **MAP G:=SERVER6_DATA:\SHARED\GENERAL**

32. Your eDirectory tree has a branch with the following hierarchy:

    O=NW65, OU=LOC1, OU=IS, CN=LASERPRN1

    Each level of this branch has the default IRF assignment. You have assigned Warren the Supervisor object right to the NW65 Organization. You have also assigned Warren the Browse object right to the LASERPRN1. You have assigned the [Public] trustee the Read and Compare property rights to the LASERPRN1. All other assignments have been revoked. What are Warren's effective rights at the IS Organizational unit?

    A. ○ Supervisor object and Supervisor property rights

    B. ○ Only the Supervisor property right

    C. ○ Browse object right only

    D. ○ Read and Compare property rights only

    E. ○ Browse object and Read and Compare property rights

33. Your eDirectory tree has a branch with the following hierarchy:

    O=NW65, OU=LOC1, OU=IS, CN=LASERPRN1

    Each level of this branch has the default IRF assignment. You have assigned Alexandra the Supervisor object right to the NW65 Organization object. What are Alexandra's effective object rights at the LASERPRN1?

    A. ○ Supervisor Entry and Supervisor Attribute rights

    B. ○ [SBCDRI]

    C. ○ [SBDR]

    D. ○ [SBDRI]

34. Which statements are true about NetWare 6.5 Search drive mappings? (Choose all that apply.)

    A. ❑ NetWare 6.5 can have a maximum of 26 Search drive mappings.

    B. ❑ NetWare 6.5 can have a maximum of 16 Search drive mappings.

    C. ❑ NetWare 6.5 Search drive mappings are primarily used to point to data.

    D. ❑ NetWare 6.5 Search drive mappings are primarily used to point to programs and executables.

    E. ❑ The NetWare 6.5 Search drive mapping, **MAP S1:=SERVER6\APPS:\SS**, appends the **SERVER6\APPS:\SS** pointer at the end of the **PATH** statement.

    F. ❑ The NetWare 6.5 Search drive mapping, **MAP S1:=SERVER6\APPS:\SS**, places the **SERVER6\APPS:\SS** pointer at the beginning of the **PATH** statement and overwrites the pointer that exists in the first position.

35. Which NetWare 6.5 file system right should you grant a user if he needs to rename a file?

    A. ○ File scan
    B. ○ Supervisor
    C. ○ Create
    D. ○ Modify
    E. ○ Access control

36. You want Emma to be able to salvage files that are deleted from the **SHARED\DEPARTMENTAL\IS** directory on your NetWare 6.5 server. Which rights should you assign to Emma that will allow her to salvage files? (Choose all that apply.)

    A. ❑ Write on the directory
    B. ❑ Create on the directory
    C. ❑ Supervisor on the file
    D. ❑ Erase on the directory
    E. ❑ Read on the file
    F. ❑ File scan on the file

37. Which NetWare 6.5 file system rights should you assign to a user who needs to copy files to a directory? (Choose two.)

    A. ❑ File scan
    B. ❑ Read
    C. ❑ Create
    D. ❑ Modify

38. You want to load the NDPS Manager on your NetWare 6.5 server. The server's name is FS6. The NDPS Manager's name is NDPSMgr. FS6 and NDPSMgr are in the same context. Which command should you enter at the server console to load NDPSMgr?

    A. ○ **LOAD NDPSM NDPSMgr**
    B. ○ **LOAD FS6\NDPSMgr**
    C. ○ **LOAD NDPSMgr**
    D. ○ **LOAD NDPSMgr NDPSM**

39. In your NetWare 6.5 network environment, you want to deploy a combined software/hardware technology that can be used to protect your internal network from outside attacks. Which technology accomplishes this?

    A. ○ DHCP
    B. ○ DNS
    C. ○ Firewall
    D. ○ Router

40. Your eDirectory tree has a branch with the following hierarchy:

    O=NW65, OU=LOC1, OU=IS, CN=FS6

    Each level of this branch has the default IRF assignment. You have assigned Marion the Supervisor object right to the NW65 Organization. Which statements correctly describe Marion's effective rights in this branch of the tree? (Choose all that apply.)

    A. ❏ Marion has the Supervisor property right at NW65.

    B. ❏ Marion has no eDirectory rights at FS6.

    C. ❏ Marion only has the Browse object right at FS6.

    D. ❏ Marion has the Supervisor object right at FS6.

    E. ❏ Marion has the Supervisor file system right for the file system stored on FS6.

    F. ❏ Marion has only the Read and File Scan file system rights for the file system stored on FS6.

41. In NetWare 6.5, what are two ways to block inherited rights in eDirectory? (Choose two.)

    A. ❏ With an IRF

    B. ❏ With a new file system assignment

    C. ❏ By deleting the Admin object

    D. ❏ With a new eDirectory assignment

42. In Figure 13.1, circle the Remote Manager option you should select if you want to reboot your NetWare 6.5 server.

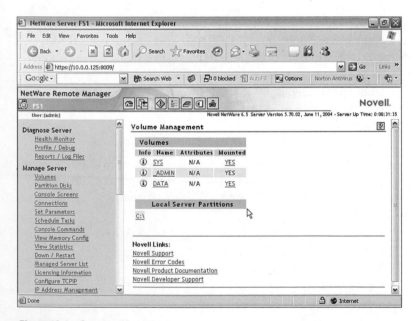

Figure 13.1 Question 42.

43. In a NetWare 6.5 Container login script, which three ways could you document your reasons for including a given line or section in a script? (Choose three.)

    A. ❑ @

    B. ❑ ;

    C. ❑ *

    D. ❑ #

    E. ❑ REM

44. In Figure 13.2, circle the iManager role you should select if you want to create a Template object?

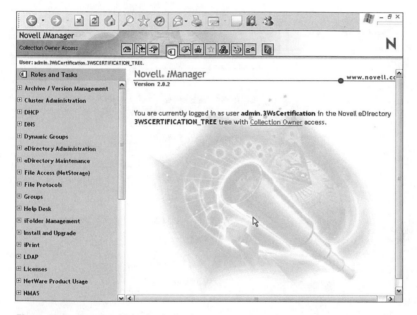

Figure 13.2   Question 44.

45. On your NetWare 6.5 server, you want to create several NSS volumes. Which tools can you use to accomplish this? (Choose three.)

    A. ❑ Remote Manager

    B. ❑ NetAdmin

    C. ❑ NetWare Administrator

    D. ❑ NSSMU

    E. ❑ iManager

46. Which of the following are NetWare system-created directories that are created on the **SYS:** volume? (Choose all that apply.)

    A. ☐ **USERS**

    B. ☐ **LOGIN**

    C. ☐ **SYSTEM**

    D. ☐ **NI**

    E. ☐ **APACHE**

    F. ☐ **SHARED**

47. In Figure 13.3, circle the option you should select if you want to display the ACL for the **DATA** volume.

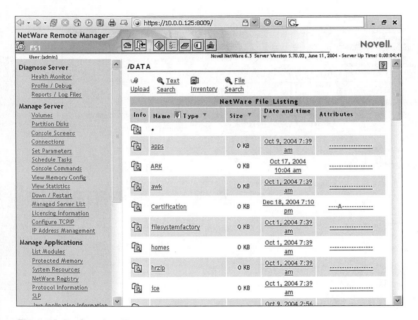

Figure 13.3 Question 47.

48. In Figure 13.4, circle the option you should select if you want to configure your client properties so that the Save PassPhrase option is hidden.

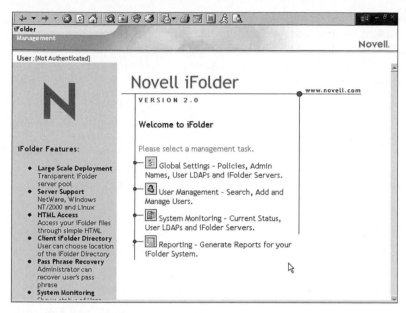

Figure 13.4   Question 48.

49. Several users on your NetWare 6.5 network need to have their print jobs moved up in the queue. You have deployed NDPS. In Figure 13.5, circle the task that you should select to reorder NDPS print jobs.

Figure 13.5   Question 49.

50. What is the default NetWare 6.5 file system rights assignment that a user is given to his home directory if it is assigned when the user object is created?

    A. ○ [SRWCEMFA]

    B. ○ [RWCEMFA]

    C. ○ [RF]

    D. ○ [RWCEF]

51. Having used earlier versions of NetWare, you are comfortable with the traditional file system. You have recently moved up to NetWare 6.5. You now are using NSS. You have a significant amount of free space on one of your storage adapters, and you want to create a storage pool. When do you create a pool?

    A. ○ Before you create a volume and after you create a partition

    B. ○ Before you create a partition or volume

    C. ○ Before you create a partition and after you create a volume

    D. ○ After you create a partition or volume

52. You want to set up iPrint in a NetWare 6.5 environment. Which NDPS entities are required in this environment? (Choose three.)

    A. ❑ Printer Agent

    B. ❑ Print Broker

    C. ❑ Print Manager

    D. ❑ Print server

    E. ❑ Print queue

    F. ❑ Gateway

53. You want to modify several file attributes on your NetWare 6.5 server. What utilities can you use to accomplish this? (Choose three.)

    A. ❑ NSSMU

    B. ❑ ConsoleOne

    C. ❑ iManager

    D. ❑ Remote Manager

    E. ❑ FLAG

    F. ❑ NDIR

54. Which NetWare 6.5 utility should you use to configure iPrint?

    A. ○ Remote Manager

    B. ○ iManager

    C. ○ ConsoleOne

    D. ○ NSSMU

55. Which NDPS Broker service allows printers to send users messages about printer events?

    A. ○ ENS

    B. ○ RMS

    C. ○ SRS

    D. ○ MTA

56. Which type of NDPS printer has an object in the eDirectory tree?

    A. ○ Public Access

    B. ○ Controlled Access

    C. ○ Gateway

    D. ○ Non-NDPS

57. If your NetWare 6.5 network has 9,500 client workstations, what protocol allows you to dynamically assign an IP address to each user's computer in the most efficient way?

    A. ○ SMTP
    B. ○ SNMP
    C. ○ FTP
    D. ○ DHCP

58. You want to access the iFolder Management Console on your NetWare 6.5 server. The server has an IP address of 10.0.0.125. What URL should you enter into your browser's location bar to access this utility?

    A. ○ http://10.0.0.125/IFOLDERAdmin/Server
    B. ○ https://10.0.0.125/Admin/iFolderServer
    C. ○ http://10.0.0.125/iFolder/ServerAdmin
    D. ○ https://10.0.0.125/iFolderServer/Admin

59. You are tasked with installing NetWare 6.5 on three identical servers. You install the operating system on the first server. You now want to utilize the Response files that are automatically generated during an installation for the other two server installations. In which NetWare 6.5 directory would you find the Response files?

    A. ○ ETC
    B. ○ PUBLIC
    C. ○ SYSTEM
    D. ○ NI

60. As the CNA for your NetWare 6.5 environment, you want to construct a login script specifically for the 10 members of the SALES group. Which type of login script should you construct?

    A. ○ Container
    B. ○ Profile
    C. ○ User
    D. ○ System

Answer Key for Practice Exam 1

1. B

2. C

3. D

4. C, E

5. A, F

6. D

7. C

8. C

9. A

10. D

11. C

12. D

13. D

14. D

15. D

16. B

17. B, C, D

18. D, F

19. A

20. C

21. B

22. Virtual Teams

23. A, C, D, E, G

24. B

25. B

26. C

27. D, E, F

28. B

29. D

30. C

31. D

32. A

33. C

34. B, D, F

35. D

36. B, E, F

37. A, C

38. A

39. C

40. A, D, E

41. A, D

42. Down/Restart

43. B, C, E

44. eDirectory Administration

45. A, D, E

46. B, C, D, E

47. The top Info button

48. Global Settings

49. Manage Printer

50. B

51. A

52. A, B, C

53. B, D, E

54. B	**57.** D	**60.** B
55. A	**58.** D	
56. B	**59.** D	

Question 1

Answer B is correct. iFolder lets users have access to their files from home, the office, or while on the road. Without copying files back and forth to a floppy disk, users can access the latest version of their data when and where they need it with an Internet connection and a browser that is Java enabled. Answer A is incorrect. Novell Cluster Services (NCS) provides high availability of critical network resources and services. A 2-node cluster ships with NetWare 6.5. Answer C is incorrect. NetWare Web Access is a NetWare 6 product that provides users with a personalized interface, controlled by gadgets, to resources on the network from a browser. Answer D is incorrect. NetWare Remote Manager is a Web-based utility that administrators can use to monitor and manage a NetWare server. It was formerly called Management Portal.

Question 2

Answer C is correct. Novell Cluster Services (NCS) version 1.6 provides high availability of critical network resources and services. A 2-node cluster ships with NetWare 6.5. NCS supports a maximum of 32 servers in a cluster.

Question 3

Answer D is correct. In NetWare 6.5, a LAN extension represents the network board driver. The network operating system uses the LAN driver to communicate with the network card. Answers A, B, and C are incorrect. Storage adapters, such as Adaptec SCSI controllers, are identified by a `.ham` extension. The extension used for storage adapters or devices before NetWare 5 is `.dsk`. It is not supported in NetWare 6.5. The `.nam` extension represents a defined namespace, such as the namespace for Macs, which is `MAC.NAM`.

Question 4

Answers C and E are correct. NetWare 6.5 requires a DOS partition that has at least 500MB of available space. The DOS partition is needed to boot the server and hold the system folder and files that load NetWare. The folder and files that boot NetWare are c:\NWSERVER and SERVER.EXE. In addition, c:\NWSERVER holds the drivers for the storage adapters, namespace modules, and STARTUP.NCF file. Answers A, B, D, and F are incorrect. After NetWare is up and running, a DOS partition is not needed. You can remove DOS from system memory by using the SECURE CONSOLE command.

Question 5

Answers A and F are correct. In a NetWare 6.5 environment, a variety of other operating systems can function as a server. Four that are widely used are Linux, Windows NT Server, Windows 2000 Server, and Windows 2003 Server. Answers B, C, D, and E are incorrect. Windows 2000 Professional, Windows NT Workstation, Windows 9.x, DOS, and Windows Me do not function as a server, in the strictest sense of the client/server server definition, in a NetWare 6.5 environment. They can, however, function as workstations or clients in a NetWare 6.5 environment. Linux, Windows 2000 Server, Windows NT Server, and Windows 2003 Server can also function as clients in a NetWare 6.5 environment.

Question 6

Answer D is correct. The folder and files that boot NetWare are c:\NWSERVER and SERVER.EXE, which is located in c:\NWSERVER. In addition, c:\NWSERVER holds the drivers for the storage adapters, such as the SCSI adapter AHA2940, namespace modules such as MAC.NAM, and the STARTUP.NCF file, which is one of the first files called after SERVER.EXE launches. Answers A, B, and C are incorrect because they do not point to the proper folder and executable.

Question 7

Answer C is correct. NetWare 6.5 requires a DOS partition that is minimally sized at 500MB. The DOS partition is needed to boot the server and hold the folder and files that load NetWare. The recommended size for the DOS partition is 1GB. The optimal size for the DOS partition is 500MB plus space equal to the amount of installed physical memory. A server that has 1024MB of installed physical memory will optimally have a DOS partition that is 1524MB. Answers A, B, D, and E are incorrect. NetWare 6 had a minimum requirement for the DOS partition of 200MB. Because the question asks for the minimum size, the correct answer is 500MB.

Question 8

Answer C is correct. Three types of requirements must be satisfied when you are preparing to install NetWare 6.5. They are System requirements, Software requirements, and Configuration requirements. The Configuration requirements are as follows:

➤ Supervisor right at the Tree root

➤ Supervisor right at the Container where the server is to be installed

➤ Read right to the tree's Security container

➤ Correctly configured network interface card and storage device

➤ An IP address, subnet mask, domain name IP address, and the IP address for the default gateway

Answer A is incorrect because a 500MB DOS partition is classified as a System requirement. Answer B is incorrect because a license/cryptography disk is classified as a Software requirement. Answer D is incorrect because the Configuration requirement for the Security container is the Read right, not the Supervisor object rights.

Question 9

Answer A is correct. Deployment Manager, which you can find at the root of the NetWare 6.5 operating system CD, is used when you want to upgrade a NetWare network to eDirectory 8, before introducing a new NetWare 6.5 server. In versions of NetWare prior to NetWare 6.5, you must extend the schema before you introduce a NetWare 6.5 server. You do this with Deployment Manager. Answer B is incorrect. NetWare Remote Manager is a Web-based utility that administrators can use to monitor and manage a NetWare server. Answer C is incorrect. iManager is a Web-based utility that lets a NetWare administrator configure and manage printing, licensing, DNS/DHCP, and Role-based administration. Answer D is incorrect. iMonitor is a new utility that you can use to monitor and diagnose servers in your eDirectory tree from any computer that has a compatible browser installed. You can use iMonitor to remotely run a DSREPAIR session on a server.

Question 10

Answer D is correct. Deployment Manager, which you can find at the root of the NetWare 6.5 operating system CD, is used when you want to upgrade a NetWare network to eDirectory 8, before introducing a new NetWare 6.5 server. In versions of NetWare prior to NetWare 6.5, you must extend the schema before you introduce a NetWare 6.5 server. You do this with Deployment Manager. The name of the Deployment Manager executable is NWDEPLOY.EXE. Answers A, B, and C are incorrect because they either point to the wrong location or do not contain the correct name for the executable.

Question 11

Answer C is correct. All answer choices are classified by Novell as Productivity-Enhancing services in NetWare 6.5. eGuide is a Web-based address book, which enables users to find names, addresses, and phone numbers that are stored in eDirectory. File Versioning, iFolder, eDirectory, iPrint, and NSS do not provide the service in question to NetWare 6.5 users.

Question 12

Answer D is correct. You can obtain a wealth of information at a NetWare 6.5 server console by using the proper console command. You use VERSION when you want to display the version of NetWare 6.5 that is installed, the installed Support Pack version, and eDirectory, server, and user license versions. Answer A is incorrect. MODULES displays the NLMs loaded on a NetWare 6.5 server. Answer B is incorrect. INETCFG configures IP, IPX, and AppleTalk on a NetWare 6.5 server. Answer C is incorrect. CONFIG displays a server's configuration, including the server's IP address.

Question 13

Answer D is correct. The AUTOEXEC.NCF NetWare configuration file typically contains most server environmental settings, including the server name, SERVERID, time zone settings, LAN card LOAD and BIND statements, and SEARCH ADD settings. You can find it in the SYS:\SYSTEM directory. Answers A and B are incorrect. The CONFIG.SYS and AUTOEXEC.BAT files are DOS configuration files, which you can find on the DOS partition. Answer C is incorrect. The STARTUP.NCF file is one of the first files called after SERVER.EXE launches. You can find it in the C:\NWSERVER directory and use it to load the necessary storage adapters, custom device modules, and namespace modules.

Question 14

Answer D is correct. iManager is a Web-based utility that lets a NetWare administrator configure and manage printing, licensing, DNS/DHCP, and Role-based administration, such as creating a role that will allow an assigned user the ability to change other user's passwords. Answer A is incorrect. iMonitor is a new utility that you can use to monitor and diagnose servers in your eDirectory tree from any computer that has a compatible browser installed. You can use iMonitor to remotely run a DSREPAIR session on a server. Answer B is incorrect. In NetWare 6.5, Web Manager is a portal to numerous Web services, including iManager, Remote Manager, and the configuration interfaces for the OpenSSH Manager. Answer C is incorrect. NetWare Remote Manager is a Web-based utility that administrators can use to monitor and manage a NetWare server.

Question 15

Answer D is correct. The correct URL for accessing Novell's Web Manager running on a NetWare 6.5 server that has an IP address of 10.0.0.125 is https://10.0.0.125:2200. Answer A is incorrect and will access the Apache Web server. Answer B is incorrect and will access the Novell Remote Manager. Answer C is incorrect and will access the default printer list that iPrint generates.

Question 16

Answer B is correct. Normally, the Novell Client installation setup routine autoruns when you insert the Client installation CD in your CD drive. However, if it does not, a user can execute the WINSETUP.EXE program from within Windows. Answers A, C, and D are incorrect because they do not correctly identify the executable that launches the Client installation routine.

Question 17

Answers B, C, and D are correct. The Novell Client installation, for Client 4.90 on a Windows XP Professional workstation, has two possible options: Typical and Custom. By default, a Typical Install installs the Novell Client for Windows, Novell Distributed Print Services, Novell Workstation Manager, and ZENworks Application Launcher. Answer A is incorrect. Remote Management is an option that is available when you elect Custom Install.

Question 18

Answers D and F are correct. In eDirectory, a Container object is an object that holds other eDirectory objects. Examples of Container objects are the Country object, the Organization object, the Organizational Unit object, the Domain object, the Security container, the License container, and Role Based Service (RBS). Answers A, B, C, and E are incorrect because they are all examples of eDirectory Leaf objects.

Question 19

Answer A is correct. In eDirectory, a Relative Distinguished Name is an object's common name relative to a workstation's current context. A Relative Distinguished Name will never have a leading period, but it might have a trailing period. Distinguished Names are similar to Relative Distinguished Names in that both use periods to separate contextual elements and both might or might not use object attribute types (abbreviations). If object attribute types are used, the name is said to be typeful. If object attribute types are not used, the name is said to be typeless. Answer A, admin.NW65, is correct because it is a typeless Relative Distinguished Name. Answer B is incorrect because it is a typeful Distinguished Name. Answer C is incorrect because it is a typeful Relative Distinguished Name. Answer D is incorrect because it is a typeless Distinguished Name.

Question 20

Answer C is correct. In eDirectory, a Relative Distinguished Name is an object's common name relative to a workstation's current context. A Relative Distinguished Name will never have a leading period, but it might have a trailing period. Distinguished Names are similar to Relative Distinguished Names in that both use periods to separate contextual elements, and both might or might not use object attribute types (abbreviations). If object attribute types are used, the name is said to be typeful. If object attribute types are not used, the name is said to be typeless. Answer C is correct because CN=EMMA.OU=TRAINING. is an example of a typeful Relative Distinguished Name. Answers A, B, and D are incorrect because they incorrectly classify this eDirectory object name.

Question 21

Answer B is correct. Current Context is also known as the name context and reflects your current position at your workstation in the eDirectory tree—in other words, where in the tree your workstation is currently positioned. Answer A is incorrect. Context is the full path to an object in eDirectory. Answer C is incorrect. An object's full name and path, distinguished by a leading period, is the definition for a Distinguished Name. Answer D is incorrect. An object's common name relative to a workstation's name context is the definition for a Relative Distinguished Name.

Question 22

The correct answer is Virtual Teams. Virtual Teams is a NetWare 6.5 Productivity-Enhancing service that lets users create a team for real-time collaboration purposes.

Question 23

Answers A, C, D, E, and G are correct. A number of Container and Leaf objects are used to simultaneously assign eDirectory rights to multiple users. Using objects that group other objects together makes eDirectory administration simpler. Examples of objects that group other objects together are the Tree object, the [Public] trustee, the Country object, the Group object, and the Organizational Role object. Answers B and F are incorrect because they only represent a single object and do not simplify eDirectory rights administration. In addition, they represent computers or servers and not users.

Question 24

Answer B is correct. You can configure Virtual Office logging using the Environment Administration link in iManager. Answer A is incorrect. Using the Services Administration link, you can configure eGuide, NetStorage, Bookmarks and many other options. Answers C and D are incorrect. They are options found in the iFolder Management Console.

Question 25

Answer B is correct. The default frame type for IPX in NetWare 6.5 is Ethernet_802.2. Answers A, C, and D are incorrect. They are not the default frame type used by IPX in NetWare 6.5.

Question 26

Answer C is correct. The [Public] trustee represents all nonauthenticated users to the tree. The main function of the [Public] trustee is that it allows users to browse the tree and the objects it contains before they log in. All objects in the eDirectory tree are security equivalent to the [Public] trustee. Answer A is incorrect because the Tree object, represented on an ACL as [Root], represents all authenticated users to the tree. Answers B and D are incorrect because they are Container objects that contain only a segment of all objects, whether authenticated or unauthenticated, in the eDirectory tree.

Question 27

Answers D, E, and F are correct. In eDirectory, there can only be one Tree object, which exists at the top of the tree. It can contain the Country object, Organization object, Security container, and Alias objects to Country, Organization, and Security. You cannot move, delete, or rename the Tree object from the tree, although you can change the tree name assigned during the initial server installation. The Tree object is created when the initial server is installed in the tree. Objects can be granted rights to the Tree object, and the Tree object can be granted rights to all other objects. Answers A, B, and C are incorrect because they incorrectly describe the characteristics of an eDirectory Tree object.

Question 28

Answer B is correct. In NetWare 6.5, rights assignments should be planned based on groups. Rights should always be assigned first to the largest possible group. Individual assignments should only be made last. As a last resort, when all other options have been exhausted, you can assign rights through security equivalence. The correct order for assigning rights is [Public] trustee, Tree object and other Containers, Groups and Organizational Roles, User object, and finally security equivalence. Novell calls this method of planning file system rights the top-down method. Answers A, C, and D are incorrect because they do not follow the top-down method of assigning file system rights.

Question 29

Answer D is correct. In eDirectory, there can only be one Tree object, which exists at the top of the tree. One of the objects that the Tree object can contain is the Country object. The Country object is not a required Container object, and it can only exist as a child of the Tree object. Answers A, B, and C are Container objects that can exist under the Country object. The Organization object can also exist in the Tree object as a child. The Organization Container object is a required eDirectory object. An Organizational Unit can exist as a child to an Organization Object or to another Organizational Unit object. It is not a required object, but a recommended one. The Domain container object can exist as a child of the Tree object, Organization, Organizational Unit, Country, or Locality objects. The Domain is not a required object. The Country will not exist as a child of a Domain, Organization, or Organizational Unit object.

Question 30

Answer C is correct. When you install the first NetWare 6.5 server in your eDirectory tree, the only user object that is created is the Admin object. Admin is a user object like all user objects. It does not have superuser characteristics, like the ROOT user in Linux or the Supervisor user in earlier versions of NetWare. You can delete, rename, move, or modify the Admin object, and you can delete and block its Supervisor object rights. You can and you should create additional user objects and assign them rights that mirror the Admin object, in case the Admin object is deleted, moved, or has its Supervisor object rights corrupted or modified. Answers A, B, D, and E are incorrect because they go counter to the characteristics of the Admin object.

Question 31

Answer D is correct. The NetWare 6.5 syntax for mapping a drive to a directory using a physical volume name is as follows:

```
Map {option} drive: = Server\Volume: Directory\
subdirectory
```

The NetWare 6.5 syntax for mapping a drive to a directory using a volume object name is as follows:

```
Map {option} drive: = Server_Volume: Directory\
subdirectory
```

The indicator used when mapping a drive using a physical volume name is the backslash (\). The indicator used when mapping a drive using a volume object name is the underscore (_). Because the file system hierarchy is SERVER6, DATA volume, SHARED, GENERAL, the correct syntax to map the G: drive to the GENERAL directory using a volume object name is as follows:

```
MAP G: = SERVER6_DATA: SHARED\GENERAL
```

Answers A, B, and C are incorrect. Answer A uses the syntax for mapping with a physical volume name. Answers B and C do not use the correct syntax for mapping a drive to the GENERAL directory.

Question 32

Answer A is correct. Because of inheritance and because the default IRFs are in place, allowing all object and property rights to be inherited down the branch of the tree, Warren has the Supervisor object right at NW65. When the Supervisor object right is assigned to a user, the user also is automatically assigned the Supervisor property right. Therefore, Warren has both the Supervisor object and property rights to NW65. By inheritance, he also has Supervisor object and property rights at LOC1 and IS. When Warren gets down to LASERPRN1, he receives a new trustee assignment, which overrides his inherited assignment. At LASERPRN1, he receives the Browse object right. However, because Warren is an implied member of the [Public] trustee, as all users are, he also receives, through Group membership, the Read and Compare property rights. Therefore, at the LASERPRN1, he has both the Browse object and the Read and Compare property rights. Answers B, C, D, and E are incorrect because they do not correctly reflect Warren's effective rights as IS.

Question 33

Answer C is correct. Because of inheritance and because the default IRFs are in place, allowing all object and property rights to be inherited down the branch of the tree, Alexandra has the Supervisor object right at NW65. Because the question is only concerned about object rights, you can ignore the property rights. By inheritance, Alexandra also has Supervisor object right at LOC1 and IS. This means that Alexandra has all object rights at NW65, LOC1, and IS, meaning Supervisor, Browse, Create, Delete, Rename, and Inheritable. At LASERPRN1, because no other explicit assignment has been made, Alexandra has the same rights. However, because LASERPRN1 is a Leaf object and not a Container object, the Create and Inheritable rights are not applicable. The Create and Inheritable rights are only applicable to Container objects. Therefore, Alexandra's effective rights at LASERPRN1 are [SBDR]. Answers A, B, and D are incorrect. Answers B and D have the Create and Inheritable rights included. Answer A is incorrect because the question only asks about object rights.

Question 34

Answers B, D, and F are correct. Drive mappings are used in NetWare 6.5 to logically point to a place in the NetWare file system. Two types of drive mappings exist: network or regular, and search. Traditionally, a network or regular drive mapping points to data, whereas a search drive mapping points to programs or executables. Twenty-six regular drive mappings and 16 search drive mappings are supported in NetWare 6.5. A search drive mapping also modifies the current Path that a NetWare 6.5 server uses. The following search drive mapping, MAP S1:=SERVER6\APPS:\SS, overwrites the first element that exists in the current server path. If you do not want to overwrite the first element but would rather insert the pointer in the first position while bumping the remaining elements down one position, use the INS option after the MAP command. If you want to add a search drive pointer to the end of the current path, use the following syntax: MAP S16:. This appends the pointer to the end of the current path. Answer A is incorrect because 16 search drives are supported. Answer C is incorrect because search drive mappings point to programs and executables, not data. Answer E is incorrect because this statement overwrites the first element that is currently in the server path.

Question 35

Answer D is correct. NetWare 6.5 file system security consists of eight rights: Supervisor, Read, Write, Create, Erase, Modify, File scan, and Access control. The Supervisor right grants a user all eight rights. This should only be given with great caution. The File scan right allows a user to see the name of a file or directory in a list. The Create right lets a user create a new file or directory. With the Modify right, a user can change the attributes on a file or directory and rename a file or directory. The Access control right lets a user assign trustee assignments. Answers A, B, C, and E are incorrect.

Question 36

Answers B, E, and F are correct. To salvage files that have been deleted in NetWare 6.5, a user needs the Read and File scan rights on the deleted file, and the Create right on the directory where the deleted file will be restored. Answers A, C, D are incorrect. The Supervisor right will provide the user with adequate rights, but that assignment is not recommended. You don't need the Write and Erase rights to salvage a file.

Question 37

Answers A and C are correct. NetWare 6.5 file system security consists of eight rights: Supervisor, Read, Write, Create, Erase, Modify, File scan, and Access control. To copy a file to a directory, a user needs the Create and File scan rights. Answers B and D are incorrect because they do not provide the necessary rights to copy files to a directory. To copy files from a directory, a user needs Read and File scan rights.

Question 38

Answer A is correct. Following is the command to load the NDPS Manager from a NetWare 6.5 console:

```
LOAD NDPSM <NDPS Manager objectname>
```
The "LOAD" portion of the statement has been implied since NetWare 5. You can enter the same statement at a server console prompt without the "LOAD" command.

In response to this question, the correct answer is this:

```
LOAD NDPSM NDPSMgr
```
Answers B, C, and D are incorrect because they use incorrect syntax for loading the NDPS Manager.

Question 39

Answer C is correct. A firewall is combined software/hardware technology that protects an internal network from outside attacks. Answer A is incorrect. Dynamic Host Configuration Protocol (DHCP) is a protocol used for dynamically assigning IP addresses to hosts on an IP network. Answer B is incorrect. Domain Name Service (DNS) is a centralized database used to translate an IP address into a user-friendly name. Answer D is incorrect. A router is a hardware device that connects a WAN to a LAN or serves as an interface between multiple networks. A router is often called a gateway to a WAN.

Question 40

Answers A, D, and E are correct. Because of inheritance and because the default IRFs are in place, allowing all object and property rights to be inherited down the branch of the tree, Marion has the Supervisor object right at NW65. By inheritance, she also has Supervisor object rights at LOC1 and IS. In addition, Marion has the Supervisor object right to the FS6 server. When a user has the Supervisor object right to a server, she also has the Supervisor file system right to the file system stored on the server. This is the only object where eDirectory rights flow into file system rights. Therefore, Marion has the Supervisor file system right to the file system stored on the FS6 server. Answers B, C, and F are incorrect because they do not correctly reflect Marion's eDirectory and file system rights in this branch of the tree.

Question 41

Answers A and D are correct. You can block inherited rights in two ways. The first way involves assigning an Inherited Rights Filter (IRF) to an object, which globally blocks selected rights from being inherited at the object. The default IRF on an object is to allow all rights to be inherited. The second way to block an inherited right is to grant a user a new explicit trustee assignment to the object. An explicit trustee assignment overwrites an inherited assignment. Answers B and C are incorrect. You cannot grant a new file system assignment in eDirectory. Deleting the Admin object can be a dangerous adventure if you have not created another user object that has Supervisor object rights to the Tree object. You could potentially lose control of your tree or of a given branch of the tree. In addition, deleting the Admin object does nothing to help you block an inherited right.

Question 42

If you circled Down/Restart under Manage Server in the left navigation bar you are correct. You can Down, Restart, or Reset a NetWare 6.5 server remotely using the Down/Restart option in Remote Manager.

Question 43

Answers B, C, and E are correct. In NetWare 6.5, login scripts are text files that set a network environment for a Container, User, or group of users. If you want to document your reasons for a line of script, you need to precede the line with either a REM, ;, or *. The line preceded by any of these three will not be executed or displayed on the screen for the user to see. Answers A and D are incorrect. The @ and # signs indicate that an external command will be launched at this point. One command that is often used with either the @ or the # signs is NAL.EXE, which launches the ZENworks Application Launcher.

Question 44

If you circled the eDirectory Administration role in the left navigation bar, you are correct. When eDirectory Administration is expanded, you can select the Create Object task to create a Template object. You would not use the eDirectory Maintenance role to create an object. The tasks available under eDirectory Maintenance include Backup, Merge Tree, Rename Tree, and Schema Maintenance.

Question 45

Answers A, D, and E are correct. Novell recommends that you use one of four possible utilities to create volumes. The four include iManager, NSSMU, Remote Manager, and ConsoleOne. Answers B and C are incorrect because they cannot be used to create NSS volumes on a NetWare 6.5 server.

Question 46

Answers B, C, D, and E are correct. The NetWare 6.5 system-created directories include LOGIN, PUBLIC, SYSTEM, MAIL, ETC, NI, and APACHE. Answers A and F are incorrect. Novell recommends that CNAs also create four user-created directories. These include a USERS or HOME parent directory, a SHARED parent directory, an APPS parent directory, and a directory for configuration files, which is often found as a subdirectory of the user's home directory or as a subdirectory of a given application.

Question 47

If you circled the top Info button on the DATA volume's file system listing, you are correct. This is the Info button just to the left of the period under the Name heading. When selected, the DATA volume's ACL and IRF are displayed.

Question 48

If you circled Global Settings, you are correct. To configure client properties, you would select Global Settings, Global Policies, Client Properties. From the Client Properties screen, you can elect to conceal the Save PassPhrase option.

Question 49

If you circled the Manage Printer task, you are correct. To move jobs ahead in the queue or to promote a print job, you select Manage Printer, select your printer, Printer Control, Jobs, select your job, Promote.

Question 50

Answer B is correct. If a user's home directory is created when the user object is created, the user is granted the Read, Write, Create, Erase, Modify, File scan, and Access control rights to the directory. Answers A, C, and D are incorrect because they do not reflect the correct rights assignments. In earlier versions of NetWare, the user was assigned the Supervisor right also to his home directory, but that is not the case in NetWare 6.5. The Read and File scan rights assignment is the default assignment to the PUBLIC directory, which is given to all users who exist in the same context as the server object. Read, Write, Create, Erase, and File scan is a safe rights assignment that many administrators use to avoid giving too many rights. This avoids granting the Supervisor, Modify, and Access control rights.

Question 51

Answer A is correct. You create a storage pool before you create a volume but after you create a partition. The correct sequence is creating a partition, creating a storage pool, and then creating a logical volume or volumes. Answers B, C, and D are incorrect because they do not follow this sequence.

Question 52

Answers A, B, and C are correct. The three required NDPS components to set up an iPrint in NetWare 6.5 are a Broker, Manager, and Printer agent. Answers D, E, and F are incorrect. A Print server and a Print queue are legacy queue-based printing entities. A Gateway is an NDPS component but is not required for iPrint.

Question 53

Answers B, D, and E are correct. A few of the utilities that you can use to view and modify file attributes are ConsoleOne, NetWare Administrator, Remote Manager, FILER, and FLAG. Answers A and C are incorrect. You cannot manage file system attributes with NSSMU or iManager. NSSMU is a utility for managing NSS volumes, pools, and partitions. iManager is a Web-based eDirectory management tool. Answer F is incorrect. NDIR is a utility used to view a file's attributes.

Question 54

Answer B is correct. The NetWare 6.5 utility of choice for configuring iPrint is iManager. Answers A, C, and D are incorrect. You cannot configure iPrint with Remote Manager, ConsoleOne, or NSSMU.

Question 55

Answer A is correct; an NDPS Broker provides three services: SRS, RMS, and ENS. The Event Notification Services (ENS) enables printers to send users and operators messages about printer events. Answer B is incorrect; the

Resource Management Services (RMS) enables resources to be located centrally. Those resources, such as printer drivers, can be accessed, downloaded, and installed easily. Answer C is incorrect; the Service Registry Services (SRS) allows Public Access printers to advertise and be discovered by users. Answer D is incorrect; the Message Transfer Agent (MTA) is a GroupWise component that is responsible for routing messages between different email systems.

Question 56

Answer B is correct; there are two categories of NDPS printers: Public Access and Controlled Access. Controlled Access printers have an eDirectory object and provide full administrative control, including eDirectory security. Public Access printers are available to everyone on a network and have no eDirectory object; therefore, answer A is incorrect. Answer C is incorrect also; an NDPS Gateway provides a means to use NDPS printing with printers that are not NDPS compliant. Answer D is incorrect; a non-NDPS printer is the term applied to a queue-based printer when using NetWare Administrator.

Question 57

Answer D is correct; Dynamic Host Configuration Protocol (DHCP) is a protocol that dynamically assigns IP addresses to hosts on an IP network. Answer A is incorrect; Simple Mail Transfer Protocol (SMTP) sends email messages across the Internet. Answer B is incorrect; Simple Network Management Protocol (SNMP) manages network devices on a TCP/IP network. Answer C is incorrect; File Transfer Protocol (FTP) transfers files from one node to another over a TCP/IP network.

Question 58

Answer D is correct. If your NetWare 6.5 server's IP address is 10.0.0.125, the correct URL for the iFolder Management Console is `https://10.0.0.125/iFolderServer/Admin`.

This URL is case-sensitive. Answers A, B, and C are incorrect because they cannot be used to access the iFolder Management Console on a NetWare 6.5 server.

Question 59

Answer D is correct. The NI directory contains the NetWare installation files, including the Response files that are automatically generated during a server install. Answer A is incorrect. The ETC directory contains sample TCP/IP files, such as hosts, gateways, and protocols. Answer B is incorrect. The PUBLIC directory contains most publicly accessible NetWare utilities. Answer C is incorrect. The SYSTEM directory contains administrative tools and most NetWare Loadable Modules (NLMs), which configure and add functionality to a NetWare 6.5 server.

Question 60

Answer B is correct; there are four login scripts in NetWare 6.5, and they execute in the following order: Container, Profile, User, and Default. The Profile script is for a group of individuals who have common needs. Answer A is incorrect; the purpose of a Container script is to configure the environment for all users in a Container. It is used to send messages, establish drive mappings, and connect to network printers. Answer C is incorrect; User scripts are written for individual users and do not apply to a group. Answer D is incorrect; there is no System script in NetWare 6.5. A System script was the equivalent of the Container script in NetWare 3 and before.

15

Practice Exam 2

1. You want to hide a Container object in your eDirectory tree. Which IRF should you configure on this Container to accomplish this?

   A. ○ [SRW F]
   B. ○ [SB R]
   C. ○ [SRC I]
   D. ○ [S CDRI]

2. You have just added a new Adaptec SCSI controller card to your NetWare 6.5 server. You will be adding several SCSI hard disks to this controller. Which driver do you have to configure so that the controller will function correctly?

   A. ○ **IDE.DSK**
   B. ○ **AHA2940.HAM**
   C. ○ **CE100B.LAN**
   D. ○ **MAC.NAM**

3. You are installing a new NetWare 6.5 server. The server has 1024MB of physical memory installed. What is the optimal size for your DOS partition?

   A. ○ 2048MB
   B. ○ 1024MB
   C. ○ 500MB
   D. ○ 1524MB

4. You want to install a NetWare 6.5 server into your existing network. The network consists of two NetWare 5.1 SP5 servers, two NetWare 4.11 SP9 servers, one NetWare 4.2 SP8 server, and one NetWare 4.10 SP3 server. You are met with an error message when you prepare the network for the new server. Which version of the NetWare operating system is causing the problem?

   A. ○ NetWare 5.1
   B. ○ NetWare 4.11
   C. ○ NetWare 4.2
   D. ○ NetWare 4.10

5. At the beginning of a new NetWare 6.5 server installation, what are the two types of installation that you can perform? (Choose two.)

   A. ❑ Custom
   B. ❑ Default
   C. ❑ Manual
   D. ❑ Express

6. During one of the initial phases of a NetWare 6.5 server installation, you create a new **SYS** volume. By default, what type of volume will the **SYS** volume be when it is created?

   A. ○ FAT32

   B. ○ FAT

   C. ○ NTFS

   D. ○ Traditional

   E. ○ NSS

7. In which file will you find a NetWare DOS Requestor section where you can configure the Preferred Server and Preferred Tree?

   A. ○ **NET.CFG**

   B. ○ **AUTOEXEC.NCF**

   C. ○ **INSTALL.BAT**

   D. ○ **CONFIG.SYS**

   E. ○ **AUTOEXEC.BAT**

8. You have decided to install the IP protocol during your NetWare 6.5 server installation. To which frame type is IP bound because of this decision?

   A. ○ Ethernet_SNAP

   B. ○ Ethernet_802.3

   C. ○ Ethernet_802.2

   D. ○ Ethernet_II

9. You want to install additional products on your NetWare 6.5 server after the operating system has been installed successfully. You want to use the GUI console screen to perform the product installation. Which command should you enter at the server console to launch the GUI console screen?

   A. ○ **AUTOEXEC**

   B. ○ **C1START**

   C. ○ **STARTUP**

   D. ○ **STARTX**

10. Which server console command should you use if you want to display the server search paths on a NetWare 6.5 server?

    A. ○ **PATH**

    B. ○ **SEARCH**

    C. ○ **DISPLAY**

    D. ○ **SEARCH ADD**

11. Which console hot keys should you use if you want to display the Emergency Console screen on a NetWare 6.5 server?

   A. ○ Alt-Esc

   B. ○ Ctrl-Esc

   C. ○ Ctrl-Alt-Esc

   D. ○ Alt-Tab

12. You want to bring your server down and automatically reboot it. Which server console command can you use to accomplish this?

   A. ○ **SEND**

   B. ○ **MOUNT**

   C. ○ **VOLUMES**

   D. ○ **RESET SERVER**

13. You installed the latest support pack on your NetWare 6.5 server. After you install the support pack, you need to edit the configuration file that loads the disk drivers. Which file do you need to edit?

   A. ○ **STARTUP.NCF**

   B. ○ **AUTOEXEC.BAT**

   C. ○ **AUTOEXEC.NCF**

   D. ○ **CONFIG.SYS**

14. Which tasks can you perform by default in NetWare 6.5 using iManager? (Choose all that apply.)

   A. ❑ Configure DHCP.

   B. ❑ Create Template objects.

   C. ❑ Delete User objects.

   D. ❑ Monitor a server's health.

15. Which two URLs can you use to access Remote Manager in NetWare 6.5 if your server's IP address is 10.0.0.125? (Choose two.)

   A. ❑ **https://10.0.0.125:2200**

   B. ❑ **http://10.0.0.125:631/IPP**

   C. ❑ **http://10.0.0.125:8008**

   D. ❑ **http://10.0.0.125**

16. Which NetWare 6.5 Web-based utility should you use if you want to display all active console screens?

   A. ○ iMonitor

   B. ○ iManager

   C. ○ Remote Manager

   D. ○ Server Management Console

17. You are installing the latest Novell Client on your Windows XP Professional workstation. Which Login Authenticator option should you select during the installation if you are logging into a tree populated with only NetWare 6.5 servers?

    A. ○ NDPS

    B. ○ NDS

    C. ○ eDirectory

    D. ○ Bindery

18. You have installed the Novell Client on all 500 workstations in your office. All servers are running NetWare 6.5. You want to modify the client properties on every workstation. Which Novell product can you use to simplify this process?

    A. ○ Nsure Identity Manager

    B. ○ ZENworks for Desktops 3

    C. ○ GroupWise

    D. ○ BorderManager

19. Which eDirectory objects are classified as leaf objects? (Choose three.)

    A. ❑ Country

    B. ❑ Server

    C. ❑ User

    D. ❑ Volume

    E. ❑ Organization

    F. ❑ Organizational Unit

20. Which of the following is an example of a typeful Distinguished Name?

    A. ○ .admin.NW65

    B. ○ .CN=admin.O=NW65

    C. ○ CN=admin.O=NW65.

    D. ○ admin.NW65

21. In eDirectory, what defines the types of objects that can exist in the tree?

    A. ○ Attributes

    B. ○ Values

    C. ○ Properties

    D. ○ Schema

22. What are the three types of objects in eDirectory? (Choose three.)
    A. ❑ Tree
    B. ❑ Container
    C. ❑ Country
    D. ❑ Locality
    E. ❑ Leaf

23. A NetWare 6.5 feature that enables you to integrate and manage different types of passwords and systems of authentication into a single common password and is *not* turned on by default is the

    _____.

24. You have recently created an Organizational Unit that you want all authenticated users in the eDirectory tree to have access to. Which object should you include in the Organizational Unit's ACL?
    A. ○ Tree
    B. ○ [Public] trustee
    C. ○ Organization
    D. ○ Country

25. You have created a new eDirectory tree and named it **NW65_Tree**. In this tree, what objects can be a child of the Tree object? (Choose three.)
    A. ❑ Admin
    B. ❑ Supervisor
    C. ❑ Server
    D. ❑ Organization
    E. ❑ Country
    F. ❑ Alias

26. Which management utility should you use if you want to remotely run DSRepair on a NetWare 6.5 server?
    A. ○ Remote Manager
    B. ○ ConsoleOne
    C. ○ iManager
    D. ○ iMonitor

27. In Figure 15.1, circle one of the directory attributes you could select if you do not want the **FileSyst** directory to be seen when users run the **DIR** command.

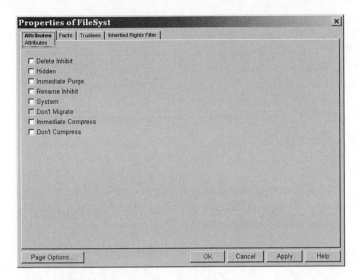

Figure 15.1   Question 27.

28. Which option should you append to the Novell Client installation executable if you need to provide special accessibility settings?

    A. ○ /2200

    B. ○ /631

    C. ○ /508

    D. ○ /8008

29. Which is a required property when you create a User object in eDirectory?

    A. ○ Description

    B. ○ First Name

    C. ○ Last Name

    D. ○ Home Directory

30. Which of the following is a security guideline that you should follow when managing NetWare 6.5 servers?

    A. ○ Place the server under your desk.

    B. ○ Remove the monitor.

    C. ○ Do not load **SCRSAVER.NLM**.

    D. ○ Load **SECURE CONSOLE**.

31. Your NetWare 6.5 server is named **SERVER6**. You have a **DATA** volume on **SERVER 6**. The **DATA** volume has a root directory that you have called **SHARED**. The **SHARED** directory has a subdirectory that you have called **GENERAL**. You have mapped the S: drive to the **GENERAL** directory using a volume object name. You need to delete the mapping to the **GENERAL** directory. Which command accomplishes this?

    A. ○ **MAP S: DEL**

    B. ○ **MAP DEL GENERAL**

    C. ○ **MAP DEL S:**

    D. ○ **DEL MAP S:**

32. You want to create a new traditional volume on your NetWare 6.5 server. You are using Remote Manager to accomplish this. In Figure 15.2, circle the option you should select to accomplish this.

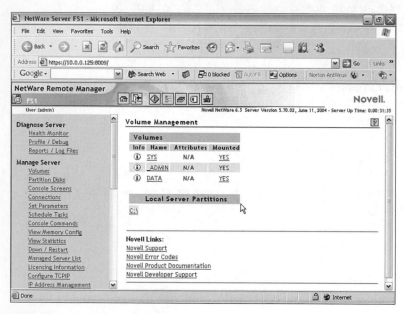

Figure 15.2 Question 32.

33. You want to display what Alexandra can effectively do at the 3WsNetWorking Organization object. In Figure 15.3, circle the role in iManager where you can accomplish this.

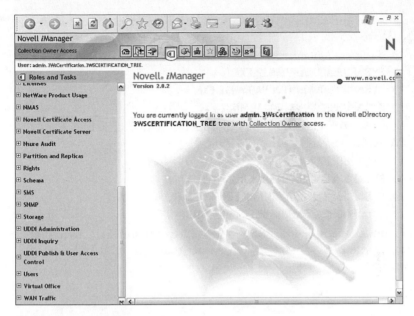

Figure 15.3   Question 33.

34. The process of rights flowing down from a higher level to a lower level in both the eDirectory tree and the NetWare 6.5 file system is

_____.

35. In Figure 15.4, circle the Organizational Role object.

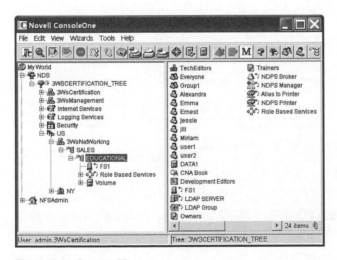

Figure 15.4   Question 35.

36. What is the correct path to the NetWare Administrator executable on a NetWare 6.5 server?

   A. ○ NetWare Administrator does not ship with NetWare 6.5.

   B. ○ **SYS:\PUBLIC\NWADMN32.EXE**

   C. ○ **SYS:\PUBLIC\WINNT\NWADMN32.EXE**

   D. ○ **SYS:\PUBLIC\WIN32\NWADMN32.EXE**

37. What is the correct path to the **CONSOLEONE.EXE** executable on a NetWare 6.5 server?

   A. ○ **SYS:\PUBLIC\WIN32**

   B. ○ **SYS:\PUBLIC\CONSOLEONE\1.2\BIN**

   C. ○ **SYS:\PUBLIC\MGMT\CONSOLEONE\1.2\BIN**

   D. ○ **SYS:\PUBLIC\CONSOLEONE\MGMT\1.2\BIN**

38. You want to open the OpenSSH Manager. In Figure 15.5, circle the option in the NetWare 6.5 Web Manager that you should select to accomplish this.

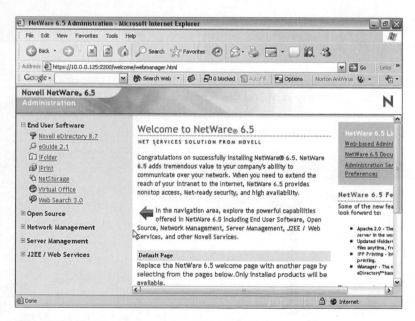

Figure 15.5 Question 38.

39. To launch OpenSSH on your NetWare 6.5 server from a server console prompt, you should enter **LOAD** _____ at the prompt.

40. You want the users on your NetWare 6.5 network to have the necessary print drivers automatically downloaded to their workstations when they log in. You have deployed NDPS. In Figure 15.6, circle the option that you should select to accomplish this.

Figure 15.6   Question 40.

41. You have been asked to plan the file system for a new NetWare 6.5 network. Which of the following guidelines should you follow as you plan the file system?

    A. ○ Store data and applications on the **SYS** volume.

    B. ○ Store data and applications on the same volume as the operating system files.

    C. ○ Store data on the same volume as the system files, but store applications on a separate volume.

    D. ○ Store data and applications on a volume other than **SYS**.

42. As part of your overall NetWare 6.5 printing environment, you want to deploy iPrint. Which NDPS component is responsible for loading the **IPPSRVR.NLM**?

    A. ○ Broker

    B. ○ Print server

    C. ○ Printer agent

    D. ○ Print Services Manager

43. By default, where is the **AUTOEXEC.NCF** file stored?

    A. ○ **C:**

    B. ○ **C:\NWSERVER**

    C. ○ **SYS:\SYSTEM**

    D. ○ **SYS:\PUBLIC**

44. Which type of NDPS printer is not represented by an eDirectory object in the tree?

    A. ○ Controlled Access

    B. ○ Public Access

    C. ○ Queue-based

    D. ○ Legacy

45. You are sitting at the server console of server FS10, a NetWare 6.5 server running OpenSSH. FS10 has an IP address of 10.0.0.10. Which command would you enter at your server console if you wanted to authenticate as admin to server FS1, which has an IP address of 10.0.0.1, and run an ssh session?

    A. ○ **SSHD.NLM**
    B. ○ **ssh admin@10.0.0.1**
    C. ○ **ssh admin@10.0.0.10**
    D. ○ **admin ssh@10.0.0.1**

46. You want to use location-based printing in your iPrint environment. To begin the configuration, you want to access the **Maptool.htm**. Your Print Service Manager has an IP address of 10.0.0.125. You do not have the Novell Client installed on your workstation. The URL that you should enter into your browser's location bar to access **Maptool.htm** is _____.

47. You are configuring your NetWare 6.5 network for NDPS. How many NDPS Managers can you load on a NetWare 6.5 server?

    A. ○ 1
    B. ○ 16
    C. ○ 256
    D. ○ Unlimited

48. You want to access Virtual Office on your NetWare 6.5 server, FS1. Your server has an IP address of 10.0.0.125. DNS has not been configured. The URL that you should enter into your browser's location bar to open the Virtual Office authentication page is

    _____.

49. Which of the following are time-tested tools for monitoring and tracking security breaches? (Choose three.)

    A. ❑ SETPASS.NLM
    B. ❑ NAAS
    C. ❑ HOL
    D. ❑ BindView Solutions

50. Which additional NetWare 6.5 products do you need to install when you install Virtual Office on your server if you want to access them from the Virtual Office interface? (Choose three.)

    A. ❑ iSCSI
    B. ❑ eGuide
    C. ❑ NetStorage
    D. ❑ iPrint

51. You are a new network administrator for a NetWare 6.5 server. You have a new installed server with the default configuration. What two things should you do to protect your network environment? (Choose two.)

    A. ❑ Create an Everyone group.
    B. ❑ Create multiple backup admins in the tree with the same explicit assignments as the Admin object.
    C. ❑ Delete the Admin object.
    D. ❑ Rename the Admin object.
    E. ❑ Create an Administrator's Local Group.

52. Which NetWare 6.5 applications make up the Open Source Services feature set? (Choose all that apply.)

    A. ❑ NCS
    B. ❑ NFAP
    C. ❑ APACHE
    D. ❑ PHP
    E. ❑ MYSQL
    F. ❑ iFOLDER
    G. ❑ TOMCAT

53. Which type of firewall technology is a proxy server that is protocol specific, for example accepting or rejecting SMTP packets based on a configured set of rules?

    A. ○ Packet filtering
    B. ○ NAT
    C. ○ Circuit-level
    D. ○ Application gateway

54. Which NetWare 6.5 technology automatically moves data from a bad block to a safe area on a drive in case one or more blocks becomes corrupt?

    A. ○ Hot fix
    B. ○ Overbooking
    C. ○ NSS Pool
    D. ○ File Versioning

55. Which of the following tasks can you perform on the Virtual Team home page? (Choose two.)

    A. ❑ Set Notify Preferences
    B. ❑ Show Blocked Users
    C. ❑ Configure the POP3 address
    D. ❑ Assign the address used by eGuide

56. In NetWare 6.5, how many Profile login scripts can be assigned to a user object?

    A. ○ 1

    B. ○ 2

    C. ○ 10

    D. ○ Unlimited number

57. Rickie is a user object in the Queens container on your NetWare 6.5 network. You have created a Queens container script. Rickie is a member of the **TECHS** group. You have created a Profile script for the **TECHS** group. You have not assigned Rickie a User script. Which login script command should you place in the container script if you do not want the Default script to execute?

    A. ○ **NO_SCRIPT**

    B. ○ **NO_PROFILE**

    C. ○ **NO_DEFAULT**

    D. ○ **DEFAULT_EXIT**

58. You have iPrint for your NetWare 6.5 environment. You have configured a DNS "A" record for your Print Service Manager. When you load the Print Service Manager NLM on your NetWare 6.5 server, which option should you append to it so that users can access your iPrint printers using common names in a Web browser?

    A. ○ **/dnsonly**

    B. ○ **/ndsonly**

    C. ○ **/ndsname**

    D. ○ **/dnsname**

59. Which NDPS component is the parent to the SRS, ENS, and RMS services?

    A. ○ Broker

    B. ○ Manager

    C. ○ Gateway

    D. ○ Agent

60. Which of the following are characteristics of a Public Access printer? (Choose two.)

    A. ❑ Full range of network security options available

    B. ❑ Does not require a great deal of administration

    C. ❑ Requires users to have necessary rights to be able to print

    D. ❑ Everyone on the network can print to it as soon as it is configured

Answer Key for Practice Exam 2

1. D
2. B
3. D
4. D
5. B, C
6. E
7. A
8. D
9. D
10. B
11. C
12. D
13. A
14. A, B, C
15. A, C
16. C
17. B
18. B

19. B, C, D
20. B
21. D
22. A, B, E
23. Universal Password
24. A
25. D, E, F
26. D
27. Hidden or System
28. C
29. C
30. D
31. C
32. Partition Disks
33. Rights
34. Inheritance
35. TechEditors object
36. D

37. C
38. Open Source
39. SSHD.NLM or SSHD
40. RPM Configuration
41. D
42. D
43. C
44. B
45. B
46. http:// 10.0.0.125:631/ IPPDOCS/Maptool.htm
47. A
48. http:// 10.0.0.125/vo
49. B, C, D
50. B, C, D
51. B, D

52. C, D, E, G	**55.** A, B	**58.** D
53. D	**56.** A	**59.** A
54. A	**57.** C	**60.** B, D

Question 1

Answer D is correct. The inherited rights filter (IRF) that you use to hide an eDirectory object is S CDRI. With this filter, you block the Browse object right, or the ability to see an eDirectory object. The default eDirectory IRF on a Container object is SBCDRI for object rights and SRCWAI for property rights. Answer A is incorrect because it is a possible file system IRF. Answer B is incorrect because it does not filter the Browse object right. Answer C is incorrect because it is a property rights IRF, not an object rights filter. You cannot filter the Browse object right using a property rights filter.

Question 2

Answer B is correct. In NetWare 6.5, storage adapters, such as Adaptec SCSI controllers, are identified by a .HAM extension. Answers A, C, and D are incorrect. .DSK is the extension used for storage adapters or devices prior to NetWare 5. It is not supported in NetWare 6.5. A .LAN extension represents the network board driver. The .NAM extension represents a defined namespace, such as the namespace for Macs, which is MAC.NAM.

Question 3

Answer D is correct. NetWare 6.5 requires a DOS partition that is minimally sized at 500MB. The DOS partition is needed to boot the server and hold the folder and files that load NetWare. The recommended size for the DOS partition is 1GB. The optimal size for the DOS partition is 500MB plus space that is equal to the amount of installed physical memory. A server that has 1024MB of installed physical memory will optimally have a DOS partition that is 1524MB. Answer A is incorrect. Although 2048MB would give you more than optimal space for the DOS partition, it does not strictly follow the logic that Novell defines for an optimal partition size. Answer B is incorrect because it is the recommended size for the DOS partition. Answer C is incorrect because it is the minimal size for the DOS partition.

Question 4

Answer D is correct. When you introduce a NetWare 6.5 server, all existing servers must be patched to a defined support pack level. The minimal support pack levels are support pack 6a for NetWare 4.11 and 4.2 servers, support pack 4 for NetWare 5 servers, and support pack 3 for NetWare 5.1 servers. You cannot have a NetWare 4.10 server on a network when you introduce a NetWare 6.5 server. The NetWare 4.10 server must first be upgraded to NetWare 4.11 or 4.2 before you introduce NetWare 6.5. Answers A, B, and C are incorrect. They exceed the minimal support pack levels defined by Novell for NetWare 4.11, 4.2, and 5.1 servers.

Question 5

Answers B and C are correct. At the beginning of the NetWare 6.5 server installation process, you need to decide on the type of installation you will carry out. You have two options: Default and Manual. Answers A and D are incorrect. These are NetWare 6 installation options.

Question 6

Answer E is correct. During a NetWare 6.5 server installation, the sys volume by default is created as an NSS volume. You have the option of making it an NSS volume or a Traditional NetWare volume at the time the volume is created. Answers A, B, C, and D are incorrect because they are not the default sys volume type at the time of volume creation. FAT32, FAT, and NTFS are Windows and DOS partition types. A Traditional NetWare volume is the type of volume that was the default used in versions of NetWare before NetWare 5.0. In NetWare 5.x, the sys volume had to be a Traditional volume, but you could create other volumes that were NSS volumes. NSS did not really come into its own until NetWare 6 and 6.5.

Question 7

Answer A is correct. You will find a NetWare DOS Requestor section in the NET.CFG file. In NET.CFG, you can configure a Preferred Server, a Preferred Tree, and your current context using the Name Context parameter. NET.CFG is used in NetWare 6.5 during an across-the-wire installation. Answers B, C, D, and E are incorrect because you will not find a NetWare DOS Requestor section in any of these files. AUTOEXEC.BAT and CONFIG.SYS are DOS configuration files that are used when a computer boots. INSTALL.BAT is the batch file that launches the NetWare 6.5 installation routine. AUTOEXEC.NCF is a NetWare file, found in the SYS:\SYSTEM directory, that is used when a server boots up.

Question 8

Answer D is correct. During a NetWare 6.5 server installation, you must configure networking protocols. You can install and configure IP, IPX, or Compatibility Mode driver. In NetWare 6.5, you must install IP. IP will be bound by default to the Ethernet_II frame. Answer A is incorrect. AppleTalk Phase II networks use Ethernet_SNAP. Answer C is incorrect. IPX automatically binds to Ethernet_802.2 during installation. This has been the default behavior in NetWare since NetWare 3.12. Answer B is incorrect. Ethernet_802.3 is the default frame type used by NetWare before NetWare 4.x. Some early versions of NetWare 3 used Ethernet_802.3 by default.

Question 9

Answer D is correct. After you have finished installing a NetWare 6.5 server, you can install additional components by using either the Deployment Manager or the server's GUI interface. If the GUI server console has not been launched, you can launch it by entering STARTX at a server console prompt. Answers A and C are incorrect. AUTOEXEC and STARTUP are two NetWare configuration files (NCF) that NetWare calls after SERVER.EXE is launched from the C:\NWSERVER directory. Answer B is incorrect. C1START is the file used to launch the server version of ConsoleOne. When ConsoleOne launches, it also launches the GUI server console. The difference between STARTX and C1START is that STARTX only launches the GUI server console, whereas C1START launches both the GUI server console and ConsoleOne.

Question 10

Answer B is correct. You can obtain a wealth of information at a NetWare 6.5 server console by using the proper console command. You use SEARCH when you want to display server search paths on a NetWare 6.5 server.

Answers A and C are incorrect. PATH is a DOS command that displays a workstation's environment paths. You use DISPLAY with a variety of commands, such as DISPLAY SLP SERVICES. You do not use it to display a server's search paths. Answer D is incorrect because you use SEARCH ADD to add a path to currently configured server search paths.

Question 11

Answer C is correct. You can make NetWare 6.5 server administration easier with some server console key sequences. One that is useful is Ctrl-Alt-Esc. You can use that one to display the Emergency Console screen when a server is hung and needs to be safely downed and restarted. Answer A is incorrect. Alt-Esc is used to toggle between console screens. Answer B is incorrect. You use Ctrl-Esc to view a menu of console screens. Answer D is incorrect. Alt-Tab is a useful key sequence in a Windows environment.

Question 12

Answer D is correct. You can gain a wealth of information and administrative control at a NetWare 6.5 server console by using the proper console command. You use the RESET SERVER command when you want to bring your server down and automatically reboot it. Answer A is incorrect. You use the SEND command when you want to send a message to all users who are logged into a NetWare 6.5 server. Answer B is incorrect. You use the MOUNT command to mount one or more volumes. You can call this command from the AUTOEXEC.NCF file or run it from the server console prompt. You can mount and dismount volumes while the file server is running. Answer C is incorrect. You use the VOLUMES command to display all mounted volumes.

Question 13

Answer A is correct. The STARTUP.NCF file is one of the first files you call after SERVER.EXE launches. You can find it in the C:\NWSERVER directory and use it to load the necessary storage adapters, disk drivers, custom device modules, and namespace modules. Answers B and D are incorrect. The CONFIG.SYS and AUTOEXEC.BAT files are DOS configuration files, found on the DOS partition. Answer C is incorrect. The AUTOEXEC.NCF NetWare configuration file typically contains most server environmental settings, including the server name,

SERVERID, time zone settings, LAN card LOAD and BIND statements, and SEARCH ADD settings. You can find it in the SYS:\SYSTEM directory.

Question 14

Answers A, B, and C are correct. iManager is a Web-based utility that lets a NetWare administrator configure, manage, and administer printing, licensing, DNS/DHCP, eDirectory tasks such as creating and deleting objects, and role-based administration. Answer D is incorrect. NetWare Remote Manager is a Web-based utility that administrators can use to monitor and manage a NetWare server, including a server's health.

Question 15

Answers A and C are correct. You can access Remote Manager in one of two ways: either directly or through Web Manager. The URLs for accessing Remote Manager directly are http://10.0.0.125:8008 and https://10.0.0.125:8009. The URL for accessing Remote Manager through Web Manager is https://10.0.0.125:2200. Answer B is incorrect. It is the URL for accessing the default printer list that iPrint generates. Answer D is incorrect. It is the URL for accessing the Apache Web server.

Question 16

Answer C is correct. NetWare Remote Manager is a Web-based utility that administrators can use to monitor and manage a NetWare server, including a server's health. One of the options that is available on Remote Manager is Console Screens, which lets an administrator display all active console screens through a browser on a workstation. Answer A is incorrect. iMonitor is a new utility that you can use to monitor and diagnose servers in your eDirectory tree from any computer that has a compatible browser installed. You can use iMonitor to remotely run a DSREPAIR session on a server. Answer B is incorrect. iManager is a Web-based utility that lets a NetWare administrator configure and manage printing, licensing, DNS/DHCP, eDirectory tasks such as creating and deleting objects, and role-based administration. Answer D is incorrect. Server Management Console is a NetWare 6.0 utility that lets you manage the accounts of iFolder users. In NetWare 6.5, Server Management Console is called the iFolder Management Console.

Question 17

Answer B is correct. Two Login Authenticator options are available during a Novell Client installation: Bindery and NDS. You use the Bindery option for NetWare 3.x servers and the NDS option for NetWare 4.x to 6.5 servers. Answer D is incorrect. There is no NDPS or eDirectory Login Authenticator options during a Novell Client installation, so answers A and C are incorrect.

Question 18

Answer B is correct. The preferred method of client configuration for a few workstations is right-clicking the red *N* in the Windows System Tray and selecting Novell Client Properties. To efficiently accomplish this on a large number of workstations, you would use ZENworks for Desktops 3 or 4 and make necessary changes through ConsoleOne. Answer A is incorrect. Nsure Identity Manager is a Novell product that lets you securely manage the access needs of your users. Answer C is incorrect. GroupWise is one of Novell's email product solutions. Answer D is incorrect. BorderManager is Novell's firewall solution. You cannot modify a large number of Novell Client properties with Nsure Identity Manager, GroupWise, or BorderManager.

Question 19

Answers B, C, and D are correct. Leaf objects in eDirectory are network resources. Examples of Leaf objects are the User object, Server object, Volume object, and Group object. Answers A, E, and F are incorrect. In eDirectory, a Container object is an object that holds other eDirectory objects. Examples of Container objects are the Country object, the Organization object, the Organizational Unit object, the Domain object, the Security container, the License container, and Role-Based Service (RBS).

Question 20

Answer B is correct. In eDirectory, a Relative Distinguished Name is an object's common name relative to a workstation's current context. A Relative Distinguished Name never has a leading period, but it might have a trailing period. Distinguished Names are similar to Relative Distinguished Names in that both use periods to separate contextual elements and both might or might not use object attribute types (abbreviations). If both naming conventions use object attribute types, they are said to be typeful. If they do not use object attribute types, they are said to be typeless. `.CN=admin.O=NW65` is an example of a typeful Distinguished Name. Answer A is incorrect because it is a typeless Distinguished Name. Answer C is incorrect because it is a typeful Relative Distinguished Name. Answer D is incorrect because it is a typeless Relative Distinguished Name.

Question 21

Answer D is correct. The schema is the set of rules that govern which objects can be created and exist in eDirectory. The schema is made up of two sets of definitions: Object class definitions that define which objects can be created in a Directory and which attributes or properties are associated with each object type, and Attribute definitions that define the structure, syntax, and limitations of an attribute. Answers A and C are incorrect because attributes and properties are characteristics of an object. Answer B is incorrect because a value is content that is assigned to an object's attribute.

Question 22

Answers A, B, and E are correct. eDirectory is made up of three major components: objects, properties or attributes, and values. There are three major object types: the Tree object, Container objects, and Leaf objects. Leaf objects are network resources, whereas Container objects hold network resources and other containers. Answers C and D are examples of Container and Leaf objects.

Question 23

The correct answer is Universal Password. The NetWare 6.5 Universal Password enables you to integrate and manage different types of passwords and systems of authentication into a single common password. It is *not* turned on by default.

Question 24

Answer A is correct. The Tree object, represented on an ACL as [Root], represents all authenticated users to the tree. Answer B is incorrect. The [Public] trustee represents all nonauthenticated and authenticated users to the tree. The main function of the [Public] trustee is that it allows users to browse the tree and the objects it contains before they log in. All objects in the eDirectory tree are security equivalent to the [Public] trustee. Answers C and D are incorrect because they are container objects that contain only a segment of all objects in the eDirectory tree.

Question 25

Answers D, E, and F are correct. eDirectory can have only one Tree object, which exists at the top of the tree. It can contain the Country object, Organization object, Security container, and Alias objects to Country, Organization, and Security. Answers A, B, and C are incorrect because they are not children of the Tree object. Admin and Server are objects that can exist in the Organization object or below. The Supervisor object is not a defined object in eDirectory. In NetWare 6.5, for Bindery purposes, Supervisor access is still available, but a Supervisor object does not explicitly exist in an eDirectory tree.

Question 26

Answer D is correct. iMonitor is a new utility that you can use to monitor and diagnose servers in your eDirectory tree from any computer that has a compatible browser installed. You can use iMonitor to remotely run a DSRE-PAIR session on a server. Answer A is incorrect. Remote Manager is a Web-based utility that administrators can use to monitor and manage a NetWare server. You can access iMonitor from Remote Manager. Answer B is incorrect. ConsoleOne is a platform-independent management utility that you can use to create, delete, and rename eDirectory objects. It is a great utility for browsing large eDirectory trees. Answer C is incorrect. iManager is a Web-based utility that lets a NetWare administrator administer, configure, and manage printing, licensing, DNS/DHCP, eDirectory tasks, and role-based administration.

Question 27

If you circled either the Hidden or the System attribute, you are correct. When either of these attributes is enabled on the FileSyst directory, users will not be able to see the directory when they run the DIR command.

Question 28

Answer C is correct. The option you should append to the Novell Client executable if you need to provide special accessibility settings is /508. The /508 option is based on Section 508 of the U.S. Federal Government Rehabilitation Act. Answers A, B, and D are incorrect. You can use port 2200 to access the NetWare 6.5 Web Manager, port 631 to access the default iPrint printer list, and port 8008 to access Remote Manager.

Question 29

Answer C is correct. *Properties* are fundamental components of eDirectory. A property is an attribute of an object. If you compare a traditional database or spreadsheet to eDirectory, an object's property is a field in a database or a column in a spreadsheet. Some properties are required, depending on the object, whereas others are optional. Some properties are single-valued, whereas others are multivalued. For example, to create a User object, depending on the utility that you use, you must give the User object a username and a last name. Answers A, B, and D are incorrect. Description, first name, and home directory are optional properties of a User object.

Question 30

Answer D is correct. Novell's guidelines for physically securing a NetWare 6.5 server include loading SECURE CONSOLE on the server. Answers A, B, and C are incorrect. Novell's guidelines for physically securing a NetWare 6.5 server call for you to 1) remove the mouse and keyboard, not the monitor; 2)place the server in a locked room; and 3) load SCRSAVER.NLM on the server.

Question 31

Answer C is correct. Following is the NetWare 6.5 syntax for mapping a drive to a directory using a physical volume name:

```
Map {option} drive: = Server\Volume: Directory\
subdirectory
```

Here is the NetWare 6.5 syntax for mapping a drive to a directory using a volume object name:

```
Map {option} drive: = Server_Volume: Directory\
subdirectory
```

The indicator used when mapping a drive using a physical volume name is the backslash (\). The indicator used when mapping a drive using a volume object name is the underscore (_). The MAP command has several options that you can use. One is the DEL option when you want to delete a drive mapping. Following is the correct syntax to delete a drive that has been mapped to the GENERAL directory, if the drive letter is S:

```
MAP DEL S:
```

You do not have to add the path when using the DEL option.

Answers A, B, and D are incorrect because they do not use the correct syntax for deleting a drive mapping.

Question 32

If you circled the Partition Disks option in the left navigation bar, the answer is correct. After you select Partition Disks, you select a device with Free Disk Space, and the Create link. You then have the option of creating either a Traditional volume and partition, or an NSS volume and pool.

Question 33

If you circled the Rights role in the left navigation bar, you are correct. When you expand the Rights role, select the View Effective Rights task, and then select Alexandra as the trustee and 3WsNetWorking as the object. You will then display Alexandra's effective rights to the Organization object.

Question 34

The correct answer is inheritance. Inheritance is the process of rights flowing down from a higher level to a lower level in both the eDirectory tree and the NetWare 6.5 file system.

Question 35

If you circled the TechEditors object in the right window, you are correct. The TechEditors object is an Organizational Role object. An Organizational Role object represents a group of users who have a common task. These are task-oriented objects whose members are defined as occupants. An Organizational Role object is represented in eDirectory by a person sitting at a desk.

Question 36

Answer D is correct. The path to the NetWare Administrator executable is SYS:\PUBLIC\WIN32\NWADMN32.EXE. Answers A, B, and C are not the correct path to the executable. NetWare Administrator is not the preferred eDirectory management utility, but it does come with NetWare 6.5.

Question 37

Answer C is correct. The path to the CONSOLEONE.EXE is SYS:\PUBLIC\MGMT\CONSOLEONE\1.2\BIN. Answers A, B, and D are incorrect. They do not represent the path to the CONSOLEONE.EXE executable on a NetWare 6.5 server.

Question 38

If you circled Open Source, you are correct. When you expand the Open Source link, you can select OpenSSH, OpenSSH Simple Administration, and the OpenSSH Manager will launch in your browser.

Question 39

The correct answer is SSHD.NLM or just SSHD. You can launch OpenSSH from a NetWare 6.5 server console by running either of these two LOAD statements. The .nlm extension is optional on a NetWare 6.5 server, but some admins prefer to include it in their statements. Both LOAD SSHD.NLM and LOAD SSHD would be correct on the CNA exam.

Question 40

If you circled RPM Configuration, you are correct. You can configure the automatic download of print drivers to a user's workstation at login using the RPM (Remote Printer Management) Configuration option under iPrint Management, found in iManager.

Question 41

Answer D is correct. The rule of thumb when planning a NetWare 6.5 file system is first and foremost to reserve volume SYS for the operating system files. Keep all volatile files, such as applications and data, on a separate volume. Answers A, B, and C are incorrect because they violate this guideline.

Question 42

Answer D is correct. Novell's iPrint requires that IPPSRVR.NLM be loaded on a NetWare server. The NDPS Manager, also called the Print Services Manager, automatically loads IPPSRVR.NLM when the first iPrint printer is configured. Answers A and C are incorrect. In NetWare 6.5, you must load and configure NDPS for iPrint to work. In addition, you must configure the NDPS Broker, Manager, and Agent for iPrint to work in NetWare 6.5. Answer B is incorrect. A print server is a queue-based printing entity. It is not part of the iPrint architecture.

Question 43

Answer C is correct. The AUTOEXEC.NCF NetWare configuration file typically contains most server environmental settings, including the server name,

SERVERID, time zone settings, LAN card `LOAD` and `BIND` statements, and `SEARCH ADD` settings. You can find it in the `SYS:\SYSTEM` directory. Answer A is incorrect. The `CONFIG.SYS` and `AUTOEXEC.BAT` files are DOS configuration files, which you can find at the root of the `C:\` drive. Answer B is incorrect. The `STARTUP.NCF` file is one of the first files called after `SERVER.EXE` launches. You can find it in the `C:\NWSERVER` directory and use it to load the necessary storage adapters, custom device modules, and namespace modules. Answer D is incorrect. You find many of the publicly available NetWare utilities in `SYS:\PUBLIC`.

Question 44

Answer B is correct. There are two categories of NDPS printers: Public Access and Controlled Access. Public Access printers are available to everyone on a network and have no eDirectory object. Answer A is incorrect. Controlled Access printers have an eDirectory object and provide full administrative control, including eDirectory security. Answers C and D are incorrect because both are synonymous with Novell's legacy queue-based printing architecture.

Question 45

Answer B is correct. The correct syntax to launch an ssh session on server 10.0.0.1, from server 10.0.0.10, is `ssh admin@10.0.0.1`. Answer C is incorrect. That is the syntax to launch an ssh session on server 10.0.0.10. Answer D is incorrect because incorrect syntax is used. Answer A is incorrect. `SSHD.NLM` loads OpenSSH on a NetWare 6.5 server.

Question 46

The correct answer is `http://10.0.0.125:631/IPPDOCS/Maptool.htm`.

Question 47

Answer A is correct. The NDPS Manager, also called the Print Services Manager, is an eDirectory object that manages printer agents. You can load only one NDPS Manager on a NetWare 6.5 server at a time. An NDPS Manager theoretically can manage an unlimited number of agents. Answers

B, C, and D are incorrect because they do not reflect the correct number of NDPS Managers that can be loaded on a NetWare 6.5 server at any one time.

Question 48

The correct answer is `http://10.0.0.125/vo`. This URL launches the Virtual Office authentication page.

Question 49

Answers B, C, and D are correct. `NAAS`, `HOL`, and `BindView Solutions` are three time-tested tools for monitoring and tracking security breaches. Answer A is incorrect. `SETPASS.NLM` and `BURGLAR.NLM` are two server-based tools that can be used to hack a NetWare 6.5 environment.

Question 50

Answers B, C, and D are correct. If you want to have access to eGuide, iPrint, and NetStorage from Virtual Office, you need to install them either before or when you install Virtual Office on your server. Answer A is incorrect. iSCSI is a NetWare 6.5 fault-tolerance technology. It is not available from Virtual Office.

Question 51

Answers B and D are correct. To protect your NetWare 6.5 environment, it is good practice to do the following:

➤ Rename the Admin object.

➤ Create multiple backup admin objects that have the same trustee assignments as the original Admin object.

Answer A is incorrect. Creating an Everyone group is a good management option if you do not want to manage users through Container administration. The Everyone group is a throwback to the NetWare 3 days of administration. Answer C is incorrect. It is a bad idea to delete the Admin object if you have not created a user(s) with rights that mirror the Admin object. You can potentially lose control of the tree. Answer E is incorrect. Creating a Local Administrator's group is not something you would do in a NetWare environment. The Local Administrator's group is a Windows NT/2000/XP/2003 entity. The NetWare object that functions similarly to a Local Administrator's group is the Organizational Role object.

Question 52

Answers C, D, E, and G are correct. APACHE, TOMCAT, PERL, PHP, and MySQL make up the Open Source Services feature set in NetWare 6.5. Answers A, B, and F are incorrect. NCS, NFAP, and iFolder are not considered part of the Open Source Services feature set.

Question 53

Answer D is correct. An application proxy is a proxy server that is protocol specific. For example, a Simple Mail Transfer Protocol (SMTP) proxy server only accepts SMTP packets and either transports them or drops them based on the rules that are configured. This is also called an application gateway, or application-level proxy. Answer A is incorrect. A packet-filtering firewall permits or denies access to packets based on the rules configured. Packets can be filtered based on source or destination IP address, port number, service type, or interface. Answer B is incorrect. Network Address Translation (NAT) is a gateway found at the network layer of the Open System Interconnection (OSI) model. NAT is primarily used to translate a private IP address to an IP address that is suitable for the Internet—the public network. Private IP addresses are IP addresses that are used primarily for private networks, or intranets. A NAT server provides a gateway to the public network for those on a private network and vice versa. Answer C is incorrect. A circuit-level gateway is similar to a NAT server, in that it translates private addresses to one or more pubic addresses. Circuit-level gateways function at the session layer of the OSI model. The circuit-level gateway does not care about upper-level issues. It is concerned only with source and destination addresses.

Question 54

Answer A is correct. The Hot Fix Redirection Area automatically stores data in a safe area on a drive in case one or more blocks becomes corrupt. The data is moved from the bad block to the Hot Fix area. A Hot Fix Area is defined automatically and is by default 2% of the available disk space. Answers B and C are not correct. An NSS storage pool is free space that is gathered from the storage devices in your NetWare 6.5 server. Overbooking is the NSS feature that allows the sum of the volume sizes to be larger than the defined size of the partition they are in. Answer D is incorrect. File Versioning lets users restore earlier versions of their files without having to call you or one of your help desk technicians.

Question 55

Answers A and B are correct. On your Virtual Team page, you can do the following:

➤ Show Team Calendar

➤ Show Team Web Page

➤ Show Team Members

➤ Invite a User

➤ Approve a Request

➤ Show Team Owners

➤ Show Blocked Users

➤ Show Team Properties

➤ Set Notify Preferences (includes preferences for new discussion posts, created events, and uploaded files)

➤ Delete This Team

➤ Display your Virtual Teams and a Virtual Team Inbox, managing your Teams' membership

Answers C and D are incorrect. These are configuration options that are performed using the Virtual Office links available in iManager.

Question 56

Answer A is correct. There are four login scripts in NetWare 6.5, and they execute in the following order: Container, Profile, User, and Default. The Profile script is used specifically for a group of individuals who have common needs. A user can only be assigned one Profile login script. Answers B, C, and D are incorrect because they do not reflect the correct number of Profile login scripts that a user can have.

Question 57

Answer C is correct. There are four login scripts in NetWare 6.5, and they execute in the following order: Container, Profile, User, and Default. If a user script exists, the default script will not execute. If a user script does not exist, the default script will execute unless the NO_DEFAULT statement is present in either the Container script or the Profile script. Answers A, B, and D are incorrect because they do not correctly identify the NO_DEFAULT statement.

Question 58

Answer D is correct. You have to configure a DNS "A" record for each server on which you want to load NDPSM.NLM. This allows clients to access your iPrint printers using common names in a Web browser. Configure this before you enable support for iPrint printers. After you have configured the DNS record, you can load NDPSM.NLM with the /dnsname option. Use this syntax:

```
LOAD NDPSM <Manager's_eDirectory_ Distinguished_Name>
/dnsname=Manager's_DNS_Name
```

Following is an example of this:

```
LOAD NDPSM .3WSMANAGER.3WSCERTIFICATION /dnsname=
3WSMANAGER.MAIL.3WSCERTIFICATION.COM
```

Answers A, B, and C are incorrect because they do not correctly identify the /dnsname option.

Question 59

Answer A is correct. An NDPS Broker provides three services: SRS, RMS, and ENS. The ENS (Event Notification Services) enables printers to send users and operators messages about printer events. The RMS (Resource Management Services) enables resources to be centrally located. Those resources, such as printer drivers, can be accessed, downloaded, and installed easily. The SRS (Service Registry Services) allows users to advertise and discover public-access printers. Answers B, C, and D are incorrect. The

Manager is the overseer of the printer agents. A printer agent represents a printer on a one-to-one basis. The Gateway provides access to printers that are not NDPS enabled, and provides backward compatibility with queue-based printers.

Question 60

Answers B and D are correct. Public Access printers are available to everyone on a network, they have no eDirectory object, and everyone on the network can print to one as soon as it is configured. Answers A and C are incorrect because they are characteristics of Controlled Access printers.

Glossary

/508

If your users have special accessibility requirements, you need to install the Novell Client on their computers so that the special accessibility settings are available. You accomplish this by appending the /508 option to the installation executable. The /508 option is based on Section 508 of the U.S. Federal Government Rehabilitation Act.

_ADMIN

When you create a storage group and NSS volume, the _ADMIN volume is created automatically. It is a read-only volume that holds a dynamic list of objects that NSS uses. At the server console, when you display the mounted volumes, you will see that the _ADMIN volume has the P attribute, which indicates that the volume cannot be deleted. In NetWare 6.5, `files.cmd` was added to the _ADMIN volume for applications such as NetStorage, which uses it to communicate with the server. Unlike past versions of NetWare, the _ADMIN volume is visible to users.

access control list

See ACL.

ACL

The ACL, or access control list, is a property of every file, directory, and eDirectory object. Objects that are added to an ACL are granted explicit rights to that file, directory, or eDirectory at that point in the hierarchy.

adaptive test

An adaptive exam is a condensed, efficient testing format in which you are presented with 15–25 questions in 30–45 minutes. The questions are presented to you based on a complex testing algorithm.

Admin object

When you install a NetWare server into a new eDirectory tree, you create a single user object called Admin. Admin is the only user object that is created in the new tree. Admin initially has all rights to manage all aspects of an eDirectory tree, including the ability to create, delete, and modify objects. You can delete Admin from the tree or rename it. Admin can lose its supervisor rights to both the Tree and Server objects.

All Property Rights

This is an eDirectory Property option that simultaneously distributes a Property Rights assignment to all object properties.

application proxy

This is a proxy server that is protocol specific. For example, an SMTP proxy server accepts only SMTP packets. It either transports them or drops them based on the rules that are configured. This is also called an application gateway or application-level proxy.

APPS

APPS is a recommended volume or directory for storing a network's available applications.

Attribute Rights

See Property Rights.

attribute types

The four most commonly used object attribute types in NetWare 6.5 eDirectory are C–Country, CN–Common Name (Leaf object), O–Organization, and OU–Organizational Unit.

AUTOEXEC.BAT

The AUTOEXEC.BAT file is a text file that, when it exists, launches configuration and initialization commands, in addition to a variety of application commands. By default, you can find AUTOEXEC.BAT at the root of the C: drive.

Bindery

Bindery is a flat-file database that is stored on each server and authenticates user accounts. It was the primary means of authentication on NetWare networks before NetWare 4. Using a bindery, users must log in to each server that they want to access.

BURGLAR.NLM

This is a hacker's tool, available on the Internet, for creating a rogue admin on a server. If you forget your admin password or someone changes it on you, you can use this tool to access the tree.

Caching server

This is a feature of some firewall packages, such as Novell BorderManager. A Caching server, also called a Web caching server, locally stores frequently contacted

URLs so that client access time to Internet data is shortened. You can retrieve frequently accessed data from the server's cache, as opposed to having to go to the Internet source and download it each time you need it.

CDE

The CDE, or Certified Directory Engineer, is one of the newest Novell certifications. It is designed for advanced support persons who need to know how to integrate and troubleshoot directory service issues. The focus of this certification is the power of directory services, regardless of the parent platform: NetWare, Unix, or Windows 2000 Server. As of June 2004, Novell is still recognizing the CDE, but it is no longer offering admission to new candidates.

Circuit-level gateway

A Circuit-level gateway is similar to a NAT server, in that it translates private addresses to one or more pubic addresses. It functions at the session layer of the OSI model. A Circuit-level gateway does not care about upper-level issues; it is concerned only with source and destination addresses.

CLE

This is one of the newest certification offerings for Novell. At the time this is being written, the Certified Linux Engineer (CLE) program is in its early beginnings.

The CLE is an advanced certification that is geared toward Linux administrators who incorporate Novell Nterprise Linux Services and eDirectory into their network environment. The CLE has no written (cognitive) exams. The only exam that a candidate must pass is a practicum (050-685), which is similar in nature to the practicum offered for the CDE.

Client Protocol Options

The Novell Client Protocol options include IP Only, IPX Only, IP and IPX, and IP with IPX Compatibility Mode.

CLP

This is the latest Novell certification offering. It it geared toward Linux administrators. Skills that are targeted include creating and managing users and groups, and installing, managing, administering and troubleshooting a SuSE Linux server, Linux kernel, and associated network processes and services. The only test that a candidate must pass to earn the CLP is the practicum (050-689).

CNA

The CNA, or Certified Novell Administrator, is the entry-level Novell certification. The CNA is designed for those who are setting up workstations, managing users and groups, administering a printing environment, and automating network access. It is a one-test, one-course certification.

CNE

The CNE, or Certified Novell Engineer, is one of Novell's premier certifications. Depending on the CNE track that you pursue, you will take either five or seven exams. The CNE is designed for networking professionals who are responsible for keeping their networks up and running. These are the folks who are charged with designing a TCP/IP internetwork and designing a directory services implementation.

CNI

The Novell CNI, or Certified Novell Instructor, certification is one of the elite technical instructor certifications that is recognized worldwide. There is no formal CNI exam, but CNIs are required to hold a current Novell CNE, such as a CNE 6, and pass all exams at a higher level than is required of CNEs, CNAs, or MCNEs.

CONFIG.SYS

CONFIG.SYS is a text file that contains system configuration instructions. One of the main commands used is device, which loads device drivers, such as the CD/DVD driver. By default, CONFIG.SYS is found at the root of the C: drive.

ConsoleOne

ConsoleOne is a Java-based eDirectory management utility for managing large eDirectory trees; creating, deleting, moving, and renaming objects; extending the schema; configuring partitions and replicas; managing the file system; and assigning rights.

Container

Container objects are one of the three major types of eDirectory objects. A Container object is a holder of other eDirectory objects. In a sense, a Container logically groups eDirectory objects. Examples of Container objects are the Country object, the Organization object, the Organizational Unit object, the Domain object, the Security container, and the License container.

Container login script

This is the first script that runs for a user. It is a property of the container object. Only users in the container are impacted by a container script. Users in subcontainers are not impacted by a container script that is not immediately configured for their container. A container script is the easiest way to simultaneously establish an environment for the maximum number of users.

Context

An object's context is where the object is located in the eDirectory tree. Context is the full path to an object in eDirectory.

Controlled Access Printer

A Controlled Access printer is a type of NDPS printer that has an eDirectory object and provides full administrative control, including eDirectory security.

Current context

A workstation's current context is where the workstation is configured to look for objects in the eDirectory. This is called the name context in some utilities. Current context reflects your current position at your workstation in the eDirectory tree.

Custom Installation

This is a method of installing the Novell Client that gives the installer full latitude in selecting the installed components.

CX

CX is a NetWare command-line utility that allows you to view or change your current context.

DATA

DATA is a recommended volume or directory for storing users' private data.

Default login script

This script is hard-coded into LOGIN.EXE and creates a basic network environment by establishing a search drive mapping to the PUBLIC directory and a first network drive mapping. You cannot edit this script. If you have a user script configured, the default script does not run. If you do not have a user script configured, this script runs automatically and overwrites any similar drive pointers. You can avoid this by having a NO_DEFAULT statement in either the container or profile script.

Deployment Manager

Deployment Manager is a set of tools that enable you to prepare your existing network for a NetWare 6.5 server, upgrade to NetWare 6.5, automate an installation, prepare for a variety of NetWare 6.5 components, consolidate servers, migrate to new hardware, create additional volumes, install NetWare 6.5 products, and install a cluster.

directory

A directory in the file system is a container for subdirectories and files. It exists on a volume.

Distinguished Name

A Distinguished Name is a combination of an object's common name and its context, beginning with the object and progressing up to but not including the Tree object. You can easily identify a Distinguished Name because it has a leading period, its contextual elements are separated by periods, and it does not have trailing periods.

DOS

NetWare relies on DOS to boot the computer. Therefore, a DOS partition is required on a NetWare 6.5 server.

DOS partition

This is a partition that NetWare uses to boot the server. The minimum size for the DOS partition on a NetWare 6.5 server is 500 MB.

Drag-and-drop question

Matching or drag-and-drop questions are graphical questions in which you click and drag a term to its associated definition. Sometimes these questions require you to reorder a series of steps to accomplish a task.

duplexing

In a duplex configuration, you have identical data being written to two drives that are on separate channels. Each channel has its own storage controller and cable. The downside to a duplex configuration is that you only have access to 50% of the overall installed storage capacity.

eDirectory

This is the latest iteration of Novell Directory Services. eDirectory can run on a multitude of platforms, including Linux and Windows 2003 Server, and it is LDAP-enabled. One of the major benefits of eDirectory is that it is scalable and has an extensible schema. Some Novell documents call eDirectory the most fundamental service that NetWare offers. It keeps track of all network resources through a hierarchical, relational database that is distributed and loosely consistent. eDirectory can be partitioned and replicated.

eDirectory Administration

One of the links on the opening iManager screen that you can use to begin the process of creating a user object is eDirectory Administration. You can use the Create Object link found under eDirectory Administration to create, delete, modify, or move most eDirectory objects, including user objects.

Effective rights

This is what a user or group can do at any given level of the file system or eDirectory tree, after any IRFs.

eGuide

eGuide is a Web-based address book, enabling users to find the names, addresses, and phone numbers that are stored in eDirectory.

ENS

The ENS (Event Notification Services) enables printers to send users and operators messages about printer events. It is a service of the NDPS Broker.

Entry Rights

See Object Rights.

explicit assignment

An explicit assignment is one in which a User, Group, Organizational Role object, Container, or [Public] trustee is added to the ACL of a file, directory, or eDirectory object and granted explicit rights at that point in either the file system tree or the eDirectory tree.

FDISK

FDISK is a DOS partition utility that allows you to create, delete, view, and activate your partitions.

File Versioning

File Versioning permits users to restore earlier versions of their files without having to call you or one of your help desk technicians.

Filer

This is a powerful workstation-based, menu-driven utility for managing the NetWare 6.5 file system, rights, and attributes.

Fill-in-the-blank question

Fill-in-the-blank questions require you to provide a missing term, command, word, phrase, or path that completes a statement.

firewall

A firewall is software/hardware technology that protects a network from outside attacks.

Flag

This is a workstation-based executable that is run from a command prompt and displays or modifies a directory or file's attributes.

form exam

A form exam is a traditional exam in which you are presented with 60–70 questions in a defined period of time.

FORMAT

FORMAT is a DOS utility that prepares the File Allocation Table on the DOS partition. With the /s option, FORMAT makes the partition bootable.

GUID

The Global User ID (GUID) is the number that is assigned to the user object upon creation. It is associated with the rights and memberships that you have assigned to the user. The GUID is deleted when you delete a user object, thereby obliterating any rights or memberships that were assigned previously.

Hidden Object Locator

This is a tool available from Novell to help locate hidden objects in the tree. Hidden users can be a major security issue in some environments.

Hot Fix Redirection Area

By default, this is 2% of the available disk space on a volume. The Hot Fix Redirection Area automatically stores data in a safe area on a drive in case one or more blocks becomes corrupt. The data is moved from the bad block to the Hot Fix area.

hot spot question

Hot spot or identification questions ask you to click on an interface option to perform a task.

iFolder

iFolder lets users have secure access to their files from home, the office, or while on the road. Without copying files back and forth to a floppy disk, users can access the latest version of their data when and where they need it with an Internet connection and a browser that is Java enabled.

iFolder Management Console

This is a browser-based tool for configuring iFolder. The generic URL for this is `https://server_ip_address/iFolderServer/Admin`. Note the capitalization in this address. It is case sensitive.

iManager

iManager is a browser-based management tool that is the tool of choice for most eDirectory tasks. The opening iManager screen shows the wide range of tasks that you can perform. These include managing DNS, DHCP, iPrint, eDirectory, roles and tasks, role-based service configuration, NSS storage devices, licenses, NMAS, rights, users, and Virtual Office.

iMonitor

iMonitor is one of the Web Services tools that ships with NetWare 6.5. You can monitor and diagnose servers in your eDirectory tree from any computer that has a compatible browser installed. Traditional NetWare diagnostic tools such as DSTRACE, DSBROWSE, DSDIAG, and DSREPAIR are incorporated into iMonitor. You can still use many of these server-based tools, although much of their functionality is now built into the workstation-based iMonitor. You can access iMonitor via `https://server_ip_address:8009/nds` or `http://server_ip_address:8008/nds`.

inheritance

Inheritance is the process of rights flowing down from a higher level to a lower level in both the eDirectory tree and the NetWare 6.5 file system.

inherited assignment

This is a rights assignment that has been granted explicitly higher access in the tree and migrated down through any intervening IRFs to your current location. If you have been granted an explicit file system assignment at a parent directory, you will have that assignment minus any rights that are filtered by intervening IRFs at lower levels in the file system. Your rights at those lower levels are inherited assignments.

IPP

iPrint uses the IPP (Internet Printing Protocol) to enable secure, Web-based printer access from anywhere in the world. Novell's implementation of iPrint is based on NDPS and its printing infrastructure. IPP is a simple, TCP/IP-based printing protocol that has been accepted as an industry standard. IPP has broad support from vendors, works over LANs and WANs, supports encryption of data, and can be used on multiple platforms, including Unix, Linux, Macintosh, and Windows.

iPrint

iPrint is Novell's anytime, anywhere printing solution based on NDPS and the IPP protocol. Users can print from their home to their office printer by using a Web browser interface.

iPrint has reduced costs, customized printer views, and unified management. For iPrint to work, you must have NDPS loaded and configured. You must configure the NDPS Broker, Manager, and Agent. Novell iPrint also requires that IPPSRVR.NLM be loaded on a NetWare server. This occurs automatically when you configure the first iPrint printer. You must also install several browser plug-ins on the Windows workstation for Novell's implementation of iPrint. You can install an optional iPrint client on a Windows workstation, but that is not required.

IRF

An inherited rights filter, or IRF, is a method of globally blocking the inheritance of rights. IRFs block rights in both file system security and eDirectory security.

iSCSI

Internet Small Computer Systems Interface (iSCSI) support provides an economically affordable Storage Area Network (SAN) using an existing Ethernet infrastructure.

leading period

A leading period is the defining indicator that an eDirectory name is a Distinguished Name.

Leaf

Leaf objects are one of the three major types of eDirectory objects. Network resources are represented in the eDirectory tree by Leaf objects. Examples of Leaf objects are the User object, the Group object, the Server object, the Volume object, the Printer object, and the Organizational Role object.

Logical volume

A Logical volume is similar to a Traditional volume in that it can store data in directories and subdirectories. However, it is different because an NSS volume can have a defined amount of space allocated to it or be allowed to grow dynamically as the need arises.

Login Authenticator

The Login Authenticator window in a Novell Client installation allows an installer to choose between NDS and Bindery as the chosen authentication method.

LOGIN directory

LOGIN is the only directory that a user can see before authenticating to the tree. This directory contains the various iterations of LOGIN.EXE and CX.EXE for changing your current context.

map

After logging into your server, when you enter the map command at a workstation command prompt, the current drive mappings are displayed. The regular or network drive mappings are at the top of the list, and the search drive mappings are at the bottom of the list. A drive mapping is simply a volatile pointer to a place in the NetWare File System. It is volatile because it exists in workstation memory as a function of the Novell Client, and it can be reassigned or lost easily when a user exits the network.

MCNE

The MCNE, or Master Certified Novell Engineer, is designed for those individuals who are responsible for integrating eDirectory and Novell Directory Services (NDS) with the platforms of other vendors. The MCNE is first and foremost an integration specialist. MCNEs are one of the most respected certified professionals involved in network management, infrastructure, and design.

mirroring

In a mirror, you have identical data being written to two drives on the same channel. If one of the drives fails, the other drive automatically takes over. The downside to a mirror configuration is that you only have access to 50% of the overall installed storage capacity.

mutiple-choice question

Multiple-choice questions have a short question or scenario and four or more response options. Multiple-choice questions come in two formats. Either the question has one correct response, which is represented by a radio button, or several correct responses, which are represented by square check boxes.

NAAS

Novell Advanced Audit Service (NAAS) is a feature of NetWare 6.5 that allows you to monitor users through eDirectory policies.

NAT

Network Address Translation (NAT) is a gateway found at the network layer of the OSI model. NAT is used primarily to translate a private IP address to an IP address that is suitable for the Internet—the public network. Private IP addresses are IP addresses that are used primarily for private networks, or intranets. A NAT server provides a gateway to the public network for those who are on a private network, and vice versa.

A NetWare 6.5 server that is configured with NAT has two interfaces: one on the private network and one on the public network. Those on the private network who want to access the public network send data through the NAT server. The NAT server routes that information through the public interface, translating the private IP address to its public IP address. The only IP address that is visible on the public network is the public IP address on the NAT server. You cannot directly access other nodes on the private network. Data that you send from the public network to the private network is translated and routed back through the NAT server.

Native File Access Protocol

Native File Access Protocol in NetWare 6.5 supports several file protocols that are native to Macs, Unix, Linux, and Windows. Clients no longer need to have the Novell Client installed to access data that is stored on a NetWare 6.5 server.

NCS

Novell Cluster Services (NCS) has been enhanced from its origin in NetWare 6.0. NCS 1.7 is a server clustering system that provides fail-back, failover, and load balancing for mission-critical environments.

NDIR

This is one of the most overlooked workstation-based executables, run from a command prompt, that displays information on files, directories, or volumes. You can display rights, attributes, IRFs, last time accessed, last time modified, and much more.

NDPS

Novell Distributed Print Services (NDPS) is a printer-based environment. Users submit jobs, not to a queue, but directly to a printer. NDPS is backward compatible to queue-based printing. Novell has combined the functionality of the printer, print queue, and print server from queue-based printing into one software entity known as a printer agent.

NDPS Manager

The NDPS Manager is an eDirectory object that manages printer agents. You can load one NDPS Manager on a NetWare 6.5 server. An NDPS Manager theoretically can manage an unlimited number of agents. The NDPS Manager NLM is NDPSM.NLM.

NDS

Novell Directory Services (NDS), the initial offering for Novell in the world of directory services, was initially released with NetWare 4. NDS is a directory naming service. It keeps track of all network resources through a hierarchical, relational database that is distributed and loosely consistent. With NDS, users no longer log in to a server, but to a tree.

NET.CFG

NET.CFG is a text file that contains configuration parameters and commands that govern how the client will interact with a NetWare server. Some of the major sections of the NET.CFG file are LINK DRIVER, LINK SUPPORT, PROTOCOL, and NETWARE DOS REQUESTOR, which configures the preferred server, preferred tree, first network drive, name context, cache size, and cache level. You can also have a Message Timeout parameter in case an errant message appears during the installation.

NetAdmin

This is a legacy NDS (Novell Directory Services) utility that you can use in NetWare 6.5 to manage eDirectory objects, rights, and IRFs.

NetStorage

NetStorage provides users with secure access to files with nothing to install or download as long as the user has an Internet connection. Users can access data with a browser or Microsoft Web Folders.

NetWare Administrator

NetWare Administrator is a Windows-based eDirectory management utility for creating, deleting, moving, and renaming objects. In NetWare 6.5, it is also valuable for configuring printing and licensing. Finally, you can use NetWare Administrator to manage the NetWare 6.5 file system.

NICI Client

NICI (Novell International Cryptographic Infrastructure) Client, which is selected by default, is one of the additional client options available when you install the Novell Client.

NLM

A NetWare Loadable Module can be loaded on a NetWare server and provide additional functionality to the core operating system.

NMAS

The NMAS (Novell Modular Authentication Service) tab in the Novell Client Login screen is where you select the appropriate login sequence that you will use for authentication.

Novell Client

The Novell Client is a software component that works with a workstation operating system platform to provide access to NetWare resources and services, enforce security, and manage communications between NetWare servers and workstations.

NSS

The NSS (Novell Storage Services) file system is Novell's answer to the current need for storing large databases, numerous files, or huge volumes, and being able to mount them quickly. NSS is a 64-bit file storage technology. An NSS volume has a maximum size of 8 TB and can store up to 8 trillion files. A NetWare 6.5 server can have a maximum of 255 NSS and traditional volumes, in addition to the SYS volume, mounted at the same time. If all volumes are NSS, you can mount an unlimited number of NSS volumes on a NetWare 6.5 server.

NWSERVER

NWSERVER is the DOS directory, found by default at the root of the C: drive where the SERVER.EXE executable launches the NetWare 6.5 operating system kernel.

object

An object is a fundamental component of eDirectory that contains information about a network resource. If you compare a traditional database or spreadsheet to eDirectory, a record in a database, or a row in a spreadsheet, is comparable to an object in eDirectory.

Object Rights

These are eDirectory rights that control what a user can do with an eDirectory object and whether he can access an object. These are called Entry Rights in some utilities. The eDirectory Object Rights are Supervisor, Browse, Create, Delete, Rename, and Inheritable.

Open Source Services

Open source implies that the source code for operating systems and associated applications is freely distributable. It is not proprietary. The five major open source services/applications that Novell ships with NetWare 6.5 are Apache, MySQL, Perl, PHP, and Tomcat.

OpenSSH

OpenSSH is an open source technology that enables you to securely access services on a NetWare 6.5 server. OpenSSH comes with ssh, sftp, and scp. These respectively replace Telnet and rlogin, FTP, and rcp.

Overbooking

Overbooking is the NSS feature that allows the sum of the volume sizes to be larger than the defined size of the partition they are in.

Packet Filtering firewall

This is a type of firewall that permits or denies access to packets based on the rules that are configured. Packets can be filtered based on source or destination IP address, port number, service type, or interface. This is a network layer firewall technology.

partition

A partition is part of a hard drive that is configured for a single operating system. When you are using NetWare volumes, you create a NetWare partition before creating a Traditional volume or an NSS pool and then one or more logical volumes. A partition is also an eDirectory term.

Passphrase

This is an iFolder option that you can use to encrypt your data on the iFolder server or when it is transmitted to your workstation. This option ensures that your data is secure and private.

Pattern Deployment

NetWare 6.5 lets you decide what type of server you want to install by providing patterns that contain a preconfigured list of components to be installed. This is the first graphical installation screen you see during the installation process. Some of the available patterns include Customized NetWare Server, Basic NetWare File Server, and Premigration Server.

pool

A pool is the space that you obtain from one or more storage devices on a server. You create a storage pool after you create a partition and before you create a volume.

practicum exam

A practicum exam has a task-oriented exam format. You are connected, across the Internet, to a bank of servers at Novell headquarters, where you have to perform a series of tasks, including installing and troubleshooting products.

Printer Agent

The Printer Agent is an NDPS component that represents each printer on a one-to-one basis. It can either be software running on a server that represents a network-attached printer or a server-attached printer, or it can represent an NDPS-capable printer that is physically attached to the network.

Printer Broker

An NDPS Broker provides three services: SRS, RMS, and ENS. By default, a Broker is installed on a network every three hops. The NLM that loads the Broker on a NetWare 6.5 server is BROKER.NLM.

Printer Gateway

A Printer Gateway provides a means to use NDPS printing with printers that are not NDPS compliant. Gateways also enable printing to queue-based printers.

profile login script

This script runs after a container script if it is configured and associated with a user. A profile script is generally used for groups of users who are in different containers. You can employ it for users who are in the same container and have similar job functions. The profile script is a property of a profile object.

property

An object has properties. Properties are fundamental components of eDirectory. A property is an attribute of an object. If you compare a traditional database, or spreadsheet, to eDirectory, an object's property is a field in a database or a column in a spreadsheet. Some properties are required, depending on the object, whereas others are optional. Likewise, some properties are single-valued, whereas others are multivalued.

Property Rights

These are eDirectory rights that control what users can do with an object's attribute values. The Property Rights are Supervisor, Read, Compare, Write, Add-Self, and Inheritable. These are the same as Attribute Rights. Some utilities use the term Property Rights, whereas others use the term Attribute Rights.

Public Access Printer

A Public Access printer is a type of NDPS printer that is available to everyone on a network, has no eDirectory object, has low security, and provides true plug-and-print capabilities.

PUBLIC directory

PUBLIC is an important directory for all Novell users. It contains a host of NetWare utilities that users and administrators rely on. You can find utilities such as MAP.EXE, NDIR.EXE, FLAG.EXE, FILER.EXE, CON-SOLEONE.EXE, and NETWARE ADMINISTRA-TOR in the PUBLIC directory.

regular drive mapping

Regular or network drive mappings traditionally are pointers to data.

Relative Distinguished Name

A Relative Distinguished Name is an object's common name relative to a workstation's current context. A Relative Distinguished Name never has a leading period, but it might have a trailing period. In addition, a Relative Distinguished Name's contextual elements are separated by periods. You can use a trailing period as a shortcut to remove the leftmost such contextual element as it exists in the current context. If more than one trailing period is used, you can remove more than one contextual element.

REM

A REM statement does not execute in a login script. It is simply a means of providing documentation in a script. You can include REM statements in a NetWare login script in four ways: Remark, Rem, ;, or *.

Remote Manager

Remote Manager is a browser-based server management tool. You can monitor your server's health, monitor and mount volumes, run server console commands, load and unload NLMs, partition disks, assign file system rights, create and remove directories and subdirectories, down and restart a server, manage the server's storage and LAN adapters, and access NDS iMonitor and DS Trace.

Rights command

This is a workstation-based executable that is run from a command prompt and displays your current rights to a file or directory or those objects that are on the ACL for a file or directory.

RMS

The RMS (Resource Management Services) enables you to centrally locate resources. You can easily access, download, and install those resources, such as printer drivers.

RPM Configuration

In iManager, you can configure the automatic download of print drivers to a user's workstation at login using the RPM (Remote Printer Management) Configuration option under iPrint.

SAN

Storage Area Network (SAN) provides access to shared storage devices over a high-speed network or a fibre-channel subnetwork.

schema

The eDirectory schema is the rule of object creation and placement. The schema dictates which properties you must assign values when an object is created, and which properties are optional. The schema is composed of two sets of definitions: an object class that defines which objects can be created in a directory and which attributes or properties are associated with each object type, and an attribute definition that defines the structure, syntax, and limitations of an attribute. The schema in NetWare 6.5 is extensible, which means that you can introduce new objects and properties into the schema to accommodate other network services and resources. An example of this is the installation of ZENworks, or GroupWise, which extends the schema and introduces a host of new objects to the base schema that ships with NetWare 6.5.

SCRSAVER.NLM

This is a server-based NLM that locks the server console and displays itself as a moving worm for every installed processor. In earlier versions of NetWare, SCRSAVER.NLM was lauched automatically when a server was idle for a brief period of time. Since NetWare 5, you must launch the screen saver manually by using this NLM and any number of associated options. You can load the screen saver by entering LOAD SCRSAVER at a NetWare 6.5 server console prompt.

Search drive mapping

Search drive mappings are traditionally pointers to applications and executables that are inserted or appended to the workstation's path statement.

Security policy

This is a corporate document detailing your practices and procedures for implementing a secure overall environment for your employees and infrastructure. This document addresses in detail your proactive and reactive measures for dealing with network security and security breaches.

Selected Property Rights

This is an eDirectory Property option that allows you to grant individual property rights to an eDirectory object. A Selected Property Rights assignment overrides an assignment that is made with the All Property Rights option.

server console prompt

At the server console prompt, you can run commands; perform a variety of management tasks; load and unload NetWare Loadable Modules (NLMs), which provide a server with added functionality above and beyond what is available in the kernel; reset or restart and down a server; and configure the server environment using SET commands. The server console prompt is similar to a DOS command prompt.

SERVER.EXE

SERVER.EXE is the executable that launches the NetWare 6.5 server operating system. Found in the c:\NWSERVER directory, SERVER.EXE launches the operating system kernel.

SRS

The SRS (Service Registry Services) enables users to advertise and discover public-access printers.

Startx

This is a server console command that launches the NetWare 6.5 graphical interface.

SYS

SYS is the first volume created on a NetWare 6.5 server. It is the only volume that is required on a NetWare server. It should be used only for operating system and non-volatile administrative applications and utilities.

SYSTEM directory

The SYSTEM directory contains most of the NLMs that control the NetWare 6.5 operating system, including utilities and administrative applications. This should be a directory that is available only to admins and the operating system. It should not be publically available.

Template object

A Template is an eDirectory object that enables you to assign similar property values to multiple users. For example, if you have 50 users being hired for the science department, all having the same phone and fax numbers, you can create a Template object called Science, fill in the Department, Telephone, and Fax Number fields, and then assign the template to each user by checking the Copy from Template or User Object box in the Create User screen. All users that you create then have those property values upon creation.

Traditional volume

A Traditional volume is the default unit of storage on NetWare servers prior to NetWare 6.x. A Traditional volume was a unit of storage that could exist on a single storage device, be spanned over multiple storage devices, or exist with other volumes on a single storage device. It has been replaced as the default unit of storage in NetWare 6.x by the NSS volume, pools, and partitions.

trailing period

A trailing period is one of the defining indicators that an eDirectory name is a Relative Distinguished Name. The other indicator of a Relative Distinguished Name is the lack of a leading period.

Tree object

The Tree object is the top of the eDirectory tree. In some management utilities, the Tree object is called the [Root] of the tree. eDirectory can have only one Tree object.

Trustee

This is a User, Group, Organizational Role object, Container, or [Public] trustee that is explicitly granted rights to a directory or file by being added to the directory or file's ACL.

typeful

Both Distinguished Names and Relative Distinguished Names might or might not use object attribute types (abbreviations). If they use object attribute types, they are said to be typeful.

typeless

Both Distinguished Names and Relative Distinguished Names might or might not use object attribute types (abbreviations). If they do not use object attribute types, they are said to be typeless.

Typical Installation

Typical Installation is a method of installing the Novell Client that automatically installs the Novell Client for Windows, Novell Distributed Print Services, Novell Workstation Manager, and ZENworks Application Launcher components.

Universal Password

This is a NetWare 6.5 feature that enables you to integrate and manage different types of passwords and systems of authentication into a single common or Universal Password. This feature is not turned on by default. Its benefit comes into play when you have users who must log in to systems using different authentication mechanisms, or when you are using Native File Access in a NetWare 6.5 environment. Instead of having to remember multiple passwords, the user can authenticate to all systems with a single password.

user login script

This is a script that establishes an environment for a single user. The user login script is a property of the user object. If a user has a user script configured for him, this script runs after the container and profile scripts. If a user script exists, the default login script does not run.

Users

One of the links on the opening iManager screen that you can use to begin the process of creating a user object is Users. You can use the Create User link found under Users only to create user objects. This capability is different from the Create Object link under eDirectory Administration in iManager.

value

The data that you assign to an object's property is a value. If you compare a spreadsheet to eDirectory, a property value is similar to a cell in a spreadsheet.

Virtual Office

Virtual Office is a collaboration and information sharing tool for remote users who work as part of a virtual team. Virtual Office allows users to communicate in real time, publish a personal Web page, back up information, manage passwords, access a team calendar and contact list, and access stored files through NetStorage.

Virtual Teams

Virtual Teams lets users create a team for real-time collaboration purposes.

volume

A volume is the fundamental unit of storage on a NetWare server.

VPN

A virtual private network (VPN) is a private network that uses the public network infrastructure for secure communication.

Workstation Manager

This is a Novell Client component that is automatically selected in a Typical install and must be installed if you are using ZENworks for Desktop Remote Management.

ZENworks for Desktops

ZENworks for Desktops is a Novell product that enables a NetWare 6.5 administrator to deploy Client Properties to numerous users in an efficient way.

NetWare 6.5 Port Reference

Many of the NetWare 6.5 applications are managed through a Web browser. A CNA who wants to locate the correct application must know which port is associated with the application by default.

Table A.1 lists many common NetWare 6.5 applications, their default port assignments, and whether the assignment is configurable.

The term "Dependent" indicates that the application depends on a subsystem, which uses the port number. The term "Unknown" indicates that it is not currently known whether the port number can be configured.

Table A.1 Common NetWare 6.5 Applications, Port Numbers, and Configurability		
NetWare 6.5 Application	Port Numbers	Configurable?
AFP	548	No
Apache	80	Yes
	443	Yes
Border Manager	21	No
	119	No
	443	Yes
	1040	No
	1045	No
	1959	No
	7070	No
	8080	No
	9090	No
CIFS	139	Unknown
CsAUDIT	2000	Yes
DirXML NDS-to-NDS	8090	Yes
DirXML Remote Loader	8000	Yes
DNS	53	No
eGuide	389	Dependent
	636	Dependent
FTP	20	No
	21	No
GW Monitor	1099	Yes
GW MTA	3800 (HTTP-6x)	Yes
	7100 (MTP)	Yes
	7180 (HTTP-55EP)	Yes
GW POA	1677 (CS)	Yes
	2800 (HTTP-6x)	Yes
	7101 (MTP)	Yes
	7181 (HTTP-55EP)	Yes
GW Web Access	80 (HTTP)	Dependent
	443	Dependent
	7205	Yes

(continued)

Table A.1   Common NetWare 6.5 Applications, Port Numbers, and Configurability (continued)

NetWare 6.5 Application	Port Numbers	Configurable?
GWIA	25 (SMTP)	No
	110 (POP3)	No
	143 (IMAP4)	No
	389 (LDAP)	No
	636 (LDAP-SSL)	No
	9850 (HTTP Monitor)	Yes
iChain	2222	Yes
iFolder	80 (HTTP)	Dependent
	389 (LDAP)	Dependent
	443 (HTTPS)	Dependent
	636 (LDAP-SSL)	Dependent
iMonitor	80	Yes
iPrint	443	No
	631	No
LDAP	389	Yes
	636	Yes
Licensing (NLSRUP)	21571	Unknown
	21572	Unknown
LPR	515	Unknown
Media Server	554	No
NAS NetDevice	2222	No
NCP	524	No
NDPS Manager	3396	No
NDPS Broker	3014	No
NDPS SRS	3018	No
NDPS ENS	3016	No
NDPS RMS	3019	No
NDPS ENS Listener	3017	No
NetWare GUI	9000	Yes
	9001	Yes
NetWare Web Access	80	Dependent
News Server	119	Yes

(continued)

Table A.1 Common NetWare 6.5 Applications, Port Numbers, and Configurability *(continued)*

NetWare 6.5 Application	Port Numbers	Configurable?
NFS	20	No
	111	No
	2049	Yes
Novell Internet Messaging System (NIMS)	25	Unknown
	80	Unknown
	81	Unknown
	110	Unknown
	143	Unknown
	389	Unknown
	443	Unknown
	444	Unknown
	465	Unknown
	636	Unknown
	689	Unknown
	993	Unknown
	995	Unknown
Novell Modular Authentication Service (NMAS)	1242	Unknown
Novonyx Web Server	80	Yes
	443	Yes
Novell Remote Manager (NRM)	80	Unknown
	81	Unknown
	8008	Yes
	8009	Yes
NTP	123	No
NetWare IP (NWIP)	396	No
Portal Services	80	Dependent
	443	Dependent
	8080	Dependent
RADIUS	1812	Yes
Remote Console DOS	2034	Yes

(continued)

Table A.1   Common NetWare 6.5 Applications, Port Numbers, and Configurability *(continued)*

NetWare 6.5 Application	Port Numbers	Configurable?
Remote Console JAVA	2034	Yes
	2036	Yes
	2037	Yes
SCMD	2302	No
SLP	427	No
SNMP	161	Unknown
Telnet	23	No
Tomcat	8080	Yes
VPN	213	No
	353	No
	2010	Yes
Web Manager	2200	Yes
WebSphere	8110	Unknown
ZFD 3	2544	Yes
	2638	Yes
	5008	Unkown
	8039	No
ZFS 2	80	Dependent
	443	Dependent
	8008	Dependent
	8009	Dependent
	1229	No
	1521	Yes
	1600	Unknown
	2544	Yes
	2638	Yes
	5008	Unknown
ZFS 3.2	80	Dependent
	443	Dependent
	1229	Yes
	1433	Yes
	1521	Yes
	2638	Yes
	8089	Yes
	65443	Yes

NetWare 6.5 File System: Effective Rights Practice Scenarios

Chapter 8, "File System Security," covered many of the nuances of the NetWare 6.5 file system security. The five scenarios addressed in this appendix pose problems similar to what you might see on the NetWare 6.5 CNA exam Foundations of Novell Networking: NetWare 6.5, where you must deduce what a user's effective rights are in a given file system structure.

File System Inheritance Scenarios

Even though the operating system is generous in clearly showing a user's effective rights, Novell expects all CNA candidates to logically conclude what a user's rights are, based on a scenario.

The first three scenarios look at simple file system inheritance based strictly on a user's explicit trustee assignments and inherited assignments.

The second two scenarios examine complex file system inheritance based on a user's trustee assignments, inherited and explicit, and any trustee assignments the user might have based on groups (including organizational roles) of which the user is a member.

Based on the scenarios, fill in the blanks with the rights that the user has at each level of the file system. For Scenario 1, you would fill in all blanks, starting at the SHARED folder, under user Emma. For Scenario 2, you would do the same under user George, and so on. An Inherited Rights Filter (IRF) is provided at each level of the file system. Your responses must consider the IRF.

The end of this appendix provides an answer key showing the correct answers for each scenario.

Simple File System Inheritance

For the following three scenarios, the file system structure is as follows:

SHARED > DEPARTMENTAL > TRAINING > EVALS.DOC

SHARED is a parent directory, DEPARTMENTAL is a subdirectory of SHARED, and TRAINING is a subdirectory of DEPARTMENTAL. EVALS.DOC is a file in the TRAINING directory.

Scenario 1

If Emma has been granted the [RF] trustee assignment to the SHARED directory, what are her effective rights at each level of the file system?

Scenario 2

If George has been granted the [S] trustee assignment to the SHARED directory, what are his effective rights at each level of the file system?

Scenario 3

If Marian has been granted the [RWCEMFA] trustee assignment to the SHARED directory and has been granted the [RWF] trustee assignment to the EVALS.DOC file, what are her effective rights at each level of the file system?

Folder/File	Rights	Emma	George	Marian
SHARED	IRF	[SRWCEMFA]	[SRWCEMFA]	[SRWCEMFA]
	Trustee Assignment			
	Effective			
DEPARTMENTAL	IRF	[SRW MFA]	[SRW MFA]	[SRW MFA]
	Inherited			
	Trustee Assignment			
	Effective			

(continued)

Folder/File	Rights	Emma	George	Marian
TRAINING	IRF	[SR F]	[SR F]	[SR F]
	Inherited			
	Trustee Assignment			
	Effective			
EVALS.DOC	IRF	[S]	[S]	[S]
	Inherited			
	Trustee Assignment			
	Effective			

Complex File System Inheritance

For the following two scenarios, the file system structure is as follows:

SHARED > DEPARTMENTAL > TRAINING > EVALS.DOC

SHARED is a parent directory, DEPARTMENTAL is a subdirectory of SHARED, and TRAINING is a subdirectory of DEPARTMENTAL. EVALS.DOC is a file in the TRAINING directory.

Scenario 1

If Robbie has been granted the [RFMA] Individual trustee assignment to the SHARED directory, and as a member of the [Public] trustee has been granted the [WCE] trustee assignment to the DEPARTMENTAL directory, what are his effective rights at each level of the file system?

Scenario 2

If Gregory has been granted the [S] Individual trustee assignment to the TRAINING directory, and as a member of the Trainers group has been granted the [WCEF] assignment to the DEPARTMENTAL directory, and as a member of the [PUBLIC] trustee has been granted the [R] trustee assignment to the SHARED directory, what are his effective rights at each level of the file system?

Folder/File	Rights	Robbie	Gregory
SHARED	IRF	[SRWCEMFA]	[SRWCEMFA]
	Individual Trustee Assignment		
	Group Trustee Assignment		
	Effective		
DEPARTMENTAL	IRF	[SRW MFA]	[SRW MFA]
	Inherited		
	Individual Trustee Assignment		
	Group Trustee Assignment		
	Effective		
TRAINING	IRF	[SR F]	[SR · F]
	Inherited		
	Individual Trustee Assignment		
	Group Trustee Assignment		
	Effective		
EVALS.DOC	IRF	[S]	[S]
	Inherited		
	Individual Trustee Assignment		
	Group Trustee Assignment		
	Effective		

File System Inheritance Scenarios—Answer Keys

The keys for the simple and complex file system inheritance scenarios are presented in the next two sections.

Simple File System Inheritance

Folder/File	Rights	Emma	George	Marian
SHARED	IRF	[SRWCEMFA]	[SRWCEMFA]	[SRWCEMFA]
	Trustee Assignment	RF	S	RWCEMFA
	Effective	RF	SRWCEMFA	RWCEMFA

(continued)

Folder/File	Rights	Emma	George	Marian
DEPARTMENTAL	IRF	[SRW MFA]	[SRW MFA]	[SRW MFA]
	Inherited	RF	S	RWMFA
	Trustee Assignment	—	—	—
	Effective	RF	SRWCEMFA	RWMFA
TRAINING	IRF	[SR F]	[SR F]	[SR F]
	Inherited	RF	S	RF
	Trustee Assignment	—	—	—
	Effective	RF	SRWCEMFA	RF
EVALS.DOC	IRF	[S]	[S]	[S]
	Inherited	—	S	—
	Trustee Assignment	—	—	RWF
	Effective	—	SRWCEMFA	RWF

Complex File System Inheritance

Folder/File	Rights	Robbie	Gregory
SHARED	IRF	[SRWCEMFA]	[SRWCEMFA]
	Individual Trustee Assignment	RMFA	—
	Group Trustee Assignment	—	R
	Effective	RMFA	R
DEPARTMENTAL	IRF	[SRW MFA]	[SRW MFA]
	Inherited	RMFA	R
	Individual Trustee Assignment	—	—
	Group Trustee Assignment	WCE	WCEF
	Effective	RWCEMFA	RWCEF
TRAINING	IRF	[SR F]	[SR F]
	Inherited	RF	RF
	Individual Trustee Assignment	—	S
	Group Trustee Assignment	—	—
	Effective	RF	SRWCEMFA

(continued)

Folder/File	Rights	Robbie	Gregory
EVALS.DOC	IRF	[S]	[S]
	Inherited	—	S
	Individual Trustee Assignment	—	—
	Group Trustee Assignment	—	—
	Effective	—	SRWCEMFA

Workstation Utilities

Although the majority of administrative tasks in NetWare 6.5 that a CNA handles are managed through a GUI interface or a Web browser, many workstation utilities and commands exist to facilitate network administration. Some of these are native to NetWare 6.5, but many are native to NetWare 3.12, NetWare 4.11, and NetWare 5.x. Even though the legacy utilities are not shipped with NetWare 6.5, if you have access to them, they will help you administer your NetWare 6.5 environment.

You can run most of these utilities from a Windows 2000/Window XP Professional client from START, RUN, or from a command prompt such as START, RUN, CMD. To discover all the possible options these commands provide, use the following syntax:

```
command /?
```

Workstation Utilities Native to NetWare 6.5

Table C.1 provides some of the valuable workstation command utilities that are native to NetWare 6.5. Table C.2 provides a list of many workstation command utilities that were native to earlier versions of NetWare but that can still work quite well in NetWare 6.5 when copied to the correct directory.

Table C.1	Useful Command Utilities	
Command	**Description**	**Path**
CX	Used to change a client's current context. Most often used with the /R /A /T switches.	**SYS:\LOGIN** **SYS:\PUBLIC**
LOGIN	Used to authenticate a user to the network from a workstation.	**SYS:\LOGIN** **SYS:\PUBLIC**
MAP	Used to map a logical drive letter to a network file system resource.	**SYS:\LOGIN** **SYS:\PUBLIC**
CAPTURE	Used to redirect a workstation's printer port to a network print queue. **CAPTURE** provides backward compatibility for non-NDPS printing environments.	**SYS:\PUBLIC**
FILER	Used to manage files, folders, and volumes on a server. **FILER** is a powerful utility that should be protected from user access.	**SYS:\PUBLIC**
FLAG	Used to determine and assign attributes to files and folders.	**SYS:\PUBLIC**
LOGOUT	Used to log out or leave a network.	**SYS:\PUBLIC**
NCOPY	Used to copy files and folders from a source directory to a destination directory. Preserves all NetWare trustee assignments and attributes.	**SYS:\PUBLIC**
NDIR	Used to list a directory's files, subdirectories, and pertinent NetWare information, including owner, effective rights, inherited rights filters (IRFs), and attributes.	**SYS:\PUBLIC**
NLIST	Used to list information about eDirectory objects and resources, including containers, users, and servers.	**SYS:\PUBLIC**
NPRINTER	Used to route printing jobs to the proper printer in a queue-based printing environment using the Internetwork Packet Exchange/Sequenced Packet Exchange (IPX/SPX) protocols.	**SYS:\PUBLIC**
NWBACK32	Used to back up and restore files, folders, and resources from target service agents, servers, and workstations.	**SYS:\PUBLIC**
RIGHTS	Used to display or change effective rights to a directory.	**SYS:\PUBLIC**

(continued)

Table C.1	Useful Command Utilities *(continued)*	
Command	**Description**	**Path**
CONSOLEONE	The main JAVA-based utility that Novell wants administrators to use to manage eDirectory and the file system on a NetWare 6.5 network.	**SYS:\PUBLIC\mgmt\ ConsoleOne\1.2\bin**
NWADMN32	The main utility that Novell wanted administrators to use to manage Novell Directory Services (NDS) and the file system in versions of NetWare prior to NetWare 5. It is still a vital tool for managing some key administrative processes, including the management of Novell Distributed Print Services (NDPS) resources.	**SYS:\PUBLIC\ WIN32**
NPTWIN95	Used on Windows 9x computers to load a port driver for queue-based printing.	**SYS:\PUBLIC\ WIN95**

Legacy Workstation Utilities That Are Compatible with NetWare 6.5

Those who have grown familiar with utilities from earlier versions of NetWare will be pleased that many of those utilities can still be used in the NetWare 6.5 environment. Those in Table C.2 do not ship with NetWare 6.5, but you can copy them from your existing SYS:\PUBLIC folder to the SYS:\PUBLIC folder in NetWare 6.5.

Many of the utilities in Table C.2 require associated message files (.MSG and .HEP) that you can find in the SYS:\PUBLIC\NLS\ENGLISH folder for the given version of the operating system. When you're copying the files to a NetWare 6.5 server, be sure to copy the executable and any associated files.

Table C.2	Command Utilities from Previous Versions of NetWare	
Command	**Description**	**Path**
FLAGDIR	Used to modify the attributes on a directory.	**SYS:\PUBLIC**
GRANT	Used to assign a trustee assignment to a user.	**SYS:\PUBLIC**
NVER	Used to display information including server name, IPX/SPX version, NDS/eDirectory version, and local area network (LAN) driver version.	**SYS:\PUBLIC**

(continued)

Table C.2	Command Utilities from Previous Versions of NetWare *(continued)*	
Command	**Description**	**Path**
MAKEUSER	Used to create numerous users and objects.	**SYS:\PUBLIC**
NETADMIN	Used in NetWare 4.x as an administrative interface for managing eDirectory objects.	**SYS:\PUBLIC**
RENDIR	Used to rename a directory.	**SYS:\PUBLIC**
RCONSOLE	Used to directly connect a workstation using the IPX/SPX protocols to start a server session from the workstation. The workstation keyboard and monitor emulate the server keyboard and monitor.	**SYS:\PUBLIC**
PURGE	Used to permanently erase files and folders from a NetWare server.	**SYS:\PUBLIC**
REMOVE	Used to remove a user or group from a file or directory's access control list.	**SYS:\PUBLIC**
REVOKE	Used to revoke a user's rights to a file or directory while leaving the user on the file or directory's access control list.	**SYS:\PUBLIC**
SALVAGE	Used to recover a file or directory that was previously deleted.	**SYS:\PUBLIC**
SEND	Used to send a message to another workstation.	**SYS:\PUBLIC**
SETPASS	Used to change a password.	**SYS:\PUBLIC**
WHOAMI	Used to display your username and connection ID and the server you are logged into.	**SYS:\PUBLIC**

Sample Response File

During the NetWare 6.5 installation, one of the first screens that a CNA encounters is the "Welcome to the NetWare Server Installation" screen. One of the options at the bottom of the screen that most CNAs overlook is the Response File option, selected by pressing the F3 key.

If you are installing numerous servers that have the same hardware and network configuration, you can use the Response File option to cut your installation time dramatically. I use it all the time when I am setting up multiple servers for advanced Novell classes. Here is how I do it.

Let's say that the classroom I am setting up needs 12 NetWare 6.5 servers in the same tree, but each server will be placed in a unique context. The first thing I do is install the first server in the tree, walking through the installation procedure step by step, responding to all the screens and waiting for all the file copies to occur. At best, when everything is going well and "Murphy" does not show up, the whole installation takes 45 minutes.

Now I have 11 more servers to install. That is where the Response File option comes in. Two response files are created during a NetWare 6.5 installation. Their names are response.sav, and response.rsp. You can find them in the SYS:\NI\DATA folder. The response.sav file is generated during the first half of the installation. The response.rsp file is generated during the second half of the installation. I copy these files to a floppy disk or the root of the C: drive. Then, using a text editor, I combine them into a single response file, called response1.txt.

Whether or not you have to do a mass rollout of NetWare 6.5 servers, it is a best practice to copy the response files that are automatically generated during an installation to a floppy disk and store the disk in a safe place. If your server ever has a major hard disk crash and you have to reinstall the operating system (OS) from scratch, you can use the response files to facilitate the process.

I then make any needed context, tree name, license, ServerID, or server name changes. For a 12-server installation, I generate 11 additional copies of this edited file, each with a unique name and with the needed changes. Normally, I end up with 12 floppy disks with a unique response file on each. Then when the "Welcome to the NetWare Server Installation" screen appears on the other 11 servers, I select the Response File option and point it to either the appropriate response file on my floppy disk, or if I have established a DOS partition prior to installation and copied the response file to the C: drive, I point the installation to the Response File option on the DOS partition. If I have made all the correct edits, the server installation is completed and I did not have to walk it through each screen.

Using this procedure, I have installed 12 servers in less than 2 hours. It is a great tool for the CNA who has too much to do and not enough time to do it in. Don't be surprised, though, if you have to re-edit the response file a little when you do your second installation. It is human nature to overlook or mistype some parameter. After you have the file just the way you want it, it is off to the installation races.

A second and much more user friendly method is available to NetWare 6.5 CNAs for creating a response file from scratch. Using the Response File Generator option, available at Deployment Manager, Install/Upgrade Options, Automate an Installation, Response File Generator, you can easily create a customized set of response files to help you automate a NetWare 6.5 installation.

After selecting the Response File Generator option in Deployment Manager, you can create your own response file using the following steps. Just follow the onscreen prompts. (Most screens link to the screen that follows by clicking on the Next button. For the sake of brevity, I am leaving that action out of each of the following steps.)

1. Accept two license agreements.

2. You can then choose to accept a default template response file location on the Enter Input Response File screen. The default template is called `Default.rsp`.

3. On the Response File Configuration screen, you can select either New Server or Blade Image installation. You can also provide a password if a remote source is being used.

4. On the Language Selection screen, you can choose the Language, Country Code, Code Page, and Keyboard Code.

5. On the Choose a Pattern screen, you can select a Customized Server, Basic NetWare File Server, Pre-Migration Server, or one of many Preconfigured server installations.

6. If you selected a Customized Server installation (as I did for this appendix because it gives the widest range of choices) on the Components screen, you can select those NetWare 6.5 components that you want installed. If you selected one of the other installation types, you will encounter a variety of different screens at this point.

7. On the Server Properties screen, you will enter the Server Name.

8. On the Protocols screen, you will configure your IP and IPX properties, including address, subnet mask, router, and IPX frame types if IPX is selected.

9. On the Encryption screen, you will configure the location of the .NFK license file. The default is A:\License, but you might want to select a different path. The wizard will check to see that the .NFK license is present when you select Next.

10. On the Licenses screen, the location of the .NLF server licenses is defined. Again, when you select Next, the wizard checks to see that the license is present. If it is not, a warning box is displayed.

11. On the SLP screen, you have the option of configuring SLP parameters, including up to three Directory Agents (DAs).

12. On the Domain Name Service screen, you configure your server's host name, domain, and up to three DNS servers' IP addresses.

13. On the Time Zone screen, you can select the correct time zone for your server.

14. On the Time Synchronization Type screen, you can select the type of time server you are installing and whether you are using TimeSync Configured Sources.

15. On the eDirectory Installation screen, you can configure whether you are installing the server into a new tree or an existing tree. Then you can configure the tree name and context, the admin name and context, and the admin's password.

16. A warning is displayed informing you that all passwords will be stored in the response file in cleartext.

17. On the Save Response File screen, you can provide a name and location for the response file. The default name is response.rsp.

Your response file is saved to the location you chose, along with the license files that you selected earlier. This is so much easier than having to manually edit, or merge, multiple response files using a text editor. It is a welcome addition to NetWare 6.5. Notice when you look at this text file that many of the parameters from the text portion of the installation are not included in this file. For the sake of completeness, you can append the configuration parameters from the response.sav file that you generate on your first server installation, or you can manually add the needed parameters, such as storage adapters and network adapters, to this response file that you generated.

Not many published resources provide a look at this valuable file. The following is the response file that was generated using the Response File Generator. If you carefully examine the sections that make up this file, you will see how your life as a CNA can be made much easier the next time you have to do a multiple server installation. A complete examination of this file could be a two-day course in and of itself.

This sample file is provided strictly as a reference, not as the definitive response file that is universally compatible with all hardware. However, if you are creative, you can edit the following file, or sections of it, to suit your particular hardware configuration. Better yet, you can use the Response File Generator available through Deployment Manager to create your own.

For a detailed discussion of the NetWare 6.5 response file, its sections, and syntax, go to http://www.novell.com/documentation/nw65/othr_enu/data/hz8pck9v.html.

If you want to see what the response.sav and response.rsp files look like for an 11-server installation of NetWare 6.0 (not NetWare 6.5), go to http://www.3wscertification.com/servers.html.

```
[NWI:Language]
Server Language=4
Prompt=FALSE

[Selected Nodes]
prompt=false
Non-Changeable Products=Script,Imonitor,Portal,ConsoleOneProducts,
➥6pkLdap,SMS,Novell Certificate Server,NWNMAS,
➥Apache2 Admin Server,Native File
Services,Tomcat4,NWEMBOX,PHP,Perl,NSN,Beans
DestinationNode=HealthChecks
HealthChecks=NetWare Services
```

```
NetWare Services=NetWare OS,Patterns,Products,NWUpdateGroup
NetWare OS=NetWare650S,NICI,Protocols,Time Zone,DS_Install,LicensePrompt,
➥W0 install,DOS_INST,SYS_INST
Patterns=CustomNetWare
Products=Novell Certificate Server,6pkLdap,Imonitor,Apache2 Admin Server,
➥Tomcat4,Apache2 Webserver,Portal,SMS,ConsoleOneProducts,NWNMAS,Native File
Services,NWEMBOX,Beans,NSN,Perl,PHP,iManager2.0 Product
Novell Certificate Server=ALL
Imonitor=ALL
Apache2 Admin Server=ALL
Tomcat4=ALL
Portal=ALL
SMS=ALL
ConsoleOneProducts=ALL
ConsoleOne=c1_core,c1_win32,c1_nw.zip
Reporting Snapin=c1_rpt
NWNMAS=ALL
Native File Services=ALL
NFSNIS=NFSNIS-NLMs
NWEMBOX=ALL
Beans=ALL
NSN=ALL
NSN install module=NSN Product zip file
Perl=ALL
Perl install module=Perl Product zip file
PHP=ALL
PHP install module=PHP Product zip file
NWUpdateGroup=NWUpdate
6pkLdap=ALL
Apache2 Webserver=ALL
iManager2.0 Product=ALL

[Product List]
Essential Products=NetWare OS,HealthChecks,NetWare Services

[NWI:Locale]
Uses Vgadisp=false
Code Page=437
Country Code=001
Keyboard=United States
Prompt=FALSE

[NWI:File Server]
Prompt=false
Servername=FS1
Server ID Number=12563112

[NWI:Server Settings]
Prompt=FALSE
Load server at reboot=TRUE
CD-ROM Driver=NetWare

[NWI:Mouse and Video]
Mouse=Auto
Video Type=PlugNPlay
Prompt=FALSE

[NWI:Boot Partition]
Prompt=FALSE
```

```
[NWI:License]
Display License Agreement=FALSE
Prompt=false
NICI Foundation Key File=A:\License\90367325.NFK
License File=A:\License\90368026.NLF
Install Licenses Later=false

[NWI:Install Options]
Upgrade=FALSE
Express=TRUE
Prompt=FALSE

[NWI:LdapConfig]
Prompt=false
ClearText=false

[SMS]
prompt=false

[NWNMAS]
Prompt=false

[Beans]
prompt=false

[NSN]
prompt=false

[Perl]
prompt=false

[PHP]
prompt=false

[Initialization]
Install State=First
Description=
DescriptionID=

[NOVELL:NOVELL_ROOT:1.0.0]
silent=true
closeScreen=SilentCloseScreen
Reboot=true
allowCloseScreen=true

[NWI:MISC]
Relogin Password=

[NWI:NDS]
Admin Language=4
Tree Name=NW65_TREE
New Tree=true
Server Context=O=NW65
Admin Login Name=admin
Admin Context=O=NW65
Admin Password=novell
Prompt=false

[NWI:Protocols]
Single Network Adapter=True
```

```
Prompt=False
Default IP Frame Type=Ethernet_II
Default IPX Frame Type=ETHERNET_802.2

[NWI:TCPIP]
Prompt=False
IP Address 1=10.0.0.125
Subnet Mask 1=255.0.0.0
Gateway 1=10.0.0.225

[NWI:IPX]
Prompt=False

[NWI:Host Name]
IP Address 1=10.0.0.125
Prompt=false
Verify=false
Host Name 1=FS1.nw65.nov

[NWI:SLP Configuration]
Prompt=false
Directory Agent=false
Multicast Routing=false
DA Server 1=
DA Server 2=
DA Server 3=
SLP Scope List=

[NWI:DNS]
Prompt=false
Domain=nw65.nov
Nameservers=10.0.0.125

[NWI:Time Zone]
Time Zone=EST
Prompt=False
Use Daylight Saving Time=TRUE

[NWI:Time Synchronization]
Time Server Type=Single
```

NetWare 6.5: New Server Installation Planning Table

Over the years that I have taught Novell CNA classes, students always want to know how I have the server(s) set up for the class. After the class is over, students want to go back to their homes or offices and set up a practice server that they can use to prepare for the live exam. That's a great plan because it provides practical hands-on experience. The same holds true for you, the reader of this book. You might want to set up your own practice server so that you can follow along.

In Chapter 3, "Installing and Configuring NetWare 6.5," I discussed the installation steps that you have to know for the exam. I did not tell you what my decisions were as I prepared the server that I used for this book. I used two servers for this book. Here is the configuration for one of them.

In Table E.1, I have detailed in the column titled FS1 Server many of the values that I provided for the variables that I encountered during the installation of the FS1 server. I have also provided a column detailing the default values that are displayed and a column that you can use to plan your own server installation.

As you prepare for the NetWare 6.5 CNA exam, Foundations of Novell Networking: NetWare 6.5, fill in the values you would give to your own practice server in the column titled Your Server. Then set up a practice server based on those values. If Murphy's law holds true, the values that will cause you the most angst will be the values you have to provide for the storage and local area network (LAN) drivers. You might have to research a vendor's Web site or Novell's support site (http://support.novell.com) to locate suitable drivers. Don't be discouraged if your first install does not go smoothly. After the first one or two installations, it's easy. Don't assume that you are using the same hardware that I am. You might have to open your test server to find out which type of storage devices and network cards you have installed.

Whenever, I am faced with a new production rollout, I plan on the installation taking several hours in a test environment until I can get all of the bugs (drivers) worked out. After I know the hardware gotchas, the rest of the installation is as easy as kissing the back of your hand. To assist you in installing your first server, see the planning table in Table E.1.

Table E.1	Planning Table		
Variable	**Displayed Default Value**	**FS1 Server**	**Your Server**
Language	English	English	
Regional settings			
Country	Default=001 (USA)	Default	
Code page	Default=437 (United States English)	Default	
Keyboard	Default=United States	Default	
Installation type	1. Default/Manual: default installation type=Default	Manual	
	2. Use Response File option	No	

(continued)

Table E.1 Planning Table *(continued)*			
Variable	**Displayed Default Value**	**FS1 Server**	**Your Server**
DOS boot partition size	Requires 500MB Recommends 1GB For the test: Novell's minimum DOS partition size for a NetWare 6.5 installation is 500MB, with 1GB being the recommended size.	500MB Recommend this value be based on 500MB plus the amount of physical memory installed in the server. For production environments (not for the test), this value should be 1GB at a minimum plus the amount of physical memory that is installed in the server. Because this is a training server and I am not worried about adequate space for core dumps, I have left this value at 500MB.	
Server ID	Randomly generated	Default ID accepted	
Load server at reboot	Yes	No	
Boot OS	Default=DOS	Default	
Allow unsupported drivers	Default=NO	Default	
Server SET parameters	Edit/Default=none	Default=none	
Video	Default=Super VGA Plug N Play	Default	

(continued)

	Displayed Default		Your
Variable	**Value**	**FS1 Server**	**Server**
Device drivers			
Platform Support Module	Default=Based on server architecture	MPS14.PSM	
Hotplug Support Module	Default=Based on server architecture	Default=None	
Storage adapters	Default=Based on server architecture	IDEATA.HAM	
Storage devices	Default=Based on server architecture	IDEHD.CDM, IDECD.CDM	
Network boards	Default=Based on server architecture	PCNTNW.LAN	
Slot number	Default=Based on server architecture	2	
Frames	Default=All frames	Only Ethernet_II	
NetWare Loadable Modules	Default:(optional)	None	
Volume SYS and partition properties	File system type=NSS Default= 4 GB	NSS 4GB	
Pattern installation type	Default=Customized NetWare Server	Default	
Components to install	Default=none	Apache2 Web Server and Tomcat4 Servlet Container iPrint Novell iFolder Storage Services Novell DNS/DHCP Services Novell NetStorage OpenSSH eGuide Novell iManager 2.0.2 Novell Virtual Office Framework	
Server Name	Default=blank	FS1	

Table E.1 Planning Table (continued)

(continued)

Table E.1   Planning Table (continued)

Variable	Displayed Default Value	FS1 Server	Your Server
Protocols			
IP	Default=not selected	Selected IP=10.0.0.165 Subnet Mask=255.0.0.0 Router (Gateway)=10.0.0.125	
IPX	Default=not selected (If selected, choose the Advanced option and select the desired frames and associated network numbers)	Not selected	
Advanced	SNMP, IPX compatibility mode, SLP details	Not selected	
Domain Name Service (DNS)			
Host name	Default=none	FS1	
Domain name	Default=none	NW65.NOV	
Up to three name servers	Default=none	10.0.0.125	
Time zone	U.S. and Canada Pacific time	U.S. and Canada Eastern time	
Time server type	Default=Secondary	Single reference	
TIMESYNC configured sources	Default=None selected	Default	
eDirectory installation	New NDS tree Default=Existing eDirectory Tree	New eDirectory tree	
Tree name	Default=none	NW65_Tree	
Context for the Server object	Default=none	.Training.NW65	
Admin name	Admin	admin	
Admin context	Default=none	.NW65	
Admin password	Default=none	A super secret password	
License file location (for NFK license file and for NLF license file)	Default=A:\License	A:	

(continued)

	Table E.1 **Planning Table** *(continued)*		
Variable	**Displayed Default Value**	**FS1 Server**	**Your Server**
License certificate context for an MLA	Default is the same as the context for the Server object	.Training.NW65	
LDAP configuration	Default: Cleartext port=389 Default: SSL/TLS port=636 Default: Require TLS	Default ports Require TLS	
Novell Modular Authentication Service	Default=NDS	Default	
DNS/DHCP	Default locations for Locator, Group objects, and RootSrvr Zone object	Defaults accepted	
iFolder Server options	Defaults for LDAP host name, ports, LDAP context for Admins, server host name, admin name, and user database path	Defaults accepted	
NetStorage configuration	Defaults for DNS name or IP address of Primary, Secondary, and Alternate eDirectory server. DNS name or IP address of iFolder server	Defaults accepted	

References (Web and Print)

The following are all of the references alluded to throughout the course of this text. Web references and print references are listed by the chapter where they were cited. This is a quick bibliography of texts that I have used in the past for students who want to do some extra research.

Of all of the references cited in this book, the absolute best source of information for the NetWare 6.5 CNA exam is the authorized courseware, be it that used in the instructor-led course or the self-study kits. Novell has some of the finest course developers in the business. I offer my compliments to them. The rest of us are just trying to get the good word out, based on the standard that they have set.

Introduction

 Novell's Testing Information Web Site:
`http://www.novell.comtraining/testinfo/theory.html`
This is Novell's definitive source for exam formats.

 Novell's Test Objectives Web Site:
`http://www.novell.com/training/testinfo/objectives/`
`3016tobj.html`
Check this out for the up-to-date objectives for the Foundations of Novell Networking: NetWare 6.5 exam.

 Novell's Test Data Web Site:
`http://www.novell.com/training/testinfo/testdata.html`
This has the up-to-date passing score for exam 050-686.

 Novell's Training Web Site:
`http://www.novell.com/training/`
This has the training locator if you are seeking a Novell authorized training partner.

 ExamForce's Web Site:
`http://www.examforce.com`
This site features the popular CramMaster practice test products.

 Self Test Software's Web Site:
`http://selftestsoftware.com`
This is Novell's authorized practice test provider.

 VMWare Workstation's Web Site:
`http://www.vmware.com/products/desktop/ws_features.html`
This is an excellent resource for setting up a test network on a single computer.

 NetWare 6.5 Documentation Web Site:
`http://www.novell.com/documentation/nw65/index.html`
This has the latest documentation on NetWare 6.5.

 Novell Press's Web Site:
`http://www.novell.com/training/books/`
This is the best Web site available for third-party Novell documentation.

Chapter 1

 Novell's Certification Web Site:
http://www.novell.com/training/certinfo/

 Novell's Training Services Locator:
http://www.novell.com/training/locator/SearchAdvanced.jsp

 Novell's Delivered Training Web Site:
http://www.novell.com/training/pep/att/def.html

 Novell's Self-Study Portal for Training Products:
http://shop.novell.com/dr/v2/ec_MAIN.Entry16?SP=10024&PN=29
&xid=27477&V1=30010406&V2=30010406&V3=1&V5=11000021&V4=10&S
1=&S2=&S3=&S4=&S5=&DSP=0&CUR=840&PGRP=0&CACHE_ID=0

 "Now What? A Certification Resource List for Self-Study Career
Changers" by Warren E. Wyrostek:
http://www.informit.com/articles/article.asp?p=29251
This provides some ideas for those who want to get certified
without spending a lot of money for instructor-led classes.

 "Now What? The Novell Certifications" by Warren E. Wyrostek:
http://www.informit.com/articles/article.asp?p=22671
This is a little dated, but it provides an overview of Novell's many
certifications.

 "Considering Bootcamp ROI—A Review of Novell's CDE
Bootcamp" by Warren E. Wyrostek:
http://www.certmag.com/articles/templates/cmag_webonly.asp?
articleid=385&zoneid=41
(To access this article, you might have to register with *Certification
Magazine*.)

Chapter 2

 Tittel, Ed, James E. Gaskin, and Earl Follis. *Networking with
NetWare for Dummies*. Foster City, California: IDG Books, 1998.
This is an excellent resource on the history of NetWare.

 Sheresh, Doug and Beth. *Understanding Directory Services*.
Indianapolis: Sams Publishing, 2002.
This is a worthy resource for understanding the world of
Directory Services, including NDS and eDirectory.

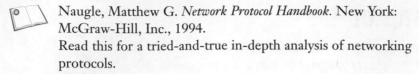

Naugle, Matthew G. *Network Protocol Handbook*. New York: McGraw-Hill, Inc., 1994.
Read this for a tried-and-true in-depth analysis of networking protocols.

NetWare 6.5 Documentation: What's New in NetWare 6.5:
`http://www.novell.com/documentation/nw65/index.html?page=/`
`documentation/nw65/install/data/all549w.html`
This is a fine overview of the new features in NetWare 6.5.

NetWare 6.5 Technical White Paper:
`http://www.novell.com/collateral/4621344/4621344.html`
This is a first-class analysis of Business Continuity Services.

Cluster Services with Novell NetWare:
`http://www.novell.com/collateral/4621200/4621200.html`
This is a solid introduction to NetWare 6.x cluster services.

Chapter 3

3WsCertification Presentations:
`http://www.3wscertification.com/install.html`
This site offers a NetWare 6.5 virtual installation.

Thomas, Robert M. *DOS 6.2 Instant Reference*. San Francisco: Sybex Inc., 1994.
If you're looking for an excellent resource for DOS commands and configuration files, look no further.

Salford Software:
`http://www.salfordsoftware.co.uk/kb/SKB62`
This site offers a detailed list of SERVER.EXE options.

Two Web sites that provide documentation on the options that can be used with FDISK:
`http://www.fdisk.com/fdisk/`
and
`http://www.macalester.edu/~fines/fdisk.html`

Lindberg, Kelley J.P. *Novell's NetWare 3.12 Administrator's Handbook*. San Francisco: Sybex Inc., 1995.
This is a great refresher on the DOS Client for NetWare.

Novell Product Updates:
`http://support.novell.com/filefinder/18197/index.html`
This allows you to download Novell support pack overlays.

Chapter 4

 Novell Product Virtual Installation Presentations:
`http://www.3wscertification.com/install.html`
Select Novell Client SP1 Install to view a virtual installation.

 Novell Download Pages:
`http:// http://download.novell.com/pages/PublicSearch.jsp`
Check out this first-rate source for the latest Novell Client.

 Harris, Jeffrey. *Novell NetWare 6.5 Administrator's Handbook.*
Indianapolis: Novell Press, 2004.
This is a very good reference source on NetWare 6.5, including all
of the Client Properties options.

 Simpson, Ted. *Hands-On Novell NetWare 6.0.* Boston: Course
Technology, 2003.
This is a superior hands-on guide to NetWare 6.x.

Chapter 5

 Harris, Jeffrey. *Novell NetWare 6.5 Administrator's Handbook.*
Indianapolis: Novell Press, 2004.
Read this for an in-depth look at NetWare 6.5, including a good
primer on eDirectory.

 Kuo, Peter, and Jim Henderson. *Novell's Guide to Troubleshooting
eDirectory.* Indianapolis: Novell Press, 2005.
This is the definitive reference for troubleshooting eDirectory. It
should be on every NetWare administrator's and engineer's desk.
It's a great reference for understanding the eDirectory schema and
object classes. For earlier versions of eDirectory and NDS, see the
earlier versions of this text by the same authors. *NDS
Troubleshooting* was published in 1995, and *Novell's Guide to
Troubleshooting NDS* was published in 1999.

 Sheresh, Beth and Doug. *Understanding Directory Services.*
Indianapolis: Sams Publishing, 2002.
This is the ultimate reference on Directory Services, including
NDS and eDirectory. It's a fantastic reference book for understanding the role of Directory Services in networking. The 2000
edition was a breakthrough text, and this version adds a volume of
information that is not available anywhere else.

Hughes, Jeffrey H. and Blair W. Thomas. *Novell's Four Principles of NDS Design.* San Jose, California: Novell Press, 1996.
Although a little dated, this is still a good book for understanding the underlying principles behind good eDirectory design.

Chapter 6

 Novell Storage Services Administration Guide for NetWare 6.5:
`http://www.novell.com/documentation/nw65/index.html?page=/`
`documentation/nw65/nss_enu/data/hut0i3h5.html`
This is the opening page to the NSS documentation.

 Comparison of NSS and Traditional File Services:
`http://www.novell.com/documentation/nw65/index.html?page=/`
`documentation/nw65/sdiskenu/data/akimeps.html#akimeps`
This site offers a summary comparison of traditional and NSS volumes.

Chapter 7

 Harris, Jeffrey. *Novell NetWare 6.5 Administrator's Handbook.* Indianapolis: Novell Press, 2004.
This is a superior reference on NetWare 6.5, including all of the Client Properties options.

 Simpson, Ted. *Hands-On Novell NetWare 6.0.* Boston: Course Technology, 2003.
Simpson's book is a good hands-on guide to NetWare 6.x.

 JRB Software:
`http://www.jrbsoftware.com/`
This is a first-class source for third-party eDirectory administration tools.

 Wolfgang's Tools Network:
`http://www.geocities.com/wstools/`
Check this out if you want a superior source for third-party eDirectory administration tools.

DreamLan Network Consulting, LTD.:

`http://www.dreamlan.com`

This is probably my favorite site for eDirectory tools of all kinds and capabilities. This site has helped my students and clients more than any of us will admit.

Chapter 8

NetWare 6.5 Universal Password Deployment Guide:

`http://www.novell.com/documentation/nw65/index.html?page=/`
`documentation/nw65/universal_password/data/front.html`

This provides a complete description and methodology for deploying the Universal Password feature in a NetWare 6.5 environment.

Simpson, Ted. *Hands-On Novell NetWare 6.0*. Boston: Course Technology, 2003.

This is an excellent hands-on guide to NetWare 6.x. Check out the section on file system security.

Harris, Jeffrey. *Novell NetWare 6.5 Administrator's Handbook*. Indianapolis: Novell Press, 2004.

Harris includes a section on file system security and attributes that is worth reading.

Clarke, David James IV. *CNA Study Guide for NetWare 6*. Indianapolis: Novell Press, 2004.

This book offers superb coverage of eDirectory security.

NetWare 6.5—Understanding Access and Usage Control for Directories and Files:

http://www.novell.com/documentation/nw65/index.html?page=/
documentation/nw65/nss_enu/data/bri5796.html

This is the definitive source for information on NetWare 6.5 file system security.

Chapter 9

Novell eDirectory 8.7-eDirectory Rights:

`http://www.novell.com/documentation/edir87/index.html?page=`
`/documentation/edir87/edir87/data/fbachifb.html`

Surf this site for Novell's classic source of documentation on eDirectory rights.

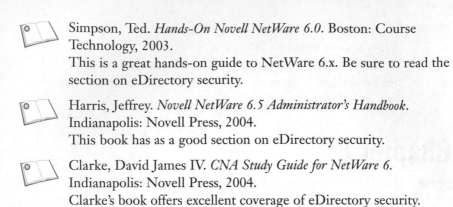

Simpson, Ted. *Hands-On Novell NetWare 6.0*. Boston: Course Technology, 2003.
This is a great hands-on guide to NetWare 6.x. Be sure to read the section on eDirectory security.

Harris, Jeffrey. *Novell NetWare 6.5 Administrator's Handbook*. Indianapolis: Novell Press, 2004.
This book has as a good section on eDirectory security.

Clarke, David James IV. *CNA Study Guide for NetWare 6*. Indianapolis: Novell Press, 2004.
Clarke's book offers excellent coverage of eDirectory security.

Chapter 10

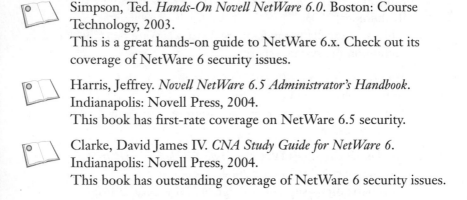

Simpson, Ted. *Hands-On Novell NetWare 6.0*. Boston: Course Technology, 2003.
This is a great hands-on guide to NetWare 6.x. Check out its coverage of NetWare 6 security issues.

Harris, Jeffrey. *Novell NetWare 6.5 Administrator's Handbook*. Indianapolis: Novell Press, 2004.
This book has first-rate coverage on NetWare 6.5 security.

Clarke, David James IV. *CNA Study Guide for NetWare 6*. Indianapolis: Novell Press, 2004.
This book has outstanding coverage of NetWare 6 security issues.

Chapter 11

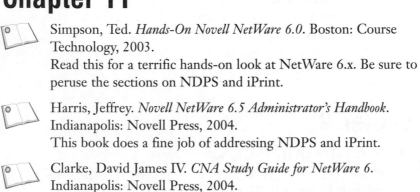

Simpson, Ted. *Hands-On Novell NetWare 6.0*. Boston: Course Technology, 2003.
Read this for a terrific hands-on look at NetWare 6.x. Be sure to peruse the sections on NDPS and iPrint.

Harris, Jeffrey. *Novell NetWare 6.5 Administrator's Handbook*. Indianapolis: Novell Press, 2004.
This book does a fine job of addressing NDPS and iPrint.

Clarke, David James IV. *CNA Study Guide for NetWare 6*. Indianapolis: Novell Press, 2004.
This book includes comprehensive coverage of NDPS and iPrint.

Novell iPrint Administration Guide for NetWare 6.5:
`http://www.novell.com/documentation/nw65/index.html?page=/`
`documentation/nw65/iprint/data/front.html`
Surf this site for the definitive source of information on iPrint.

Chapter 12

iFolder 2.1:
`http://www.novell.com/documentation/ifolder21/index.html`
This is Novell's documentation Web site on iFolder 2.1. It is the
ultimate source for information on iFolder.

Novell Virtual Office for NetWare 6.5 Configuration Guide:
`http://www.novell.com/documentation/nw65/index.html?page=/`
`documentation/nw65/virtualoffice/data/ac6spye.html`
This is Novell's state-of-the art online documentation on Virtual
Office.

Harris, Jeffrey. *Novell NetWare 6.5 Administrator's Handbook.*
Indianapolis: Novell Press, 2004.
This book does a good job of addressing iFolder and Virtual
Office, especially the step-by-step setup.

Appendixes

`http://support.novell.com/cgi-bin/search/searchtid.cgi?/`
`10065719.htm`

`http://novell.unc.edu/netware/PortMatrix.htm`

NetWare 6.5 Response File Installation Guide:
`http://www.novell.com/documentation/nw65/othr_enu/data/`
`hz8pck9v.html`
Visit here for a detailed discussion of a NetWare 6.5 response file,
its sections, and its syntax.

3WsCertification.com: 3001 Servers Sample Response Files:
`http://www.3wscertification.com/servers.html`
Check this out if you want to see what the `response.sav` and
`response.rsp` files look like for an 11-server installation of
NetWare 6.0 (not NetWare 6.5).

Commonly Used NetWare 6.5 Management URLs

With the advent of NetWare 6.0 and 6.5, Novell has continued its migration of server and network management utilities away from those that are platform-dependent to those that are easily accessed through a browser. You need to know the following NetWare 6.5 Management URLs for your everyday administrative tasks and for the exam.

Table G.1 includes a list of those URLs that you will be responsible for on the Foundations of Novell Networking: NetWare 6.5 exam. For purposes of illustration, I have listed the URLs using a private IP address that is assigned to one of my test servers. If you have Domain Name System (DNS) configured, you can substitute a fully qualified domain name (FQDN) for the IP address 10.0.0.125. For example, if 10.0.0.125 resolves to fs1.mail.nw65.nov, the URL for iManager, using a FQDN, is `https://fs1.mail.nw65.nov/nps/iManager.html`.

Feel free to substitute your own IP address, or DNS name, in the URLs in Table G.1 as you prepare for the exam. Remember: Practice is the only way you will commit these to memory.

This is in no way a comprehensive list of all management URLs that are available to you on NetWare 6.5. Rather, it is a list of the critical ones for daily administration and for becoming a CNA in NetWare 6.5.

You can access all of these URLs by using Internet Explorer (IE) 5.5 and above. Some are accessible using other browsers, including those available from Netscape and Mozilla. Others are still quirky in their reliance on IE.

Table G.1 Commonly Used NetWare 6.5 Management URLs	
Management Utility	**URL**
eGuide on a remote server (configure in VO)	**https://10.0.0.125/eGuide/**
iFolder client installation site	**http://10.0.0.125/iFolder**
iFolder Management Console	**https://10.0.0.125/iFolderServer/Admin**
iManager	**https://10.0.0.125/nps/iManager.html**
iMonitor	**http://10.0.0.125:8008/nds** (8008 = http stack) **https://10.0.0.125:8009/nds** (8009 = http secure stack)
iPrint client installation site	**http://10.0.0.125:631/ipp**
iPrint maps for location-based printing	**http://10.0.0.125/ippdocs/<the map file you created>**
iPrint Maptool (when the Novell client is not installed)	**http://10.0.0.125:631/ippdocs/ Maptool.htm**
iPrint on a remote server (configured in VO)	**https://10.0.0.125/iPrint/**
iPrint printing using a secure port	**http://10.0.0.125:443/ipp** **https://10.0.0.125/ipp**
NetStorage on a remote server (configured in VO)	**https://10.0.0.125:443/NetStorage/**
Remote Manager	**http://10.0.0.125:8008/** **https://10.0.0.125:8009/**
Virtual Office	**http://10.0.0.125/vo** **https://10.0.0.125/vo/**
Web Manager (starts and configures OpenSSH and a host of other utilites; can also be used to access iManager and Remote Manager)	**https://10.0.0.125:2200**

CD Contents and Installation Instructions

The CD features a state-of-the-art exam preparation engine from ExamForce. This uniquely powerful program will identify gaps in your knowledge and help you turn them into strengths. In addition to the ExamForce software, the CD includes an electronic version of this book in Portable Document Format (PDF) format, a "Need to Know More?" PDF file of useful resources, and the Adobe Acrobat Reader used to display these files.

The CramMaster Engine

This innovative exam engine systematically prepares you for a successful test. Working your way through CramMaster is the fastest, surest route to a successful exam. The presentation of questions is weighted according to your unique requirements. Your answer history determines which questions you'll see next. It determines what you don't know and forces you to overcome those shortcomings. You won't waste time answering easy questions about things you already know.

Multiple Test Modes

The CramMaster test engine, from ExamForce, has three unique testing modes to systematically prepare you for a successful exam.

Pretest Mode

Pretest mode is used to establish your baseline skill set. Train CramMaster by taking two or three pretests. There is no review or feedback on answers in this mode. View your topic-by-topic skill levels from the History menu on the main screen. Then, effective exam preparation begins by attacking your weakest topics first in Adaptive Drill mode.

Adaptive Drill Mode

Adaptive Drill mode enables you to focus on specific exam objectives. CramMaster learns the questions you find difficult and drills you until you master them. As you gain proficiency in one area, it seeks out the next with which to challenge you. Even the most complex concepts of the exam are mastered in this mode.

Simulated Exam Mode

Simulated Exam mode approximates the real exam; by the time you reach this level you've already mastered the exam material. This is your opportunity to exercise those skills while building your mental and physical stamina.

Installing CramMaster for the Novell NetWare 6.5 Exam

The following are the minimum system requirements for installation:

➤ Windows 95, 98, Me, NT4, 2000, or XP

➤ 64MB of RAM

➤ 18MB of disk space

NOTE

If you need technical support, please contact ExamForce at 800-845-8569 or email support@examforce.com. Additional product support can be found at www.examforce.com.

To install the CramMaster CD-ROM, follow these instructions:

1. Close all applications before beginning this installation.

2. Insert the CD into your CD-ROM drive. If the setup starts automatically, go to step 6. If the setup does not start automatically, continue with step 3.

3. From the Start menu, select Run.

4. Click Browse to locate the CramMaster CD. From the Look In drop-down list in the Browse dialog box, select the CD-ROM drive.

5. In the Browse dialog box, double-click Setup.exe. In the Run dialog box, click OK to begin the installation.

6. On the Welcome screen, click Next.

7. To agree to the End User License Agreement (EULA), click Next.

8. On the Choose Destination Location screen, click Next to install the software to C:\Program Files\CramMaster.

9. On the Select Program Manager Group screen, verify that the Program Manager group is set to CramMaster, and click Next.

10. On the Start Installation screen, click Next.

11. On the Installation Complete screen, verify that the Launch CramMaster Now box is checked, and click Finish.

12. For your convenience, a shortcut to CramMaster will be created automatically on your desktop.

Using CramMaster for the Novell NetWare 6.5 Exam

An Introduction slide show will start when CramMaster first launches. It will teach you how to get the most out of this uniquely powerful program. Uncheck the Show on Startup box to suppress the Introduction from showing each time the application is launched. You may review it at any time from the Help menu on the main screen. Tips on using other CramMaster features can be found there as well.

Customer Support

If you encounter problems installing or using CramMaster for the Novell NetWare 6.5 exam, please contact ExamForce at 800-845-8569 or email support@examforce.com. Support hours are from 8:30 a.m. to 5:30 p.m. EST Monday through Friday. Additional product support can be found at www.examforce.com.

If you would like to purchase additional ExamForce products, telephone at 800-845-8569, or visit www.examforce.com.

Index

/508 option, 76

A

Access Control right, 171
ACLs (access control lists), 175
  adding/deleting objects, 179-180
  explicit assignments, 175
  viewing
    with ConsoleOne, 176-177,
      211-212
    with iManager, 210-211
    with NetWare Administrator,
      176-177, 213
    with Remote Manager, 176
    with Rights command, 178
    with Windows Explorer, 177-178
Add/Remove Self property right, 208
address books. *See* eGuide
Admin object, 134-135
  security guidelines, 242-243
_ADMIN volume, 114-115
adminsrv directory, 122
AFP port assignment, 398
Alias objects, 98
All Property Rights, 208-210
AMP (Apache, MySQL, Perl/PHP), 16
answers
  practice exam 1, 323-341
  practice exam 2, 357-374

Apache Web Server, 15
  port assignments, 398
apache2 directory, 122
Application and Services layer, 47
Application objects, 98
application proxy, 247
application server (Novell exteNd), 16
application port assignments, 397-401
APPS directory, 126-127
Attribute types (typeful names), 100-101
attributes
  directory attributes, 193-198
  file attributes, 193-198
authentication
  Login Authenticator window, 77
  universal password, 169
AUTOEXEC.BAT file, 36-39, 53
AUTOEXEC.NCF file, 53-56

B

backdoors, 244
backups, 410
Bamboo Tree, 99
BIND command, 49
bindery (NetWare 3.x), 10
BindView Solutions for Novell, 245
blocking inherited rights, 218-220
boot disks, 35-39
Border Manager port assignments, 398

BROADCAST command, 49
Browse object right, 207
BURGLAR.NLM, 244-245
Business Continuity services, 14

C

caching servers, 247
CAPTURE command, 410
CDE (Certified Directory Engineer)
  certification, 5-6
certification, Novell, 2
  CDE (Certified Directory Engineer),
    5-6
  CLE (Certified Linux Engineer), 7
  CLP (Certified Linux Professional), 7
  CNA (Certified Novell
    Administrator), 2-3
  CNE (Certified Novell Engineer), 3-4
  CNI (Certified Novell Instructor), 6
  MCNE (Master Certified Novell
    Engineer), 4-5
  NAI (Novell Certified Instructor), 7
  online resources, 427-435
  references cited in book, 427-435
CIFS port assignment, 398
circuit-level gateways, 247
CLE (Certified Linux Engineer)
  certification, 7
Client Policies page (iFolder Global
  Settings), 287
clients
  definition of, 18
  iFolder Client
    installing, 283-285
    management URL, 438
  iPrint clients
    configuring support, 269
    installing, 272
  NetWare 6.5 platforms, 18
  Novell Client, 70
    bind order, reordering, 77
    features, 70-71
    installing, 75-78
    login methods, 73-75
    login options, 78-82
    login scripts, 72-73, 79
    operating system platforms, 18
    properties, setting, 83-84

protocol options, 71-72
  special accessibility settings, 76
CLP (Certified Linux Professional)
  certification, 7
clustering, 14
CNA (Certified Novell Administrator)
  certification, 2-3
CNE (Certified Novell Engineer)
  certification, 3-4
CNI (Certified Novell Instructor)
  certification, 6
Command.com file, 17
commands. *See also specific commands*
  console commands, 48-50
  legacy NetWare 6.5 utilities, 411-412
  native NetWare 6.5 utilities, 409-411
  NSS commands, 124
Compare property right, 208
Compatibility Mode Driver (NetWare
  5.x), 12
CONFIG command, 49
CONFIG.SYS file, 36-39, 53
CONFIGURATION directories, 126
configuration files, 57
ConsoleOne, 106
  access control lists
    adding/deleting to/from objects,
      179
    viewing, 176
  directory/file attributes, managing,
    195
  eDirectory rights, managing, 211-212
  effective rights, displaying, 183-184
  volumes, creating, 145-147
CONSOLEONE command, 411
Container login script, 159
Container objects, 95-98
context, 99-104
Controlled Access printers, 258
copying
  NCOPY command, 410
  response files, 414
  traditional volumes to NSS volumes,
    124
Country object, 96
CPQIDECD.SYS file, 37
CPUCHECK command, 49
Create object right, 207
Create right, 171

creating
  DOS partitions, 34-40
  location-based maps, 273
  NDPS Manager, 263
  NDPS Printer Brokers, 261
  objects
    template objects, 137-138
    User, 135-139
  printer agents, 264-265
  volumes
    NSS volumes, 144-146, 149-152
    Traditional volumes, 144-149
CsAUDIT port assignment, 398
current context, 101-102
Custom Installation (Novell Client),
  76-77
CX command, 410
CX utility, 103-104

D

DATA volume, 120, 125-126
databases
  flat-file databases, 10
  MySQL Database, 16
default
  eDirectory rights, 214-215
  object rights, 207
  printer list, 272
  printer security setting, 267
  property rights, 207-209
  rights assignments, 173
  volume, 114
Default login script, 160
Delete object right, 207
DELETED.SAV directory, 123-124
Delpart.exe utility, 27
Deployment Manager
  preparing networks for NetWare 6.5,
    32-33
  Response File Generator
    creating response files, 414-416
    sample file, 416-419
DHCP servers, modifying client
  properties, 84
dial-up connections, configuring, 81-82
Dial-up tab (Novell Login), 81-82

directories, 115
  attributes, 193-198
  NWSERVER, 17
  structure, evaluating, 127-128
  SYS volume, 121-123
  types, 125-126
Directory Map objects, 98
DirXML NDS-to-NDS port assignment,
  398
DirXML Remote Loader port
  assignment, 398
DISMOUNT command, 49
DISPLAY SERVERS command, 49
DISPLAY SLP SERVICES command, 49
DNS port assignment, 398
Domain object, 97
domains, root, 92
DOS
  boot disks, 35-39
  NetWare 6.5 interaction, 17-18
  partitions, creating, 34-40
  unloading from server memory, 50
DOWN command, 49
DR-DOS, NetWare 6.5 interaction, 17
drive mappings, 153-158
Drivers layer, 46
duplex configurations, 121

E

eDirectory
  benefits, 90-91
  components, 93-94
  context for login, defining, 78-79
  defined, 14
  features, 92
  login server, defining, 78-79
  management tools, 105-107
  NetWare 6.5 platforms, 18-19
  objects. *See* objects (eDirectory)
  platform support, 92
  role of, 91
  schema, 93
  security, 169, 204-206
    blocking inherited rights, 218-220
    compared with file system security,
      205
    default rights, 214-215

effective rights, 220-226
guidelines, 241
inheritance, 217
management utilities, 210-213
object rights, 206-207
property rights, 207-209
rules governing rights, 215-216
troubleshooting, 226
tree
design, 99
login options, defining, 78-79
organization of, 91-92
eDirectory Administration link
(iManager), 135
EDIT.NLM, 54
effective rights, 182-185
eDirectory effective rights, 220
calculating, 221-226
displaying, 220
file system effective rights
calculating, 188-192
displaying, 183-185
rules governing, 187-188
practice scenarios, 403-408
eGuide
accessing from Virtual Office, 294
defined, 15
management URL, 438
port assignments, 398
ENS (Event Notification Services), 259
entry rights, 205
Erase right, 171
ETC directory, 122
Event Notification Services (ENS), 259
EVERYONE group (NetWare 3.x), 11
explicit assignments, 175
exteNd application server, 16

F

F3 key (Response File option), 413
FDISK utility
DOS partitions, creating, 35-36
hard drives, cleaning, 27
features of NetWare 6.5, 13
business continuity services, 14
open source services, 15-16
productivity-enhancing services,
14-15
Web Application services, 16

File Scan right, 171
FILE SERVER NAME command, 49
file system
components, 114-116
drive mappings, 153-158
planning, 119
file system security, 169-170
access control lists, 175-179
compared with eDirectory security,
205
file/directory attributes, 193-198
management utilities, 174-175
policy guidelines, 234-235
rights, 171-173
common assignments, 172
default assignments, 173
effective rights, 182-185, 188-192,
403-408
planning, 192
rules governing, 187-188
trustees, 175, 178-179
changing assignments, 181-182
inheritance, 180-181
File Versioning, 15
FILER utility, 123, 175, 410
attributes, managing, 195-196
files
attributes, 193-198
AUTOEXEC.BAT, 36-39, 53
AUTOEXEC.NCF, 53-56
BURGLAR.NLM, 244-245
Command.com, 17
CONFIG.SYS, 36-39, 53
configuration files, 57
EDIT.NLM, 54
Ibmbio.com, 17
Ibmdos.com, 17
INETCFG.NLM, 51
INSTALL.BAT, 37
Io.sys, 17
IPPSRVR.NLM, 271
MAKESU.NLM, 134
MONITOR.NLM, 51
MSCDEX.EXE, 37
Msdos.sys, 17
NCFs (NetWare Configuration Files),
53-56
NDPSM.NLM, 259
NET$OBJ.DAT, 10

NET$PROP.DAT, 10
NET$VAL.DAT, 10
NET.CFG, 39-40
NWCONFIG.NLM, 54
response files, 413-419
    copying, 414
    creating, 414-416
    response.rsp file, 413
    response.sav file, 413
    response1.txt file, 413
    sample file, 416-419
SCRSAVER.NLM, 234
SSHD.NLM, 62
STARTNET.BAT, 39
STARTUP.NCF, 53-54
VCU.NLM, 124
firewalls, 245-247
FLAG command, 196-198, 410
FLAGDIR command, 411
flat-file databases, 10
FORMAT.COM utility, 36
FTP
    port assignments, 398
    secure sessions, 63

G

gateways
    application gateways, 247
    circuit-level, 247
    NAT (Network Address Translation),
      246
General Information page (iFolder
  Global Settings), 287
Global Policies page (iFolder Global
  Settings), 287
Global Settings (iFolder Management
  Console), 286-289
Global User ID (GUID), 142
GRANT command, 411
Group objects, 98
GUID (Global User ID), 142
GW Monitor port assignment, 398
GW MTA port assignment, 398
GW POA port assignment, 398
GW Web port assignment, 398
GWIA port assignment, 399

H - I

hard drives, cleaning, 27
hardware requirements, NetWare 6.5
  installation, 28-29
HELP command, 50
Hidden Object Locator (HOL), 245
history of Novell NetWare, 10-13
HOL (Hidden Object Locator), 245
HOME directory, 125
Hot Fix Redirection Area, 149

Ibmbio.com file, 17
Ibmdos.com file, 17
iChain port assignment, 399
iFolder, 14, 280
    benefits, 280-281
    Client
        installing, 283-285
        management URL, 438
    features, 280-281
    installing, 281-282
    Management Console
        accessing, 284
        Global Settings, 286-289
        management URL, 438
        Reporting, 291-292
        System Monitoring, 291
        User Management, 290
    optimizing, 291-292
    port assignments, 399
    system requirements, 281-282
iManager, 57-58, 106-107
    accessing, 58
    eDirectory Administration links, 135
    eDirectory rights, managing, 210-211
    management URL, 438
    User objects
        creating, 135-139
        deleting, 143-144
        modifying, 139-140
        moving, 141-142
    Virtual Office, configuring, 294-300
iMonitor, 107
    accessing, 107
    management URL, 438
    port assignment, 399

INETCFG.NLM, 51
Inheritable object right, 207
Inheritable property right, 208
inheritance, 104
    eDirectory rights, 217
    file system rights, 180
inherited rights filters. *See* IRFs
inherited rights masks (IRMs), 181
INSTALL.BAT file, 37
installing
    iFolder, 281-282
    iFolder Client, 283-285
    NetWare 6.5 servers
        configuration requirements, 30-31
        decision tables, 27
        new server requirements, 30-32
        planning table, 421-426
        preparing designated computer,
          33-40
        preparing environment, 32-33
        prerequisite requirements, 26-28
        process, 40-46
        response files, 413-419
        software requirements, 29-31
        support packs, 29
        system requirements, 28-31
        test environments, 27
    Novell Client, 75-78
    Novell Distributed Print Services
      (NDPS), 260-261
    Virtual Office, 293-294
Internet root domains, 92
Internet Small Computer Systems
  Interface (iSCSI), 14
IntraNetWare, 12
Intruder Lockout, 238-239
Io.sys file, 17
IP and IPX option (Novell Client), 72
IP Only option (Novell Client), 72
IP with IPX Compatibility option
  (Novell Client), 72
IPP, 271
IPPSRVR.NLM, 271
iPrint, 14, 270
    accessing from Virtual Office, 294
    client
      configuring support, 269
      installing, 272
    components, 271
    configuring, 271-272

features, 270-271
    location-based maps, creating, 273
    management ULRs, 438
    port assignment, 399
IPX INTERNAL NET command, 50
IPX option (Novell Client), 72
IPX servers, displaying, 49
IPX/SPX
    configuring, 56
    NetWare 5.x and, 12
IRFs (inherited rights filters)
    eDirectory rights, 218-220
    file system rights, 181-182
IRMs (inherited rights masks), 181
iSCSI (Internet Small Computer Systems
  Interface), 14

J - K - L

J2EE Web application servers, Novell
  exteNd, 16
JAVA directory, 122
javasave directory, 122
Journaling File System, 117

Kernel, 46

LDAP (Lightweight Directory Access
  Protocol)
    port assignments, 399
    LDAP Group objects, 98
    LDAP Server objects, 98
Leaf containers, 98-99
Leaf objects, 95-96
legacy workstation utilities, 411-412
License Container objects, 97
LOAD command, 50-51
logical volumes, 118
login
    Novell Client, 78
      dial-up options, 81-82
      NDS options, 78-79
      NMAS options, 81-82
      Windows options, 80-81
    Novell Client methods, 73-75
    scripts, 72-73, 158-160
      configuring, 79
      map statements in, 160-161
      variables, defining, 79-80
    login security, 169, 235-239

Login Authenticator window, 77
LOGIN command, 410
LOGIN directory, 122
LOGOUT command, 410
LPR port assignment, 399

M

MAIL directory, 122
MAKESU.NLM, 134
MAKEUSER command, 412
Management Console (iFolder), 284
   accessing, 284
      Global Settings, 286-289
      management URL, 438
      Reporting, 291-292
      System Monitoring, 291
      User Management, 290
management URLs, 437-438
map command, 154-158, 410
Map Designer (iPrint), 273
Maptool.htm, 273
MCNE (Master Certified Novell
   Engineer) certification, 4-5
Media Server port assignment, 399
MEMORY command, 50
messages, sending, 49
mirror configurations, 121
Modify right, 171
MODULES command, 50
MONITOR.NLM, 51
MOUNT command, 49
mounting volumes, 49, 117
moving User objects, 141-142
MS-DOS, NetWare 6.5 interaction, 17
MSCDEX.EXE file, 37
Msdos.sys file, 17
multivalued object properties, 93-94
MySQL Database, 16

N

NAAS (Novell Advanced Audit Services),
  245
NAI (Novell Certified Instructor)
  certification, 7
name context, 101

naming
   eDirectory objects, 99-103
   volumes, 116, 120, 156
NAS NetDevice port assignment, 399
NAT (Network Address Translation), 246
Native File Access Protocol, 15
native TCP/IP protocol stack, 12
NCFs (NetWare Configuration Files),
  53-56
NCOPY command, 410
NCP port assignment, 399
NCS (Novell Cluster Services), 14
NDIR command, 197-198, 410
NDPS (Novell Distributed Print
  Services)
   components, 258-260
   installing, 260-261
   managing, 267-269
   Printer Brokers, 259
      creating, 261
      loading, 262
      port assignment, 399
   printer types, 257-258
   printing, 256-257
   RPM (Remote Print Management),
     266-267
   setting up environment, 261
ndps directory, 122
NDPS ENS port assignment, 399
NDPS ENS Listener port assignment,
  399
NDPS Manager, 259
   creating, 263
   loading, 263-264
   port assignment, 399
NDPS RMS port assignment, 399
NDPS SRS port assignment, 399
NDPSM.NLM, 259
NDS (Novell Directory Services), 11
NDS tab (Novell Login), 78-79
NET$OBJ.DAT file, 10
NET$PROP.DAT file, 10
NET$VAL.DAT file, 10
NET.CFG file, 39-40
NetAdmin, managing eDirectory rights,
  213-214
NETADMIN command, 412

NetStorage
  accessing from Virtual Office, 294
  management URL, 438
NetWare, history of, 10-13
NetWare 3.x, 10
NetWare 4.x, 11
NetWare 5.x, 12
NetWare 6.5
  client platforms, 18
  configuration files, 54-57
  DOS interaction, 17
  eDirectory server platforms, 18-19
  features, 13
    business continuity services, 14
    open source services, 15-16
    productivity-enhancing services,
      14-15
    Web Application services, 16
  interaction with other operating
    systems, 16-18
  legacy workstation utilities, 411-412
  management URLs, 437-438
  native workstation utilities, 409-411
  operating system components, 46-47
  server installation
    configuration requirements, 30-31
    decision tables, 27
    new server requirements, 30-32
    planning table, 421-426
    preparing designated computer,
      33-40
    preparing environment, 32-33
    prerequisite requirements, 26-28
    process, 40-46
    response files, 413-419
    software requirements, 29-31
    support packs, 29
    system requirements, 28-31
    test environments, 27
NetWare 6.x, 13
NetWare Administrator, 105-106
  access control lists
    adding/deleting to/from objects,
      179
    viewing, 176-177
  directory/file attributes, managing,
    195

eDirectory rights, managing, 213
effective rights, displaying, 184-185
NetWare Configuration Files (NCFs),
  53-56
NetWare GUI port assignments, 399
NetWare Web Access port assignment,
  399
network adapters, binding/unbinding, 49
Network Address Translation (NAT), 246
network drive mappings, 153-157
News Server port assignment, 399
NFS port assignments, 400
NI directory, 122
NIMS port assignments, 400
NLIST command, 410
NLMs (NetWare Loadable Modules),
  51-53
  BURGLAR.NLM, 244-245
  displaying loaded modules, 50
  EDIT.NLM, 54
  INETCFG.NLM, 51
  IPPSRVR.NLM, 271
  loading, 50-51
  MAKESU.NLM, 134
  MONITOR.NLM, 51
  NDPSM.NLM, 259
  NWCONFIG.NLM, 54
  SCRSAVER.NLM, 234
  SSHD.NLM, 62
  unloading, 50-51
  VCU.NLM, 124
NLSRUP port assignments, 399
NMAS port assignment, 400
NMAS tab (Novell Login), 81-82
Novell Advanced Audit Services (NAAS),
  245
Novell Authorized Instructor (NAI)
  certification, 7
Novell certification, 2
  CDE (Certified Directory Engineer),
    5-6
  CLE (Certified Linux Engineer), 7
  CLP (Certified Linux Professional), 7
  CNA (Certified Novell
    Administrator), 2-3
  CNE (Certified Novell Engineer), 3-4
  CNI (Certified Novell Instructor), 6

MCNE (Master Certified Novell Engineer), 4-5
NAI (Novell Certified Instructor), 7
online resources, 427-435
references cited in book, 427-435
Novell Client, 70
  bind order, reordering, 77
  features, 70-71
  installing, 75-78
  login methods, 73, 75
  login options, 78
    dial-up connections, 81-82
    NDS, 78-79
    NMAS, 81-82
    Windows, 80-81
  login scripts, 72-73, 79
  operating system platforms, 18
  properties, setting, 83-84
  protocol options, 71-72
  special accessibility settings, 76
Novell Cluster Services (NCS), 14
Novell Directory Services (NDS), 11
Novell Distributed Print Services. *See* NDPS
Novell exteNd, 16
Novell Gateway, 259
Novell Login window
  accessing, 73-75
  Dial-up tab, 81-82
  NDS tab, 78-79
  NMAS tab, 81-82
  Script tab, 79
  Windows tab, 80-81
Novell Storage Services. *See* NSS
Novonyx Web Server port assignments, 400
NPRINTER command, 410
NPTWIN95 command, 411
NRM (Novell Remote Manager) port assignments, 400
Nsn directory, 123
NSS (Novell Storage Services)
  defined, 15
  overbooking, 118
  volumes
    component creation, order of, 118
    creating, 144-146, 149-152
    logical, 118
    management commands, 124
    mounting, 117
    namespace support, 120
    status, checking, 152-153
NSSMU utility, 145
NTP port assignment, 400
NVER command, 411
NWADMIN32 command, 411
NWADMIN32.EXE , 105
NWBACK32 command, 410
NWCLIENT directory, 38-39
NWCONFIG.NLM, 54
NWIP (NetWare IP) port assignment, 400
NWSERVER directory, 17

O

objects (eDirectory)
  adding to access control lists, 179-180
  Admin, 134-135
  Container, 95-98
  context, 99-104
  definition of, 93
  deleting from access control lists, 179-180
  inheritance, 104, 180
  Leaf, 98-99
  naming, 99-103
  rights, 206-207
  template objects, creating, 137-138
  Tree, 95-96
  User
    creating, 135-139
    deleting, 142-144
    modifying properties, 139-140
    moving, 141-142
open source services, 15-16
OpenSSH, 61-63
operating systems
  as NetWare 6.5 clients, 18
  as NetWare 6.5 eDirectory servers, 18-19
  NetWare 6.5 interaction, 16-18
Organization object, 97
Organizational Role objects, 98
Organizational Unit object, 97
overbooking, 118

P

packet-filtering firewalls, 246
parameters (SET), 50
partitions
    DOS, 34-40
    NSS, 118
partitions (NSS)
    creating, 150
passphrase (iFolder), 280
password security, 239-241
Perl 5.8, 16
perl directory, 123
PHP 4.2.3 for NetWare, 16
php directory, 123
physical
    security, 169, 234
    volume names, 116, 156
planning
    file system, 119
    security rights, 192
    volumes, 119-121
Portal Services port assignment, 400
ports, default assignments, 397-401
practice exam 1
    answers, 323-341
    questions, 307-321
practice exam 2
    answers, 357-374
    questions, 344-356
Print Queue object, 98
Print Server object, 98
printer agents, 259
    creating, 264-265
Printer Brokers (NDPS), 259
    creating, 261
    loading, 262
Printer Gateways, 259-260
Printer object, 98
printers
    Controlled Access printers, 258
    default printer list, 272
    iPrint support, enabling, 271
    Public Access printers, 257
    security, configuring default setting, 267
    spool location, modifying, 269

printing
    iPrint
        clients, installing, 272
        components, 271
        configuring, 271-272
        features, 270-271
        location-based maps, creating, 273
    NDPS (Novell Distributed Print Services)
        components, 258-260
        features, 256-257
        installing, 260-261
        managing, 267-269
        printer types, 257-258
        RPM (Remote Print Management), 266-267
        setting up environment, 261
    reordering print jobs, 267
productivity-enhancing services, 14-15
Profile
    login script, 159
    objects, 98
properties
    eDirectory object properties, 93-94
    Novell Client properties, setting, 83-84
    User object properties, modifying, 139-140
property rights, 207-209
PROTOCOL command, 50
protocols
    native TCP/IP protocol stack, 12
    Novell Client options, 71-72
proxy servers, 247
Public Access printers, 257
PUBLIC directory, 123
[Public] trustee, 179, 206
PURGE command, 412
PVSW directory, 123

Q - R

questions
    practice exam 1, 307-321
    practice exam 2, 344-356
QUEUES directory, 123
Quick Links (Virtual Office), 300-301

RADIUS port assignment, 400
RAID, 121
RCONSOLE command, 412
Read property right, 207
Read right, 171
regular drive mappings, 153-157
Relative Distinguished Names, 102-103
REM statements, including in login
   scripts, 160
Remote Console DOS port assignment,
   400
Remote Console JAVA port assignments,
   401
Remote Manager, 58-59, 61
  accessing, 58
  access control lists (ACLs)
    adding/deleting to/from objects,
     179
    viewing, 176
  directory attribute management, 193
  effective rights, displaying, 183-184
  file attribute management, 193-194
  management URL, 438
  volumes, creating, 146-147
    NSS volumes, 150-152
    Traditional volumes, 147-149
Remote Print Management (RPM),
   266-267
remote server management
  iManager, 57-58, 106-107
    accessing, 58
    creating User objects, 135-139
    deleting User objects, 143-144
    eDirectory Administration links,
     135
    eDirectory rights, managing,
     210-211
    management URL, 438
    modifying User objects, 139-140
    moving User objects, 141-142
    Virtual Office, configuring,
     294-300
  OpenSSH, 61-63
  Remote Manager. *See* Remote
   Manager
REMOVE command, 412
REMOVE DOS command, 18
Rename object right, 207

RENDIR command, 412
Reporting (iFolder Management
   Console), 291-292
RESET ROUTER command, 50
RESET SERVER command, 50
Resource Management Services (RMS),
   259
Response File Generator (Deployment
   Manager)
    creating response files, 414-416
    sample response file, 416-419
response files, 413-419
  copying, 414
  creating, 414-416
  sample file, 416-419
response.rsp file, 413
response.sav file, 413
response1.txt file, 413
RESTART SERVER command, 50
restores, 410
REVOKE command, 412
rights
  eDirectory rights
    blocking, 218-220
    default rights, 214-215
    effective rights, 220-226
    inheritance, 217
    rules governing, 215-216
    troubleshooting, 226
  file system rights, 171-173
    common assignments, 172
    default assignments, 173
    effective rights, 182-185, 188-192
    IRFs (inherited rights filters),
     181-182
    planning, 192
    practice scenarios, 403-408
Rights command, 185-187, 410
RIGHTS utility, 175
RMS (Resource Management Services),
   259
rogue admin, 244
Role Based Services, 170
Role-Based Service objects, 98
root, 91
root domains, 92
routing tables, resetting, 50
RPM (Remote Print Management),
   266-267

S

SALVAGE command, 412
schema, 93
SCMD port assignment, 401
Script tab (Novell Login), 79
SCRSAVER.NLM, 234
SEARCH ADD command, 50
SEARCH command, 50
SEARCH DEL command, 50
search drive mappings, 153-158
search paths, 50
SECURE CONSOLE command, 17, 50
secure shell, launching, 62
security
    eDirectory security, 169, 204-206
        blocking inherited rights, 218-220
        compared with file system security,
          205
        default rights, 214-215
        effective rights, 220-226
        guidelines, 241
        inheritance, 217
        management utilities, 210-213
        object rights, 207
        property rights, 207-209
        rules governing rights, 215-216
        troubleshooting, 226
    equivalence, 180-181
    file system security, 169-170
        ACLs (access control lists),
          175-179
        compared with eDirectory security,
          205
        effective rights practice scenarios,
          403-408
        file/directory attributes, 193-198
        management utilities, 174-175
        planning, 192
        policy guidelines, 234-235
        rights. *See* rights, file system rights
        rules governing, 187-188
        trustees, 175, 178-179
    firewalls, 245-247
    login security, 169, 235-239
    OpenSSH, 61-63
    policies, 232-233
        administrative access guidelines,
          242-243
        eDirectory rights guidelines, 241

        file system guidelines, 234-235
        login guidelines, 235-239
        password guidelines, 239-241
        physical security guidelines, 234
        virus protection guidelines,
          243-244
    printer security, configuring default
        setting, 267
    server console security, 169, 234
    troubleshooting internal problems,
        244-245
    types provided by NetWare, 168-170
    universal password, 169
Security Container objects, 98
Selected Property Rights, 209-210
SEND command, 49, 412
server console, 47
    commands, 48-50
    NLMs, loading/unloading, 51
    security, 169, 234
Server objects, 98
    rights assignments, 173
Server Policies page (iFolder Global
    Settings), 287
SERVER.EXE command, 17, 56-57
servers
    caching servers, 247
    definition of, 18
    installing NetWare 6.5 servers
        configuration requirements, 30-31
        decision tables, 27
        new server requirements, 30-32
        preparing designated computer,
          33-40
        preparing environment, 32-33
        prerequisite requirements, 26-28
        process, 40-46
        software requirements, 29-31
        support packs, 29
        system requirements, 28-31
        test environments, 27
    proxy servers, 247
    restarting, 50
    warm boots, 50
Service Registry Services (SRS), 259
SET command, 50
SETPASS command, 244-245, 412
SETUPNW.EXE, 76
SHARED directory, 125, 127

single-valued object properties, 93-94
SLP
  displaying SLP services, 49
  port assignment, 401
SLP DA command, 50
SNMP port assignment, 401
software requirements (NetWare 6.5
  installation), 29
SPEED command, 50
SRS (Service Registry Services), 259
ssh utility, 62
SSHD.NLM, 62
STARTNET.BAT file, 39
STARTUP.NCF file, 53-54
STARTX command, 282, 293
storage pools, 118-119
  creating, 150
storage volumes. *See* volumes
subdirectories, 115
Supervisor, 134
  object right, 207
  property right, 207
Supervisor right, 171-172
support packs, 29
SWAP command, 50
SYS volume, 114
  planning guidelines, 119
  system-created directories, 121-123
SYSTEM directory, 123
System Monitoring (iFolder Management
  Console), 291
system requirements
  iFolder, 281-282
  NetWare 6.5 installation, 28-31

T

TCP/IP, native protocol stack, 12
Telnet port assignment, 401
template objects, 98
  creating, 137-138
TIME command, 50
tomcat directory, 123
Tomcat Servlet Engine, 16
  port assignment, 401
Traditional File Services, 117
Traditional volumes, 117
  copying to NSS volumes, 124
  creating, 144-149

mounting, 117
namespace support, 120
status, checking, 152-153
trailing periods
  Distinguished Names, 100-101
  Relative Distinguished Names), 102
Tree objects, 91, 95-96
Tree trustee, 206
trees (eDirectory)
  designs, 99
  login options, defining, 78-79
  organization of, 91-92
troubleshooting security
  eDirectory, 226
  security internal problems, 244-245
trustees, 175, 178-179
  changing assignments, 181-182, 218
  inheritance, 180-181
  managing with ConsoleOne, 211
  [Public], 179, 206
  Tree, 206
typeful names, 100
typeless names, 100
Typical Installation (Novell Client), 76

U

UNBIND command, 49
universal password, 169
UNLOAD command, 50-51
User login script, 159
User Management (iFolder Management
  Console), 290
User objects, 98
  Admin, 134-135
  creating, 135-139
  deleting, 142-144
  modifying properties, 139-140
  moving, 141-142
  properties, 94
USERS directory, 125, 127
utilities
  legacy NetWare 6.5 utilities, 411-412
  native NetWare 6.5 utilities, 409-411

V

values (eDirectory objects), 94
variables, defining login script variables,
  79-80

VCU.NLM, 124
VERSION command, 50
Virtual Office, 292-293
   configuring
      using iManager, 294-300
      using Virtual Office interface,
        300-302
   installing, 293-294
   management URL, 438
virtual private networks (VPNs), 247
Virtual Teams, 15
virus protection, 243-244
Volume command, 152-153
Volume objects, 99
   names, 116, 156
volumes, 114-115
   _ADMIN, 114-115
   creating
      NSS volumes, 144-146, 149-152
      Traditional volumes, 144-149
   DATA, 120, 125-126
   default, 114
   drive mappings, 153-158
   mounting, 49
   namespace support, 120
   naming, 116, 120, 156
   NSS, 117-119
      component creation, order of, 118
      creating, 144-146, 149-152
      management commands, 124
      mounting, 117
      status, checking, 152-153
   planning guidelines, 119-121
   SYS, 114
      planning guidelines, 119
      system-created directories,
        121-123
   Traditional, 117
      checking status, 152-153
      copying to NSS volumes, 124
      creating, 144-147, 149
      mounting, 117
VPNs (virtual private networks), 247
   port assignments, 401

W - Z

warm boots, 50
Web Application services, 16
Web Manager
   management URL, 438
   port assignment, 401
Web proxies, 247
WebSphere port assignment, 401
WHOAMI command, 412
Windows 2000 Professional, eDirectory
   and, 19
Windows Explorer, 175
   access control lists (ACLs)
      adding/deleting to/from objects,
        180
      viewing, 177-178
Windows tab (Novell Login), 80-81
Windows XP Professional, eDirectory
   and, 19
WINSETUP.EXE, 76
Write property right, 208
Write right, 171

ZENworks for Desktops, client
   properties, modifying, 84
ZFD 3 port assignments, 401
ZFS 2 port assignments, 401
ZFS 3.2 port assignments, 401

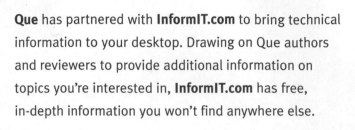